THE WORLD'S
GREATEST
PLACES

THE MOST AMAZING
TRAVEL DESTINATIONS ON EARTH

THE WORLD'S
GREATEST
PLACES

THE MOST AMAZING
TRAVEL DESTINATIONS ON EARTH

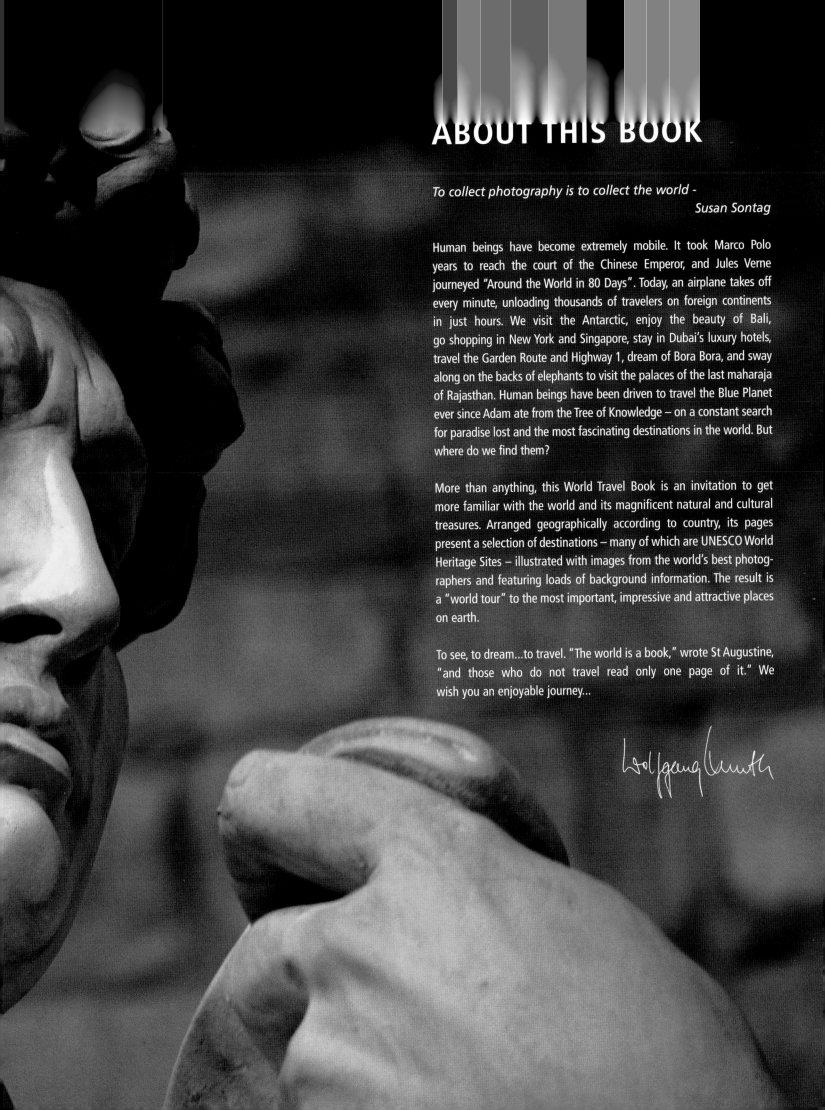

ABOUT THIS BOOK

To collect photography is to collect the world -
Susan Sontag

Human beings have become extremely mobile. It took Marco Polo years to reach the court of the Chinese Emperor, and Jules Verne journeyed "Around the World in 80 Days". Today, an airplane takes off every minute, unloading thousands of travelers on foreign continents in just hours. We visit the Antarctic, enjoy the beauty of Bali, go shopping in New York and Singapore, stay in Dubai's luxury hotels, travel the Garden Route and Highway 1, dream of Bora Bora, and sway along on the backs of elephants to visit the palaces of the last maharaja of Rajasthan. Human beings have been driven to travel the Blue Planet ever since Adam ate from the Tree of Knowledge – on a constant search for paradise lost and the most fascinating destinations in the world. But where do we find them?

More than anything, this World Travel Book is an invitation to get more familiar with the world and its magnificent natural and cultural treasures. Arranged geographically according to country, its pages present a selection of destinations – many of which are UNESCO World Heritage Sites – illustrated with images from the world's best photographers and featuring loads of background information. The result is a "world tour" to the most important, impressive and attractive places on earth.

To see, to dream...to travel. "The world is a book," wrote St Augustine, "and those who do not travel read only one page of it." We wish you an enjoyable journey...

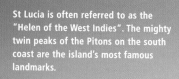

St Lucia is often referred to as the "Helen of the West Indies". The mighty twin peaks of the Pitons on the south coast are the island's most famous landmarks.

Previous pages: the Golden Gate Bridge in San Francisco and Michelangelo's *David* in Florence.

CONTENTS

Minakshi-Sundareshvara Temple in Madurai in the southern Indian state of Tamil Nadu possesses formidable dimensions. The complex is dedicated to the "fish-eyed" goddess Minakshi, Shiva's bride. Shiva is honored here as Sunarshvara, the "Beautiful God".

CONTENTS

The fjords and cliffs of Scandinavia, the rolling forest landscapes of Central Europe, the snow-covered peaks of the Alps, the sun-filled shores of the Mediterranean, the legacy of the ancient Greeks and Romans, the monumental Medieval cathedrals, the magnificent baroque castles ... Europe! For Pope Boniface VII, Tuscany (here the Val d'Orcia) was in fact "the quintessence of the world".

KRAFLA

Situated just to the north-east of Mývatn, the countryside around Krafla, an active, 818-m (2,684-ft) volcano (above and main picture), is tectonically one of the least stable regions in Iceland. Believed for almost 2,000 years to be extinct, Krafla suddenly exploded to life at the beginning of the 18th century, smothering the region in a thick layer of lava and ash. What remained was a sparkling, emerald-green crater lake. In 1975 Krafla erupted yet again, this time for almost a decade. Its sulfur mud pots have been bubbling and steaming ever since. They are now a popular attraction as well as the most visible beacon of Iceland's continuing volcanic activity.

GODAFOSS

About 40 km (25 mi) to the east of Akureyri, traveling from the Sprengisandur gravel and lava desert toward the ocean, the Skjálfandaðfljót River thunders over a 10-m-high (33-ft) cleft in the terrain. The Goðafoss (right, top) owes its name, Waterfall of the Gods, to Thorgeir, speaker of the Althing, Iceland's parliament. In the year 1000, he is said to have thrown the statues of the former pagan gods into the river because the Icelandic parliament had decreed that Iceland should become Christian. The decision followed a threat from Norwegian King Olaf to stop the trade in timber, a move that would have endangered a vital industry for Iceland, shipbuilding.

DETTIFOSS

The Dettifoss (right) in Iceland's north-eastern corner is an impressive 100 m (328 ft) wide and 44 m (144 ft) high waterfall with a flow of up to 1,500 cu m (52,972 cu ft) per second, the most powerful in Europe.

The landscape surrounding the 818-m (2,684-ft) volcano just a few miles north-east of Lake Myvatn is one of the most tectonically unstable areas of Iceland.

MÝVATN

Roughly 30 km (17 mi) east of Goðafoss is "Mosquito Lake" (right), formed by the escaping lava from volcanic eruptions as recently as about 2,000 to 3,500 years ago. The lake covers an area of 37 sq km (14 sq mi) but it is only 4 to 5 m (13 to 16 ft) deep and fed by hot springs. Hardly anywhere else on the planet does such a diversity of fauna and flora exist at such northern latitudes. A great variety of mosses, grasses, ferns, herbs and birches grow along the lakeshore and on its numerous islands. During the summer months, huge swarms of mosquitoes buzz, giving the warm waters their name. Together with the insect larvae in the water, they provide nutrition for rich stocks of fish as well as several thousand waterfowl that nest in the network of bays.

The Mývatn also counts as one of Iceland's most spectacular landscapes due to its location in a zone of extreme volcanic activity. Strolling along the well-marked footpaths you will see an array of unusual lava formations. Especially bizarre are the Dimmu-borgir (Dark Castles), a series of fantastic formations that feature small caverns and arches.

You can get the best view of the pseudocraters in and around Mývatn from the rim of Hverfjall, an ash cone that rises roughly 170 m (558 ft).

SKAFTAFELL

Skaftafell National Park, founded in 1967 and part of the Vatnajökull National Park since June of 2008, stretches from the center of the Vatnajökull, Iceland's largest glacier, to the south as far as the Ring Road. Signposted footpaths lead through dense forests (for example, near Núpsstadaskógar), along extensive swamps, moorlands and meadows to farms – some no longer in use, some still operational – and a grand waterfall surrounded by lava columns.

VATNAJÖKULL

This national park covers a vast area of roughly 12,000 sq km (4,632 sq mi) and has a variety of attractions: moors, swamps, birch groves, scree fields and sandy terrain all against the magnificent backdrop of the Vatnajökull, or Water Glacier (top), which consists of a larger volume of ice than any of the glaciers in the Alps. Above: Glaciers reflected on a lake in the national park. Since June of 2008, the Skaftafell and Jökulsárgljúfur parks have also been integrated into the protected area, which now constitutes the largest national park in Europe.

The waters of the Svartifoss – or Black Waterfall – tumble over an impressive basalt cliff shaped like an amphitheater (main picture).

VÍK

The great attraction at Iceland's so-called South Cape are the bird rocks on the Dyrhólaey Peninsula near Vík. Many common species of North Atlantic waterfowl live on several different levels of the landscape here: at the top are the puffins, which dig their corridors into the grassy knoll; below, on the rocky ledges, are the kitti wakes and northern fulmars. You can reach the black sand and lava beach by boat where the rock for mations rise a good 120 m (394 ft above the strand. A lighthouse marks a famous viewpoint.

BERGEN, GEIRANGERFJORD, SOGNEFJORD

Dalsnibba (1,476 m/4,843 ft) offers amazing panoramic views of the Sunnmøre mountain region (main picture) into which the Geirangerfjord slashes a more than 1,000-m-deep (3,281-ft) valley. You can also reach the mountain by car on a 5-km (3-mi) toll road.

BERGEN

From the 14th to the 16th centuries, it was mostly German merchants who controlled business dealings in the trading and port town of Bergen, Norway. The Germans ran the salt trade, an important ingredient needed to conserve the fish catches from the Norwegian Sea. In those days, salted fish was sold as far away as the Mediterranean and, thanks to its extensive commercial ties, Bergen eventually became one of the most important towns in the Hanseatic League.

On the Tyske Bryggen Quay – which means German Bridge and plainly reveals its use among Hanseatic merchants – gabled warehouses still bear witness to the former prosperity of this once mighty trading port. The 58 wooden houses that have been carefully preserved in the historic district, however, are not actually left over from medieval times. They were rebuilt in the original style after a fire in 1702. Fires have caused continuous damage in Bergen, which is still an important Norwegian port. The most recent fire was in 1955.

GEIRANGERFJORD

If statistics are proof, then the Geirangerfjord is one of the most impressive landscapes on the planet: The innermost arm of the Storfjord is roughly 120 km (75 mi) long and visited by more than 150 cruise ships from around the world each year. From the ship you will be able to see three famous waterfalls, among other things: Seven Sisters (above), Suitor and Bridal Veil. In summer, the Hurtigruten ships also dock in Geiranger, a village of about 250 people at the end of the fjord. The Ørneveien pass (or Eagle Road), from the Geirangerfjord to the Norddalsfjord farther north, is one of the most breathtaking roads in all of Scandinavia featuring hairpin turns and stunning vistas. The most spectacular viewpoint, however, can only be reached on foot at 1,112 m (3,648 ft) above the fjord: the nearly vertical Flydalshornet.

The Marina and the Old Town (left) are among the loveliest attractions in Bergen, Norway's second-largest city. Situated on the Byfjord, Bergen enjoys a mild climate as it is sheltered from the colder inland temperatures by mountains reaching up to 2,000 m (6,562 ft).

SOGNEFJORD

The Sognefjord (top) is not only Europe's longest fjord at 204 km (127 mi), but also the deepest on earth at 1,308 m (4,292 ft). Both Nærøyfjord (above left), flanked on both sides by rock cliffs up to 1,800 m (5,906 ft) high, and Aurlandfjord (above right) are arms at the south-eastern end of Sognefjord.

The Melkevollbreen Glacier flows down a steep valley into Lake Oldevatnet on the edge of Jostedalsbreen National Park. It is just one arm of the largest glacier in mainland Europe, the Jostedalsbreen.

JOSTEDALSBREEN

DOVREFJELL-SUNNDALSFJELLA

JOTUNHEIMEN

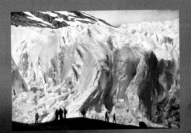

Jostedalsbreen is the largest glacier in mainland Europe. From the interior arms of the Sognefjord, this plateau glacier stretches about 100 km (328 mi) into the north-east at widths of up to 15 km (9 mi). The ice is 500 m (1,640 ft) thick in places.

In the middle of the glacier stands the Høgste Breakulen, a 1,957-m (6,421-ft) glacial cone covered in ice. Only a few rocky islands break through the ice cover, the highest of these being the Lodalskåpa at an impressive 2,083 m (6,834 ft). You can take Route 604 to the Jostedalen Valley, which runs for 50 km (31 mi) and contains a network of valleys with glacial fingers stretching toward the east. Brigsdalsbreen is the best-known glacier arm on the sunnier north-west side.

Guided glacier tours (above) offer added security during your discovery of this icy realm. They start at the visitor center, which was built to resemble a crevasse.

Dovrefjell-Sunndalsfjella National Park combines expansive Vidda plateaus (top right) and the glacial high mountain range of the Snøhetta. In the steep tributary valleys of the Sunndalsfjord, the plateau tumbles down an impressive series of 100-m-high (328-ft) rock formations (top).

The animal world is as diverse as the spectacular landscape here. At thirteen degrees latitude, in the south it is hardly distinguishable from that of Central Europe, while the mountain plateaus and the northern reaches have a more Arctic feel. The muskox (above), the iconic animal of the Arctic, has been reintroduced all the way from Greenland to the tundra Dovrefjell. Above middle: A white-tailed eagle during a precision catch. Above bottom: A reindeer.

Jotunheimen National Park, home to Northern Europe's highest summits, is the most easily accessible hiking and mountain sports region in all of Norway. Galdhøpiggen at 2,469 m (8,101 ft), is the highest peak in Scandinavia and more than two hundred other summits surpass the 2,000 m (6,562 ft) mark in this glacial mountain range.

On the Vestland side the area is characterized by an alpine ruggedness while the Østland side features much gentler, undulating landscapes. Overall, approximately 1,151 sq km (444 sq mi) of these central highlands are protected by the national park.

Known as the North Cape, the rocky promontory in the north of Magerøya Island is the point which, for centuries, has been falsely considered the northernmost spot in mainland Europe.

NORTH CAPE

The rocky promontory on the north side of Magerøya Island, known as North Cape, has for centuries wrongly been regarded as mainland Europe's northernmost point. To be fair, the actual northernmost point is not far away: the next spit of land, Knivskjellodden (above). Jutting about 1.5 km (0.9 mi) farther northward into the sea, it is comparatively flat and not quite as spectacular as its more famous neighbor, which is a tall headland protruding 307 m (1,000 ft) into the Norwegian Sea. It was Englishman Richard Chancellor, navigator of a fleet of seven ships on the first journey to find the North-East Passage in 1554, who spotted the rocky bluff and, believing it to be the northern tip of the continent, named it the "North Cape".

LOFOTEN

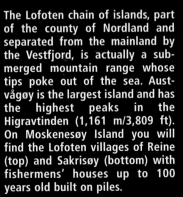

VESTERÅLEN

The Lofoten chain of islands, part of the county of Nordland and separated from the mainland by the Vestfjord, is actually a submerged mountain range whose tips poke out of the sea. Austvågøy is the largest island and has the highest peaks in the Higravtinden (1,161 m/3,809 ft). On Moskenesøy Island you will find the Lofoten villages of Reine (top) and Sakrisøy (bottom) with fishermens' houses up to 100 years old built on piles.

The Vesterålen archipelago off the coast of Troms extends over an area of 150 km (93 mi), and in the south merges almost seamlessly into the Lofoten archipelago. The Raftsund strait and the Trollfjord on the Lofoten side are seen as the dividing line. The overall landscape resembles that of Lofoten: fjords, straits, bays, skerry islands, rivers, lakes, moors, valleys, plains, alpine summits and sandy beaches like those in the south. The main islands are Hinnøya, the

largest island in Norway covering 2,205 sq km (851 sq mi), Langøya and Andøya.
In 2003, the lakes and highlands on Hinnøya island were made into the Møysalen National Park (above). The 51-sq-km (20-sq-mi) area extends from Indrefjord to the Møysalen (1,266 m / 4,154 ft), the highest peak on the Vesterålen. Administratively, only a part of Hinnøya is in Troms, despite its geographical proximity. The rest belongs to Nordland.

DROTTNINGHOLM

Completed in around 1700, Drottningholm Palace (or Queen Island) is majestically located on Lovön Island in Lake Mälar, on the site of an earlier building dating back to the 16th century. Commissioned in 1662, by Hedwig Eleonora, wife of the late King Charles X Gustav, it is the largest baroque palace in Sweden and widely regarded as the most important work by architect Nicodemus Tessin.

The main façade of the rectangular structure faces the water. The palace was enlarged after 1750, and numerous rooms were furnished in the lavish style of the rococo. When the palace was increasingly used for state visits, starting in 1777, some of the important rooms were remodeled in elegant neoclassical style. King Gustav III (1771–92) had the gardens laid out in English landscape style.

Aside from the splendid rooms from a range of style periods, visitors are especially fascinated these days by the China Pavilion and the Drottningholm Theater, one of very few rococo theaters still in use.

Royal Stockholm: the first Swedish regent, King Adolf Fredrick, moved into the castle (Kungliga Slottet) in 1754. Its 600 rooms making it one of the largest residences in the world (main picture).

Drottningholm Palace, residence of the Swedish royal family, is surrounded by several gardens and has been delightfully incorporated into the aquatic scenery around Lake Mälar (left).

STOCKHOLM

Founded in 1252, and the capital since 1634, Stockholm has long been a dynamic and international city, and its wonderful mix of grandiose buildings, parks, waterways and bridges give the vibrant metropolis a unique ambience. All of the major sights can easily be visited on foot during a stroll through the Old Town (Gamla Stan), and overall there are roughly one hundred museums. In addition to the Nationalmuseet, which has the country's most

important art collection, and the Moderna Museet, with contemporary art, it also features Skansen, the world's oldest open-air museum, and the Vasamuseet. The latter exhibits the Vasa, King Gustav II Adolf's flagship, which sank upon its launch in 1628.
The picture shows Riddarholmen Island with the steeple of Riddarholmskyrka church. This former place of worship is now a museum and the last resting place of the Swedish kings.

ÖLAND, VISBY (GOTLAND), FÅRÖ

Gotland and Öland are Sweden's largest islands and were originally settled by the Vikings. Gotland's capital is Visby, whose fortifications extend for 3.4 km (2 mi). During the time of the Hanseatic League, it was considered one the most important trading ports in the entire Baltic.

ÖLAND

Öland, Sweden's second-largest island after Gotland, features steep, jagged cliffs on its western side, while the eastern side enjoys a more gentle descent toward the sea. The south-east possesses soil deposited by glaciers and is the only part of the island that can be cultivated. The rest of Öland's plateau to the south is dominated by sandstone, slate and chalk.

The Stora Alvaret area, a 40-km (25-mi) stretch of treeless limestone heathland, acquired its present appearance from centuries of over-grazing and deforestation that exposed bare limestone in some areas. Despite these difficult topographic and climatic conditions, humans have been able to inhabit South Öland for at least 5,000 years.

South of the Mysinge hög, the largest Bronze-Age burial mound in Sweden, is a passage grave where thirty people were buried roughly 4,000 years ago. Numerous burial fields from the Iron Age and several ring fort refuges from the time of the Great Migration even indicate permanent settlement.

VISBY (GOTLAND)

The main town on Gotland's north-western coast was settled as early as the Stone Age. In the 12th century, Visby served initially as a stopping point for German merchants in their highly lucrative trade with Novgorod, but soon it became the launch pad for an extension of the Hanseatic League cities into the east.

In the 13th century, Visby was regarded as probably the most important trading town in the north of the European continent aside from Lübeck in Germany. It even minted its own coins, and it was here that the so-called Visby Rules were agreed, an international maritime treaty binding for the entire Baltic region. This gold-en age came to a relatively abrupt end, however, when Gotland was conquered by Danish King Waldemar IV in 1361.

Today, the mighty fortifications still bear witness to the town's former prosperity. Thirty-eight historical defense towers have been preserved, but the port of Visby has since silted up.

Herbs, grasses and flowers flourish on Öland, including the pasqueflower (left). The large stones, which probably mark burial places (far left with windmill in the background) indicate at least one prehistoric settlement, possibly during the last Ice Age.

FÅRÖ

The most famous inhabitant of Fårö was Swedish director Ingmar Bergmann, who was buried here after his death on July 30, 2007. Separated from Gotland only by a narrow sound, this tiny island is a quiet summer paradise with lovely beaches that are popular among visitors from the mainland. There is a ferry from Fårösund on

Gotland and the island's military installation has been shut down since the mid-1990s.

Highlights in the countryside are the nature reserve of Ullahau in the north with its sand dunes, and the limestone stacks (left) of Digerhuvud, Gamle Hamn and Langhammars, given their bizarre shapes by wind and erosion.

The sculpture of the Little Mermaid in the port of Copenhagen (main picture) was created by sculptor Edvard Eriksen based on the main figure in Hans Christian Andersen's fairytale. His models were the prima ballerinas who danced the part of the mermaid in a ballet interpretation of the fairytale, and his own wife.

NYHAVN

Since Denmark and Sweden were connected by the ambitious Öresund Bridge, it has become even easier to travel between the two "united kingdoms". One of the strangest, and yet somehow still accurate, travel recommendation for Denmark came from the much-loved and down-to-earth Queen Margrethe II: "No country is as much Denmark as Denmark itself." Indeed, it is an ideal travel destination for people who love the sea. Where else can you find 7,400 km (4,598 mi) of mostly undeveloped and freely accessible coastline combined with a choice of the blue shimmering Kattegat, the mild Baltic, the rough Skagerrak or the tidal North Sea?

And in Copenhagen, which has been the capital of Denmark since 1443, visitors encounter history and tradition around virtually every corner. The ambience is at once cosmopolitan and pleasantly tranquil, and

most of the sights can be comfortably visited on foot.

The city on the Öresund experienced its first period of prosperity back in the late Middle Ages as a trading port. A new golden age developed in the 16th and 17th centuries, in particular under King Christian IV, who did a lot to expand and further enhance the capital.

The Nyhavn Canal district (above) is particularly charming with its old wooden sailboats and a slew of cafés. Canal and harbor cruises begin here and take visitors to the popular Little Mermaid (Lille Havfrue, Copenhagen's most famous icon, main picture) on a rock in the bay. The statue was donated by Carl Jacobsen, a brewer and patron of the arts, and was finally unveiled in the year 1913.

AMALIENBORG

North of Nyhavn is the Amalienborg, city palace of Danish Queen Margrethe II commissioned by King Frederick V and completed between 1749 and 1760. It was based on designs by Nicolai Eigtved and has been the residence of the Danish royal family since 1794.

FREDERIKSKIRKE

Many visitors to Frederikskirke are reminded of St Peter's Basilica in Rome when they see its dramatic cupola (33 m/108 ft in diameter). Also known as the Marble Church, it was designed by Nicolai Eigtved, begun in 1749, and not completed until 1894.

CHRISTIANSBORG

Today, the Folketing, the 179-member Danish Parliament, holds its sessions in the former royal palace, which did not take on its present form until 1928. It was built on the site of two former structures, both of which were destroyed by fire.

HELSINKI

Roughly 500,000 people live in Finland's capital, a city originally founded by King Gustav I of Sweden in 1550. After a series of fires, Czar Alexander II commissioned Berlin architect Carl Ludwig Engel with the neoclassical reconstruction of Helsinki. Twenty of the monumental edifices from that time, 1820 to 1850, are still standing today and, along with other famous buildings in styles from Art Nouveau to modern, they lend the capital on the Gulf of Finland a unique urban landscape.

Worth seeing are Engel's Senate Square with the cathedral and the statue of Czar Alexander II (main picture), the Government Palace, the main university building and the university library, as well as the Orthodox Uspenski Cathedral, built in 1868 and boasting rich interior flourishes. Other attractions include the market square and the historic market building on the south side where the ferries dock that take visitors to the island fortress of Suomenlinna and the skerry islands. Numerous Art Nouveau buildings can be seen on Luotsikatu, one of Helsinki's most elegant streets. The esplanade, the capital's pedestrian zone, is bordered by parks. This is also where you will find Stockmann's flagship department store, the largest of its kind in all of Scandinavia.

The best panoramic view across Helsinki can be enjoyed from the Katajanokka Peninsula.

SAIMAA

With its countless fingers, bays and satellite lakes, the Saimaa region forms the largest connected lake district in Finland. Saimaa Lake itself (above, with Loikansaari Island) is also known as the "lake of a 1,000 islands". Up to 90 m (295 ft) deep in parts, it covers a vast area of about 1,300 sq km (502 sq mi), not including the islands. Spread out over several lakes is Savonlinna, the region's main town.

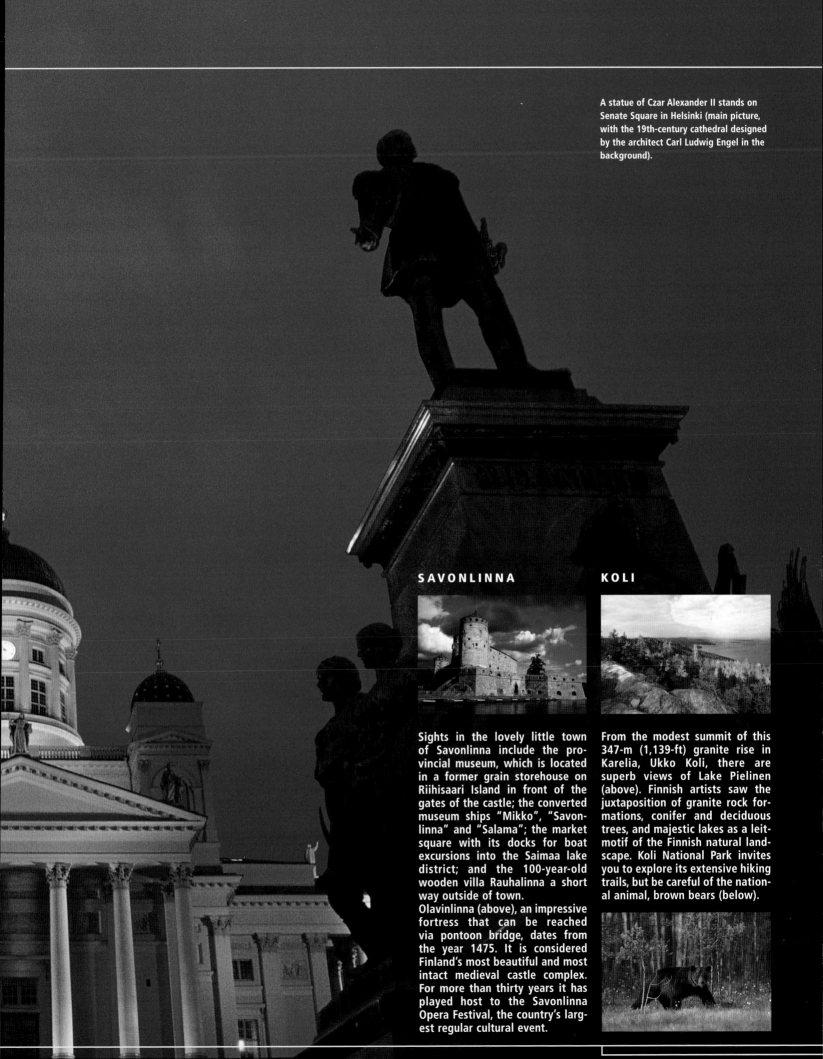

A statue of Czar Alexander II stands on Senate Square in Helsinki (main picture, with the 19th-century cathedral designed by the architect Carl Ludwig Engel in the background).

SAVONLINNA

Sights in the lovely little town of Savonlinna include the provincial museum, which is located in a former grain storehouse on Riihisaari Island in front of the gates of the castle; the converted museum ships "Mikko", "Savonlinna" and "Salama"; the market square with its docks for boat excursions into the Saimaa lake district; and the 100-year-old wooden villa Rauhalinna a short way outside of town.

Olavinlinna (above), an impressive fortress that can be reached via pontoon bridge, dates from the year 1475. It is considered Finland's most beautiful and most intact medieval castle complex. For more than thirty years it has played host to the Savonlinna Opera Festival, the country's largest regular cultural event.

KOLI

From the modest summit of this 347-m (1,139-ft) granite rise in Karelia, Ukko Koli, there are superb views of Lake Pielinen (above). Finnish artists saw the juxtaposition of granite rock formations, conifer and deciduous trees, and majestic lakes as a leitmotif of the Finnish natural landscape. Koli National Park invites you to explore its extensive hiking trails, but be careful of the national animal, brown bears (below).

TALLINN

This Baltic town was founded by Danes and developed into a center of the Hanseatic League in the Middle Ages. Many of the patrician houses and churches still bear witness to this time of prosperity, such as St Olav's Church, which dominates the city (below, seen from Cathedral Hill, with fortification towers in the foreground).

After being severely damaged in World War II, the historic center of the Estonian capital was rebuilt in the style of the 18th century. Originally called Reval (a Latin reference to the surrounding area) by the Swedish, Danish and the Germans, the city has been known as Tallinn since 1920, a name whose meaning is debated. The Old Town is on Cathedral Hill.

Sites worth seeing include St Mary's Cathedral (from 1230), the Church of the Holy Spirit (12th/13th centuries), St Nicholas' Church (13th to 14th centuries), and St Olav's Church (13th century) with its 123-m-tall (404-ft) steeple that for many years served as a lighthouse. St Mary's Chapel was built from 1512 to 1523. The trade guilds here also commissioned grand

buildings for themselves as symbols of civic pride. The Great Guild, for example, supplied the members of the municipal council and moved into its hall in 1410. The two-story town hall, built in the early 15th century, is surrounded by well-preserved medieval homes. The baroque Kadriorg Palace was built as a royal summer residence in the years between 1717 and 1725.

The historic center of Tallinn resembles other small medieval towns in Central Europe. The narrow alleyways, dominated by the towers of St Nicholas' Church (far left) and the town hall (center), create a romantic atmosphere especially at night. Left: Raekoja Square.

The magnificent House of Blackheads stands on Town Hall Square (main picture). It was once a meeting place for unmarried foreign merchants. They were named "blackheads" after their patron saint, Mauritius, who was often represented as a Mauritanian.

Riga is situated on the Baltic Sea at the mouth of the Daugava River. Among the many important churches in the city, the cathedral, which was begun in the year 1211 and only completed in its present form in 1775, stands out along with the octagonal wooden steeple of the Lutheran Jesus Church (1819–22). Of the once-mighty fortifications, the 14th-century Powder Tower and the 13th-century Ramer Tower have been very well preserved. The Citadel was begun in 1760, while the area was under Swedish rule, and the Swedish Gate also dates back to that time.

The Guildhall is the only remaining medieval administrative building in Riga. The Small Guild, built around the middle of the 14th century and remodeled in 1866, is one of the most prestigious buildings in the city. The Latvian Stock Exchange was built between 1852 and 1855 in the style of a Venetian palazzo with a playful façade. Other architectural delights include splendid patrician houses such as the Reutern House, begun in the year 1683, and some outstanding Art Nouveau buildings by Mikhail Eisenstein.

You can enjoy beautiful panoramic views of Riga's Old Town from the left bank of the Daugava River (left). The skyline here is dominated by the towers of the cathedral (in the center) and St Peter's Church (on the right).

Like many medieval cities, the Old Town of this former trading settlement spreads out from the base of Vilnius Castle, on the left bank of the Neris River near its confluence with the Vilnia River. The city experienced its heyday in the 15th and 16th centuries as a mediator between the cities of the Russian czardom and what were then strongholds of the Hanseatic League. As a result of its location, the Lithuanian capital features some remarkable urban architecture that mirrors the turbulent history of this small nation. Among the older buildings, a number of late-Gothic churches such as St Anne's Church, St Nicholas' Church, and St Bernhard's Church, as well as some baroque era noblemen's palaces are of particular historical interest. The 17th-century Church of Saints Peter and Paul is also baroque in style.

The center of the Old Town, however, is dominated by St. Stanislaus Cathedral, which received its present appearance between 1783 and 1801. Neoclassical in style, it resembles a Greek temple. The cathedral's bell tower was originally the defensive tower of the Lower Castle, which was built in the 13th century. During the Soviet period, the church was used as a large exhibition space. Vilnius Town Hall was also later remodeled in neoclassical style.

The neoclassical Vilnius Cathedral (main picture) was consecrated in 1801. As is typical for many churches in the Baltic states, it has a separate steeple. The upper story of the 16th-century "Gates of Dawn" has a chapel dedicated to the "Blessed Virgin Mary Mother of Compassion" (right).

LONDON

The whole world in one city – not just a great advertising slogan but a reality. London is truly a global city, created and defined by people from all over the world who have brought their cultures with them to create the unique urban mélange that is the British capital. The diversity of the city, however, is not solely a result of the interplay between different cultures, which among other things has given London a great variety of cuisines and some of the most exciting restaurants in Europe, for example. No, what also makes London special is its spirit of innovation and creative energy, which in turn contributes enormously not only to European but also world culture and business in general. The world comes to London, and London welcomes the world with open arms.

BUCKINGHAM PALACE

Built in 1703 as a residence by John Sheffield, the first Duke of Buckingham and Normandy, Buckingham Palace came into royal family ownership in 1761 under King George III and, has been the residence of the English kings and queens since 1837. Buckingham Palace, Westminster Abbey and the Palace of Westminster – better known as the Houses of Parliament – are historical landmarks in the United Kingdom and it is here, in the center of the City of Westminster borough, where the political heart of the United Kingdom beats. Both the lower house (House of Commons) and the upper house (House of Lords) meet here at the British seat of government. The Queen has also inherited a position in the House of Lords and she attends during important events such as the Queen's speech. In personal union law, Elizabeth II is the Queen of the United Kingdom of Great Britain and Northern Ireland as well as of the member states of the Commonwealth of Nations. As head of state in the United Kingdom, however, she fulfils a purely ceremonial function.

BIG BEN

The clock on Big Ben is the largest in Britain. Each of its four faces measures 8 m (26 ft) in diameter. Although the bell tower of Westminster Palace itself is commonly referred to as Big Ben, this is in fact the name of the largest of the tower's five bells, which has become known simply as the Great Bell instead.

WESTMINSTER

View of Big Ben from Trafalgar Square. In the foreground are two of the four lions at the foot of Nelson's Column.

The Thames is London's lifeline. The river (above) connects historical sights such as Big Ben at the Palace of Westminster with modern attractions like the giant London Eye Ferris wheel.
Construction of the Palace of Westminster and Westminster Abbey began in 1045, under King Edward the Confessor (1003–1066). The church, which was replaced by a Gothic cathedral in the 13th century, served as a burial place for Edward and subsequent rulers until 1760. It is still used as the coronation church of the monarchs. Royal weddings and funerals also take place in Westminster Abbey. Right: The 30-m-long (98-ft) main aisle.
In 1097, the Palace of Westminster, begun by Edward the Confessor, was enlarged by William II. In 1547 it became the seat of the English parliament. The complex was rebuilt between 1840 and 1888 by Charles Barry following a fire in 1834 that had destroyed the Palace and only spared Westminster Hall and St Stephen's Chapel. Its current neo-Gothic design was intended to match

the façade of nearby Westminster Abbey, which is dominated by Big Ben to the north.
Many of the palaces rooms were partially renovated in the 19th century. St Margaret's Church, built and consecrated in the 11th century, is the parish church of parliament and received its present look as early as the beginning of the 16th century.

During construction of the neo-Gothic Tower Bridge, the towers were clad with limestone from the Isle of Portland for aesthetic reasons as well as to hide the steel used in the bridge's substructure.

THE TOWER OF LONDON

After his successful invasion of England in 1066, William the Conqueror commissioned the Tower of London as a fortified residence and observation post for the boats and barges plying the Thames. It was given its present appearance in the 13th century.

The Tower remained the royal residence of English monarchs until the year 1509, when the fortress was transformed into the state prison. Many famous citizens were held here, among them Thomas More, two of Henry VIII's wives, and the future Queen Elizabeth I.

The building is primarily a museum these days and has an extensive collection of European military items and torture devices. The Jewel House contains the crown jewels.

London's oldest church, the Norman Chapel of St John from 1080, is also on the grounds. Prisoners executed in the Tower, including two wives of Henry VIII (Anne Boleyn and Catherine Howard) and the Queen For Nine Days Lady Jane Grey, were buried in the St Peter Royal Chapel, restored in 1512 after a fire.

TOWER BRIDGE

Tower Bridge opened in 1894, and combines bascule and suspension bridge design. It is not only one of London's most famous landmarks, but is also an important testimony to the already advanced engineering capabilities of the time.

Originally, steam engines were used to operate the hydraulics, which allowed the bridge to be opened within just a few minutes. Today it is operated by electricity.

Both towers contain exhibitions on the structure's history, and from the glassed-in walkway high above the bridge you can get spectacular views of the city.

The castle complex, also known as the "White Tower" (left), is Britain's best-preserved fortress. With walls up to 3 m (10 ft) thick, it prevented breakouts as much as break-ins.

ST. PAUL'S CATHEDRAL

II's coronation in 2002. In 1981, Lady Diana Spencer and Prince Charles were married at St Paul's. Built between 1675 and 1710 on the site of a previous cathedral that was destroyed in the Great Fire of 1666, St Paul's is considered Christopher Wren's most important work.

St Paul's Cathedral rises above the city about 300 m (328 yds) north of the Thames. It is the main church of the Anglican Diocese of London and the venue for important state occasions, from the funeral of Lord Nelson in 1806 to the festivities celebrating the Golden Jubilee of Queen Elizabeth

FINANCIAL DISTRICT

London is one of the world's most important centers of business and finance. The prosperity of the city is reflected in its innovative architecture, for example in Richard Roger's Lloyd's building (above), which has all its service tracts, stairways and elevators on the outside of the structure.

JURASSIC COAST, EASTBOURNE, BRIGHTON

The seaside resorts along the English Channel coast are in constant competition to outdo each other with their impressive Victorian pier pavilions. The one in Eastbourne (main picture), from the 1870s, is one of the most attractive.

JURASSIC COAST

The 150 km (93 mi) of coastline that stretch between Old Harry Rocks near Swanage and Orcombe Point in Devon is like an open history book of the Mesozoic period, with layers of deposits dating from the Triassic, Jurassic and Cretaceous periods. It is basically an uninterrupted view of the three layers of what could be considered the Earth's Middle Ages. Geomorphologists first took note of this coastline in the year 1810, when Mary Anning, an eleven-year-old girl, discovered a "dragon" in the rocks near the fishing village of Lyme Regis (now Dorset). In fact, it was the first complete fossil imprint of an Ichthyosaurus and resembled a cross between a giant fish and a lizard. Since then, ever new finds are being made along the Dorset and East Devon coasts as erosion of the rocky landscape continues to take place at breathtaking speed – geologically speaking of course. A relaxing stroll along this wild coast becomes a journey of discovery taking you through the different stages of evolution and the Earth's history.

EASTBOURNE

Originally built east of the Bourne, a small stream, Eastbourne declared itself the "Sunshine Coast" and began attracting visitors with a promise of more hours of sunshine than anywhere else in England. It wasn't long before grand hotels shot up along the elegant beach promenade to service holidaymakers from the cities.

BRIGHTON

In the middle of the 18th century, Doctor Richard Russell described the positive benefits of seawater, and in particular the water off of the coast of Brighton, in curing certain diseases. His endorsement sparked unexpected popularity for the fishing village. In 1786, when Prince Regent and future King George IV built the faux-Oriental Royal Pavilion, it was tantamount to giving the village a royal seal of approval and increasing numbers of people began visiting. Brighton is still a popular destination for daytrippers thanks to its proximity to London. Brighton Pier (left) was built in 1899 and juts far into the sea. Its official name was originally "Brighton Marina Palace and Pier". The pavilion (below) was remodeled in 1815, by John Nash in the style of an Indian Mogul's palace.

Superb views of the coast in Dorset and East Devon can be enjoyed on a walk along the South West Coast Path, which follows the lovely cliffs (left). With its fossil remains, the coast offers a unique overview of around 185 million years of the earth's history.

CORNWALL

ST. MICHAEL'S MOUNT

According to legend, a fisherman saw the archangel Michael appear on this tidal rock island in the year 495. Since then the island has been known as Michael's Mount, and a church was built there in the 15th century. A monastery was also built here before it was transformed into a country mansion by subsequent owners. At low tide, the island can be reached on foot via a causeway. Historians assume this to be the island of Ictis, which was an important center for local trade in tin during the Iron Age.

LAND'S END

The westernmost point in England features a number of archeological sites including tombs from the Iron and Bronze Ages, stone circles, Celtic crosses and entire villages from the time before the birth of Christ, all of which bear testimony to thousands of years of settlement in the area. The waves of the Atlantic crash incessantly against the peninsula, which was given the name Belerion by the Romans, or "seat of storms". From Land's End to John O'Groats in northern Scotland it is 1,406 km (900 mi) overland – the farthest distance between any two points in the United Kingdom.

ISLES OF SCILLY

About 40 km (25 mi) off the coast of southwest Cornwall are the 140 Isles of Scilly, which you can reach by ferry from Penzance. Some 2,000 people live mostly from tourism and flower exports and are spread out over five inhabited islands, each with steep granite cliffs, white sand beaches and turquoise bays that are great for exploring on foot or by bike. The mild climate even allows palm trees and exotic plants to flourish here. A collection of exotic plants that are indigenous to these islands can be seen at the Abbey Garden in Tresco.

ST. IVES

St Ives has a history of attracting painters and sculptors looking for inspiration in the enchanting light and landscapes here. Small, grey granite houses characterize this former fishing village that is home to one of Cornwall's most attractive beaches.
Towering above Porthmeor Beach in the north, the Tate Gallery has opened a museum featuring the works of local St Ives artists. They include, for example, the pictures of Patrick Heron and Ben Nicholson, who lived here with his wife, artist Barbara Hepworth.

Lighthouses like this one built in 1859 on Godrevy Island are common along Cornwall's wildly romantic coast.

DARTMOOR

Dartmoor is most famously known as the location where Sir Arthur Canon Doyle's Sherlock Holmes encounters the Hound of the Baskervilles. The landscape is virtually untouched and can be very romantic as well as a bit spooky, especially when it is cloaked in the typically dense fog. The so-called "tors", enormous granite towers that have managed to withstand the forces of erosion, are typical of the area. Dartmoor National Park, which covers more than 950 sq km (367 sq mi), is noted for its vast meadow and moor landscapes.

The megaliths of Stonehenge near Salisbury are arranged in a circle of pillars connected by capstones (main picture). The stones of the inner circle came from the Preseli Hills in Wales, some 400 km (249 mi) away.

Stonehenge, an inspiring arrangement of megaliths in the county of Wiltshire, is still a mystery to us today. How were these giant stones transported? And what was the true purpose of the formation? The stones each weigh in at several tons and tower to heights of up to 7 m (23 ft) while an impressive trench 114 m (374 ft) wide surrounds the entire site.

During the final phase of construction, in roughly 2000 BC, the monoliths were transported hundreds of miles to this location, some having come from what is now Wales. They were then apparently oriented toward certain heavenly bodies, giving rise to the theory that the complex may have served both religious as well as astronomical purposes over the millennia.

The stone circle of Avebury east of Bath has the same orientation as Stonehenge and was built between 2600 and 2500 BC. According to an 18th-century British scholar, the Neolithic sanctuary was a druid temple, later destroyed under orders from the Church during the 1300s. Many of the megaliths were then used to build homes in the region.

The sun and the moon were probably the orientation points for the sanctuary at Stonehenge. Seen from the central altar stone, the sun once rose in between two sarsen stones, exactly aligned with the Heel Stone. Since then, it has shifted slightly with the gradual shift in the Earth's axis.

Of the former 154 stones at the Avebury site, only 36 have been preserved. Of those, 27 formed part of the large outer stone circle (left); they were inserted into the ground to a depth of 15 to 60 cm (6 to 24 in). In the 1930s, members of the National Trust began to re-erect the stones in their original positions.

YORK

York Minster is the largest Gothic church north of the Alps and boasts the largest number of medieval stained-glass windows. The 163-m-long (525-ft) structure was begun in 1220 and completed in 1472. York, one of the most attractive cathedral cities in Britain, is also known for its narrow lanes and half-timbered houses.

YORKSHIRE COAST

One of Yorkshire's greatest attractions is its natural beauty, which can be enjoyed along the coast in a variety of forms: villages such as Staithes (above), and picturesque coves like Saltwick Bay (right and main photo) and Robin Hood's Bay (far right, bottom). Right, top: The view from Sutton Bank.

Saltwick Bay on the Yorkshire Coast (main picture) displaying the type of dramatic summer evening light that makes the coast a real dream destination.

LAKE DISTRICT

The Lake District has been a national park since 1951, but it was more than 200 years ago that the "Lake Poets", part of the Romantic movement that included the likes of Wordsworth, began extolling the beauty of this stunning landscape. Hiking, climbing, sailing, or windsurfing enthusiasts will be well served in this varied park area comprising twelve large lakes and numerous small ones such as Lake Buttermere (above). Great Langdale is one of the more beautiful lakes, and the two Langdale Pikes, the higher of which rises to 730 m (2,395 ft), can be reached on a trail that is just under 10 km (6 mi) long. A road with hairpin turns will take you to the remains of a Roman fort at the Hardknott Pass, where superb views unfold into the Eskdale Valley below.

During his campaigns in the 13th century, King Edward built nine castles in Wales within a period of nine years. Conwy Castle (main picture) was the first of them. It boasts walls up to 4.5 m (15 ft) thick and eight flanking towers.

SNOWDONIA

Densely wooded valleys, mountain lakes, expanisve moors and picturesque ocean inlets all juxtaposed with a fascinating series of ragged peaks. That is Snowdonia National Park. Founded in 1951, it was the first Welsh national park and is still the largest of three (the Pembrokeshire Coast National Park was founded one year later, and the Brecon Beacons National Park in 1957). Snowdonia extends from Conwy in the north up to the peaks of Machynlleth in the south. Its highest point is Mount Snowdon at 1,085 m (3,560 ft), which is also the highest mountain in Wales. The many hills and mountains in the national park are often draped in clouds and mist. It is a paradise for ramblers and rockclimbers, and there are a number of rare plants and animals to discover in this excitingly diverse area, for example the golden eagle and the merlin. A pleasantly nostalgic way to explore the park is a trip on one of the narrow-gauge railways. At Caernarfon it is also possible to take the ferry to the island of Anglesey off the northwestern coast of Wales.

CONWY, HARLECH, CAERNARFON

After conquering Wales in the year 1284, English King Edward secured his positions in the area with the construction of three strongholds on the English border. Conwy, begun in 1283 and completed in the incredibly short time of just four and a half years, is considered a masterpiece of medieval military architecture. It was built by James of St George, a leading fortifications architect who also supervised work on the castles at Harlech and Caernarfon,

Begun in 1283, Caernarfon Castle (top) was built at the mouth of the river Seiont. It was to serve not just as a fortress but also as the residence of the king and the seat of his government. Harlech Castle (bottom) was conquered in 1404 by the Welsh captain Owain Glyndwr.

both of which were started in the same year.
Together with the later castles of Aberystwith, Beaumaris and Flint they formed a chain of fortresses along the coast of North Wales. Conwy Castle was to become a monument to English rule and a starting point for the planned settlement of Wales by the English. The medieval castle has been immortalized in countless paintings by English artists.

Left: Snowdonia National Park's English name derives from the highest mountain in Wales, the 1,085-m-high (3,560-ft) Snowdon peak. In Welsh, the area is known as Eyrie (Eagle's Nest), and if we could soar above it like an eagle, we would be able to enjoy a fascinatingly rich and diverse natural panorama.

DUNOTTAR

SLAINES

CRATHES

A journey through Scotland is also a journey through prehistory. The earliest evidence of hunters and gatherers in the far north dates back to about 7,000 BC. Later, when the clan system had taken hold, Scottish chiefs continued their battles to control the rugged, expansive landscape. In the Highlands alone there were roughly 180 clans. They had the land cultivated by farmers, made pacts with royal houses while simultaneously conspiring against them, and built castles and palaces as a symbol of their power. As a result of their successes, they were able to erect the impressive structures now considered typical of Scotland, all amidst this breathtaking natural environment, which is intricately and beautifully linked with the culture here.

Dunnottar Castle, for example, near the small port town of Stonehaven, enjoys a panoramic backdrop of grand rock cliffs and is so picturesque that it could be the creation of a talented set designer. Slaines Castle, on the coast north of Aberdeen, is the property of the 19th Earl of Errol and inspired Bram Stoker to pen his world-famous "Dracula" novel in 1895. Crathes Castle, situated to the east of Banchory in Aberdeen's hinterland, is famous for its beautiful gardens.

Once heavily disputed, then forgotten:
Oliver Cromwell laid siege to Dunnottar
Castle for eight months in 1651/52 in
order to obtain the insignias of the
Scottish crown. After capitulation he
found out that they had long been
smuggled out of the castle.

BEN NEVIS

Ben Nevis rises majestically from the Grampian Mountains to a height of 1,344 m (4,410 ft), the highest mountain in the British Isles. It is one of 284 "munros", a name in Scotland given to mountains that are more than 3,000 ft (915 m) high and whose summits stand out noticeably from others. While the mountain's north-west slope is relatively easy for hikers to climb, the steeper north-east side, with its 460-m (1,509-ft) rock face is still a challenge even for experienced climbers.

GLENCOE

Glencoe is a beautiful and wildly romantic valley. A handful of its peaks, such as the Buachaille Etive Mór (top), rise above the 1,000 m (3,281 ft) mark.

RANNOCH MOOR

Rannoch Moor is the largest expanse of moorland in Great Britain and as such one of the last virtually untouched natural habitats in Europe.

Storm clouds gather at dusk above
Ben Nevis and Loch Eil.

The largest island of the Inner Hebrides, the Isle of Skye, is considered one of the wildest, most rugged and most beautiful in all of Scotland. Ranges like the Cuillin Hills at 1,009 m (3,311 ft), the Quiraings and other bizarre geological formations such as the Old Man of Storr give the island its unique character. Fog, the occasional brief shower and rainbows make the remote coastal roads an unforgettable adventure.

The green meadows with herds of cattle and flocks of sheep (top) are mostly concentrated in the south of the Isle of Skye. Dunvegan Castle (above, middle), in the north-western part of Skye, has been the ancestral seat of the MacLeod clan since the 11th century. Portree (bottom) is the island's capital.

The Trotternish Peninsula on the Isle of Skye features some of the most spectacular scenery in the United Kingdom and has a hiking trail covering its entire length. Beinn Edra (main picture) towers up to 611 m (2,005 ft).

DONEGAL

FANAD

The Fanad Peninsula offers visitors a variety of scenery and features a coastline with beautiful sandy beaches, wooded areas and truly amazing rock formations.

In the nearby Carmelite Friary at Rathmullan, an event took place in 1607 that was to be a turning point in Irish history: The counts O'Neill and O'Donnel, hugely out-numbered by the English Army, fled the scene, thus clearing the way for Northern Ireland to be settled by Scottish Protestants.

NORTH COAST

The north coast of Donegal is a sparsely populated, lonely stretch of land. From top to bottom: Five Finger Beach; 16th-century Doe Castle, surrounded by the sea on three sides; and the Atlantic surf washing against the jagged coast.

WEST COAST

The cliffs of Slieve League fall a dramatic 601 m (1,972 ft) into the sea and are among Europe's high-est. Oddly, Donegal's hinterland is as infertile as the west coast is spectacular.

The lighthouse on the northern tip (Fanad Head) of the Fanad Peninsula was built at the beginning of the 19th century and enjoys a particularly spectacular setting (main picture).

GLENVEAGH

At some point in the 19th century, a speculator named John George Adair bought this piece of land and drove off the peasants who lived there. Breeding sheep, he had figured out, was more profitable than rental income. In the 20th century, Henry P McIlhenny, an American of Irish descent, bought and donated the land to the state. Today it is a national park once again open to the public.

DINGLE, BEARA, IVERAGH, KILLARNEY

Idyllic coastlines, picturesque villages, enchanting lake districts, steep cliffs, islands cloaked in myth and legend, remnants of ancient civilizations, and towns that are as historically exciting as they are vibrant – that is what awaits you in Munster, Ireland's largest province.

DINGLE

The Dingle Peninsula is the northernmost of five spits of land in County Kerry that point westward like fingers. With its gorgeous mountains, romantic rocky coast, and magnificent beaches it is one of Ireland's most beautiful and most popular regions. The mountains on either side of the Connor Pass, which at 456 m (1,496 ft) is the highest pass in Ireland, are a paradise for ramblers, while surfers will find excellent if cold conditions on the 5-km (3-mi) Surfer Beach near Inch on the peninsula's south coast.

Like everywhere in the west of Ireland, Dingle boasts relics of early Christendom. Especially impressive are the "beehive cells" of the early Irish hermit monks. In the early 6th century, Kerry's patron saint, St Brandon, allegedly prayed atop Mount Brandon (953 m/3,127 ft) before starting on his legendary journey to America in a curragh, a traditional sailing boat, with fourteen other monks. Mount Brandon is Ireland's second-highest mountain after Carrauntoohil, which checks in at 1,041 m (3,416 ft).

BEARA

Beara was the ancestral home of the O'Sullivans, the lords of Dunboy Castle near Castletownbere. When English troops took the castle in 1601, 1,000 clan members began a march across Ireland to the remote county of Leitrim; only 35 of them made it. Subsequent waves of emigration further reduced the population and today Beara is still a sparsely populated area.

In a bay near Castletownbere, the ruins of the Victorian Puxley Mansion are a reminder of the former copper mines of Beara. The home of a hated family of mine owners, it was burned down in the 1920 by the Irish Republican Army.

Right, top: The narrow road around the rocky Beara Peninsula offers superb views over more than 140 km (87 mi). Below that is a view of beautiful Ballydonegan Bay near Allihies.

IVERAGH

The drive around the Ring of Kerry takes you 170 km (106 mi) along the Iveragh Peninsula and is a highlight of any trip to Ireland. The ever-changing views of mountains and bays are simply breathtaking. A popular starting point for the tour of the Ring is Kenmare, a picturesque town with pastel-colored houses at the end of Kenmare Bay. Founded in 1775, Kenmare was known for its silk production.

Puffin Island (right) just off the west coast near the Bay of St Finan, is a popular nesting place for puffins, gannets and boobies.

Right, bottom: In a valley about 4 km (2.5 mi) from the south coast of Iveragh is the 2,000-year-old ring fort of Staigue. It once served as the residence of the kings of Munster and is today one of the best-preserved monuments of its kind in all of Ireland.

The Dingle Peninsula enchants with its wildly romantic coastal scenery (left). In the background is Mount Brandon shrouded in clouds. Behind it on the left, are the Three Sisters cliffs facing the opposite coast.

KILLARNEY

Ice Age glaciers formed the Killarney region, a mountainous lakeland area comprising more than 8,000 hectares (19,768 acres) near the town of the same name. Parts of the region have been made into a national park where the roads are free of cars. Any visit to the national park should include a trip by horse-drawn coach through the Gap of Dunloe, a mountain pass in the

On a swath of land near Lough Leane stands the late 15th-century Ross Castle (top).
Southwest of the town of Killarney is a region with three attractive lakes (middle, bottom and right).

shadows of Purple Mountain, which owes its name to the heather that flowers here in late summer. More demanding is the tour to the top of Carrauntoohil, Ireland's highest peak at 1,041 m (3,416 ft).
The oak and yew trees that grow in the park are fairly rare in Ireland, since most of the woods were cut down centuries ago. The strawberry tree is part of the unusual flora of the region, a shrub with red, edible fruits that normally only grows in the Mediterranean.

Tree masts were rammed as much as 30 m (98 ft) deep into the peaty ground to form the foundations of Amsterdam's Old Town. The result was not only seventy islands on stilts, but also the romantic ambience of a town on the water.

At the height of the "Golden 17th Century", construction began on the Three-Canal-Belt (left) whose half-moon shape includes the Keizersgracht canal (main picture). Four hundred bridges now criss-cross the historic center alone, and the water level is kept constant with the help of a system of locks and pumps. Even commercial loads are still transported on the city's canals.

Hundreds of houseboats lie in anchor on the quays of Amsterdam's 160 waterways as well. They have become an iconic element of city life, just like the bicycles and the flower stalls selling "tulips from Amsterdam".

KINDERDIJK, KEUKENHOF

KINDERDIJK

The landscape of the Kinderdijk-Elshout is characterized by reservoirs, dykes, pumping stations, administrative buildings and the beautifully preserved wooden windmills. In the early 17th century, the Belgian Simon Stevin refined the technology for draining the polders. By erecting a neat row of windmills at Kinderdijk, he was able to create an ingenious system in which the water was "milled" away. It took place in two stages. First, water was transported from a lower canal to one that was higher up. Then, it was moved to a system of locks that would remove it.

Today, such windmills still stand tall along the canals between Kinderdijk and Alblasserdam farther south. This cultural landscape so typical of Holland is the largest and best-preserved collection of historic windmills in the country. And they are not just there for show. A majority of these windmills have been in constant use since the 18th century. Just one of them was transformed into a museum that is now open to visitors.

KEUKENHOF

Visitors to the Bollenstreek, or "bulb region", between Haarlem and Leiden, can enjoy a drive through a sea of flowers. The fields of 8,000 nurseries specializing exclusively in the wholesale trade of flowers are on display here. The Tulip Route, as it is also known, takes you to the famous Keukenhof, founded in 1949.

BRUSSELS

GRAND-PLACE

The Grand Place, or great market square, in the Belgian capital is a modest-sized square by European standards at 110 m (345 ft) by 68 m (220 ft), but it is surrounded by glorious rows of guild houses and a beautiful town hall that make it one of the most attractive of its kind on the entire continent. In the 15th century, when the powerful and prosperous guilds in Brussels replaced traditional aristocratic rule of the city, they created this square with its exquisite patrician houses as a monument to their newly found wealth.

Narrow guild houses with ornately
structured façades surround the Grand
Place (top). Equally impressive are the
Gothic Town Hall (bottom right), the
Maison du Roi (bottom left) and the
Italianate Maison des Ducs de Brabant
(bottom middle).

BRUGES

In the Middle Ages, the prosperous trade in textiles between England and the European continent went primarily via Bruges. Merchants from seventeen countries owned factories there. Thanks to generous patrons, Jan van Eyck and Hans Memling then transformed Bruges into a center of art and culture. Bruges reached its zenith in the 15th century when the dukes of Burgundy, active supporters of late-Gothic court culture, took up residence within its walls. International trade, however, soon began to decline when the river Zweyn silted up, thus blocking access to the sea.

The town, oval in its planning, is accessed by numerous canals and long streets with rows of gabled houses. These patrician mansions, the counting houses of the merchant princes, and the magnificent town hall (left) – where the counts of Flanders "liberated" the people – tell of the former prestige of the city. Its proudest icon is the belfry of the Cloth Hall (below)

GHENT

The city's most famous sights are nestled in the well-preserved historic heart of the city, between the Grafenburg and the 14th-century St Bavo's Cathedral, which is slightly elevated and visible from afar. Its greatest religious treasure is the famous "Ghent Altar" by the brothers Hubert and Jan van Eyck (15th century). The 95-m-high (312-ft) bell tower opposite the church was a symbol of the rising bourgeoisie in the 14th century.

Ghent, the capital of the Belgian province of East Flanders, is located at the confluence of the rivers Schelde and Leie.

ANTWERP

The lifeblood of Antwerp, Belgium's second-largest city, is its bustling port. An array of automotive and chemical companies are based there, and as one of the busiest ports in the world it has cultivated an atmosphere of openness to the world for centuries – a fact that has contributed significantly to the rise of Antwerp as a world center for diamonds.

Antwerp boasts a number of historic monuments and an exceptionally vibrant cultural life. Most of its sights are in the city center, which forms a semi-circle on the right bank of the Schelde. The most remarkable sight in Antwerp is probably the Steen, a former castle complex whose oldest parts date back to the 9th century. Today it houses the National Maritime Museum, which features a fascinating Flemish warship from the 15th century.

The castle's viewing platform offers superb views across the Schelde – more than 500 m (1,650 ft) wide at this point – of the bridges, the old quay, and the countless derricks scattered across the horizon down at the port.

The French capital is steeped in history, and yet always ahead of the times. It is breathtaking in size, and yet seductive in its charm. One of few genuine world cities, Paris boasts a bewildering array of historic buildings and cultural landmarks.

Especially rich in history are the areas along the banks of the Seine, between Pont de Sully and Pont d'Iéna, beginning with the Île St Louis where the statue of Paris's patron saint stands, Ste Geneviève. Farther west, on the Île de la Cité, is the heart of Catholic Paris, with its Gothic Notre Dame Cathedral and Ste Chapelle, a filigree masterwork of High Gothic style.

Continuing along, opposite the Concièrgerie you come to one of the world's most important art museums, the Louvre. Farther down the Seine you arrive at the Musée d'Orsay, the Grand and Petit Palais, and the National Assembly. At the end of this stretch you reach the Eiffel Tower, a revolutionary steel structure completed in 1889 for the Exposition Universelle.

The Seine excursion boats, or "bateaux mouches," go right past the cathedral Notre Dame de Paris on the Île de la Cité in the Seine.

NOTRE DAME DE PARIS

Construction of the Gothic cathedral Notre Dame de Paris began on the Île de la Cité, an island in the Seine, in 1163. Among the new architectural elements were the transept and the rose windows, in the Rayonnant style (right), and the spectacular flying buttresses (main picture) on the east side of the church, each with a span of 15 m (49 ft). The main portal tympanum still features some of the original decoration, with figures portraying scenes from the Last Judgment. Notre Dame's interior is accentuated by five aisles with clustered columns and crossed-rib vaulting.

SAINTE CHAPELLE

Praised as a "miracle of the High Gothic," this former royal palace chapel was built in less than three years, presumably by Pierre de Montreuil, at the behest of King Louis IX. Comprising an upper (right) and lower (right, bottom) chapel, it represented a "gate to heaven" for the faithful in the Middle Ages. Thanks to nearly 360 degrees of 12-m-high (39-ft) stained glass windows, the Upper Chapel is a masterpiece of lighting that still mesmerizes visitors to this day. Completed in 1248, the chapel was to be a shrine for the holy relics that the pious Louis IX had bought (not "acquired") from the Emperor of Constantinople. In fact, he paid three times more for them than the entire cost of the chapel complex itself. These precious relics, which include the Crown of Thorns and a nail from Christ's Crucifix, are now kept in the treasury of Notre Dame.

The Louvre has been rebuilt several times over the centuries. The most recent addition, completed in 1989, was the glass and metal pyramid in front of the building (main picture). The structure was designed by Ieoh Ming Pei to allow more light into the museum below.

LOUVRE, JARDIN DES TUILERIES

The Louvre was originally to be "a museum for the people" that required no admission fee for visitors. That was the decree of the revolutionary government when the museum was opened in 1793 – the year Louis XVI and his wife Marie Antoinette were executed by the guillotine. From the 14th century until 1682, when Louis XIV moved his court to Versailles, the Louvre was actually the Paris residence of the kings of France. After that, the former town palace was transformed into one of the world's most important art museums. On the occasion of its 200th anniversary, the Louvre was remodeled as the "Grand Louvre," the largest museum in the world (the exhibition space was doubled to roughly 60,000 sq m/645,600 sq ft).

At the same time, the long-neglected Tuileries also received a facelift. During their redesign, architects Wirtz, Cribier and Benech preserved the long perspectives that royal landscape gardener Le Nôtre had originally created in the 17th century.

OPÉRA NATIONAL – PALAIS GARNIER

Opened in 1875, the national opera house reflects the opulence of the Second Empire. Thirteen years previous, in 1862, a vote had been taken to select among 171 tendors for the building's design. The unanimous winner was a hitherto unknown architect, Charles Garnier. However, construction on the project was delayed when the ground water rose unexpectedly. In order to maintain the water, a giant underground

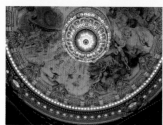

The full splendor of Garnier's opera house only becomes apparent once you are inside. Marc Chagall did the auditorium's ceiling fresco.

concrete basin was built, the ceiling of which provided support for the entire opera house. This "lake" below the opera served as inspiration for Gaston Leroux's novel, *Phantom of the Opera* (1910), a piece that has since been very successfully adapted as a musical by Andrew Lloyd Webber.

After the French Revolution, the Louvre's valuable collections were opened to the general public. Today, some 300,000 exhibits are on display there, including (above, from left) Michelangelo's *The Dying Slave*, Leonardo da Vinci's *Mona Lisa*, and the Greek sculpture *Venus de Milo*, discovered on the Cycladic island of Melos in 1820.

The Louvre's glass pyramid, flanked by the Denon and Richelieu wings, as seen from the Sully Wing. To the left of the pyramid stands an equestrian statue of Napoleon (left).

PLACE DE LA CONCORDE

Conceived as a "royal square" in 1755 by Jacques-Ange Gabriel during the reign of Louis XV, it was here in 1794 that the "Reign of Terror" unleashed its full wrath during the French Revolution – over 1,300 people, among them Louis XVI, were put to the guillotine. One year later the square was given its more reconciliatory name, Place de la Concorde. The roughly 3,200-year-old obelisk from Luxor has stood at its center since 1836.

The two bronze fountains on Place de la Concorde were designed by German architect Jacob Ignaz Hittorf (1792–1867).

CHAMPS-ÉLYSÉES, ARC DE TRIOMPHE

The Champs-Élysées is Paris' most famous avenue. It begins at Place de la Concorde and ends at Place Charles de Gaulle, the latter of which is home to the 50-m-high (164-ft) Arc de Triomphe (1836), built to commemorate Napoleon's victorious army. Unlike the gates from antiquity upon which it was modeled, Arc de Triomphe architect Jean-François Chalgrin dispensed with the arrangement of columns that was customary at the time and instead constructed a single, 29-m-high (95-ft) opening in the arch.

Napoleon's triumphal arch is the focal point of the Avenue des Champs-Élysées.

Alexandre Gustave Eiffel got the idea for the Eiffel Tower from his colleagues, Maurice Koechlin and Emile Nougier. Architect Stephen Sauvestre divided the tower into three sections and gave it rounded arches, creating transparency. An enthusiastic Eiffel directed and executed the project.

MUSÉE D'ORSAY

In many ways, the building opposite the Jardin des Tuileries that houses the Museé d'Orsay is itself the first work of art to be admired by visitors. A daringly engineered structure made of iron and glass, it features magnificent façades and is a textbook example of fin-de-siècle (turn-of-the-century) architecture. Originally a train station built for the Exhibition Universelle in 1900, trains departed here for south-western France up until 1939. Not until forty-seven years later, on December 9, 1986, did it become the museum that it is today. Complementing the collections in the Louvre, it houses masterpieces of French art from the years 1848 to 1914.

EIFFEL TOWER

Built in 1889 for the Paris Exhibition Universelle, the Eiffel Tower was a pioneering achievement in its day. In just over two years, 3,000 Gustave Eiffel Company metal workers, under the supervision of architect Stephen Sauvestre, assembled the tower, which is made of approximately 20,000 prefabricated parts and about 2.5 million rivets.

It was originally supposed to remain standing for only 20 years, but its usefulness as a radio tower ensured its longevity. The fact that the steel structure is still standing also speaks for the quality of the flexible "puddled" steel that was used in its construction.

The Eiffel Tower, visible from great distances and beautifully illuminated at night, was initially rejected by the populace. Today, it is impossible to imagine Paris without it.

Eiffel (1832–1923), a descendant of German emigrants from the Eifel region, had an excellent nose for business. Working with his Paris office, where he employed only first-class architects and engineers, Eiffel was not only responsible for the world-famous tower in Paris that is named after him, but was also active in many other projects both in France and abroad, some as far afield as Africa and South America. They build viaducts, train stations, engine and trade fair halls, and the scaffolding system for another equally world-famous piece: the Statue of Liberty in New York. Eiffel projects were oriented toward new "graphic styles" and were therefore always in step with the aesthetics of the time.

The Pont Alexandre III was built for the 1900 World Exhibition and the Eiffel Tower for the one in 1889.

At the time of its construction, the Eiffel Tower, which was built in two years, was the highest tower in the world.

The Musée d'Orsay cannot hide its former incarnation as a train station (left). Between 1980 and 1986, the building was transformed into a museum that specializes in French art. One of its exhibits is the historical painting *The Romans of the Decadence* (far left) by Thomas Couture (1815–79).

HÔTEL DES INVALIDES

As can be surmised from the name, Louis XIV built the Hôtel des Invalides for the victims of his many wars. Today it houses one of the world's largest military museums. In 1767, a dome was added as a royal vault, but it is Napoleon who now lies buried there instead of the Sun King.

The shiny golden cupola of the dome of Les Invalides rises above Napoleon's sarcophagus of red porphyry.

PALAIS BOURBON

The Palais Bourbon near the Pont de la Concorde is the seat of the National Assembly. The building, erected around 1730 for one of the daughters of Louis XIV, was given a neoclassical portico and an array of sculptures during its many remodels. In 1827, it was bought by the Chamber of Deputies. The library housed there holds about 350,000 volumes, the most important of which is the original protocol of the trial of Joan of Arc.

Michel de l'Hôpital, a 16th-century lawyer and statesman, stands guard in front of the National Assembly.

The Palace of Versailles outside of Paris is the archetype of an absolutist sovereign's residence and became a model for many European royal palaces. Main picture: Wrought-iron fencing separates the Place d'Armes from the palace.

FONTAINEBLEAU

In the 12th century, King Louis VII commissioned a small hunting lodge in the forest of Fontainebleau, about 60 km (37 mi) south of Paris. After being abandoned for a while, François I had it rebuilt in 1528. Now only a single turret from the original building remains standing.

For the interior design work he hired Italian artists including Rosso Fiorentino and Francesco Primaticcio, both of whom were well known for their adaptations of the mannerist style known as the "School of Fontainebleau." The palace was subsequently remodeled on a number of occasions, in particular during the reigns of Henry IV and Napoleon.

Today Fontainebleau houses some outstanding baroque, rococo and neoclassical works of art from Italy and France. The palace was eventually extended to contain five courtyards, all with differing designs. Among its most impressive rooms are the horseshoe-shaped staircase and the luxurious ballroom. The palace gardens are also well worth seeing.

VERSAILLES

In 1661, King Louis XIV began the expansion of his father Louis XIII's hunting lodge, a location that would soon serve him as his permanent seat of government. The two leading architects, Louis Le Vau and later Jules Hardouin-Mansart, created a palace complex comprising roughly 700 rooms and vast manicured gardens that is a work of art in and of itself with plants, fountains and sculptures as well as the auxiliary garden palaces Petit and Grand Trianon.

For 100 years, Versailles was the political heart of France. At times,

This portrait by Hyacinthe Rigaud (today in the Louvre) was intended to help further glorify this absolutist monarch.

as many as 5,000 people lived at the palace, including a considerable number of French aristocrats, and up to 14,000 soldiers resided in the outbuildings and in the actual town of Versailles.

Of the many magnificent staterooms at the palace, the Hall of Mirrors has historically been seen as the most important. The room, which bewilders visitors with its size, is so named for the seventeen giant mirrors that reflect the light from the windows opposite. It is here that the German emperor was crowned in 1871 and the Treaty of Versailles was signed in 1919.

The Hall of Mirrors at the Palace of Versailles (left) measures 73 by 11 m (240 by 36 ft) and is one in a sequence of rooms created in 1678 that extends along the entire garden façade. It is a masterpiece of the baroque decorative arts. The Sun King held his morning and evening audience in his bedchamber (middle) and the palace had its own opera house (right) and theater.

In 1645, landscape architect André Le Nôtre – creator of the park at Versailles – designed the Grand Parterre at the Palace of Fontainebleau, a terraced garden with low-lying plants intended primarily for representational purposes (left).

The museums at Versailles (left, the Musée des Carosses with its historic coaches) help to recreate a grandiose past. An important conceptual component of the parks are the water gardens – canals and fountains adorned with sculptures (right). Particularly spectacular is the Apollo Basin, from which the god rises in his sun chariot pulled by horses (middle).

Reims represents the starting point for the Christianization of Gallia (Latin for Gaul), and it remained a bulwark of the Catholic Church for centuries, as is symbolized by the abbey church of St Rémi (main picture).

AMIENS

Situated about 115 km (71 mi) north of Paris, Amiens is both a university town and a bishop's see. The cathedral, Notre Dame d'Amiens, is one of the great churches of the French High Gothic, and its dimensions are awe-inspiring. Covering a total area of 7,700 sq m (82,852 sq ft), it is the largest church in all of France, and became the model for the famous cathedral in Cologne, Germany.

Bishop Evrard de Fouilloy laid the foundation stone for the church in 1220 and within about fifty years, by the end of the 13th century, Robert de Luzarches' plans had been nearly completed. Construction here began not with the choir but with the west towers. The cathedral consists of a three-aisled nave rising to an astonishing height of 43 m (139 ft). The west front is divided into three portals and crowned by two wide towers. It also features a large, artfully designed rose window. The portals are decorated with scenes from the Old and New Testaments, a highpoint of medieval sculpture.

REIMS

Reims is in the heart of the Champagne region and enjoys a glorious history. In around 500, Clovis was anointed first King of the Franks here by St Remigius. The archbishop's bones are interred in the 11th-century St Rémi Abbey Church, where an early-Gothic choir adjoins the narrow nave and the windows date from the 12th century.

Notre Dame Cathedral, the coronation church of the French kings,

The high-Gothic cathedral of Reims has a richly decorated western façade as well as beautiful stained-glass windows by Marc Chagall.

was erected starting in 1211 on the site of an earlier church that had burned down. The building is adorned with expressive stone sculptures and the lovingly restored stained-glass windows (including some by Chagall) are vibrant masterpieces of light and color.

The archbishop's Palais du Tau, built around 1500, served as a stopping post for the French kings. Its interior features superb tapestries.

About a dozen archbishops, cardinals and other church dignitaries are buried in Notre Dame d'Amiens (left).

CHARTRES

Notre Dame de Chartres is the cathedral par excellence of the High Gothic. Unlike many other cathedrals, it boasts an array of fully preserved original furnishings. The triple-aisled basilica with transept and five-aisled choir is considered one of the first purely Gothic structures and was the model for the cathedrals in both Reims and Amiens. Construction here began in the early 12th century, and the church was consecrated in 1260. Below the choir is the

The two contrasting spires of Notre Dame de Chartres (top) date from the 12th and the 15th centuries. The emphasis on vertical lines is characteristic. Middle and bottom: The church's nave and the ambulatory.

Crypt of St Fulbert (1024) – with a length of 108 m (354 ft) it is the largest Romanesque crypt in France.
New construction technologies were employed at Chartres, for example the use of flying buttresses. This permitted the walls to be interrupted by large window surfaces. This led to the use of stained-glass windows in the 12th and 13th centuries, which provide a unique light inside the building.

CHALKSTONE CLIFFS OF NORMANDY, MONT-SAINT-MICHEL

On a rocky island out in the English Channel, in an exclusive spot about 1 km (1,100 yds) off the Normandy coast, is the former Benedictine Abbey of Mont-Saint-Michel, the most famous landmark in the region (main picture).

CHALKSTONE CLIFFS OF NORMANDY

It is not exactly delicate, this countryside stretching along the English Channel in the north-west of France. But the wind-battered coast and verdant green hinterland have their own undeniable magic that it is impossible to escape.

The Atlantic surf, the rugged shoreline, the gleaming white chalkstone cliffs and the long sandy beaches scattered in hundreds of bays along the spectacular Normandy coast present a nature full of brute force and primordial beauty. Strewn throughout the area are sleepy fishing villages and lively port towns as well as elegant seaside spas and pleasant holiday resorts. The zenith of the Normandy chalkstone cliff landscape can be found at Étretat. This tiny fishing village was "discovered" by artists in the 19th century who thought it was particularly picturesque. Situated in a quaint cove, it is romantically framed by alabaster-white cliffs with bizarre rock formations that stretch along the steep coastline.

MONT-SAINT-MICHEL

The story of Mont-Saint-Michel began in the 8th century with the Vision of St Aubert: the Archangel Michael appeared before the bishop, and in return the bishop had a small prayer hall built for pilgrims. In 1022, a new structure that incorporated the original walls was built atop the earlier church of Notre-Dame-sous-Terre. The crypt and choir, possibly the first choir ambulatory without radial chapels, were built first. After its collapse, the church was rebuilt in the late-Gothic style. In the 11th century, under Abbot Randulf of Beaumont, work continued on the crossing piers and transept, and the nave was completed at the beginning of the

12th century, under Abbot Roger I. The cross-ribbed vaults of the side aisles and central nave walls have been preserved only on the south side. The west front, with its twin towers, was completed in 1184, but burned down in 1776. People eventually settled at the foot of the abbey and some houses from the 14th century are still standing. Due to driving sands and strong currents, Mont-Saint-Michel was difficult to reach even at low tide – it was besieged but never conquered.

The coast between Le Havre and Le Tréport is known as the Alabaster Coast – Côte d'Albâtre – after its white chalk cliffs. In some parts, they reach more than 100 m (328 ft) in height. The eroded arch west of Étretat (left) is particularly famous; it resembles an elephant's trunk plunging into the water.

Brittany was home to a civilization even before the Common Era that puzzles scientists to this day. Who were the people of this megalithic culture? Did the menhirs, large stones erected between 5,000 and 2,000 BC, function as solar or lunar calendars? Or were they symbols of fertility, cult sites or markers for processional routes? We can't even begin to answer these questions.

The veil of mystery only begins to lift as of the year 500 BC. Around that time, the Celts had arrived and settled in Brittany, a region they appropriately called "Armor": land at the sea. Although they eventually converted to Christi-anity, many of their pre-Christian customs and legends have pre-vailed, as has the Breton lan-guage. Certain character traits of the Celts also live on: Bretons are quite imaginative people, and are known to be strongheaded and proud.

Brittany, which covers roughly 27,200 sq km (10,499 sq mi) of northwestern France, is dominated by fishing and agriculture – just about every single sea bass or monkfish ("loup de mer") that lands on European plates comes from the Breton coast. Other areas of strength here include the export of early vegetables as well as the processing of meat and milk. In addition, with 1,200 km (746 mi) of coastline, it ranks as one of the country's most popular tourist regions after the Côte d'Azur. The windswept shores, the craggy rock formations, the lush green meadows and the powerful Atlantic surf are all highlights.

Oddly, the region first achieved international fame through Asterix and Obelix. The best-known Celts since King Arthur, these cartoon characters have delighted readers around the world since 1959, when the first story by René Goscinny and Albert Uderzo was published. Unfortunately for would-be seek-ers, the villages they visited were only imaginary.

POINTE DE SAINT-MATHIEU

About 20 km (12 mi) west of Brest, a unique architectural complex stands atop a promontory that rises 30 m (98 ft) from the ocean (main picture): a 36-m (118-ft) lighthouse, a rectangular signaling tower, the nearby village church of Saint Mathieu, and the ruins of the former Benedictine abbey church of Notre Dame de Grâce, parts of which date back to the 12th century (west front) while most of the church goes back to the 13th to 16th centuries. The lighthouse was built in 1835, partly using the stones from the ruined church. It guides ships and sailors along the Côte des Abers, one of the most dangerous strecthes of the Breton coast.

ST. MALO

CÔTE DE GRANIT ROSE

POINTE DU RAZ

This old Corsair town, which was restored to its original state after World War II, has a lot to see including the Old Town and promenade along the fortifications.

Off the coast from the fishing port of Paimpol lies the Île-de-Bréhat, a bird reserve. The stony shorelines and the surrounding eighty-six islands consist of red granite, which gave its name to the entire coast: Côte de Granit Rose.

Pointe du Raz, near Cape Sizun, is a narrow spit of land jutting out into the Atlantic. It is almost 80 m (262 ft) high and the view across the cliffs is breathtaking.

LOIRE VALLEY

A unique collection of historic monuments is concentrated along the roughly 200-km (124-mi) stretch of the Loire Valley between Sully-sur-Loire in the east and Chalonnes in the west, a short way downstream from Angers. France's longest river meanders through sensational countryside toward the Atlantic, traversing the historic regions of the Orléanais, Blésois, Touraine and Anjou.

The establishment of towns along the Loire Valley began between 371 and 397 with St Martin, Bishop of Tours and patron saint of the Franks. After his death, his tomb in Tours became an important pilgrimage site. In 848, Charles the Bald was crowned in Orléans, and in the 10th and 11th centuries the river valley became the preferred place of residence for the Capetians. There are several important Romanesque landmarks on the Loire, among them the abbey churches of St Benoît-sur-Loire with 11th-century narthex and crypt, Germigny-des-Prés (with a mosaic from the 12th century), frescoes in Liget and Tavant, and Notre-Dame de Cunault. Fontevraud Abbey is one of Europe's largest monasteries and the burial place of the Plantagenets.

The coronation of Henry Plantagenet as King of England in 1154 created a massive empire whose centers of power were at Angers and Chinon. It was there, in 1429, during the Hundred Years' War, that Joan of Arc met the still uncrowned Charles VII and set off to liberate the town of Orléans, which was under siege by the English. Many beautiful châteaux were rebuilt or remodeled under Francis I, including the magnificent Château Azay-le-Rideau (1527) on the Indre; Chambord, the model for all Renaissance châteaux on the Loire; Blois and Amboise; and the bridge château of Chenonceaux. Villandry and Saumur are also worth seeing and there are numerous vineyards scattered throughout the region.

BLOIS

A mighty bridge leads across the Loire into the old town of Blois, which is dominated by an imposing château. In 1498, under Louis XII, Blois became the royal residence of the House of Valois, and for a few years it enjoyed status as the capital of France. The château was enlarged on several occasions, which is why the individual tracts are fashioned in different styles. Catherine de Medici, who died here, is remembered by her Oratory.

AMBOISE

Château Amboise, atop a promontory overlooking the Loire, was commissioned in 1490, by Charles VIII who hired Italian artists and landscape gardeners to build the magnificent palace on the foundations of an older castle. Francis I based his glamorous court there. An avid patron of the arts, the king invited Leonardo da Vinci to spend his last years in Clos Lucé, a mansion connected to the château via tunnel. He is allegedly buried in the château chapel.

CHENONCEAUX

Château Chenonceaux is unique thanks to the location of its extraordinary two-story gallery, which straddles the charming Cher. Built by Philibert Delorme, this important Renaissance structure was commissioned by Catherine de Medici, but the château itself had already been completed in 1521. Its isolated donjon is a relic of an earlier building, the keep, which was a characteristic element of French castles.

CHAMBORD

Chambord (left and main picture), about 15 km (9 miles) east of Blois in what used to be extensive hunting grounds, is the largest of the Loire Valley castles.

Chambord (main picture and above) is the largest of the Loire châteaux. Francis I commissioned this extravagant structure in 1619, as a hunting lodge, with stout towers and chimneys. It has more than 400 rooms and can accommodate up to 10,000 guests during festivities and hunts. Conceived as a symbol of the king's absolutist powers, the château was actually deserted most of the time. Even later its usefulness was inversely proportional to its size. Particularly noteworthy among the furnishings are four stoves with Meissen porcelain tiles and a double-helix staircase that is said to have been designed by Leonardo da Vinci.

VILLANDRY

The magnificent Renaissance gardens are the main attraction at Château Villandry, completed in 1536 and situated 15 km (9 mi) west of Tours. Laid out in large squares, the 7-hectare (17-acre) complex is subdivided into water, music, pleasure, vegetable and herb gardens. Even the different vegetables are grouped such that their colors create geometric patterns. The plants are irrigated by an elaborate underground watering system.

AZAY-LE-RIDEAU

This château on the Indre, built in 1524, boasts harmonious proportions and a romantic location on the water – which originally served as a moat. But it did not bring good fortune to its sponsor, Gilles Berthelot, then the mayor of Tours. King Francis I was very particular when his subjects displayed their wealth too openly. Shortly after its completion, the king accused Berthelot of disloyalty and summarily confiscated his château.

CHINON

Chinon, at the confluence of the Vienne and the Loire, is dominated by a mighty castle whose origins date back to the 10th century. Henry II, King of England, enlarged the complex and made it into his residence. Only the castle's ruins remain, but it is well known as the location where Joan of Arc met with Charles VII in 1429 with the intention of persuading him to entrust her with an army to drive the English out of France.

SAUMUR

Château Saumur became world-famous as an illustration on a calendar page in the Duke du Berry's book of hours, the Très Riches Heures. Despite later enlargements, the defensive structure with four towers standing on a rocky promontory has been more or less preserved its original 14th-century state. Today, in addition to the Musée des Arts Décoratifs, the palace houses the Musée du Cheval, which documents the history of equestrianism.

The astronomical clock on Strasbourg Cathedral (main picture) is a miracle of precision and depicts the apostles passing in front of Christ.

STRASBOURG

The icon of Strasbourg is its stunning cathedral, one of the most important sacred buildings of the European Middle Ages. Begun in about 1015, it was originally Romanesque in style, but as construction work spanned several centuries, the cathedral also features elements of the Gothic.

The west front, praised for its sheer proportions and ornate portal sculptures, is an especially important element of the structure. It was a way for the citizens to create a monument for themselves after having taken on the financing of mammoth edifice in 1286. Further highlights of the cathedral are the magnificent stained-glass windows and its astronomical clock.

The cathedral square is lined with half-timbered houses, some of which are up to five stories high, including House Kammerzell and Palais Rohan, built around 1740 in Louis XV style. The historic cityscape also includes the picturesque tanners' district, La Petite France, from the 16th/17th centuries, the Ponts Couverts (a formerly covered bridge), and the Vauban Weir.

COLMAR

Colmar, the capital of the Département Haut-Rhin, combines all of the delights of the region. The river Lauch flows through the Old Town, which boasts some very picturesque and romantic sights such as the St Martin Collegiate Church, the tanners' district, and "Little Venice." Art lovers typically head straight for the renowned Unterlinden Museum. At the heart of its collection of medieval art is Matthias Grünewald's Isenheim Altar (above), created between 1512 and 1516. The highlight of the nearby Dominican Church is Martin Schongauer's grand *Virgin at the Rosebush* (1473).

RIQUEWIHR

The older inhabitants of Riquewihr often refer to their town as the "pearl of the vineyard." And rightly so: No other wine village has preserved its 16th-century appearance as well as Riquewihr. Mighty gate towers, long rows of stately Renaissance homes, and no fewer than five museums bear witness to its centuries of prosperity. Not even the line of kitschy souvenir shops along Rue de Gaulle detract from the village's charm.

The four defiant towers of the Ponts Couverts (left) are the last of originally eighty towers placed along the walls of the old imperial town of Strasbourg. The bridges linking them were covered until the 18th century, hence the name "covered bridges".

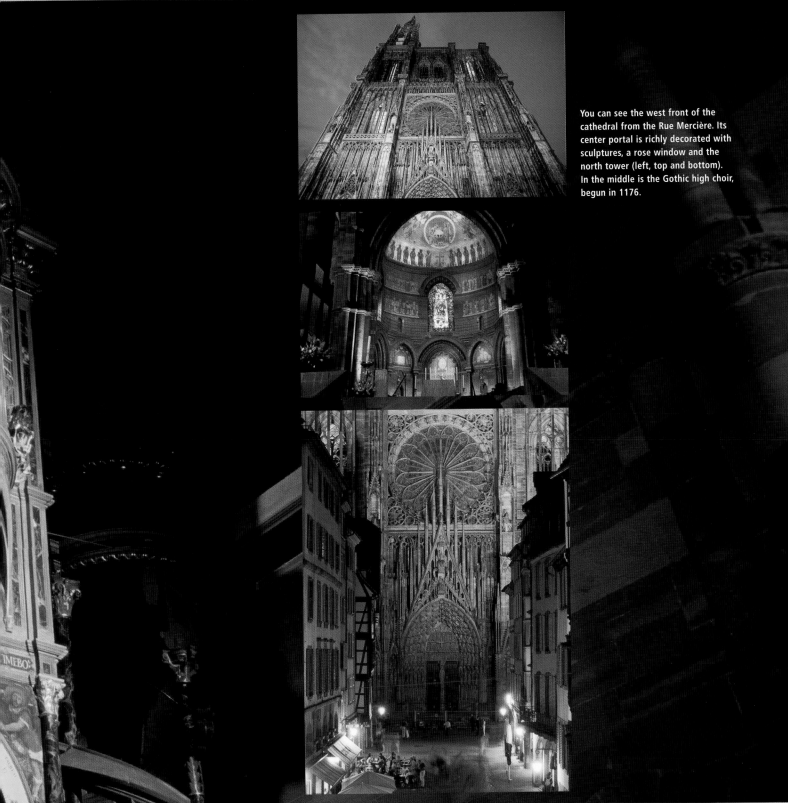

You can see the west front of the cathedral from the Rue Mercière. Its center portal is richly decorated with sculptures, a rose window and the north tower (left, top and bottom). In the middle is the Gothic high choir, begun in 1176.

Cannes (main picture) is a popular stomping ground among the rich and famous, and one of the most glamorous towns on the Côte d'Azur. Luxury yachts line the port like pearls on a string.

SAINT-TROPEZ

Dense pine, oak and chestnut forests push their way down to the coastline between Fréjus and Hyères, two hills that drop off steeply toward the sea and leave no room for construction and development along the Corniche des Maures. The coastal road is all the more attractive thanks to this, winding along the wooded hills often half way up the incline and frequently offering superb views across the sea. In the numerous coves and bays, small former fishing villages huddle together having lost little of their original charm.

The motto in Saint-Tropez is to see and to be seen. The exclusive village first became famous through the film "And God Created Woman," which was shot here in 1956 by director Roger Vadim and featured his wife at the time, Brigitte Bardot. The idea of a decadent life by the sea first lured the youth of the world before the throngs of high-end tourists came rushing in. On her 40th anniversary, "BB" celebrated her retirement from cinema on the beach of Pampelonne just a couple miles from Saint-Tropez.

NICE

This secret capital of the Côte d'Azur is a town full of contrasts. While the grand boulevards cling to memories of the Belle Époque, life in parts of Nice's Old Town resembles the scenes in a village in Italy.

The Greeks founded what they referred to as Nikaia, the "victorious town", in the 5th century BC, while the Romans preferred a location higher up in the hills for their settlement, Cemenelum, present-day Cimiez. The trademark icon of Nice is the Promenade des Anglais, built in the 1830s along the waterfront by wealthy English folks who

Top: The legendary Hotel Négresco adorns the eight-lane, 5-km (3-mi) seaside promenade in Nice.
Bottom: One of the most beautiful squares in the city, Cours Saleya.

had already recognized the benefits of Nice as a desirable place to retire in the mid-19th century.

The most impressive edifices from that period are the famous Hotel Négresco and the Palais Masséna. The Old Town features narrow, winding alleyways and houses with a distinctly Italian feel. The main square, Cours Saleya, has an attractive farmers' market. From the Castle Hill you can enjoy amazingly beautiful views of the Old Town and the Mediterranean.

Jet-setters discovered the dreamy fishing village of Saint-Tropez (left) in the early 1950s. The town is said to have been named after a Roman soldier who had died a martyr's death as a Christian under Nero.

CANNES

The Celts and Romans had already established settlements around the Golfe de la Napoule in their times, but the bay did not become a popular destination until the 19th century, with the arrival of the British. Initially, they built beautiful villas for themselves before the upscale hotels followed. The Boulevard La Croisette was built around the entire bay.

Le Suquet, the Old Town, covers Mont Chevalier, a tiny hill that rises above the old port and whose summit is crowned by a watchtower dating back to the 11th century. Next to it, the Musée de la Castre displays relics from antiquity. The Gothic Notre Dame de

The luxury Carlton Hotel on the Croisette in Cannes.

l'Espérance dates from the year 1648. Magnificent views of the entire bay of Cannes unfold from the viewing platform behind the church, and on the edge of the Old Town is a giant hall that houses the Forville Market.

Cannes is of course also a town of festivals: the month of May is firmly set aside for the Film Festival, when the Golden Palm is awarded for the best film; in June, the international advertising industry meets in Cannes to select the best cinema and TV advertising spots; and in the fall, TV bosses from around the world gather there to buy and sell their programs. The venue for these activities is the Palais du Festival, at the western end of the Croisette.

The Abbaye de Sénanque (main picture) was founded by Cistercians in 1148, and had its heyday in the early 13th century before being destroyed in 1544. In 1854, seventy-two monks chanced a new beginning: Lavender fields now frame the abbey complex with its church and cloisters.

LUBÉRON

East of Avignon, halfway between the Alps and the Mediterranean, is the expansive limestone plateau of the Lubéron, a rocky landscape with lonely oak groves, small mountain villages and stone houses that has done well to preserve its impressive natural beauty. The mountains reach 1,125 m (3,691 ft) and contain some largely uninhabited stretches of land with more than 1,000 different species of plants. The "Parc Naturel Régional du Lubéron" was founded in 1977 to protect this unique environment.

The present-day isolation of many parts of the Lubéron is, however, deceptive – the limestone ridge, which was formed in the Tertiary period, has actually always been settled. The villages huddled in the hollows and valleys sprung up in the Middle Ages. Houses here have thick walls and churches served as both places of worship and refuge. The inhabitants of the Lubéron mostly depended on meager agriculture. When the harvests were no longer sufficient, the villages on the north side were abandoned.

AIX-EN-PROVENCE

In 122 BC, the Romans founded the hot springs colony of Aquae Sextiae Saluviorum on the ruins of the Celtic-Liguric settlement of Entremont. It later enjoyed the status of capital of Provence for centuries. During the Middle Ages, Aix first became an important center for the arts and learning after the 12th century.

The Old Town extends from the Cours Mirabeau, an avenue with

Developed as early as 1651, the Cours Mirabeau (top: Atlas on a house façade) forms the southern edge of the Old Town.

sycamore trees and beautiful city mansions from the 18th century, to the St Sauveur Cathedral, which has a baptistery dating back to Merovingian days. Other sights worth seeing are the 17th-century town hall, the Musée des Tapisseries and Paul Cézanne's studio. The favorite motif of the city's most famous son was Mont St Victoire to the east of Aix-en-Provence, which is worth a detour.

Flowering lavender fields are the trademark of Provence. Here, the proverbial "light of the south" is combined with beguiling scents and a riot of colors.

Arles was founded by the Romans due to its strategic position on the Rhône (main picture). The city also has a place in art history as the home of Vincent van Gogh, who painted some of his most famous works here.

PONT DU GARD

This famous bridge aqueduct was built between AD 40 and 60, during the reigns of the emperors Claudius and Nero, in order to supply water to the fast-growing ancient town of Nemausus, present-day Nîmes. The bridge, which spans the Gard Valley, was considered a daring feat of engineering at the time and is still a very impressive sight even in the days of glass skyscrapers.

The bottom level has a road between its six arches, which vary in width from 15 to 24 m (49 to 79 ft). The middle level has a total of eleven arches. The thirty-five arches on the top level are about 5 m (16 ft) wide and support the actual water duct, which transports roughly 40,000 cu m (1,412,587 cu ft) to Nîmes every day during high demand. The uppermost level of the bridge is about 275 m (900 ft).

The aqueduct increasingly fell into disrepair after the 4th century, and during the Middle Ages the central level was tapered so it could be used for traffic of various kinds. The structure was finally restored in the 18th century.

ARLES

Among the oldest Roman structures in Arles are the subterranean corridors of the Cryptoporticus, below the Roman Forum. More than 100 m (328 ft) long and about 70 m (230 ft) wide, the vast tunnels were likely used to store grain.

Two amphitheaters from the 1st and 2nd centuries also date back to the Romans. One of them measures

The Arena in Arles (top) is a relic of Roman days; the mighty St Trophime Cathedral (center; above: the Place de Forum) a jewel of the romanesque style.

135 m (443 ft) wide and 100 m (328 ft) long, the largest remaining open-air stage from antiquity. Its vast arena is now used for bullfights. The thermae on the right bank of the Rhône date from the late-Roman period and are part of an approximately 200-m-long (656-ft) palace complex.

The necropolis of Alyscamps and its well-preserved sarcophagi provide insight into burial customs of pre- and early-Christian days. Meanwhile, the nave at St Trophime Cathedral dates from the 11th century and is one of France's most remarkable Romanesque buildings.

The Roman aqueduct over the river Gardon (left) is a masterpiece of Roman engineering. It is part of a roughly 50-km (31-mi) pipeline that runs from the Fontaines d'Eure springs to Nîmes. The limestone blocks were placed without mortar – pressure and shape hold them together.

ORANGE

Orange enjoys a history of more than 2,000 years going back to the Romans who originally founded the town of Arausio on the site of a conquered Celtic settlement in the Rhône Valley. It is not only home to one of the best-preserved Roman amphitheaters, but it is also the largest from antiquity with a stage backdrop that measures 103 m (330 ft) by 37 m (150 ft). The theater accommodated up to 10,000 spectators to watch shows in front of the beautifully adorned wall.

Also worth seeing is the Arc de Triomphe, completed in about AD 25. It is the most completely preserved Roman archway in the region of Gallia and once marked the entrance to the town on the Via Agrippa.

NÎMES

Nîmes, a town of temples, thermae and theaters, was founded in the year AD 16 by Emperor Augustus. The most impressive Roman structure here is the amphitheater with its oval arena and rising rows of stone seats that accommodate to 25,000 spectators. The Maison Carrée, or "square house" (above) – also from the time of Augustus – features Corinthian columns and an impressive decorative freeze. It is one of the best-preserved Roman temples in Europe. The Jardin de la Fontaine has a large number of hot springs, temples and a theater.

Camargue horses (main picture) have a compact build, slightly angular heads and a dense mane. The coats on these half-wild horses are not white until their fifth year.

AVIGNON

Catholic Church history was made in the 14th century in this southern French town on the Rhône: Between 1309 and 1376, the Roman Curia found refuge here from the political turmoil in Rome and went into "Babylonian exile." In 1348, Pope Clement VI bought the sovereignty of Avignon from Joan of Naples and it became the center of Christianity. Seven popes and later two antipopes resided here in the roughly 100-year period that eventually led to the Western Schism.

The papal residence consists of an Old and a New Palace. On the north side is the 12th-century Roman cathedral Notre Dame des Doms. Also part of the bishops' district is the Petit Palais, built in 1317, which was intended to compensate the archbishop for the demolition of his original palace.

From the 14th century, Avignon was surrounded by an imposing town wall that was strengthened with fortified towers such as the Tour des Chiens and the Tour du Châtelet. The latter controlled access to the world-famous Pont d'Avignon.

MARSEILLE

France's second-largest city and the most important port in the country, Marseille boasts more than 2,500 years of history. Its importance as a major gateway for incursions into North Africa is also mirrored in the composition of its population.

The town of Massalia was originally founded by Greeks from Asia Minor on the hill where Notre Dame de la Garde stands today. Initially Rome's allies, it was not until 49 BC that Caesar finally conquered the Greek republic. The port town experienced its first major period of prosperity in the 12th century when armies of crusaders brought lucrative business to the city for their trips from Marseille to Jerusalem. In the centuries

Notre Dame de la Garde watches over the port of Marseille.

that followed it was the most important port in the Mediterranean.

Today, the heart of Marseille still beats in the old harbor. It is from there that La Canebière, the city's main boulevard, starts its way through the entire city. It was once the symbol of a vibrant city with a penchant for extravagance. The entrance to the port is flanked on the north side by Fort St Jean and on the south side by Fort St Nicolas.

The basilica Notre Dame de la Garde is Marseille's most enduring landmark and is visible from quite a distance. The square in front of it, the Plateau de la Croix, affords the best views of the port and city. Another excellent vista point across the water to Marseille is from the summit of the Château d'If rock.

Also worth seeing are the St Victor Basilica, Notre Dame de la Garde, Château d'If on a rocky island offshore from the port, and the Citadel.

View of Avignon, capital of the Département Vaucluse, from the opposite bank of the Rhône. Only four original arches remain of the much-celebrated Pont St Bénézet bridge (left). The medieval city is surrounded by 4.5 km (3 mi) of heavy fortifications.

CAMARGUE

The estuary between the two main distributaries of the Rhône comprises 140,000 hectares of swamps, meadows and grazing land as well as dunes and salt marshes – it is one of Europe's largest wetlands. Agricultural use, mostly for the cultivation of rice, is concentrated in the northern part of the Camargue; in the south-eastern portion salt is harvested in shallow lagoons. The south, however, is a nature paradise unique in Europe, with half-wild horses, bulls, and aquatic birds and waders.

The grassy meadows of the estuary are a home to the Camargue horses (top) as well as to many waterfowl and waders: about 10,000 pairs of flamingos (bottom) breed here.

More than 350 species of migratory bird stop at the "Parc Ornithologique du Pont-de-Grau" in the south-west of the Camargue. The main distinctive feature of the black Camargue bulls are their lyre-shaped horns. The white horses of the Camargue were even depicted in the ancient cave paintings of Solutré. When trained to take saddle and tack, they are untiring companions and can be of great service for herding livestock. A number of operators also offer guided excursions on horseback even for inexperienced riders that lead into the swamps, out to the beaches and to see the bulls. They allow you to see some of the normally less accessible parts of the Camargue to be enjoyed.

CARCASSONNE

Even before the Romans, Iberians had settled on the hill above the river Aude along the old trading route linking the Mediterranean and the Atlantic. In 418, the Gallo-Roman town of Carcasso fell to the Visigoths, who built the inner town fortifications in 485. In 725, the Moors conquered the town, followed by the Franks in 759. In 1229, Carcassonne fell to the French crown.

The impressive Romanesque St Nazaire Basilica was built from 1096 to 1150, during the course of the town's expansion in the Middle Ages. It was remodeled in the Gothic style in the 13th century, and the magnificent stained glass windows date from the 14th to 16th centuries. Around 1125, Château Comtal was integrated into the inner town wall complex. Construction of the outer wall and its fortified towers began at the end of the 13th century. An imposing gate, the Porte Narbonnaise, was added later, and the Pont d'Avignon is from the 12th century. The fortifications fell into a state of disrepair after about 1660 but they were reconstructed in 1844. The project was not completed until 1960.

With the white limestone near Bonifacio (main picture), red granite rock in the Calanche and green wilderness of the Castagniccia, it is not surprising that the Greeks once called Corsica "Kalliste", meaning "the beautiful". The island not only features wide beaches and small swimming coves along a strikingly beautiful coastline, but it also has mountains and green forests that have somehow retained their unspoiled state despite the continued encroachment of civilization.

Napoleon, Corsica's most famous native son, was born in Ajaccio in 1769, but he left his island home only ten years later, in 1779. After his military successes he assumed power in France and, in 1804, had himself crowned Emperor. After the "great Corsican" failed in his Russian Campaign of 1812 and the Battle of Nations at Leipzig in 1813, he was exiled to Elba. He escaped and returned to power a year later, but lost at Waterloo in 1815. He eventually died in exile on the island of St Helena.

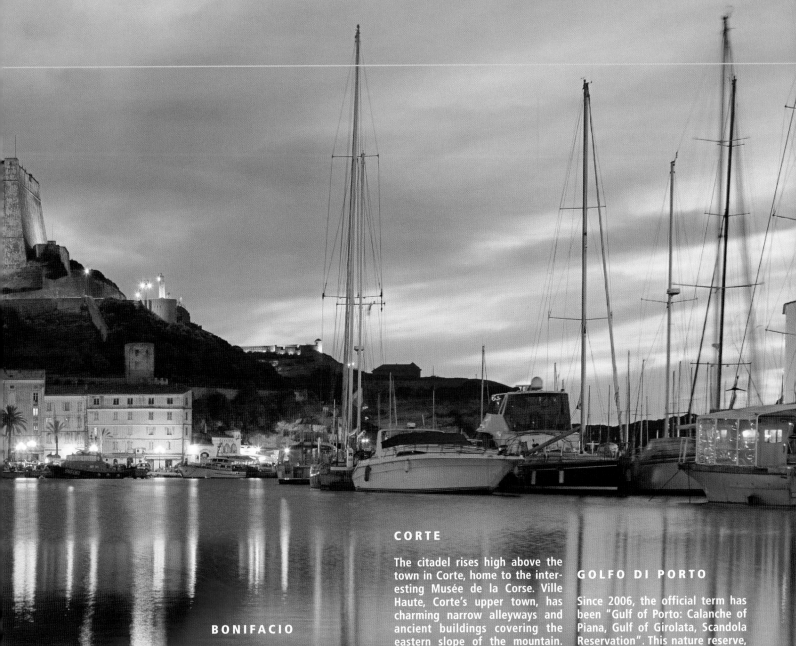

CORTE

The citadel rises high above the town in Corte, home to the interesting Musée de la Corse. Ville Haute, Corte's upper town, has charming narrow alleyways and ancient buildings covering the eastern slope of the mountain. Corte also boasts the only university on the island, which gives the village a very special ambience. During the struggle for Corsican independence, coastal Corte was the site of many a dramatic event

GOLFO DI PORTO

Since 2006, the official term has been "Gulf of Porto: Calanche of Piana, Gulf of Girolata, Scandola Reservation". This nature reserve, part of a larger regional park on Corsica, is an ideal nesting and breeding area for many species of waterfowl such as seagulls, cormorants and the now rare white-tailed eagle. Large sections of the

BONIFACIO

The most southerly town on the island of Corsica is perched precariously on a narrow rock that has been hollowed out from below by the waves over the centuries. The bluff is surrounded by water

CAPU PERTUSATO

Along the cliffs of the "Promenade des Falaises" near Bonifacio, a coastal path leads southward for 5 km (3 mi) from the Chapelle St Roch to the Pertusato promontory. Ramblers will be rewarded by a relaxing swimming beach, a lighthouse and a beautiful view of the chalkstone cliffs. The way back is particularly impressive in the late afternoon, when the light of the setting sun illuminates the old town on the craggy coast.

on three sides. Down in the bay of Bonifacio is the district of La Marine with the small harbor. Ville Haute, as the Old Town itself is called, features narrow alleyways and tower-like buildings that bear witness to earlier sieges. Many homes still have wells and cisterns along with food storage rooms. Steep wooden stairs that could be quickly pulled up in moments of danger lead to the first story of the houses.

because the island's interior was considered a stronghold of fierce Corsican nationalists. Pasquale Paoli, the "General of the Nation", made Corte the capital of the island from 1755 to 1769. Corte is also the main starting point for excursions into the surrounding mountains. At least one day should be set aside for a visit to the magnificent Restonica Valley, which extends to the south-west town.

rocky La Girolata peninsula are covered with natural woodland where it is still possible to see vast expanses of macchia pine, which is typical of the Mediterranean. Dense eucalyptus groves also fringe the sandy beaches. The coves and grottoes on the rugged rocky coastline possess a variety of underwater fauna and flora, including some rare algae species. The area has been wonderfully preserved.

SANTIAGO DE COMPOSTELA

The cathedral of Santiago de Compostela was consecrated in the year 1211 and later enlarged with chapels, a cupola and cloisters. The master-stroke and final element was the late-baroque façade. The magnificent entrance hall, Pórtico de la Gloria, dates from the Romanesque period.

Legend has it that in the 8th century pious Christians rescued the bones of the apostle St James the Greater from the Saracens in St Catharine's Monastery on Mount Sinai and brought them to Galicia. The relics were buried in a church that was built especially for that purpose. It was around the church that the town of Santiago (derived from Sanctus Jacobus) de Compostela then developed. In Spain, James became the patron saint of the Christians in their struggle against the Moors, and victory in the Battle of Clavijo in 844 was credited to his divine intervention. The news spread quickly through Europe and Santiago soon became the most important pilgrimage destination after Rome and Jerusalem. Today, thousands of pilgrims come here in July for James's Day to venerate their saint. The cathedral above the Apostle's grave dates from the 11th and 12th centuries and is Romanesque in style, but it was enlarged and remodeled several times until the 18th century. Behind the portal of the façade is the masterpiece "Pórtico de la Gloria," a narthex by Master Mateo with a Romanesque group of sculptures completed in 1188.

Pilgrims' mass is celebrated several times each day in the cathedral. The Capilla Mayor was set up above the supposed tomb of the saint. It is a splendid main altar that features a silver-plated sculpture of St James. One of the church treasures is the altar with the crucified figure of Christ.

BARRI GÒTIC, LA RAMBLA, PLAÇA DEL REI, LA BOQUERIA

Barcelona, bustling metropolis with 1.7 million inhabitants, is the capital of Catalonia and for some the true capital of Spain. A Mediterranean city, it has a romantic Old Town as well as a New Town with wide boulevards that invite strollers and shoppers. The city has a lively history: Hannibal's father is said to have originally founded it, and it eventually became an important stronghold for the Romans. During the Middle Ages it was in the hands of the caliph of Córdoba before becoming the residence of the kings of Aragón. Today, Barcelona is a city of culture, industry and trade. The Barri Gòtic, the Gothic Old Town, invites you to wander the alleyways; la Rambla leads down to the port where a monument to Columbus has been erected. On the medieval Plaça del Rei is the palace of Catalan and Castilian kings. The nostalgic La Boqueria market presents an overwhelming selection of goods.

PALAU DE LA MÚSICA

The Palau de la Música Catalana (Palace of Catalan Music) is the most important concert hall in Barcelona. Designed by Domènech i Montaner in 1908 for the "Orfeo Catalá" chorus, the steel frame of this Art Nouveau building is clad in shiny, colorful materials, including ceramics and stained glass. Some famous artists of the Catalan Art Nouveau style joined in the design of the interior as well, making the harmonious combination of light and space a particularly impressive element. Also noticeable are the lavish flowers and climbers ornamenting the ceiling, walls and columns of the hall along with dragons' heads and other sculptures.

LA SEU

In the very heart of the Barri Gòtic is Barcelona's cathedral, which dates from the 14th century. Following a very long tradition, geese are the guardians of the graves in its cloisters.

The Art Nouveau style is embodied in a special way by the Sagrada Familia (main picture), which features spindly turrets and organic shapes inspired by nature.

SAGRADA FAMILIA, PALAU GÜELL, PARQUE GÜELL, CASA MILÀ, CASA BATLLÓ, CASA VICENS, COLONIA GÜELL

Architect Antoni Gaudí i Cornet is considered an outstanding representative of Modernism, or Catalan Art Nouveau. He created some of his most magnificent buildings in Barcelona such as the Sagrada Familia (main picture), a church that was originally designed in the neo-Catalan style in 1882, and which has still not been completed. For Eusebi Güell, a generous patron of the arts, Gaudí designed an idiosyncratic city mansion, the Palau Güell, which was completed in 1889 after four years of construction. Typical for the artist, ornamentation and organic forms dominate here.

The Parque Güell was conceived as a small garden city. Although the park was created according to detailed plans from 1900 to 1914, it seems to have grown naturally. The Casa Milà (left), built between 1905 and 1911, is a multi-story apartment block whose bizarre design makes it hard to distinguish architecture and sculpture. The Casa Batlló (right) is a magnificent city mansion with a roof designed by Gaudí to represent a large dragon and adorned with mosaic chimneys. For the interior design of the Casa Vicens, Gaudí adapted some ideas from Mudéjar architecture. Of the Colonia Güell Church, he was only able to complete the crypt, but a drawing by the master exists that gives you an idea of how the structure was supposed to have looked in its final form.

Plaza Mayor de Salamanca (main picture) is a square surrounded by arcades laid out in the baroque style according to plans by Alberto Churriguera. All buildings have four stories and balustrades.

SEGOVIA

The medieval Old Town of Segovia straddles a mountain ridge and boasts a rich architectural heritage that includes more than twenty Romanesque churches. In order to channel fresh water from the Río Frío to Segovia over a distance of 18 km (11 mi), the Romans built an impressive aqueduct with a total length of 730 m (750 yds). The bridge, erected in the 2nd century AD, rests on 118 arches and was built from specially designed granite blocks that do not require the use of mortar. The complex was last renovated in the late 15th century.

The city's many Romanesque churches are remarkable for their characteristic ambulatories, which served as meeting places for guilds and fraternities. Work on Segovia's late-Gothic cathedral was begun in 1525 on the site of an earlier structure that had been destroyed by fire.

In 1474, Isabella of Castile's coronation took place in the Alcázar fort, which stands high above the town on a rock and received its present Gothic look in the 13th century.

SALAMANCA

Salamanca was conquered by the Romans in the 3rd century BC and destroyed later on several occasions by the Moors. It achieved great importance after 1085, when it was reconquered by King Alfonso VI of Spain. The university, founded in 1218 by Alfonso IX, was regarded as one of the four most important universities in the West along with Oxford, Paris and Bologna. Its façade is a masterpiece of the plateresque Renaissance style.

Plaza Mayor (top) is the heart of Salamanca and is dominated by the baroque façade of the town hall. Center and above: New and Old Cathedrals harmonize despite their different architectural styles.

Salamanca is also rich in Romanesque and Gothic buildings. The 12th-century Old Cathedral is one of few preserved churches showing Romanesque-Byzantine influences. The church was eventually incorporated into the complex of the New Cathedral, which was begun in 1513 and features late-Gothic, plateresque and baroque elements.

ÁVILA

Ávila is perhaps the most attractive example of a medieval town in all of Spain. Ávila's Gothic cathedral rises like a bastion above the battlements of the nearly flawlessly preserved town fortifications. Construction of the town walls was started as early as about 1090, but it was not until the 12th century that they received their present appearance, which reflects a rather simple rectangular plan. The "ciborro" is the mightiest of its towers, and serves at the same time as the church's apse.

Ávila's town walls feature nine gates and eighty-eight towers (top). The interior of the church is spectacularly high (center). Bottom: The interior of San Vicente, one of the most beautiful churches in the town.

The church, which is incorporated into the fortifications like a bulwark, is one of the oldest cathedrals in Spain. Its interior houses masterly sculptures. There are also some remarkable medieval churches outside the town walls, the most interesting of which is probably the 12th-century San Vicente with its historically significant collection of Romanesque sculptures.

EL ESCORIAL

In 1561, eager to express his hunger for power and bolstered by his successes in the war against France, Philip II commissioned the construction of a vast palace in Escorial, some 60 km (37 mi) northwest of Madrid. The original architect was Juan Bautista de Toledo; after his death, Juan de Herrera took over in 1567, supervising construction until near completion in 1584. The rectangular complex (above) covers a vast area of more than seven acres and provides space for sixteen courtyards. It is equipped with nine towers.

The composition of the buildings was inspired by the Temple of Jerusalem, and thanks to its perfect symmetry it remained for a long time the prototype for many other extravagant palaces across Europe.

The magnificently furnished royal mausoleum houses the remains of all Spanish monarchs since Philip II. In addition to the countless private and staterooms of the royal family, the comprehensive library (main picture) is an impressive feat that contains many priceless volumes.

MADRID

The capital of Spain is not only the geographic heart of the Iberian peninsula, but it was at one point also the center of an empire in which "the sun never set." Over centuries, dynasties such as the Habsburgs and the Bourbons each left their own mark on the city. Accordingly, the cityscape is wildly diverse even in the center. Since the end of the Franco dictatorship in 1975, Madrid has undergone a rapid change and developed from a sleepy administrative town into a pulsating world city.

As the capital, Madrid has been a big draw for artists and merchants since the 16th century. Velazquez and Goya were invited as painters to the Spanish royal court, during which time they created some of their famous masterpieces. A com-

prehensive collection of paintings from them and other artists can now be admired in the Museo del Prado, one of the most famous classical collections in the world. It comprises more than 9,000 works of art including Goya's 1814 piece *The shooting of the rebels on May*

3, 1808 (above), 5,000 illustrations and 700 sculptures. The capital naturally has a wealth of other world-renowned museums as well. In terms of its architecture, Madrid features a great variety of styles ranging from the Renaissance in the "Madrid de los Austrias" district (for example, the Monasterio de las Calzas Reales, right) to the baroque and neoclassicism in the Palacio Real (top) and a range of Art Deco and postmodernist edi-

fices around town. The impressive main square of the city – and the model for many other Spanish squares – is the 17th-century Plaza Mayor (top left with the equestrian statue of Philip III). San Francisco el Grande (left bottom) is a domed church built in 1770 on the site of an earlier Franciscan monastery and holds important paintings by Goya, Velázquez and others.

Documentation shows that a church was built as early as the 9th century where today the Nuestra Señora de la Almudena Cathedral (top right) stands. Incidently, the cathedral was not consecrated until 1993, after more than 100 years of construction.

TOLEDO

Toledo's Old Town straddles a rock surrounded on three sides by the river far below in a deep gorge (right). Toledo is a veritable treasure chest of Spanish architectural jewels. The town's icon is the Cathedral, built from the 13th to the 15th centuries on the site of a former Visigoth church and an old Moorish mosque. While its exterior displays the typical features of pure French Early Gothic, the building's interior, which

is a stately 110 m (350 ft) in length, is a textbook example of Spanish Late Gothic. The three portals on the main façade are richly adorned with reliefs and sculptures. The Capilla Mayor shows a multitude of biblical scenes in which the life-size figures are carved from larch pine and then painted or gilded. At the highest point in the town is the Alcázar. The façade of this almost square

building dates mostly from the 16th century. The way up to the fortress starts from the Plaza de Zocodover and the centrally located triangular square is the true heart of the city.

Other attractions in Toledo include the Franciscan San Juan de los Reyes Monastery (15th–17th centuries) and the Casa El Greco; the painter lived in Toledo for nearly forty years.

LA MANCHA, CUENCA

Hardly any other region in the world is so closely linked to the name of a literary figure and its author as La Mancha, the setting of Miguel de Cervantes Saavedra's novel Don Quixote (above right). The "knight of the sad countenance" waged battle against the windmills in this barren region. The La Mancha plateau is a desolate landscape but its cornfields also make it the country's breadbasket.

Above Belmonte (right, bottom), birthplace of the writer Fray Luis de León, is the Castillo built on a hill in around the middle of the 15th century. One of the three gates is resplendent with scallops and a cross, symbol of the pilgrims on the Way of St James. The star-shaped complex with six

round towers is enclosed by a double ring of walls, while the three sections of the fortress are grouped around a triangular

courtyard. The fortress was built by the Marquis of Villena, to whom the town was assigned in 1456, and the interior is deco-

rated with panelled ceilings and Mudéjar stucco work. Cuenca's old town was built on a steep cliff that drops down abruptly on both sides to the canyons of the Río Júcar and the Río Huécar. The town is especially famous for its "hanging houses" (casas colgadas), one of which is home to the Museo de Arte Abstracto Español, and has one of the largest collections of modern Spanish art. The nearby Museo Arqueológico exhibits items relating to the region's history. The impressive Gothic-Norman cathedral, built in the 12th/13th centuries on the site of a former mosque, was rebuilt after collapsing at the beginning of the 20th century.

Bordered by two rivers, Cuenca's old town (main picture) is situated on a steep cliff and is known for its unique "hanging" houses.

Moorish invaders from North Africa built the Great Mosque after their initial conquest of Seville in 712, but it was ultimately destroyed during the Reconquest in the year 1248. Only the Giralda minaret survived, indeed a masterpiece of Almohade architecture from the late 12th century, but it was converted into the steeple of the new cathedral, the largest Gothic structure of its kind in the world. Its chapels house important paintings by Murillo, Velazquez and Zurbarán.

The mighty Alcázar (from the Arabic for fortress) obviously also goes back to Moorish times and features detailed ornamentation in its beautiful courtyards. In the 13th century, the palace became the seat of the king and in subsequent centuries it was enlarged in the Mudéjar style (a name given to Muslims who stayed but did not convert to Christianity). Its beautiful gardens are an example.

Casa Lonja (1598) was once the main market for goods from the colonies. In 1785, it was converted into the Archivo General de las Indias, where documents about the history of Latin American exploration are kept.

The Casa Lonja Archive (main picture) houses documents that provide an insight into the relationship between Spain and its former colonies.

Of the mosque that once stood here, only the La Giralda Minaret (above) has been preserved – now the steeple of the city's cathedral.

The Alcázar (left), begun in 1364 on the remains of another Moorish fortress, is one of the best-preserved examples of the Mudéjar style, which combines elements of Islamic architecture with Gothic influences. The cathedral's organ and the sarcophagus of Columbus are impressive pieces (below).

MEZQUITA

Córdoba was an important center of politics and culture even in Roman times, as is evidenced by the Puente Romana bridge across the river Guadalquivir (above). With its sixteen arches, it was once part of the Via Augusta, a road stretching from Cádiz to the Pyrenees. One of Córdoba's most important sons was the Roman philosopher Seneca. In the year 929, the Caliphate of Córdoba also rose as the shining star of Al-Andalus and thus competed for fame with Baghdad, also a major world city. As in many cities at the time, Jewish, Arabic and Christian cultures lived peacefully together here while science and philosophy flourished.

In the Old Town, around the Mezquita, some of this spirit can still be experienced today. At its height, Córdoba was a powerful city of one million inhabitants with great influence within the Caliphate. It is now a provincial capital with a population of only about 300,000, but Córdoba is still a magical city in white. In particular, the Old Town with its narrow alleyways, whitewashed houses and flowery courtyards is truly idyllic. In the center stands the Mezquita, the mighty fortress that was once a mosque and is now a cathedral.

The vast former prayer hall (main picture) of the Great Mosque has 856 ornate columns and creates an wonderful ambience. Nineteen naves and thirty-six transepts, splendid Moorish adornments and mysterious light between the columns make any visit to the Mezquita an unforgettable one.

JUDERÍA

Immediately next to the Mezquita is the Judería, the former Jewish quarter with its narrow alleyways and flower bedecked balconies (above). Also worth a visit are the former synagogue and the bullfighting museum. The Alcázar de los Reyes Cristianos, the royal palace built as a fortress in the 14th century, has beautiful gardens. The Museo Arqueológico Provincial, housed in a stunning Renaissance building, displays Roman, Visigoth and Moorish relics. Not far away, in the quarter around the Christian churches, stands the inviting Palacio de Viana, a manor house with twelve courtyards.

GRANADA

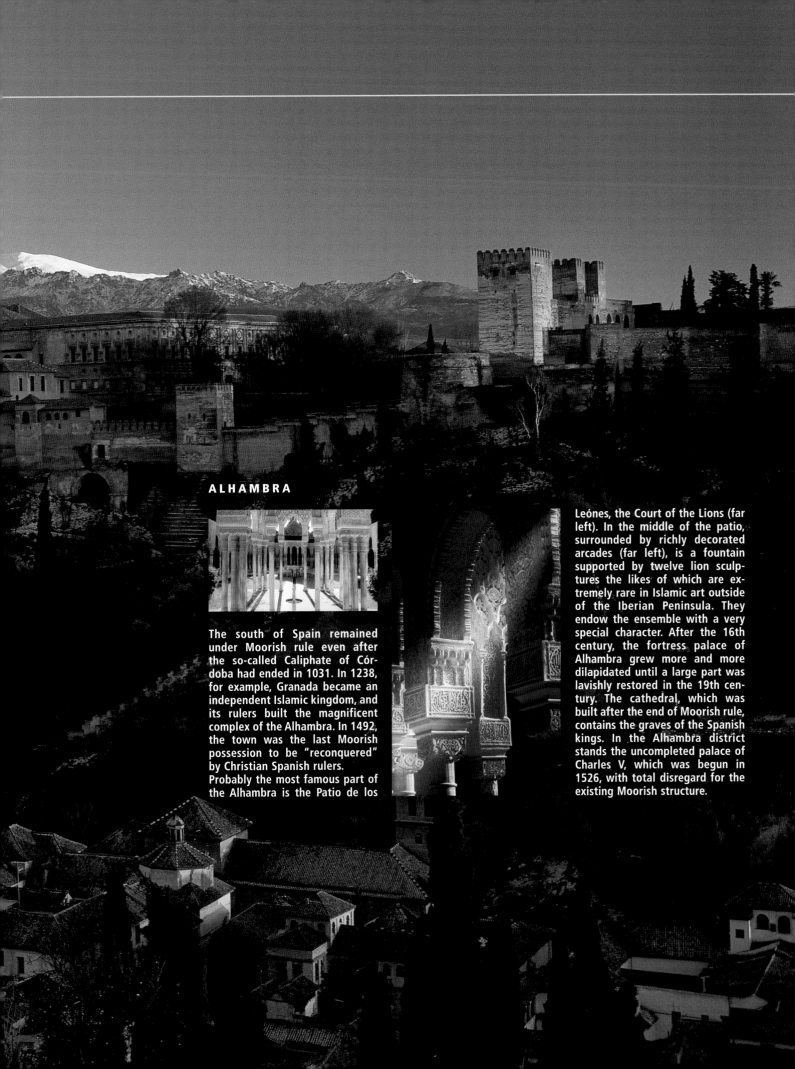

ALHAMBRA

The south of Spain remained under Moorish rule even after the so-called Caliphate of Córdoba had ended in 1031. In 1238, for example, Granada became an independent Islamic kingdom, and its rulers built the magnificent complex of the Alhambra. In 1492, the town was the last Moorish possession to be "reconquered" by Christian Spanish rulers.

Probably the most famous part of the Alhambra is the Patio de los Leónes, the Court of the Lions (far left). In the middle of the patio, surrounded by richly decorated arcades (far left), is a fountain supported by twelve lion sculptures the likes of which are extremely rare in Islamic art outside of the Iberian Peninsula. They endow the ensemble with a very special character. After the 16th century, the fortress palace of Alhambra grew more and more dilapidated until a large part was lavishly restored in the 19th century. The cathedral, which was built after the end of Moorish rule, contains the graves of the Spanish kings. In the Alhambra district stands the uncompleted palace of Charles V, which was begun in 1526, with total disregard for the existing Moorish structure.

Steep cliffs are typical of the Cap de Formentor in the north-east of Mallorca. Wind and water have created a spectacular coastline here.

MALLORCA

"If you like Paradise," wrote Gertrude Stein, "Mallorca is paradise." Every year, this Mediterranean island is visited by millions of tourists, and yet it still has some quiet bays and breathtaking landscapes. Mallorca is an island like an entire continent, with wilderness and surprisingly high mountains in the north, vast almond plantations and cornfields in the interior, and miles and miles of beaches and coves in the south. A holiday paradise with an area of 3,640 sq km (1,405 sq mi) and surrounded by turquoise seas, its capital Palma (right center with the La Seu Cathedral towering high above the port) is the most prosperous town in

Spain by gross national product. And those who wish to escape the bustle of the coastal resorts between Andratx and Arenal, and discover the beauty of nature and meet the people in the small villages, will only have to go a short way inland. The mountain village Valldemossa (right bottom), for

example, boasts a charterhouse whose monks' cells were converted into small apartments in the 19th century. In 1838/39, Frédéric Chopin and George Sand lived there, a fact that has attracted music lovers from around the world ever since. Near the Port de Valldemossa is the majestic Son

Marroig (far left top), former summer residence of the Austrian Archduke Ludwig Salvator on the "Costa Brava Mallorquina." An excursion to Cap de Formentor, the northernmost point of this spectacular island, is indeed breathtaking (above and main picture).

MENORCA

Covering an area of 716 sq km (276 sq mi), Menorca is only about one-fifth the size of Mallorca. And it is this fact to which it owes its name, Menorca (the "smaller one"). "La Isla verde y azul", or "the island of blue and green", is divided into two regions named after the prevailing north and south winds: the Tramuntana in the north and the Migjorn in the south. The border between these two regions, which are very different geologically, runs along the road from Maó (above), the island's capital, to Ciutadella (top right). Around sixty per cent of the roughly 87,000 people on Menorca live in these two towns. It is the least densely inhabited island in the archipelago with less than ten per cent of the total Balearic population.
The Cala Macarelleta (below) is one of Menorca's paradisical bays. Many visitors come by boat and drop anchor in the bay, which can only be reached via footpath.

IBIZA

Ibiza and Formentera form the western end of the Balearic Islands, which together form an autonomous region (and province) of Spain. High above the steep coast at Cap Jueu on the south-western tip of the island, you can see the uninhabited islands of Vedranell and Es Vedrá from the "Torre del Pirata".
Eivissa, the official Catalan name for Ibiza (above) is the island's main town, administrative center and also a bishops' see. Though it is most famous for having the most lively party scene and night-clubs in the Mediterranean, Ibiza also has an imposing fortress in the upper town.

GRAN CANARIA

Gran Canaria is an island of contrasts. The poet Miguel de Unamuno called its wildly rugged central mountain range, with V-shaped valleys ("barrancos") converging like rays on the island's edge, the "tempestad petrificada," or the "petrified thunderstorm". The Tamadaba Nature Park on the west coast of the island is a superb adventure.
The main picture shows the "Dedo de Dios," the "finger of God" – tall needles that have withstood the waves of the Atlantic for millennia. The subtropical north with its lush vegetation is contrasted by the desert landscape of Maspalomas (bottom) in the south.

"It is as if the volcano forming the basis of the small island is also crushing it; it rises out of the sea three times higher than the clouds in summer. If its crater, semi-dormant for centuries, were to emit flashes of fire like Stromboli…then the peak of Tenerife would serve as a lighthouse for ships within a radius of more than 1,170 km (727 mi)," wrote Alexander von Humboldt of the highest peak in the Canary Islands (main picture).

TENERIFE

The landscapes of Tenerife are as varied as its climate zones, and range from verdant green in the north to rugged mountains and desert-like expanses in the south. Life in the coastal towns is modern European. San Cristóbal de La Laguna is a lively university town and the cultural capital of the island. In the more isolated mountain villages, people still lead more traditional lives.

Thanks to its species-rich vegetation, many visitors regard Tenerife as the most beautiful of the Canary Islands. The Teide National Park, for example, is not only home to Spain's highest mountain, Pico del Teide (left) at 3,718 m (12,199 ft), but also to a fascinating volcanic landscape with a vast variety of flora and fauna.

TORRE DE BELÉM

The richly adorned tower of Belém (main picture) was built in 1521 on the orders of Manuel I as a watchtower to protect the Tagus estuary, the location where Portuguese sailors once embarked on their journeys of exploration. With its many balconies and battlements, Belém is an impressive example of Manueline architecture and also one of Lisbon's most famous landmarks.

The massive multi-story building, which in later periods served as both a weapons arsenal and a state prison, displays Moorish, Gothic and Moroccan influences. Its grand presence was meant to welcome home the captain and crew of richly loaded ships and at the same time, because of its similarity with a ship's bow, persuade potential enemies that the armada had left the harbor for a counterattack.

Over centuries, the Tagus silted up so much that the tower today no longer stands at the estuary but on the riverbank. There are superb views from the highest platform at 35 m (115 ft).

ALFAMA, BAIRRO ALTO, BAIXA

A sea of houses climbs from the wide estuary of the river Tagus up the steep hills of the "white city". Lisbon, the capital of Portugal, has a superb location that attracts visitors from around the world who, like the locals, travel aboard the city's "eléctricos", rickety old trains that squeak their way through town. Particularly worth seeing is the Alfama, Lisbon's oldest and most picturesque neighborhood, a labyrinthine Old Town on Castle Hill, which is crowned by the ruins of the Castelo de São Jorge. Between the castle ruins and the medieval Sé Cathedral are two of many miradouros, attractive viewing platforms that Lisbon is famous for and from which you can enjoy spectacular views across the city. Author Fernando Pessoa, a native of Lisbon, said of his city there exists "no flowers that can match the endlessly varied colors of Lisbon in the sunlight.". Lisbon is divided into an upper town (the bairro alto) – the entertainment quarter with its lively pubs, traditional restaurants and fado bars – and a lower town (the baixa), which was rebuilt after the devastating earthquake of 1755 according to the city's original plans and is today the banking and shopping district.

The best view of the baixa can be enjoyed from the Elevador de Santa Justa, a cast-iron lift between lower and upper town that was built in 1901 (left).

Belém is an abbreviation for Bethlehem. Once equipped with canons, the Torre de Belém still watches over the port and recalls the age of the great seafarers and explorers (main picture).

HIERONYMITE MONASTERY

tery on the site where the Infante (Prince) Henry the Navigator had earlier built a chapel. The plan for the overall complex dates back to Master Boytac and the column-less transept is a late work by João de Castilho. An impressive testimony of contemporary statuary is the sculpted decoration in the church's south and west portals. The spectacular church itself (left), a hall church with late-Gothic and early-Renaissance styles, measures 92 m (300 ft) in length and 25 m (85 ft) in width.

Many important figures from history were buried in the Hieronymite Monastery. It holds, for example, the tomb of Vasco da Gama (below, the sarcophagus), whose discovery of the sea route to India secured the finance for furnishing the monastery.

Emanuel I the Fortunate, king of Portugal from 1495 to 1521, was an avid supporter of the country's maritime explorations, in particular those of Vasco da Gama and Pedro Cabral, credited with the discovery of the sea route to India and Brazil, respectively. Indeed, during his reign, the arts and sciences flourished. To honor Vasco da Gama, in 1502, he commissioned the enormous Hieronymite Monas-

ALTO DOURO

Grape vines have been cultivated in the Alto Douro region for roughly 2,000 years now. As a result of this tradition, an extraordinarily beautiful natural and cultural landscape has emerged whose most famous product is port wine.
The basis of port consists of twenty-one grape varieties that are grown on the rocky slopes of the upper Douro river. Since these wines did not travel well across the Atlantic, British merchants added brandy or marc during the fermentation process and this is how, eventually, in the 17th century, port wine was invented.
Vines have grown in the upper Douro since Roman days. Not only the landscape with its steep, terraced slopes, but also the streets and villages with their churches and quintas, or wineries, have been defined by this 2,000-year-old tradition. The full-bodied, robust red wines of the Alto Douro region are still matured in oak barrels.

The Ponte de Dom Luís I railway bridge was designed in the offices of Gustave Eiffel (main picture).

PORTO

This port city on the Rio Douro estuary on the Atlantic has much to offer its visitors. Five bridges link Porto with Vila Nova de Gaia, its sister city on the opposite banks and home to most of the port wine cellars (the town hall on the hill above the Avenida dos Aliados in the background).

The streets and houses of Porto's Old Town cling tightly to the steep granite rocks beneath it. In the heart of the town, at the bottom end of the Avenida dos Aliados, is the Praça Liberdade with the Torre dos Clerigos, the highest church steeple in Portugal at 75 m (246 ft). At the top of the hill is the town hall with its 70-m (230-ft) bell tower.

At the São Bento station, the giant azulejo murals are especially worth seeing. The name of these brightly hand-painted and glazed floor and wall tiles, which decorate all types of buildings in Porto including the Capela das Almas (below), is probably derived from the Arabic word "al-zulayi", meaning small polished stone, or possibly from the word "azul", meaning blue.

On the way to the Ponte de Dom Luis I you come to the cathedral with its superb silver altarpiece. From there you can descend into the Bairro da Sé quarter, Porto's oldest district.

The Praça da Ribeiro and the Praça Infante Dom Henriques are the center of the Ribeira district, rich and poor clash harshly – the stock exchange sits among narrow dingy alleyways.

ALGARVE

The town of Lagos (on top the fascinating sandstone formations at the Praia de Dona Ana beach and the rocky cliffs on the Ponta da Piedade about 2 km (1.3 mi) south of there) was once a major staging point for Portuguese explorers setting sail for the New World, and since the days of Henry the Navigator (1394–1460) it has been a center of shipbuilding. The darker side in its history involved the transshipment of captured African slaves. The first recorded auctions in fact took place here on the Praça da República in 1443. Sagres was once the location of Henry the Navigator's legendary nautical school, remembered by a giant stone compass with a diameter of 43 m (141 ft), on the rocky Ponta de Sagres, not far from the Fortaleza de Sagres. Cabo de São Vicente (above) is almost visible from Sagres jutting out to sea with its 24-m-high (79-ft) lighthouse. It is Europe's south-westernmost point. The cliffs, which are up to 60 m (197 ft) high, were still thought of as the "end of the world" in the days of Christopher Columbus.

ÉVORA, MONSARAZ

The Corinthian columns of a temple dedicated to Diana (above) still stand at the heart of the Roman settlement of Évora. In addition to that, the preserved remains of an aqueduct and a castellum also remind us of the town's former significance in Roman commerce. The town also has some Moorish influence from hundreds of years of rule that ended in 1165.

The mighty cathedral here (right) was started in 1186, and with its two colossal steeples the Romanesque-Gothic structure looks like a fortress. In the 14th century, some

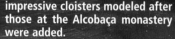

impressive cloisters modeled after those at the Alcobaça monastery were added.

The royal palace, built in its present form under Emmanuel I, is arguably the most beautiful building in Évora. The Jesuit University is now home to a Collegium and a valuable collection of ancient manuscripts. Other important buildings in the town are the São Brás Chapel, the Church of St John the Evangelist, built in the Mudéjar style and the St Francis Church. The medieval village of Monsaraz (below) is just 50 km (31 mi) east of Évora and is worth an excursion.

The dream destination for many a holidaymaker lies in southern Portugal: the Algarve, with its beaches and blue ocean (main picture).

BERLIN

KURFÜRSTENDAMM

"Great Berlin, the open city – it should not be just a German city," wrote Mexican author Carlos Fuentes, before adding, "It is our city, a city of the whole world." And in fact, Berlin stands at the heart of the world like virtually no other city. History was, and still is, made in this city on the river Spree, and the past and the present connect with whatever the next future may be. As the capital and seat of government, home to muses and museums, and as a multicultural center, Berlin is a city like no other. Or more precisely: "a city of the whole world."

The capital of the German Empire should have a grand boulevard modeled after the Champs-Elysées in Paris. That was the decision by Chancellor Otto von Bismarck upon his return from the French capital after the Franco-Prussian War. And so the former corduroy road to the hunting palace in Grunewald forest was transformed into a 3.5-km (2-mi) long, 53-m (174-ft) wide avenue where only those who could afford it lived. Today, the shops here compete with the up-and-coming Mitte (center) district, but as a shopping street, Kurfürstendamm (above) is still number one in Berlin.

Two warriors guard the forecourt of Charlottenburg Palace with its equestrian statue of the Great Elector Friedrich Wilhelm (main picture).

SCHLOSS CHARLOTTENBURG

In the heart of the Charlottenburg district and originally conceived as a summer residence for Electress Sophie Charlotte, this grandiose edifice was built in several stages between 1695 and 1746. The domed tower rises almost
50 m (164 ft) above the palace forecourt with its equestrian statue of the Great Elector. After World War II, the historic rooms in the central building – the oldest part of the complex, which also comprises extensive palace gardens – were rebuilt in their original splendor.

KAISER WILHELM MEMORIAL CHURCH

"Everything passes" was the main theme of the sermon in the Kaiser Wilhelm Memorial Church on November 22, 1943. It was the last Sunday before Advent, commemorating the dead. Bombs soon after reduced the church to the now famous ruin (above, through the sculpture "Berlin" in Tauentzien Street). The damaged west steeple, reduced from 113 to 63 m (371 to 207 ft), was then given the nickname "hollow tooth" by locals. Despite their irreverence, however, Berliners did not allow the destroyed church to be demolished and in 1961, Egon Eiermann built a monument church over the ruins.

Covering an area of roughly 890 sq km (344 sq mi), the German capital is the largest and, with just under 3.4 million inhabitants, also the most populated city in the republic.

BRANDENBURG GATE

Carl Gotthard Langhans began construction of the iconic Brandenburg Gate in 1788 as the triumphal end to the grand boulevard Unter den Linden. Completed in 1791, this severe sandstone structure is 26 m (85 ft) high and 65 m (215 ft) wide, a stout edifice indeed. Twelve Doric columns divide the double portico into five passages, with the center reserved for the king's coach and the narrower passages used by the infantry.

The relief on top of the attica, the Quadriga, depicts the entry of the gods of peace into the city while the reliefs in the passage feature the labors of Hercules. The gods Mars and Minerva stand guard in the side halls.

THE REICHSTAG

The Reichstag building, designed by Paul Wallot and opened in 1894, was meant to symbolize the vastness and power of the German Empire. After being badly damaged in World War II, it was restored as a conference venue after 1961. From 1995 to 1999, a modern, more environmentally-friendly parliamentary building was created behind the historic façade of the old Reichstag building according to plans by Sir Norman Foster. The glass dome, which is open to the public, quickly became a new landmark for the capital.

POTSDAMER PLATZ

For years, visitors from around the world were awed by Europe's largest urban building site as the internationally acclaimed architects altered the skyline of Berlin. The likes of Renzo Piano, Richard Rogers, Arata Isozaki, Hans Kollhoff, Helmut Jahn and Giorgio Grassi created a 21st-century city that is both admired and criticized. Construction began in October 1994; in 1996, Daniel Barenboim conducted dancing cranes for the topping-out ceremony; and in 1998, ten new streets and seventeen buildings became operational.

HOLOCAUST MEMORIAL

Near Brandenburg Gate is an ensemble of 2,711 dark concrete blocks in uneven, narrow rows of varying heights. According to its creator, Peter Eisenman, the memorial is meant to disorient visitors while inspiring reflection. The space below contains important facts about the Holocaust and in the "Raum der Familien" (Room of Families) are some exposés about the lives of European Jews before the Holocaust. In the "Raum der Namen" (Room of Names), the names and short biographies of missing Jews are read aloud.

GENDARMENMARKT

The Gendarmenmarkt, named after the "gens d'armes," a regiment of cuirassiers, is one of Berlin's most attractive plazas. It is surrounded by the Schauspielhaus (national theater), Deutscher and Französischer Dom (German and French cathedrals) and the Schiller Monument. In the 18th century, Frederick II had built a comedy theater on the square and commissioned Carl von Gontard to add the mighty domes to the churches, which had been erected nearly eighty years earlier. The Schiller statue before the theater was done by Reinhold Begas.

MUSEUMSINSEL

Museum Island, between the Spree and Kupfergraben, covers an area of less than 1 sq km (247 acres) but contains five outstanding museums that together representing more than 5,000 years of human history – a concentration of art and artefacts that is unique in the world. On the island are: the Altes Museum (Old Museum, right), one of the first museums in Germany built in 1828; Neues Museum (New Museum, 1855); Alte Nationalgalerie (Old National Gallery, 1876); Bodemuseum, opened in 1904; and the spectacular Pergamonmuseum (1930).

BERLINER DOM, ALEXANDERPLATZ

Berlin Cathedral, the burial church of the Hohenzollern family (far right), was built between 1893 and 1905 on the orders of Emperor Wilhelm II. The vaults hold ninety-four tombs and sarcophagi of the ruling dynasty that span four centuries. Alexanderplatz developed as an ox market in front of the Oderberg Gate around 1700. In 1805, it was renamed to honor the Russian Czar Alexander I. Not much remains of its original structures, but worth seeing are the World Time Clock and the Fountain of Friendship between Peoples (both 1969).

The Brandenburg Gate (left) was based on the propylaea of the Acropolis in Athens. The Quadriga (far left) was created in 1789 to 1791, to a design by Johann Gottfried Schadow.

SYLT

Sylt, known for its see-and-be-seen ambience, is the northern-most island in Germany. At the northern tip of the island is the tiny community of List, the north-ernmost place in the republic. Sylt splitt off from the mainland some 8,000 years ago when the seas began rising. In 1927, the two were linked again by the Hinden-burgdamm.

Since then, up to 650,000 holiday-makers a year cross the dam to the 39-km-long (24-mi) island which, at its widest point is just over 1 km (0.6 mi) wide. While the west coast is lashed by the wind and the waves of the North Sea, the eastern Wad-den Sea coast is much quieter and calmer. It is also home to Wadden Sea National Park, famous for its diversity of flora and fauna as well as its tidal mud flats.

FÖHR

Christian VIII, King of Denmark and Norway, had already discov-ered the beneficial effects of the fresh air, beautiful scenery and the almost 15 km (9 mi) of sandy beaches in the south of the island of Föhr back in the middle of the 19th century. The center of the nearly circular island, 82 sq km (32 sq mi) in size, is the North Sea resort of Wyk.

The west and south of Föhr was formed by a moraine – a glacial relic from the Ice Age. It is higher and drier than the marshlands of the north and east, which only gradually grew with increased land reclamation.

AMRUM

South-west of Föhr lies the quiet island of Amrum, about 20 sq km (8 sq mi) in size and featuring dunes up to 30 m (98 ft) high. Amrum also has a sandy beach that is up to 2 m (1.3 mi) wide and 15 km (9 mi) long – the famous Kniepsand beach. The small island has a population of roughly 2,200 people living in five villages, of which the Friesian village of Nebel is the best known and most pop-ular. To get an good view of the island with its dunes, forests and marshlands, it is best to climb the 66-m-tall (217-ft) lighthouse between Nebel and Wittdün. From there you can see the entire island and sometimes as far as neigh-boring Föhr.

HELGOLAND

You have to catch a boat if you want to visit Helgoland, with its famous buntsandstein (red sand-stone) formations and breeding grounds for guillemots and kitti-wakes. Germany's only solid rock, high-seas island was actually in British hands for many years before becoming German in 1890, when it was swapped for the island of Zanzibar. During World War II, Helgoland was a military base, and as such was frequently bombed. After the war, the island was used as a bombing range by the British but by 1952 it was given back to Germany and by the mid-1950s, the first inhab-itants had begun returning to the island, rebuilding their lives, and welcoming the first visitors, who came to enjoy the fresh air and duty-free shopping. Daytrippers still arrive in large numbers.

SCHLESWIG-HOLSTEIN – WADDEN SEA

The Wadden Sea is an annual stopover for more than two million migratory birds as well as a summer retreat for about 100,000 breeding shelducks, eider ducks, seagulls and swallows. In addition, the tidal area is a breeding ground for herring, sole and plaice as well as a habitat for gray seals, harbor seals and harbor porpoises.

In an area covering more than 4,000 sq km (1,544 sq mi), from the Danish border to the estuary of the river Elbe, Wadden Sea National Park provides more than 3,000 different animal and plant species with an ideal environment. Schleswig-Holstein was the first German state to place the northern stretches of the Wadden Sea under protection, declaring it a national park in 1985, and then a biosphere reserve in 1990. The Wadden Sea National Park is divided into three protection zones. The first zone includes the seal colonies, where humans are either not allowed at all, or only allowed on designated paths. Part of the second zone is the whale protection area. The third zone is open to fishing, tourism and even oil drilling.

The Wadden Sea is a perfect ecosystem that is rich in nutrients. Many animal and plant species have even adapted to living in the salt marshes, the best-known among being is the lugworm.

An estimated 10,000 lighthouses still exist around the world, and some of the most attractive ones can be found on the German North Sea coast. This one stands on the Ellenbogen Peninsula, the northernmost tip of the island of Sylt.

LÜBECK, WISMAR, SCHWERIN, ROSTOCK, STRALSUND

LÜBECK

Lübeck's most famous icon is the Holstentor, built in 1478 and one of only two remaining city gates (the other one is the Burgtor). Part of the mighty fortifications, this Gothic gate is so heavy that shortly after construction the subsoil began to sink. Since then, the southern tower has had a slight lean. Today it houses a permanent exhibition on the Hanseatic League. Visitors to Lübeck's Old Town will enjoy a journey back in time to the Middle Ages through a maze of alleyways from Holstentor to Burgtor and the cathedral district. Behind the old merchants' homes and warehouses, narrow passages run through secluded courtyards. Aside from the splendid Marienkirche (Saint Mary's church), there are five other historic churches that are worth visiting as well as the St Anne's Monastery Art Museum and one of the oldest hospitals in northern Europe. From St Petri, fascinating views unfold over the sea of magnificent structures including the town hall, the various churches and the two surviving town gates.

WISMAR

Wismar is a town that resembles an open-air museum of the Hanseatic League. Many of its churches, burghers' mansions and the market square (right) date back to this period, as do the harbor basin and the "Grube," an artificial waterway to the Schwerin lake. All have survived virtually unchanged and it was here that the bulky cogs entered and left the port. The remains of one such ship were found off the island of Poel in 1999 – the "Wissemara" in the port is a faithful reconstruction at 31 m (100 ft). After the Hanseatic League came the Swedes who ruled Wismar for 250 years. Some buildings such as the baroque arsenal of 1701, or the "Baumhaus" are from that period. The tall steeples of the parish churches of St Mary and St Nicholas demonstrate that the town was oriented toward the sea. They served as orientation markers for ships.

SCHWERIN

After the fall of the Berlin Wall, the state of Mecklenburg-West Pomerania needed to designate a new capital for itself. As a result, the small town of Schwerin was chosen despite Rostock's greater size. But if you visit this smallest of the German state capitals, you will easily understand why the choice went the way it did.

Schwerin was and still is a ducal residence and with a picturesque location amid charming lakes, a largely restored Old Town, and a fairy-tale palace on the Schlossinsel island, it resembles an extravagant film set.

In 1990, Schwerin Palace (right, in the background) became the seat of regional government – the "residency" continues, albeit in less glamorous style than during the days of the dukes of Mecklenburg-Schwerin. It is also a cultural center with a state theater, an art gallery in the regional museum, and an open-air summer festival on the grounds.

"Concordia Domis Foris Pax" – "Harmony inside, Peace outside," is the motto on the portal of Lübeck's Holstentor since 1863 (far left). Lübeck's beautiful Old Town (left) is surrounded by water and features the brick architecture typical of northern Germany. In the background is St Mary's Church.

ROSTOCK

Rostock has an obsession with seven. The "Rostocker Kennewohrn", or the seven symbols of Rostock, is a poem from 1596 that extolls the seven icons that define the cityscape, each of those in turn having seven telltale features. Among them are the originally medieval town hall with seven spires, for example.

Indeed, Rostock is a fine example of a flourishing medieval town. After Danish King Valdemar destroyed it in 1161, this former Slav castle village was given its town charters in 1218. Soon after, in 1229, it became the main principality in the Mecklenburg Duchy of Rostock and by the 14th century had become the most powerful member of the Hanseatic League after Lübeck. The remains of the city wall with its three gates, the tall Gothic St Mary's Church, and a row of old warehouses bear witness to its former importance. After heavy damage during World War II, much of the city has thankfully been lovingly restored.

STRALSUND

Millions of rectangular roof tiles make up the distinctive face of Stralsund (left the Old Market with town hall and St Nicholas Church). It is one of the most attractive examples of northern German Brick Gothic.

The town on the Strelasund is situated between the Baltic Sea and the Greifswalder Bodden, opposite Germany's most popular holiday island, Rügen. Since 1936, the Rügendamm has connected the mainland with both Rügen and Dänholm, once known as Strela, the name given to the island's main town founded in 1234.

In the time of the Hanseatic League, Stralsund became one of the mightiest cities in the Baltic Sea, with splendid buildings such as the St Nicholas Church and the town hall with its elaborately ornamented gable all dating from that period. During the Thirty Years' War, Stralsund was able to defend itself against General Wallenstein by allying itself with Sweden. It is from this period that the baroque Commandantenhus stems.

RÜGEN

Rügen, Germany's largest island, has an area of 976 sq k (377 sq mi), and actually comprises five islands that have grown together over the course of centuries. Jasmund, isolated between sea and shallower coastal waters is only reachable via two spits of land and was the first of the five.

The forested northern half of Rügen is home to the Jasmund National Park established in 1990. At only 30 sq km (12 sq mi) it is Germany's smallest. The highlight here are the chalk cliffs (top left). Cape Arkona juts far into the Baltic Sea and is one of the sunniest places in Germany. Its exposed location on Rügen's northernmost tip make it important for shipping. When visibility is low or navigation errors occur, ships are in danger of running aground there. No wonder then, that Cape Arkona is home to the oldest lighthouse on the Baltic Sea (above). Built by Schinkel in 1826, the 21-m (69-ft) tower was operated until 1905. Beside the neoclassical old tower is its successor, which is still in use. More than 100 years old, it isn't exactly a new feature here either.

Apart from lively holiday resorts, Rügen also boasts many hidden gems where romantics can find a bit of seclusion, for example by the Gager Marina, on the hilly Thiessow Peninsula in the southeast of the island (above).

The Sellin pier on Rügen was destroyed by ice drift in 1941, and finally rebuilt in 1998, in the style of the Art Nouveau original. From the 30-m-high (100-ft) cliffs on which the Baltic Sea resort of Sellin is located you can get lovely views of the beach and the pier.

FISCHLAND-DARSS-ZINGST

Fischland, Darss and Zingst were once three separate islands that grew together over time and were finally linked by dykes in the 19th century. "Fischland is the most beautiful place in the world," said the female protagonist, Gesine Cresspahl, in Uwe Johnson's book, *Jahrestage*. But it is small, and the water laps conspicuously up on both sides of this narrow piece of land that is home to the Baltic Sea resort towns of Ahrenshoop (left) and Wustrow. The Darss peninsula forms the central part of the present-day Fischland-Darss-Zingst chain, an island wilderness that served as a pirate's bolt hole until the end of the 14th century. The Zingst peninsula and the Baltic Sea resort of the same name form its easterly continuation. Parts of Darss and Zingst belong to the Vorpommersche Boddenlandschaft National Park (West Pomerania Lagoon Area National Park) that was set up shortly after German reunification. Large parts of it are covered by water that is only knee-deep ("bodden" means shallow lagoon). For many species of animals, especially cranes, this is a unique habitat. Every year, up to 60,000 of the proud birds stop over at the national park, the "kingdom of cranes".

HIDDENSEE

"Dat söte Länneken," is how this small island is lovingly described in Low German, and a "sweet little land" it is indeed. Hiddensee and its four villages, Grieben, Kloster, Neuendorf and Vitte, is a miniature world of its own without cars, spa resorts or even a pier. Just under 1,100 people live here in what some would consider self-imposed isolation. Many outsiders like it here as well, however, and visit the island to find peace and tranquility, as Gerhard Hauptmann once did. In 1930, he purchased "House Seedorn" in Kloster and came every summer until 1943. A memorial remembers the Nobel Prize winner. West of Rügen is Hiddensee, a flat island in the Vorpommersche Boddenlandschaft Park, that has virtually no forest, but features salt marshes, reed belts and heathland. The sea buckthorn also grows here, which is used to make Hiddensee specialties such as jam, juice and liqueur.

In the age of satellite navigation, lighthouses have become increasingly obselete, but as historical landmarks many of them still serve dual functions as both icon and maritime orientation point. This is also true for the "Dornbusch" Lighthouse on Hiddensee, built in 1888 (above left).

"Sanssouci" ("without worries") – that is how Frederick the Great wished to live in his summer palace in Potsdam. With that goal in mind, he had Georg Wenzeslaus von Knobelsdorff build him a graceful retreat (right top) among the vineyard terraces of Potsdam in 1747, partly according to his own designs. A single-story structure, it is considered a masterwork of the German rococo and the most important sight in Potsdam. Adorned with ornate sculptures and rich furnishings, the palace also bears witness to its occupant's lively interest in the arts: in his music room the king liked to play his flute; in his magnificent library he would hold debates with Voltaire, the French philosopher of the Enlightenment.

Maxims such as the following bear witness to his literary interests: "Thus do I say sedulously / Enjoy every moment / Today the heavens may smile upon us / We do not know if they will grumble tomorrow."
More buildings were added later such as the New Chambers and the New Palace (left bottom, with performers during the popular "Night of the Palaces"). Frederick's successors were active as well, adding the Orangery and the Charlottenhof Palace.
In 1816, landscape architect Peter Joseph Lenné began the elaborate transformation of the spacious park, which extends all the way up to the Pfaueninsel (Peacock Island) and the parks of Glienicke and Babelsberg.

The Chinese Tea House, built in 1757 by Johann Gottfried Bürin, is a pavilion in Sanssouci Park. Outside, the rococo tea house is adorned with six groups of figures and twelve individual figures.

DRESDEN

Baroque and neoclassical buildings still characterize the cityscape of Dresden today. From down on the Elbe you get spectacular views of the Brühlsche Terrasse with the Academy of Art, the Ständehaus (Guild Hall), Hofkirche and Semper Opera House as well as of the rebuilt Frauenkirche.

"Venice of the East", "Saxon Serenissima", "Florence on the Elbe", "Pearl of the Baroque" – the epithets that have been used to describe the capital of the Free State of Saxony over the centuries are as numerous as they are effusive. And with good reason, for the former seat of the Great Elector is without doubt one of the great European centers of culture. Seat of the Albertiner government from 1485, it developed into one of the most magnificent baroque centers of power in the German states under Elector Augustus the Strong. In the late 18th and early 19th centuries, intellectuals even made Dresden a center of German Romanticism. However, the devastating bombing raids of World War II brought the glorious city to her knees.

In February 1945, Dresden's Old Town was irrecoverably destroyed. Thankfully, many buildings have been lavishly rebuilt including the city's most famous icon, the Frauenkirche (Church of Our Lady), the Zwinger, the Semper Opera House, the Residenz (Dresden Palace), the Hofkirche (St Trinitatis Cathedral), and the Brühlsche Terrasse on the banks of the Elbe.

Augustus the Strong commissioned architect Matthäus Daniel Pöppelmann and sculptor Balthasar Permoser to build the Zwinger (left), a masterpiece of courtly baroque in 1709. Completed in 1732, the palace gardens are framed by galleries and pavilions that today house museums.

Three words sum up Germany's westermost metropolis: churches, art and kölsch beer. A Roman settlement was the original nucleus of this cosmopolitan city on the Rhine. During the reign of Charlemagne, Cologne became an archbishopric, and by the early Middle Ages it had become one of Germany's leading cities.

Romanesque and Gothic churches still bear witness to the former spiritual and intellectual importance of Cologne, most of all of course the famous Kölner Dom (Cologne Cathedral). Art also seems more present here than anywhere else in Germany. Its important galleries and museums are numerous and include the Museum Ludwig and the Wallraf Richartz Museum. The local joie de vivre is also legendary all year round, not just during the Rose Monday (Carnival) celebrations.

People from Cologne often sum up their philosophy of life with two sentences: "Et kütt, wie et kütt." and "Et hätt noch immer jot jejange" ("Things happen the way they do" and "In the end things have always turned out alright"). People take things the way they come in Cologne because they are convinced that in the end all will turn out just fine. If you look back on 2,000 years of history, apparently you can afford such equanimity. After all, the locals have outlasted the ancient Romans as well as the occupation by the French in the 19th century.

Cologne's lifeline is the Rhine and its heart is the Cathedral. In the evening, the panorama is particularly beautiful and the view from the Deutzer Bridge to the church of Gross St Martin and the Cathedral is brilliant (main picture).

COLOGNE CATHEDRAL

Begun in the year 1248, the Kölner Dom (above, view over Hohenzollern Bridge) was not completed until 1880, after an interruption of more than 300 years from 1530 to 1842. It is considered a masterpiece of French Cathedral Gothic. The focal point of the cathedral is the Shrine of the Three Kings (left, priests celebrating holy communion), the largest reliquary ever created. It was made in around 1200 by Nicholas of Verdun, the most famous goldsmith of the Middle Ages, and holds the bones of the Three Magi. The Gero Cross is about 200 years older; its figure of Christ was one of the earliest monumental sculptures created after antiquity. Around 1440, Stephan Lochner painted the Altar of the City Patrons, a highlight of German Gothic art. When the sun shines, the interior of the cathedral is flooded with light thanks to its 10,000 sq m (107,600 sq ft) of windows.

MOSEL VALLEY

The Mosel is one of Germany's most capricious rivers, despite the fact that it rises in France, where it is called the Moselle. With its source in the heart of the Vosges Mountains, the Mosel snakes past Metz before reaching Luxembourg and finally enters German territory for the last 243 km (151 mi) of its 544-km (338-mi) total length. More than 2,000 years ago, the river was part of the Roman realm and called the Mosella. Caesar had conquered the land and mountains along its course at that point, but even earlier, the Celtic Treveri had named it Mosea. Indeed, the Mosel probably has a longer history than any other "German" river. After all, Germany's oldest town, Trier, was founded on its banks. The Mosel is a meandering river (left top, near Bremm) that flows past famously steep vineyards (left bottom, Landshut Castle near Bernkastel-Kues amid the vines) and numerous castles such as Cochem (above), originally built in 1100, destroyed by French soldiers in 1688, and rebuilt in its present neo-Gothic style in the 19th century. It sits perched above the town of the same name. The natural beauty of the region combined with the meandering river and its abundance of fish was even celebrated in song by the Roman poet Decimus Magnus Ausonius (310–395) in the 4th century.

TRIER

Records document that Trier was founded in the year 16 BC by the Romans during the reign of Emperor Augustus, and subsequently named "Augusta Treverorum," the town of the Treveri. Initially, Trier was the main town in the Roman province of Belgica, but during the reign of Emperor Diocletian it became the capital of the Westen Roman Empire and ultimately remained in Rome's possession until 475.

Numerous historical buildings in Trier were erected during that time, including the famous Porta Nigra (left), the best-preserved Roman town gate north of the Alps, the Roman bridge spanning the Mosel, the amphitheater, the basilica, the aqueduct from the Hunsrück Mountains, and of course the imperial thermae (below), begun in the early 4th century and one of the largest spas in the entire Roman Empire.

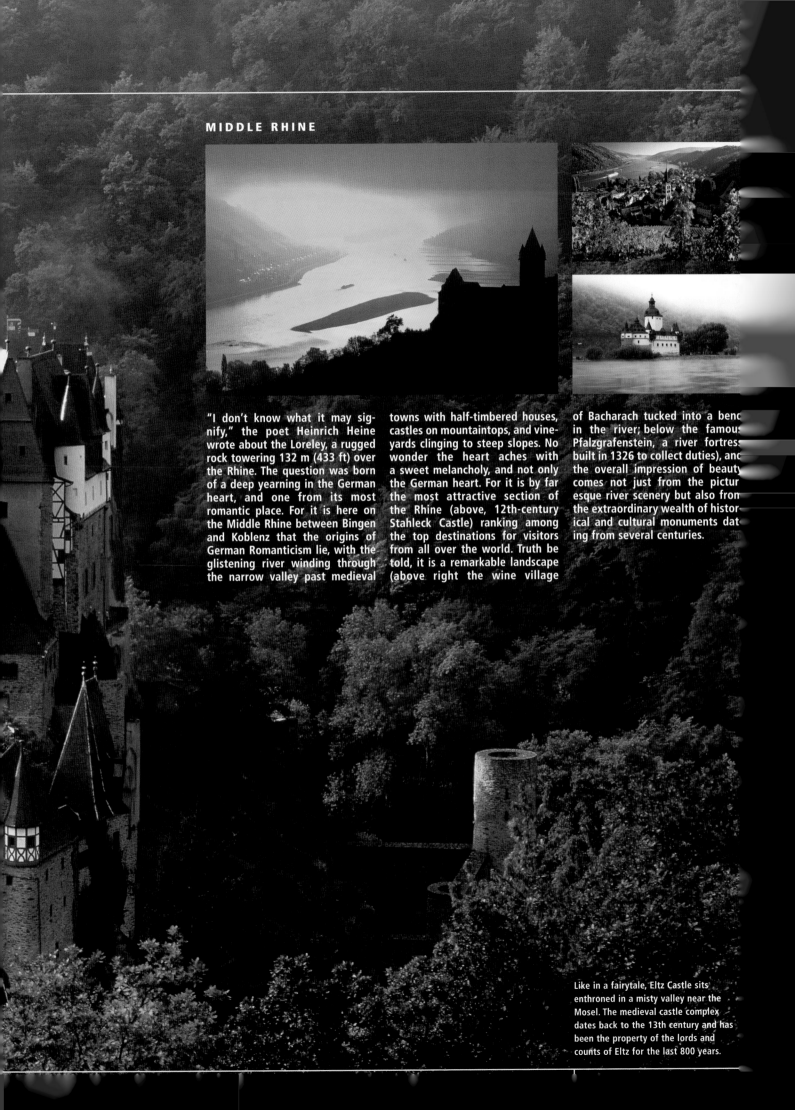

"I don't know what it may sig-nify," the poet Heinrich Heine wrote about the Loreley, a rugged rock towering 132 m (433 ft) over the Rhine. The question was born of a deep yearning in the German heart, and one from its most romantic place. For it is here on the Middle Rhine between Bingen and Koblenz that the origins of German Romanticism lie, with the glistening river winding through the narrow valley past medieval towns with half-timbered houses, castles on mountaintops, and vine-yards clinging to steep slopes. No wonder the heart aches with a sweet melancholy, and not only the German heart. For it is by far the most attractive section of the Rhine (above, 12th-century Stahleck Castle) ranking among the top destinations for visitors from all over the world. Truth be told, it is a remarkable landscape (above right the wine village of Bacharach tucked into a bend in the river; below the famous Pfalzgrafenstein, a river fortress built in 1326 to collect duties), and the overall impression of beauty comes not just from the pictur-esque river scenery but also from the extraordinary wealth of histor-ical and cultural monuments dat-ing from several centuries.

Like in a fairytale, Eltz Castle sits enthroned in a misty valley near the Mosel. The medieval castle complex dates back to the 13th century and has been the property of the lords and counts of Eltz for the last 800 years.

BAYREUTH

Wilhelmine von Bayreuth (1709–1758) was an enlightened margravine and active but cautious reformer of her small fiefdom, an architect and philosopher, a composer and writer, as well as the favorite sister of Frederick the Great. From her privileged position she was able to influence the look of her namesake town, Bayreuth, with her style of choice, rococo. From 1736, she enlarged the Hermitage, the Old and the New Palaces as well as the splendid palace gardens. It was on her initiative, too, that the Margraves' Opera House was built in 1748, a masterpiece of the European baroque built according to plans by Joseph Saint-Pierre. Its magnificence was what attracted Richard Wagner to Bayreuth when his own plans for a festival hall in Munich had failed. With the help of his patron, King Ludwig II of Bavaria, Richard Wagner was able to fulfill his dream in 1872. Every year since then, the international community of Wagner enthusiasts makes the pilgrimage to the festival with its important opera productions.

Goethe's enthusiasm for Franconia was not exhausted solely by his admiration for the natural beauty of the region between the Main and Danube. What he loved were the art treasures and Franconian wines, which he took to with gusto.

WÜRZBURG

In a beautiful location at the foot of Fortress Marienberg and the lovely municipal vineyards, Würzburg extends around the market square with its late-Gothic St Mary's Chapel and the House of

Top: Würzburg's old Main Bridge dates back to 1133. In the 18th century, twelve statues, including St Kilian (here), were added.
Middle: Fortress Marienberg.
Bottom and right: The Würzburg Residence (palace).

the Falcon with its rich rococo stucco work. Many of its treasures are hidden, for example the small Lusam Garden behind the baroque Neumünster, final resting place of the minstrel Walther von der Vogelweide.
The Residence (1720) is a masterpiece of the baroque built by Lukas von Hildebrandt and Johann Balthasar Neumann. Inside is a grand staircase with a ceiling painting by Giambattista Tiepolo.

The Margraves' Opera House in Bayreuth (left) is one of the most beautiful baroque theaters in Europe; another gem in the town is the Hermitage (far left).

BAMBERG

This town of emperors and bishops is more than 1,000 years old and cozily situated on seven hills in the valley of the river Regnitz. Unlike Nuremberg or Würzburg, the former "caput orbis" (head of the world) was only lightly damaged in World War II and in some ways still feels like an old engraving. This is why Bamberg and its Old Town with the world-famous symphony orchestra are certainly worth a visit. There are many sights to see, including the old town hall from the 14th century, the "little Venice" fishermen's quarter and the late-Gothic cathedral with the *Bamberg Horseman*.

Top: Bamberg's Cathedral is one of the most important churches of the German Middle Ages.
Above: The *Bamberg Horseman*.
Right top: View of the Old Town.
Right: The town hall on the Regnitz.

The Emperor's Tomb inside the cathedral was created by Tilman Riemenschneider between 1499 and 1513, and the Marian Altar is by Veit Stoss. In the west choir lies the only papal tomb in Germany (Clement II), and the Diocesan Museum holds precious cathedral treasures.

ROTHENBURG OB DER TAUBER, AUGSBURG

ROTHENBURG OB DER TAUBER

Rothenburg ob der Tauber is a gem of late-Gothic architecture, each square more romantic than the last, and crooked alleyways and buildings. The Siebersturm at the junction of Plönlein and Untere Schmiedgasse (main picture) is one of the towers in the old town wall.

This small town is the absolute epitome of German Romanticism. If a medieval European setting is required for a film, Rothenburg is often the town of choice. Its medieval ambience has remained more or less unchanged to this day and once inspired the painter Ludwig Richter to call it a "fairy-tale of a town". The town's unique appearance, with its red tile roofs, towers and turrets, the town hall (left), large market square with fountain, town gates, churches, half-timbered houses, and a 2-km (1.5 mi) town wall simply transports you back to another time. And if that isn't enough, you can futher immerse yourself in the Middle Ages in one of the museums, for example in the Reichsmuseum, where the "Meistertrunk-Humpen", the elector's tankard from the Thirty Years' War, is on exhibit, or in the Medieval Crime Museum, where the darker sides of the Middle Ages are explained in lurid detail.

AUGSBURG

Augsburg is inseparably linked with the Fuggers, one of the richest merchant dynasties in history, to whom the city owes many celebrated buildings including the Renaissance town hall flanked by the Perlach Tower (left), and the magnificent Golden Hall ceiling in the town hall.

The first settlement in what is now Augsburg goes back to the year 14 BC making it Germany's second-oldest town after Trier. It had its heyday in the 15th and 16th centuries as an important trading city on the trans-Alpine route that served southern Germany, Italy and lands beyond.

In a spectacular location upon a promontory at the foot of the Ammer Mountains near Füssen stands the "fairytale" castle of Neuschwanstein (main picture, upper left). Hohenschwanstein Palace (lower right) was bought by Ludwig II's father Maximilian II in 1832.

WIESKIRCHE

The "Wies" Pilgrimage Church is dedicated to a wondrous event: in 1730, monks from nearby Steingaden Abbey produced an image of Christ for the Good Friday procession on a farm near the hamlet of Wies that belonged to the abbey. Then, on June 14, 1738, the statue suddenly began to shed tears, a miracle that immediately transformed the church into a pilgrimage site. A cult soon developed around the Scourged Savior of Wies, resulting in the commissioning this church, perhaps the most exuberant rococo church in all of Germany. The architects were the brothers Dominikus and Johann Baptist Zimmermann and it was built between 1745 and 1754.

NEUSCHWANSTEIN

Ludwig II commissioned Neuschwanstein Castle in 1860. It was built in neo-Romanesque style according to plans by theater set designer Christian

Jank to replace the ancient ruins of Vorder-Hohenschwangau. Its model was Wartburg Castle in Thuringia – the setting for the famous Wagner opera "Tannhäuser". Ultimately, Ludwig would only spend a few days at the castle before being arrested and deposed, among other reasons because of the high construction costs of the castle and the resulting debts of the state. Today, Neuschwanstein is one of the most-visited castles in the world, and the income it generates has by far paid the debt it once created.

LINDERHOF

Linderhof was an agricultural estate near Ettal that King Ludwig II knew from hunting trips

with his father Maximilian II. It became his wish to erect a copy of the palace and gardens at Versailles, but his plans proved far too ambitious for the narrow valley where Linderhof is situated. As a result, in 1869, construction began on his father's former hunting lodge, which at the time stood on the what is now the palace forecourt. Linderhof Palace is the only larger palace that Ludwig II was able to see completed. The grounds also include smaller "refuges" such as the Venus Grotto (above) and the Moorish Kiosk.

HERRENCHIEMSEE

The Old Palace on Herrenchiemsee, one of the two islands in Lake Chiemsee, is where the Basic Law of the Federal Republic of Germany was written in 1948. Far more famous, however, is the "fairytale King's" New Palace. The foundation stone for the building, whose garden façade is almost identical to that of the one in Versailles, was laid in 1878. But the project remained unfinished for financial reasons. Only twenty of the originally planned seventy rooms were completed, among them the impressive Hall of Mirrors (above).

Visible from a great distance, the Church of Wies (left) sits on a hill at Pfaffenwinkel, not far from Füssen. Its interior is exceptionally beautiful and features lavish stucco work and rich ceiling frescoes. The paintings are by Johann Baptist Zimmermann.

Founded in 1158, Munich owes much of its meteoric rise to Napoleon, who in 1806 made Munich the capital of Bavaria. King Ludwig I brought architectural splendor to the city while his son Maximilian II promoted the arts. The Alps seems to begin just beyond the city limits (main picture).

THE RESIDENZ

The Residenz is the historical seat of power in Munich and it is from here that Bavaria's counts, electors and kings ruled. It was built in the 16th century to replace the Neuveste Castle (from the 14th), which had replaced the Old Court as the ducal seat. Between 1568 to 1619, a Renaissance complex was built that was later expanded to include baroque, rococo and neoclassical styles.

Since World War II, the Residenz now comprises ten courtyards and 130 rooms. The Court Church of All Saints as well as the former Residenz Theater (now the Cuvilliés Theater), a splendid, newly restored rococo building, are also part of the complex.

The Residenz still plays an important role in Munich. It houses museums (including the Porcelain, Silver and Treasure Chambers in the Königsbau, Cabinet of Miniatures, State Collection of Coins, Collection of Egyptian Art) and is a prestige building for festive occasions and receptions, for example in the Antiquarium, the largest Renaissance hall north of the Alps.

MARIENPLATZ

Munich's urban center is framed by the neo-Gothic New Town Hall from 1909 (above) with its famous Glockenspiel, as well as the Old Town Hall from 1480. When Ludwig the Bavarian granted the market charter to Munich in 1315, he stipulated that the Marktplatz remain "free from building for all eternity". In 1638, Elector Maximilian I had the Marian Column erected there in gratitude for the city being spared during Swedish occupation in the Thirty Years' War. Since 1854, the center of Munich has been known as Marienplatz, named after the Madonna on top of the column.

FRAUENKIRCHE

The onion domes of the Frauenkirche are the most recognizable icons of Munich, the capital of Bavaria. They also mark an important limit: no building in the city center can be higher than their 99 m (338 ft). The Church of Our Lady, more accurately called "Cathedral of Our Blessed Lady", has ten bells. Susanna, the largest bell, dates back to 1490, and weighs eight tons. Built in what would have been a record time of twenty years by Jörg Halspach, the Gothic church is 109 m (358 ft) long, 40 m (131 ft) wide, and accommodates roughly 20,000 people. It has been the cathedral church of the archbishops of Munich and Freising since 1821.

The Antiquarium (far left, 1568–1571) is the oldest preserved room in the Munich Residenz. The name refers to the antique sculptures that decorate the space. The Cuvilliés Theater (left) is the most attractive loge theater of the Rococo age.

HOFBRÄUHAUS

Hundreds of visitors from around the world stream in and out of the Hofbräuhaus on a daily basis. It accommodates up to 1,300 guests and has become a venue of cultish proportions. The beer hall goes back to 1589, when Duke Wilhelm V had a brewery built to supply his court and servants. In 1828, Ludwig I began selling the beer at prices soldiers and working class people could afford, so they too could enjoy this "healthy" drink. The most famous regular here is an angel, Alois Hingerl, from Ludwig Thoma's 1911 story "Ein Münchner im Himmel". After too many beers he forgot his task and still sits there to this day.

NYMPHENBURG

In 1662, Electress Henriette Adelaide bore her husband, Elector Ferdinand Maria, a son and long-awaited heir to the throne of Bavaria, Max Emanuel. To show his gratitude, the ruler gifted her the extravagant Nymphenburg Palace. Unfortunately, she would not live to see its completion in 1757.

The palace's baroque façade is 700 m (766 yds) wide. Behind that, the palace park covers over 3 sq km (1 sq mi), with greenhouses, the Badenburg and Pagodenburg pavilions, and the Amalienburg hunting lodge. The summer residence of the Wittelsbachs and birthplace of Ludwig II, Nymphenburg boasts stately rooms, the Gallery of Beauties, a Nymphenburg Porcelain exhibit, and the Museum of Carriages and Sleighs in the former royal stables.

STEIN AM RHEIN, SCHAFFHAUSEN, ST. GALLEN

The Rhine Falls near Neuhausen, with Laufen Castle on the southern side (main picture), are spectacular at any time of the year but they are especially impressive in early summer when the river is swollen.

STEIN AM RHEIN

Sometimes also called the "Rothenburg of the Upper Rhine" due to its medieval townscape characterized by timbered gables and bay windows, Stein am Rhein is situated where the Rhine exits the lower section of Lake Constance (Untersee). Its main gem is the town hall from 1539, which boasts a variety of painted motifs taken from the history of the region and the town. Stein's most striking appeal, however, comes from its numerous meticulously maintained medieval houses. Opposite the town hall, for instance, is the late Gothic Weisser Adler (White Eagle) with its painted Renaissance façade, while the Hirsch and Krone buildings feature magnificent five-sided wooden bays. The Rote Ochsen (Red Ox) was built in 1446 and painted in 1615. Also worth a visit is the former Benedictine monastery of St Georg, with buildings from the 14th to the 16th centuries that are open to the public. They give an impression of monastic life in the late Middle Ages. The real showpiece is Abbot David von Winkelsheim's picture gallery completed in 1516.

SCHAFFHAUSEN

The Rhine Falls are Europe's largest waterfall in terms of water volume – the drop in height is only 25 m (82 ft). Without the falls, Schaffhausen would not have developed into a town as it did early in the Middle Ages when the goods transported along the Rhine were offloaded onto wagons here for a few miles, from which the waggoners, merchants, aldermen and toll keepers all profited. The large cathedral is testimony to the town's former

Top: View of the Old Town over the Rhine with the Munot fortress and the steeple of St John's Church. Bottom: The Fountain of the Moors on the central Fronwagplatz.

wealth and, dating from the 11th/12th centuries, it is a fine example of a very pure form of the Romanesque style. The former Benedictine All Saints Monastery, which today houses the comprehensive All Saints Cultural History Museum, was added later to the cathedral (large cloister and herb garden). The town's landmark is the Munot fortress dating from the 16th century.

Stein am Rhein is considered to be the best intact medieval town in Switzerland after Murten. It features a charming Old Town (far left) with painted façades such as this one on Rathausplatz (town hall square, left).

ST. GALLEN

St Gallen has been an important cultural center in the Lake Constance region since the early Middle Ages, and the textile and weaving industries later made it an economically important town as well. The collegiate church and monastery were rebuilt in the mid-18th century in late-baroque style – only in the crypt can remains of the original 10th-century building still be seen – and the library contains books from the monastery's early days. The monastery was founded by Abbot

Top: Gallusplatz to the south-west of the cathedral is lined with magnificent townhouses.
Bottom: Room in St Gallen Abbey Library.

Otmar in the 8th century after the Irish traveling preacher and monk Gallus had settled here as a hermit in 612. The library's inventory has been expanded continuously since the early Middle Ages. Thankfully, the dissolution of the princely abbey in 1805 took place without incident and the library now contains more than 130,000 volumes as well as about 2,000 manuscripts, around 400 of which date back to before the year 1000. The most valuable of these include the "St Gallen monastery plan", a plan for the ideal monastery drawn up in about 820, as well as the Codex Abrogans, a Latin lexicon of synonyms named after its first entry and which, having been compiled in German in about 765, is considered the oldest known work in the German language.

ZURICH

It is a cliché, and an incorrect one at that, to assume that the country's economic metropolis on Lake Zurich, with its more than 100 banking headquarters, is just a boring, old-fashioned financial center. Zurich boasts numerous architectural gems such as the Fraumünster church in the Old Town west of the river Limmat , which has a set of five windows by Marc Chagall. Next door is the 13th-century parish church of St Peter with Europe's largest clock face. The Grossmünster on the other side of the river, its neo-Gothic tower cupolas dominating the cityscape, entered the annals of church history as the domain of the reformer Huldrych Zwingli (1484–1531).

Magnificent city gates and arcades are the landmarks of Bern's historic city center. The main picture shows the view along the Kramgasse and the Marktgasse to the Käfigturm (Prison Tower) and Zytgloggeturm (Clock Tower).

BERN

Once the largest city-state north of the Alps, Bern's historic center clearly depicts the chronological order of its different periods of expansion. The stately guild and townhouses with arcades extending for a total of 6 km (4 mi) are characteristic of the city center. Construction of the late Gothic St Vincent Cathedral began in 1421 and was only completed in 1573; the magnificent main portal was designed by Erhard Küng. The late-

The highly expressive Pfeiferbrunnen Piper's Fountain) in Bern.

Gothic townhouse was erected between 1406 and 1417 and renovated in 1942. The Heiliggeistkirche (Church of the Holy Spirit), from 1729, is one of the country's most important examples of Protestant baroque architecture. Bern's landmark, however, is the Zytglogge-turm (Clock Tower) city gate.

The ensemble of lovely historic residential buildings in the Gerech-tigkeitsgasse stands out from the multitude of beautiful buildings in Bern, and some of them date back to the 16th century. Bern's Renaissance fountains with their lovely expressive figures are also worth seeing, three of them having been created by the Freiburg sculptor Hans Gieng.

The twin towers of Zurich's Grossmünster dominate the skyline of this, the "smallest large city in the world", situated at the northern end of Lake Zurich seen with the river Limmat – a tributary of the Aare – running through it (far left and left).

The Bernese Oberland is the cradle of Swiss tourism, which was instigated by three famous figures: Rousseau, Haller and Goethe. They sparked an enthusiasm for nature that became a trend among high society types to escape to the mountains. The Bernese were quick to react. The first official "Unspunnenspiele" (a festival uniting town and country) took place near Interlaken in 1805, set against the Alpine backdrop with yodelers, Fahnenschwingen (flag throwing), Steinstossen (stone throwing), and traditional garb – a huge open-air event two centuries ago! Visitors arrived via Lake Thun, some – like the Rothschilds for instance – with their own boats, and it is still a nice way to view the spectacular scenery. And by the time you reach Interlaken with the Eiger-Mönch-Jungfrau triumvirate, there is only one thing you will want to do: head off into the mountains!

GRINDELWALD

This health spa town nestled among the mighty Eiger at 3,970 m (13,026 ft), Wetterhorn (above) at 3,701 m (12,143 ft) and Schreckhorn at 4,078 m (13,380 ft) has been the main attraction in the Bernese Oberland for more than 150 years. A trip with the Jungfraubahn (above) from Kleiner Scheidegg through the Eiger and Mönch to Europe's highest train station, the Jungfraujoch tunnel station at an altitude of 3,454 m (11,333 ft), is a unique experience.

From left to right:
The Eiger (3,970 m/12,026 ft),
the Mönch (4,099 m/13,449 ft) and
the Jungfrau (4,158 m/13,642 ft), plus
the Männichen (2,345 m/7,694 ft) in
the foreground make up the Jungfrau
region of the Bernese Oberland.

The Morteratsch Glacier (main picture) is the largest glacier in the Bernina Range. It is framed by imposing mountains and the Piz Bernina which, at 4,049 m (13,285 ft) is the only mountain in Engadin over 4,000 m (13,124 ft).

UPPER ENGADIN

The Inn (Rhaeto-Romanic "En") Valley is lined with massive mountain chains and is around 90 km (56 mi) long. It extends from the Maloja Pass at the far eastern end of Switzerland to the Austrian border near Martina. Engadin (Rhaeto-Romanic "Engiadina") is generally taken to refer to Upper Engadin:

"This Upper Engadin is the loveliest stopover in the world," claimed Thomas Mann, who "almost" believed himself to be happy there. The Upper Inn Valley from Zuoz as far as Maloja is indeed a landscape beyond compare in the Alps. There is no oppressive sense of confinement even in the high mountains near the edge of the forest. It is a broad, open area and in the midst of all this are the Upper Engadine Lakes which, together with the larch forests glowing golden in the autumn and the white snowcapped peaks beneath the bright blue sky, produce an alpine scenery that was a draw for nature enthusiasts even in the days of the stage coach, inspiring Nietzsche to the conclusion that: "All desire longs for eternity."

ST. MORITZ

This upscale health resort in the heart of Upper Engadin enjoys special status: famous for having twice been the venue for the Winter Olympics (1928 and 1948), it has cleverly promoted itself as the "Top of the World". As the gateway to a unique landscape of lakes (Lake St Moritz, Lake Silvaplana, Lake Sils) the village, first documented in 1139, offers a wide range of sporting options with its much-lauded "champagne climate" in both winter and summer.

BERGELL

Two adjacent areas could hardly be more different than the Upper Engadine lake plateau and the Bergell valley: at the 1,815-m-high (5,955-ft) Maloja Pass, the wide valley, which rises no more than 50 m (164 ft) from the Inn ravine near St Moritz, suddenly drops dramatically to the south-east as far as the Italian border. The mountains then suddenly close up on one another, but not far away is the "threshold to paradise", as the painter Giovanni Segantini (1858–1899) named the village of Soglio (above), situated on a sunny peak above the narrow valley – one of the most popular tourist destinations in Bergell.

Nietzsche spent several summers at Lake Sils (left), where he wrote significant parts of his philosophical work *Also sprach Zarathustra* (*Thus Spake Zarathustra*). He said to a friend who visited him there that he needed to have the blue sky above him in order to gather his thoughts.

LOWER ENGADIN

The appeal of this wide valley landscape at the foot of the Silvretta Range lies in its primeval nature. Zernez, at the confluence of the Inn and the Spöl, was almost burnt to the ground in 1872 and has hardly any old buildings left at all. It is nevertheless a starting point for hikes into Swiss National Park (170 sq km/67 sq mi), which was opened on August 1, 1914, the first of its kind in Europe.

Guarda and Ardez are considered the loveliest towns in Lower Engadin. They are both subject to strict preservation orders and comprise exceptionally appealing Engadine buildings, many of which feature century-old courtyards

Tarasp Castle, built in around 1040 and towering atop a shale cliff top, is Lower Engadin's landmark.

with sophisticated scraffiti and bay windows, as well as tremendously thick walls protecting meticulously paneled living rooms and bedrooms. The valley broadens after Ardez and it is here that Scuol, its tourist center dominated by the Tarasp Castle, is situated. Until 1915, the village was considered the "spa queen of the Alps" thanks to its hot springs, but fell into oblivion thereafter only to be revived again in the 1990s with the opening of a modern version. The valley narrows again to the east and becomes more rugged and remote. A number of small villages such as Sent, Ramosch or Tschlin hug the narrow, sunny terraces before both the road and the river cross the Austrian border at Martina, close to the Finstermünz Pass ravine.

Enchanting in shape and with a magical light, it is no wonder that the Matterhorn is also referred to as the "crown jewel of the Alps". A particularly lovely view is with Riffel Lake in the foreground (main picture). The normal route up to the 4,478-m (14,692-ft) summit is via the distinctive Hörnligrat.

What hasn't already been written about this mountain! Bombarded regularly with superlatives, the Matterhorn's incomparable shape is much vaunted, having been referred to as the "advertising mountain" due to its use in promoting just about everything.

Who would have thought? The Matterhorn adorns not only Swiss yoghurt containers and Belgian beer bottles, it has also found itself on wine labels and on Japanese confectionery, on a cigarette carton from Jamaica and even on a poster for a Rolling

Stones European tour in 1976. Luis Trenker made a tearjerker of a film out of the tragic first ascent of the mountain (1865) by Edward Whymper, in which the four-man crew lost their lives, and in Zermatt the souvenir shops are full of Matterhorn kitsch. A mythical mountain and yet so much more than just pyramid-shaped rock?

Well, "Horu" (as it is called by locals) has brought great prosperity to the country village of Zermatt (1,616 m/5,302 ft). The hotel pioneer Alexander Seiler was the first to recognize the huge significance of this unique mountain backdrop for his tiny village. And indeed, the "mountain of mountains" has been captivating visitors since Whymper's time. They come from all over the world to marvel at this magnificent monument to Alpine altitudes, some of them even coming to climb it.

LAVAUX, GENEVA, LAUSANNE, CHILLON

LAVAUX

Grapes have been cultivated on the Lavaux Vineyard Terraces for at least 1,000 years. This landscape, arguably one of the most beautiful in Switzerland, stretches roughly 30 km (19 mi) along the northern shore of Lake Geneva, from the eastern outskirts of Lausanne up to the Château de Chillon.

Three suns, so say the locals, warm the grapes there: the sunshine of the day, the reflection of the sun's rays on the lake's surface and the sun's heat that is stored by the stone walls during the day and released at night.

The present terraced landscape dates back to the Benedictine and Cistercian monks of the 11th and 12th centuries. The grape variety that is grown on the shores of Lake Geneva is called the Gutedel – a variety that is generally known as "Chasselas" or "Fendant" in Switzerland. The fourteen communes of the Lavaux produce exclusively white wines, all of them with one of the following "appellations contrôlées": Villette, Saint-Saphorin, Dézaley, Epesses and Chardonne. The wines are a major part of the economy here.

Château de Chillon, the most frequently visited historical monument in Switzerland, is famous for its location upon a rock on the shores of Lake Geneva.

GENEVA

Geneva lies where the Jet d'Eau fires its plume of water 145 m (476 ft) into the sky, framed by the Jura and Savoy Alps and huddled into a bay on Lake Geneva. The "Protestant Rome", where around 450 years ago John Calvin propagated his rigorous ideas for reform and Henri Dunant founded the Red Cross in 1864, is today a truly international city. A third of its inhabitants are foreign; over 200 organizations including the United Nations (UN) and the World Health

Geneva is the second-largest city in Switzerland. It lies where the Rhône flows out of Lake Geneva.

Organization (WHO) have their headquarters there. But beyond the diplomats, expensive watches and Cuban cigars, there are also some worthwhile architectural attractions: St Peter's Cathedral including its archaeological excavations and adjacent Place du Bourg-de-Four; the richly stocked Museum for Art and History; the Palais des Nations – headquarters of the UN; and the memorial to philosopher and Geneva native son Jean-Jacques Rousseau. Geneva is also an Alpine city, as can be seen in the Geneva altar of Konrad Witz from 1444, in his painting *Petrus Altar* (today in the Museum of Art): depicted is a marvelous haul of fish from Lake Geneva with Mont Blanc as a backdrop.

The Lavaux Vineyard Terraces descend dramatically down to Lake Geneva (left). The lake and the Alps form a unique backdrop for the vineyards in this historic wine-growing region.

LAUSANNE

This city in Canton Vaud is on the north shore of Lake Geneva and is an important center of education and trade fairs as well as the seat of the Federal Supreme Court – the highest court in Switzerland – and of the International Olympic Committee. Scattered with villas and spread across several hills is the Old Town, which can also be reached cog railway from the port district of Ouchy. The main attraction is the early-Gothic cathedral. Consecrated in 1275, it was Switzerland's most attractive church in its day.

CHILLON

Château de Chillon, the epitome of a romantic moated castle, is roughly 5 km (3 mi) south-east of Montreux, the sophisticated holiday resort on the north shore of Lake Geneva that has become famous for its international jazz festival. Built in the 11th and 12th centuries by the counts of Savoy, the castle controlled the route from Burgundy over the Great St Bernard Pass to Italy. It became famous mainly thanks to Lord Byron's ballad, "The Prisoner of Chillon". The poet – who had visited the castle in 1816 – had been inspired to write the ballad by the fate of Geneva prior François Bonivard, who was imprisoned in Chillon for six years because of his reformist tendencies before being liberated from his chains in 1536.

TICINO

Ticino is known as the "sunny side of Switzerland", and every school-child there knows that on the other side of the Gotthard peak, the sun shines more often than in Zurich. Ticino is a popular holiday region, and some may ask themselves whether this is in fact the southern part of Switzerland or the northern part of Italy. At any rate, the Alpine world here already exudes an air of Mediterranean promise.

Hermann Hesse described Ticino, his adopted home, as "wonderfully rich and beautiful", and it is surely the diversity of contrasts that still fascinates visitors today.

LOCARNO

The heart of Ticino beats on the Swiss side of Lake Maggiore. One of the most beautiful towns on the north shore of the lake is Locarno, not far from where the Maggia River flows into the lake from its high mountain source. Locarno has been famous since 1946 for its annual film festival.

With approximately 2,300 hours of sunshine a year, the people of Locarno enjoy the mildest climate in Switzerland. The historic center of the town, first documented around the year 789, was originally directly on the lake, but over the course of centuries, the Maggia has deposited immense amounts of sediment between Locarno and Ascona that today occupies about half the former width of the lake. The icon of the town is the Madonna del Sasso Pilgrimage Church, situated on top of the wooded Belvedere Hill (above), where in 1480 the Blessed Virgin is said to have appeared to a monk, wearing a halo of bright light.

ASCONA

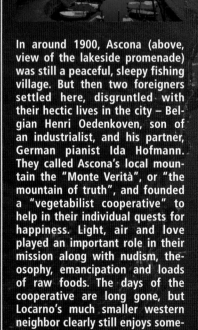

In around 1900, Ascona (above, view of the lakeside promenade) was still a peaceful, sleepy fishing village. But then two foreigners settled here, disgruntled with their hectic lives in the city – Belgian Henri Oedenkoven, son of an industrialist, and his partner, German pianist Ida Hofmann. They called Ascona's local mountain the "Monte Verità", or "the mountain of truth", and founded a "vegetabilist cooperative" to help in their individual quests for happiness. Light, air and love played an important role in their mission along with nudism, theosophy, emancipation and loads of raw foods. The days of the cooperative are long gone, but Locarno's much smaller western neighbor clearly still enjoys something of a reputation as a mecca for the avant-garde – and for art. It is also still a very good place to pursue happiness: the mountains, wonderful light and fresh air at least are guaranteed.

LAKE LUGANO, LUGANO

Where today subtropical vegetation and the most northerly olive trees in Europe flourish, 15,000 years ago was permafrost. The basins of the lakes were dug out by glaciers, which then formed terminal moraines when they receded. That allowed the valleys to fill with water. The shores rise steeply here due to this glacial activity. The same is also true of Lake Maggiore, which is fed mainly by the Maggia, a river rising in the northern Ticino Alps.

Etruscans and Gauls had already settled on Lake Lugano long before the Romans came. The lake is around 35 km (22 mi) long, up to 3 km (2 mi) wide and up to 288 m (945 ft) deep. A view of the lake from one of Lugano's two mountains – Monte Bré (above) at 925 m (3,035 ft) or Monte San Salvatore at 912 m (2,992 ft), which rises like a sugarloaf out of the water – is spectacular. The largest part of the lake, which is 217 m (712 ft) above sea level, belongs to the Swiss canton of Ticino while the smaller part belongs to the Italian provinces of Como and Varese.

Lugano, whose Old Town square is surrounded by arcades, was the capital of Ticino from 1803 to 1878, alternating in a six-year cycle with Locarno and Bellinzona. Today it is considered the "capitale morale", the "heartfelt" capital of the Ticino, and the region around Lake Lugano, with its rolling hills and cypress trees, is known as "Tuscan Switzerland". Hermann Hesse spent almost half his life in Montagnola above the lake; a museum near his former home, the Casa Camuzzi, is dedicated to the Nobel Laureate in Literature.

VIENNA

Vienna is one of the continent's most historic metropolises and has been able to retain its splendor in the face of much adversity. The imposing St Stephen's Cathedral sits majestically in the heart of the city (main picture).

ST CHARLES' CHURCH

It is the symbolic building of those euphoric centuries after the second Turkish Siege in 1683, when Vienna was transformed into the elegant metropolis that it is today. St Charles' Church was commissioned in 1713 by the emperor of the same name, Charles VI, at the end of a plague epidemic. Its creators, Fischer von Erlach Sr and Jr, combined the classic forms of Greek, Roman and Byzantine architecture to construct the church. A temple portico rises up under the patina-green dome, while triumphal pillars decorated with spiral reliefs and a bell tower soar up on both sides. A magnificent dome fresco by J. M. Rottmayr adorns the oval interior.

ST STEPHEN'S CATHEDRAL

St Stephen's Cathedral, Vienna's most important religious building and the city's emblem, is visible from afar and affectionately known by locals as "Steffl". It is a masterpiece of stonemasonry made from 20,000 cu m (706,293 cu ft) of sandstone. It dates back a good 750 years. Its west front still originates from the previous Romanesque building; the rest is High Gothic. The

Top: The southern spire of St Stephen's Cathedral towers over Vienna.
Middle: "Pummerin", the third-largest church bell in Europe.
Bottom: The high altar, by brothers Tobias and Johann Jakob Pock.

southern spire, the third-highest in Europe, measures 137 m (449 ft) and soars gloriously towards the heavens. From its viewing deck, which is reached by climbing 343 steps, you get a panoramic view of the city. The solemn interior is peppered with artistic treasures from the past. The most prominent of these are the marmoreal tomb of Emperor Friedrich III, the New Town Altar, the so-called Servants' Madonna, and Anton Pilgram's pulpit and organ stand.

"I want to keep my vow before those who fear God" is the inscription on St Charles' Church (left). The monumental building is almost 80 m (262 ft) long, 60 m (197 ft) wide 72 m (236 ft) high at the top of the dome.

IMPERIAL CRYPT

An attraction just as curious as it is popular is the Imperial Crypt, also known as Capuchins' Crypt, on Neuer Markt square. From the early 17th century, the Habsburg rulers and their next of kin were buried in a total of 138 metal caskets in the deep vaults here, traditionally guarded by Capuchin friars, at the foot of the rather unimposing Ordenskirche. Maria Theresa and her husband Francis Stephen of Lorraine were laid to rest

Behind the tomb of Emperor Joseph II is the double casket of Maria Theresa and Francis I Stephen.

here – in a double sarcophagus that was lavishly adorned with life-size figures in rococo style. Next to them lies the reformist Emperor Joseph II in a simple copper casket much more in keeping with his humble character. Emperor Franz Joseph I also has his final resting place here, as do his wife Elisabeth of Bavaria (known more commonly as "Sissi"), his son Rudolf, his brother Maximilian, who was murdered in Mexico, and, from 1989, Austria's last empress: Zita.

HOFBURG

The Hofburg was for many centuries the Habsburg monarchy's seat of political power and served as the imperial family's main residence. It also houses the present-day National Library (above, the ceremonial room), which Emperor Charles VI had built by Johann Bernhard Fischer von Erlach and his son in 1722. It was the first part of the court library.

COURT RIDING SCHOOL

The Spanish Riding School was not opened to the general public until after World War I. It is one of the oldest establishments for classic dressage. The performances of the legendary Lipizzaner stallions – elegant, snow-white horses originally bred in Spain – were one of the highlights of court entertainment from the 16th century.

The Hofburg, radiant in the evening light, still bears witness to the opulence with which the emperors of the Habsburg dynasty adorned their capital until the end of the monarchy in 1918.

MUSEUM OF ART HISTORY AND NATURAL HISTORY

The "twin museums" on the Burg-ring were designed in the early 1870s by Hamburg-born architect Gottfried Semper and Vienna native Carl von Hasenauer. The buildings look identical from the outside, but their content could hardly be more different: while the thirty-nine rooms of the Museum of Natural History (top right, a dinosaur skeleton) are home to great collections of minerals, meteorites, fossils, and skeletons as well as present-day plant and animal species, the Museum of Art History (top left, the Dome Hall) houses one of the most valuable painting galleries in the world – from Dürer and Breughel, to Rembrandt and Rubens and Tintoretto. Added to this are the Kunstkammer, coin cabinets, antiques and the Egypt-ian and Oriental collections.

VIENNA

The "Gloriette" (main picture) in the park at Schönbrunn Palace provides an excellent view over the vast "Austrian Versailles". The park is home to sculptures and fountains, as well as a Palm House and zoological garden.

SCHÖNBRUNN

The ultimate symbol of imperial, baroque Vienna will always be Schönbrunn Palace, located outside the city center in the western villa district of Hietzing. As an early 18th-century creation, it reflects the desire to express architectural exuberance, which inspired aristocratic builders after the triumph over the Turks. In its current form, the sunny-yellow palace complex is the result of a massive renovation led by Nikolaus Pacassi and Fischer von Erlach between 1744 and 1749. Schönbrunn was the summer residence of the Habsburgs until 1918. Today, up to 11,000 admirers visit the magnificent imperial apartments, the historic coaches in the carriage collection, the Palm House, and the zoological garden every day during the high season. Like Versailles, a walk through the vast park with its artistically landscaped flower beds, hedges, ponds, fountains and statues feels simply decadent.

BELVEDERE

One of Vienna's main baroque monuments is the Belvedere, by Lukas von Hildebrandt. The legendary commander and conqueror of the Turks, Prince Eugene of Savoy, had this summer palace – actually comprising two palaces – built between 1714 and 1723. The more opulent Upper Belvedere (left) was once the scene of a significant moment in Austrian history: in 1955, in the Marble Hall, foreign ministers of the four occupying powers sealed independence for the young republic by signing the State Treaty. Masterpieces by Waldmüller, Klimt, Kokoschka and others in the palace's other rooms testify to the heyday experienced by the world of fine art in the 19th and early 20th century. The Lower Belvedere (right), which was clearly simpler on the outside but appointed almost as lavishly as its twin on the inside, is primarily reserved for special exhibitions.

KAISERGEBIRGE

What a contrast! At one end of the Kaisergebirge range are the bizarre pinnacles of the Wilder Kaiser (or "Wild Emperor", top), and at the other, the green ridges of the Kitzbühel Alps. Generations of climbers have left traces of their efforts in the light, firm limestone of the Kaisergebirge. Ludwig Purtscheller, the great alpinist, wrote about these fascinating mountains: "Other mountains may tower over them in terms of absolute height or sheer immensity, but the Kaisergebirge is unparalleled [...] when it comes to the wonderful arrangement of their bizarrely fissured peaks and horns."

KITZBÜHEL

Geologically part of the schistous and greywacke zone, the Kitzbühel Alps, located in the Eastern Tyrol on the border with Salzburg, are a low mountain range characterized by forests and gentle grassy meadows. The name comes from the district capital of Kitzbühel, winter meeting place of the international jet set since the sporting successes of Toni Sailer, the "Blitz from Kitz". The famous Hahnenkamm Races come under the sporting and social media spotlight every year toward the end of January.

KARWENDEL

This section of the Northern Tyrolean Limestone Alps, which soars up from the Seefelder Sattel in the west to Lake Achensee in the east, gets its name from the rocky gray walls and the hollows dug out of the stone by the glaciers – so-called cirques (or Kare). The highest peak in the Karwendel range, which includes the rock faces of the Laliderer (left) and the Überschalljoch (below) is the Birkkarspitze (2,756 m/9,042 ft). Cable cars are the easiest way to access the 2,334-m-high (7,658-ft) Hafelekar from Innsbruck, or the Karwendelspitze from Mittenwald in Germany. The massif, whose northern foothills transition into Upper Bavaria, is subdivided into four ranges, running from east to west. The valleys in between, with their mountain pastures covered in Swiss stone pine, are blocked off to private traffic. The region where the Isar (Munich's river) has its source is rather sparsely settled and, along with the peaks, is largely a nature reserve.

DACHSTEIN

where the three states of Styria, Salzburg and Upper Austria meet. The Dachstein group (left, the Bischofsmütze or Bishop's Cap) is a karstified limestone high plateau with several jagged peaks and the easternmost glaciers in the Alps.

HALLSTATT

This pretty little town (below) lent its name to an entire culture, the "Hallstatt Culture". When Johann Georg Ramsauer began the first excavations on the pre-history of Central Europe in the shadow of the Dachstein Mountains (left) in 1846, he and his team unearthed upwards of ten thousand priceless discoveries documenting the transition from the European Bronze Age to the early Ice Age.

The highest peak here – the Dachstein, at 2,995 m (9,827 ft) – towers over the extreme western end of the region of Styria. The mighty massif marks the point

Tavonaro Cross on the Stripsenjoch in the Wilder Kaiser range, the southern part of the Kaisergebirge mountains.

SALZBURG

Hugo von Hofmannsthal called the Salzburg state capital the "heart of the heart of Europe". This city not only produced Wolfgang Amadeus Mozart, but has also inspired artists from all over the world for centuries. Hohensalzburg Fortress, its Cathedral, Collegiate Church, residence, St Peter's and Mirabell

Palace – the collective urban works of art on the Salzach between the hills of the Kapuzinerberg, Mönchsberg and Festungsberg dazzle the senses with their intense baroque atmosphere and fascinating range of cultural attractions. This urban gem that is the Getreidegasse (left) largely has Archbishop Wolf Dietrich von Raitenau to thank for its present-day appearance. Around 1600, the Archbishop had half of the city's medieval center demolished and the expansive central open spaces laid out. His successor, who was just as extravagantly minded, subsequently completed the unique architectural ensemble.

Hohensalzburg Fortress sits atop the Mönchsberg, below which nestles the charming Old Town.

MIRABELL

HELLBRUNN

Mirabell Palace (meaning nice view) was originally called Altenau, after Simone Alt, the mistress of Archbishop Wolf Dietrich von Raitenau, who had the palace built for his beloved in 1606. At the time its location was still outside Salzburg city limits. The palace (above, with Mirabell Garden), which was converted between 1721 and 1727 into a baroque complex by Lukas von Hildebrandt, Austria's most famous builder along with Fischer von Erlach, has been the registered office of the mayor and the magistrate since 1950.

Markus Sittikus, Count of Hohenems, the cousin and – from 1612 – successor of Archbishop Wolf Dietrich von Raitenau, built his "villa suburbana" between 1613 and 1615. It was a country pleasure palace with park complex and water features in the present-day district of Morzg. "May his successors have pleasure" is inscribed above the entrance. One of the murals in the Music Room (above), known as the "Octagon", which has ornate frescos by Donato Mascagni, depicts the Archbishop as a pink cavalier.

GROSSGLOCKNER

The Grossglockner, Austria's highest peak, is a mighty 3,798 m (12,461 ft) and best admired from the lookout on Kaiser Franz Josefs Höhe. The high alpine road named after it, which leads into the Salzburg Fusch Valley from Heiligenblut, winds its way through twenty-six hairpin turns and over sixty bridges to an altitude of 2,500 m (8,203 ft). Built in the 1930s, it has brought more than fifty million visitors closer to these exhilarating mountains since its opening in 1935. The 50-km (31-mi) stretch of road is only open from April to November, depending on the snow conditions, and features a number of museums, educational tracks and signposted viewing points.

Lake Wangenitzsee (large picture) is at an altitude of 2,464 m (8,084 ft) in the Hohe Tauern National Park, a natural landscape and habitat for ibexes, marmots, bearded vultures, chamois and golden eagles (insets, from left).

HOHE TAUERN

There are six national parks in Austria. The one in the Hohe Tauern is by far the largest (1,836 sq km/ 709 sq mi) and also the highest. Apart from the Grossglockner, the Grossvenediger checks in at 3,666 m (12,028 ft) some 30 km (19 mi) further west, armored with the largest interconnecting glacier district in the Eastern Alps. This region supplies the headstream of the Salzach (which flows through Salzburg) and the Isel, as well as

Top to bottom: Edelweiss, gentian and campion, the wonderful blossoms of the Hohe Tauern, give this landscape its unique appearance.

two of the mightiest waterfalls in Europe: the 380-m-high (1,247-ft) Krimmler Falls in Upper Pinzgau, and the Umbal Falls in the gorgeous Virgental valley.

Some 150 years ago, mountaineering pioneer Ignaz von Kürsinger described the Hohe Tauern as a "magical world" of mountain pastures, rock and ice, "full of great, wild natural scenery and beautiful flowers". The national park protects the last, pristine natural landscape in the Eastern Alps – and not least its unique flora and fauna.

A picture-postcard view: the Grossglockner (left), located on the border between Carinthia and East Tyrol, with the Pasterze at its base, the largest glacier in the Eastern Alps (far left).

The Wachau Valley is known for Dürnstein, with its castle ruins, Renaissance palace, baroque monastery and former Poor Clare Convent (main picture). On a rocky promontory over the Danube is Melk Abbey, with its ornate baroque church and famous monastic library (inset).

The steep, narrow valley road that leads through Wachau begins in the west with the grandiose, baroque monastic residence of Melk which, with its imposing twin-spired domed church, is the "crown jewel" of this area. A number of castles, castle ruins, palaces and churches adorn the river valley between the pretty villages of Obstbauerndorf and Winzerdorf.

This area is also home to the small township of Willendorf, made famous by what was the most important discovery from the Old Stone Age – the Venus of Willendorf. After the wine-growing towns of Spitz and Weissenkirchen you reach Dürnstein, where a hike up to the monastery beneath the castle ruins is worth the effort. The slender late-baroque tower of the

monastery is one of the most elegant of its kind. The valley widens after Dürnstein, and provides a clear view as far as Krems, the medieval town with the Gothic buildings of the Gozzo-Burg, the Dominican Church and the Church of the Piarist Order. The Göttweig monastery perched ceremoniously on a hilltop marks the end of the Wachau Valley.

On a rocky promontory over the Danube is Melk Abbey, with its ornate baroque church and famous monastic library.

Just a short distance away from Dürn-stein is the wine-growing town of Weissenkirchen (left), dominated by a mighty fortified church dating back to the 14th century.

ROME

The center of the present-day metropolis of Rome – located at a bend in the Tiber River – was first settled around 3,000 years ago. The people who settled here left traces of their civilizations from the very start, providing Rome with tremendous appeal for anyone interested in art, architectural and cultural history.

The presence of the city's mythical founders, Romulus and Remus, can be felt during a walk through its fascinatig streets just as much as that of the other well-known Roman emperors and popes who resided in this, the capital city of Christianity, during the Renaissance and baroque periods. More than any other city, Rome is testimony to the advanced development of European culture and it is indeed here that some of the deepest roots of western civilization are to be found.

THE CAPITOL

In ancient times, there was a temple on the Capitoline Hill that was dedicated to Jupiter, king of the gods. It was reached by a winding path leading south-east from the Forum. Today you climb the hill from the west on a flight of stairs designed by Michelangelo. At the top is a piazza, also designed by Michelangelo, and which is paved with a geometric pattern. The bronze equestrian sculpture of Marcus Aurelius in the center of the square (above, today a copy) is the only one of its kind to have escaped being melted down in the Middle Ages because the rider was thought to be Constantine I, defender of Christianity. The Palazzo Senatorio on the piazza is the seat of the mayor of Rome.

FORUM ROMANUM

Located between the Palatine Hill and the Capitoline Hill, the Roman Forum and the other buildings dating from the 6th century BC were the site of religious ceremonies and political gatherings. It was here, for example, that speeches were held and all manner of merchandise offered for sale. During the day it was said to have been a bustling areal full of buyers and sellers.

The fall of the Roman Empire saw the deterioration of Forum buildings (above) such as the triumphal arch of Septimius Severus, the Temple of Saturn and the Temple of Vespasian in front of the baroque Santi Luca e Martina Church, which then fell into disuse. In the Middle Ages the Forum was known as the Campo Vaccino, the cow's meadow.

THE COLOSSEUM

Among the highlights on Capitoline Hill are the remains of a colossal statue from the 4th century BC in the courtyard of the Palace of the Conservators. It depicts Emperor Constantine I and once stood in the apse of the Basilica of Constantine on the Roman Forum. The unclothed body parts were made of marble while the rest was of bronze-clad wood.

THE PANTHEON

The site where the towering ruins of the largest amphitheater in antiquity now stand was once occupied by a wooden construction that fell victim to the great fire of AD 64. Nero's included those grounds in his new palace and even had an artificial pond built. His successor Vespasian then commissioned a three-story stone arena in about the year AD 72, a magnificent building financed in part by the gold and other treasures that fell into Roman hands following the plundering of the temple in Jerusalem. The consecration of the colosseum was marked by games that lasted one hundred days during which a multitude of people and thousands of animals were killed in the name of mass entertainment.

The Piazza della Rotonda to the west of the Via del Corso boasts one of the most impressive buildings of antiquity: the Pantheon. Built in 27 BC, the Pantheon was a temple dedicated to all of the gods, as its name implies. The round opening in the dome was of mythical significance, creating a link with the heavens. Inside the former temple are the tombs of the painter Raphael and the first king of unified Italy, Victor Emanuel II.

Bernini's Allegory of the Ganges (main picture) is one of four allegories of the four main continents – in this case Asia – known to Renaissance geographers. It adorns the Fontana dei Quattro Fiumi (Fountain of Four Rivers) built in the middle of the Piazza Navona in 1651.

PIAZZA DI SPAGNA

This square is so named because it was here that the Spanish ambassador to the Holy See had his residence in the 17th century. This area was alleged to be unsafe for young Romans at the time, some of whom apparently disappeared without a trace here – presumably forced into serving in the Spanish army. The popular name "Spanish Steps", which refers to the first part of the staircase built in 1726 linking Piazza di Spagna with the Trinità dei Monti church higher up, is misleading because its construction was initiated by a French cardinal. The staircase in the middle of Rome was actually intended to proclaim the greatness of the French monarch.

PIAZZA NAVONA

This piazza was not originally built as such, but rather emerged as the result of organic growth over the centuries. Its oblong outline is testimony to the fact that this was once the site of a stadium built by Julius Caesar and subsequently expanded under Domitian in about AD 85. In the early Middle Ages a church was built here on the purported site of St Agnes' death as a martyr. Living quarters and shops eventually rose where the lower

The Fontana del Nettuno created by Antonio del la Bitta between 1873 and 1878 depicts the Roman god of the sea killing an octopus with a spear.

sections of the former grandstand lay, and they gradually developed into larger buildings. Sixtus IV established a market here in 1477, and in 1495 the square, which also used to be a horse racing venue, was paved over.

In the mid-17th century, Bernini and Borromini were commissioned with the expansion of the square. Bernini's creations included the Fontana di Quattro Fiumi while Borromini took on the construction of Sant' Agnese. The Fontana di Quattro Fiumi was financed by a special tax levied on bread, among other things, a measure that was wildly unpopular at the time.

The official name of the Spanish Steps (left) is "Scalinata della Trinità dei Monti". They are a popular meeting place. The Fontana della Barcaccia (far left) at the foot of the steps features a bark by Piero Bernini in commemoration of the flooding of the Tiber in 1598, when boat traffic was still possible.

FONTANA DI TREVI

Rome's most famous fountain is the Fontana di Trevi. Nicola Salvi started to build it in 1751. In fact, Anita Ekberg's legendary "bath" in this fountain – from a scene in Fellini's film *La Dolce Vita* (1960) – made a significant contribution to the fountain's fame. There are also superstitions involving the fountain, for example, that anyone who throws a coin into the fountain, whose central figure depicts the god of the sea flanked by tritons, is sure to return to Rome. At around 26 m (85 ft) in height and 20 m (66 ft) in width, the Fontana di Trevi is the largest fountain in Rome.

PIAZZA DEL POPOLO

The Piazza del Popolo used to provide access to the city from the north. Having undergone several conversions, the appearance of the "people's square" is today the work of architect Giuseppe Valadier, who wanted to "open up" Rome. When he began the conversion of the piazza in 1816, Valadier left the 1,500-year-old Porta del Popolo gate and the adjacent Santa Maria del Popolo Church standing along with the two 17th-century churches Santa Maria in Montesanto and Santa Maria dei Miracoli. The center of the square is crowned by an ancient Egyptian obelisk that is around 3,200 years old.

ST PETER'S

Facing St Peter's Square (above) is the mighty façade of St Peter's Basilica, officially known as San Pietro in Vaticano and which was built in the 16th century on the site of the apostle Peter's crucifixion. It is also where Emperor Constantine built Rome's first basilica. The present-day building is some 45 m (148 ft) high and 115 m (126 yds) wide. The height of the lantern crowning the dome is 132 m (433 ft) and the interior covers an area of 15,000 sq m (16,145 sq ft). It can accommodate around 60,000 worshippers. Naturally, the most famous artists of the age were involved in its construction: architects Bramante and Sangallo, sculptors Bernini and Maderno, and master painters Michelangelo and Raphael (both of whom were employed as architects as well). St Peter's grave is said to be located in the so-called "grotto" beneath the church.

St Peter's Basilica is an oblong building in the shape of a Latin cross. The central dome high above the crossing lets in light.

THE SISTINE CHAPEL

The Sistine Chapel, commissioned in 1477 by Pope Sixtus IV, was not just a place of worship but also a fortress with walls that are 3 m (10 ft) thick. It also continues to serve as the venue for the papal conclave, in which the College of Cardinals elects a new pope. Upon the completion of construc-tion work in 1480, Lorenzo de' Medici, the "ruler" of Florence, sent a number of his city's leading artists to Rome to decorate the interior of the chapel with frescoes. Having waged war against the pope in the preceding years, he now wanted to make a gesture of peace. The artists included Pietro Perugino, Sandro Botticelli and Domenico Ghirlandaio. The walls were decorated with scenes from the lives of Jesus and Moses, while the ceiling of the dome was trans-formed into a luminescent blue sky with golden stars. It was only later, from 1508 to 1512, that it was painted over by Michelangelo.

LAKE GARDA, LAKE COMO, LAKE MAGGIORE, LAKE ORTA

Alexandre Dumas once described these northern Italian lakes as "... a place of incomparable beauty". Indeed, his words still apply to all of them: Garda (main picture), Como, Maggiore and Orta.

LAKE GARDA

LAKE COMO

Lake Garda (above, the town of Gardone) was known as "Lacus benacus" in antiquity, after the Neptune-like divinity Benacus. The lake, which is 52 km (32 mi) long and up to 346 m (1,135 ft) deep, is fed by the Sarca, Ponale and Campione rivers. It has long been a popular holiday destination and is particularly popular among windsurfers.

Lake Como is 51 km (32 mi) long and 4 km (2.5 mi) at its widest point and is situated between the Lugarno and Bergamo Alps. Bellagio (above) is the loveliest town this stunning body of water, carved into the narrow valley by the Adda glacier and still fed by the Adda River. Comer divides into the Como and Lecco arms to the south.

LAKE MAGGIORE

LAKE ORTA

Lake Maggiore extends from the southern Alps to the Po River plain and is fed by the Ticino River, a tributary of the Po. Four-fifths of the lake are in Italy and the rest is in Switzerland. It is 66 km (41 mi) long and has four islands (Isole Borromee) situated in the Gulf of Verbania. The most famous of them is Isola Bella.

Measuring just 13 km (8 mi) in length, Lago d'Orta is one of the smallest, but also one of the most idyllic of the north Italian lakes. The resort town of Orta San Giulio (above) with its lovely Palazzo della Comunità – the old 16th-century town hall – is located on a narrow peninsula that extends far out into the lake.

THE DOLOMITES

The primeval Tethys Ocean is said to have once covered the area where the towering Dolomites now stand. It was a tropical region at that time and as a result, huge limestone coral reefs flourished along the flat coastlines. Over the course of the millennia this limestone changed into dolomite, a mineral named after the French mineralogist Dieudonné de Gratet de Dolomieu. Forty million years ago, the Tethys basin was thrust upwards and the Dolomites are one of the consequences of that momentous development. The high plateaus have huge peaks, some with craggy, blade-like pinnacles. The Marmolada is the highest of them at 3,342 m (10,965 ft).

"The loveliest mountains in the world? The Dolomites!" – Le Corbusier. Indeed, Mother Nature provided us with some truly magnificent shapes and colors here between the Isarco and Marmolada, and the Pusteria Valley and Feltre.

The Tre Cime di Lavaredo, Italian for "three peaks of Lavaredo" (on the right), form the most famous profile of the Dolomite Range. The range actually comprises five peaks, however. They were first ascended by the Innerkoflers from Sexten, a famous dynasty of mountain guides. Within mountaineering circles they are as legendary as the north wall routes.

VENICE

SAN GIORGIO MAGGIORE

Benedictine monks lived San Giorgio Maggiore Island as early as the 10th century. The relics of St Stephanus of Constantinople are said to have been brought here in 1109, the result being that the church and monastery adjacent to the grave of the apostle Mark subsequently became an important pilgrimage site in the lagoon city. In 1223, the monastery was destroyed by an earthquake, but its buildings were rebuilt between the 15th and 17th centuries and those are what you see today. The Benedictine Church was designed by Andrea Palladio in 1565, its white façade having been designed to be seen from afar and its ground plan being in the shape of a Latin cross. The monks' choir and campanile were built after Palladio's death and the high altar was created by Girolamo Campagna. Two large paintings in the side aisles depict the Miracle of Manna and The Last Supper, among the last of Tintoretto's works.

ST MARK'S CATHEDRAL

Construction on St Marks Cathedral began in the 11th century on the site of two previous buildings. In allusion to the Church of the Holy Apostles in Constantinople, its ground plan is in the form of a Greek cross. The intersection and each of the arms feature vaulted domes. The cathedral's oriental aspect derives from a second construction phase that followed the Byzantine conquest. The church took on a Gothic element between the 14th and 16th centuries and the façade, situated in front of a porch, is divided into five arched portals

crowned with Byzantine-style mosaics and incorporating the treasure from Venetian raids. Above the portals is a gallery with gilded horse sculptures that the Venetians looted from Constantinople in 1204. The history of the cathedral is inextricably linked to the legend of St Mark, according to which the evangelist's remains were once miraculously transported from Alexandria to Venice where they are said to be kept to this day – in a sarcophagus far below the high altar.

THE DOGE'S PALACE

Starting in 9th century, the Doge's Palace was the residence of the Venetian head of state and the seat of the Venetian government. The present day appearance of this marble and stone masterpiece dates from the 14th and 15th centuries.

From the Piazzetta the view over the
Canale di San Marco takes in the luminescent, white marble façade of the San
Giorgio Maggiore church on the small
island of the same name (main picture).

THE CANAL GRANDE, THE RIALTO BRIDGE

The Canale Grande is roughly 4 km (2 mi) long and lined with magnificent palaces built and owned by nearly five centuries, of merchants and nobility. It is the main traffic artery in Venice upon which a throng of gondolas and vaporetti ply their way. The end of the canal is marked on the right bank by the baroque Santa Maria della Salute Church with its wonderful dome. The roofed Rialto Bridge (above) spans the canal at about its halfway point. Originally a wooden bridge, between 1588 and 1592 it was built of stone with its present design, including two rows of shops.

THE CATHEDRAL, GALLERIA VITTORIO EMANUELE II, LA SCALA

The trio of Milan includes the cathedral (main picture), the Galleria (below) and La Scala (below, with the Leonardo da Vinci memorial statue on the left). During Late antiquity the Roman Empire was at times ruled from Milan, and the city became one of the focal points of the new Italy in the Middle Ages. Its greatest sightseeing attraction is the cathedral, a masterpiece of Italian Gothic 157 m (515 feet) in length and 92 m (302 feet) at its widest point. It is one of the world's largest Gothic churches and the marble façade is decorated with no less than 2,245 individual statues.

The Piazza del Duomo forms the heart of Milan and is linked to the Piazza della Scala by the Galleria Vittorio Emanuele II, which has been an exemplary model for many modern shopping center architects. The Teatro alla Scala is Milan's famous opera house, owing its reputation as the "best opera house in the world" to the wonderful acoustics, and its existence to Empress Maria Theresia.

SANTA MARIA DELLE GRAZIE

Santa Maria delle Grazie was constructed between 1465 and 1482 by Guiniforte Soari as a high Gothic Dominican convent. In 1492, Renaissance master builder Donato Bramante began work on a new choir with semi-circular apses. Just five years later, in 1497, Leonardo da Vinci then completed his monumental wall painting *The Last Supper* (below) in the abbey's refectory. The piece depicts the moment in which Jesus utters the famous words: "One of you will betray me".

The cathedral in Milan can comfortably accommodate around 40,000 people (main picture, left, a lion flanking the mounted statue of King Victor Emmanuel II on the cathedral square). The roof of the cathedral is crowned with 135 small Gothic towers (pinnacles), while the façade displays Renaissance and neo-classical elements in addition to some Gothic touches.

MARIAE NASCENTI

THE CINQUE TERRE

The five villages (Cinque Terre) of Monterosso, Vernazza (main picture), Corniglia, Manarola and Riomaggiore are simply striking, clinging to the cliffs and bays of the steep Ligurian coast between Levanto and Portovenere.
Though hard to believe, there is still no direct road along the coast that connects the five sleepy hamlets. But perhaps it is for the better. In the past the impassable coastline was accessed using footpaths and steps. The Via dell'Amore, which seems to hug the craggy rocks, links Riomaggiore (top), the most eastern Cinque Terre village, with Manarola (middle), where the Natività di Maria Vergine Church boasts a Carrara marble rose window on its façade. Corniglia (above) is the only one of the five villages about 100 m (328 ft) above the sea.

PORTOVENERE

Portovenere at the western end of the La Spezia Gulf is just one of the architectural gems to be found along the Ligurian coast. Situated on a cliff above the town is the 13th-century San Pietro Church with its black and white marble façade, as well as a Genoese fortress dating back to the 12th century. The Cinque Terre strip of coast extends to the north-west of Portovenere.

In Vernazza (Cinque Terre), the port features a small piazza with bright buildings and the Romanesque Church of Santa Maria di Antiochia. Parts of the Genoese fortifications still exist.

RAVENNA

From outside, the Church of San Vitale in Ravenna is a plain, octagonal brick building, which makes the opulence of its interior all the more overwhelming. The main picture depicts the unique mosaics in the cross-ribbed vaults of the presbytery.

SAN VITALE

Ravenna was once the capital of the Western Roman Empire, later became the center of power of the Goths before developing into the focus of the Byzantine part of Italy until it was conquered by the Lombards in 751. A number of buildings from that era survive in nearly original form in Ravenna and feature fascinating mosaics. They are among the most important remnants of early Christianity. Close to the old city wall is the San Vitale Church (main picture, the capped vault of the presbytery), which was built between 525 and 547, based on the Hagia Sophia in Constantinople (now Istanbul).

The unique mosaics depict scenes from the Bible as well as of the imperial couple Theodora and Justinian with their entourage. The dome vault of the apse features Christ seated on a luminescent blue globe framed by two angels, Bishop Ecclesius and the church's namesake, St Vitalis.

SANT'APOLLINARE
IN CLASSE

The Basilica of Sant'Apollinare in Classe, situated about 5 km (3 mi) outside of Ravenna and built between 533 and 549, has an especially impressive interior consisting of twenty-four columns made of Greek white marble, each linked via arches that separate the nave (above) from the side aisles. The mosaics in the apse dome are from the 6th century are definitely worth taking a look at. They depict an intaglio cross in the night sky symbolizing Christ's transfiguration, flanked by the Old Testament prophets Moses and Elias. Beneath that is St Apollinare, to whom the church is dedicated, standing in the midst of a blossoming paradise landscape.

PISA

LUCCA

The cathedral, the baptistery, the Camposanto, and the Leaning Tower ("Campanile") constitute a unique ensemble in Pisa known as the Piazza del Duomo. The tower here began to lean in 1185, due to the marshy subsoil, twelve years after construction had begun – and with only the first three floors completed. One hundred years passed before efforts were made to counter the leaning by means of a significant slant in the opposite direction.

The cathedral exhibits the characteristic light and dark stone stripes of the Pisan style. The most eye-catching feature of the nave (above) is the mosaic by Francesco di Simone and Cimabue in the apse depicting the seated Christ, flanked by Mary and John.

Lucca originally developed on a tiny island in the marshes of Serchio – "luk" means marsh in the Ligurian language. Situated on the Via Francigena, Lucca enjoyed economic importance even as a Roman colony. The fortifications of the town began in 1544, and anyone wanting to reach the city center today has to pass through one of the eleven fortified gates. The city wall, which is 4 km (2.5 mi) in length and up to 30 m (98 ft) thick, has trees growing on it. The buildings around the Piazza del Mercato (above) were originally built around the former Roman amphitheater.

The Leaning Tower of Pisa is around 5 m (18 ft) off center. After several years of renovation work it was once again opened to the public in 2001. The cathedral's cross-shaped layout is also unusual, with its blind arches and loggia floors making it the epitome of Tuscan Romanesque style (main picture with the Fontana dei Putti in the foreground).

The Tuscan capital on the Arno (right) is considered the birthplace of the Renaissance and humanism, which began in roughly 1400 and is paramount to the history of European art. The elevated Piazzale Michelangelo provides an amazing view (main picture) of the city including the mighty red dome of Santa Maria del Fiore built by Filippo Brunelleschi between 1420 and 1436 as a central highlight of the city center. Inset: The Arno flows through Florence toward the setting sun, past the buildings in the evening light with the wide Ponte Vecchio and the tower of the Palazzo Vecchio watching over.

THE BAPTISTERY, CATHEDRAL, AND CAMPANILE

Upon seeing the baptistery (top left) Michelangelo is purported to have said that, "only the gates of paradise could be so wonderful." The church, which dates back to the 4th century and is the location of Dante's baptism, is among the oldest buildings in the city. Magnificent 13th-century mosaics (right) adorn the cupola above the baptismal font. The baptistry is also renowned for its splendid portals depicting scenes from the Old and New Testaments.

Construction of the Santa Maria del Fiore Cathedral began in 1296. Consecrated in 1436, Florence's most famous landmark is 153 m (502 ft) long, 90 m (295 ft) wide in the transept and, with the lantern on the octagonal dome, 116 m (381 ft) high, making it the fourth largest church in the Occident after the cathedrals in Rome, London and Milan. Construction of the freestanding bell tower, almost 85 m (279 ft) in height and clad in marble of different hues, was begun by Giotto in 1334.

FLORENCE

PIAZZA DELLA SIGNORIA, PALAZZO VECCHIO

The secular center of Florence is the Piazza della Signoria, home to the Loggia dei Lanzi, with its priceless sculptures, and the Palazzo Vecchio, the seat of the mighty Medici government completed in 1322.

The foundation stone for the Palazzo Vecchio (top) was laid in 1299. Sculpture later enjoyed a golden age in the Florence of the Medicis, and Michelangelo's world-famous *David* puts in two appearances in the city: the original in the Galleria dell'Accademia (middle left) and a replica in front of the Palazzo Vecchio (middle right shadow). Ammannati's *Fountain of Neptune* (bottom left) and Bandinelli's *Hercules and Cacus* at the Piazza della Signoria are also masterpieces to behold.

THE UFFIZI

The Medici family determined the city's fate for generations. Their rise began with Giovanni (1360–1429), who was able to increase his fortune through banking, the pope being his best customer. The Uffizi, begun in 1560, was initially used as administrative buildings for the Medicis.

The Galleria degli Uffizi is one of the world's most important art collections. Bernardo Buontalenti was commissioned by Francesco I de' Medici to create the octagonal, gold- and red-hued Tribuna, where the collection's most important treasures were originally kept in a shrine. Giorgio Vasari's *Ideal Portrait* (above left) was based on Lorenzo I de' Medici's death mask, while Agnolo Bronzino painted the Grand Duke Cosimo de' Medici 1545/1546 (above right9, both of which hang in the Uffizi Gallery.

Cityscapes and battle scenes by Vasari and his atelier adorn the Hall of Five Hundred (Salone dei Cinquecento, 1495, main picture) on the first floor of the Palazzo Vecchio in Florence.

PONTE VECCHIO   PALAZZO PITTI

Only goldsmiths used to be permitted to ply their trade on this world-famous bridge with its tiny shops. In Roman times a wooden bridge spanned the Arno here.

The Palazzo Pitti (top, with a sculpture by Roberto Barni; bottom, a bedroom) was built between 1457 and 1819 for the banker Luca Pitti. It combines several styles due to its centuries of building phases. In 1550, the Medicis made the palace their main residence. The adjacent Boboli Garden from 1590 is a gem of Italian garden design. Today the palace and garden are home to seven museums and galleries, including the world famous Galleria Palatina.

SIENA

Siena was originally an Etruscan settlement, later became a Roman colony (Saena Iulia), and eventually sided with the Ghibellines in the Middle Ages, thus becoming Florence's arch rival. The city reached the height of its political power in the 13th century, after which it was ruled by a council of nine merchants between 1287 and 1355. Siena was conquered by the Spanish in 1555, who then ceded it to the Grand Duchy of Tuscany. The city is dominated by the Gothic cathedral with its interior of black and white marble (left and main picture). The Piazza del Campo (below) has been the venue of the biannual Palio since the Middle Ages, a horse race with a magnificent medieval ambience that always takes place on July 2 and August 16. Siena's opposing city districts compete against one another in the race, and the residents don historic costumes.

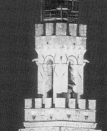

CHIANTI

The center of the Chianti region lies north of Siena. The area is famous for its idyllic, gently undulating landscape (right). Extensive vineyards, wine estates and attractive cypress and pine alleys characterize the scenery. And yes, Chianti Classico wine estates with their Gallo Nero – black cockerel – emblem as a quality guarantee are everywhere, tucked into misty valleys down narrow country roads.

The word "chianti" originally stems from the ancient Etruscan language and referred then to a high-quality product before it became synonymous with an entire wine-growing region. The turning point came in 1841, when Bettino Ricasoli developed his idea of an "original" chianti at Brolio Castle, and it was he who established the best ratio of grapes.

SAN GIMIGNANO

This area was once the scene of civil war and the families had tower houses built in order to outdo one another. Of the original seventy-two towers only fifteen are still standing. They guard over the Piazza della Cisterna in the center of the Old Town and give San Gimignano its characteristic skyline.

VOLTERRA

The former Etruscan town of Volterra is situated about 45 km (30 mi) from the coast on a cliff amidst the Tuscan hills. Excavations indicate that the town was extremely prosperous during the 4th century BC. A 7-km (4-mi) wall encompassing fields and pastures surrounded Volterra at the time, meaning the residents were able to fend for themselves when under siege.

MAREMMA, MASSA MARITTIMA

Maremma, the coastal region between Livorno and Monte Argentario, has been settled since Etruscan times. The Romans also knew how to make use of this area but their drainage systems were later forgotten. Parco Naturale della Maremma was set up in 1975 and reforestation with pines, poplars and cork oaks has ensured beneficial water circulation and also created an appropriate habitat for deer, badgers, foxes, wild boar – and the wild Maremma horses. Massa Marittima (left) lies on the edge of the Maremma region at an altitude of about 830 m (2,723 ft). It became a bishop's see in the 12th/13th centuries, to which a number of magnificent medieval buildings remain testimony to this day.

The Crete Senesi landscape is typically Tuscan: earth tones, cypress trees and isolated farmhouses.

VAL D'ORCIA

PIENZA

Situated between Montepulciano and Montalcino in the Val d'Orcia, Pienza was designed by Bernardo Rossellino on the orders of Pope Pius II as the "ideal Renaissance town". The focal point of the historic center is the Piazza Pio II, which is lined with a number of impressive buildings. You can see the cathedral (above) through the colonnades of the Palazzo Civico. The square is bordered to the left and right by the Palazzi Vescovile and Piccolomini.

The Val d'Orcia – roughly 50 km (31 mi) south of Siena– embodies a Renaissance landscape. Over centuries, graphic depictions of this area had a major influence in the history of European art with regard to our notions of the ideal landscape.

MONTEPULCIANO

CRETE

Situated on top of a picturesque hill between Valdichiana and the Val d'Orcia, Montepulciano (top) at 605 m (1,985 ft) is one of the highest towns in Tuscany.
As is often the case in this area, Etruscans first settled here in 715, calling the town "Castrum Politianum". Although mostly famous for its wine, Montepulciano is also home to a classic example of a centralized Renaissance church, situated somewhat outside of the town: San Biagio (above).

"Crete", not to be confused with the island, designates an area to the south-east of Siena, between Vescona and Asciano. It is an area that has unfortunately been heavily deforested and overgrazed, but the grey and yellow boulders, a result of erosion, are still a beautiful feature of this surrealist lunar landscape. Here – and a little further south in the Val d'Orcia (main picture) in particular – was where the first landscape artists found the inspiration for their frescoes. Cypresses, isolated farmhouses and a little church on a hill like the one close to Pienza (above) are considered typical of Tuscany.

ORVIETO

Orvieto's origins go way back to Etruscan times when the town was settled on the 200-m-high (656-ft) block of tuff stone above the Paglia Valley, where it remains today. During the course of some 3,000 years of human activity here, a labyrinth of caves both large and small has developed within the depths of the mountain, interconnected via stairs and passages. The first to dig their way into the mountain were of course the Etruscans. The town's inhabitants later dug into the soft rock to remove "pozzolan", which can be mixed with water to make a cement-like material. The subterranean columns and vaults were simply a side effect. The town's focal point is now the piazza with the cathedral (main picture), considered to be one of the loveliest Gothic churches in Italy. Its construction went on for around 500 years up until the end of the 17th century. The town owes both its founding and its magnificent adornments to the Miracle of Bolsena, which also forms the basis of the Feast of Corpus Christi. Blood is said to have dripped from the Host during a celebration of mass in Bolsena, a town adjacent to Orvieto, in 1263 – the corporal, the cloth bearing the blood stains, is on display in a chapel in the Cathedral of Orvieto.

ASSISI

Assisi lies on a hillside below Monte Subasio and is Umbria's most important pilgrimage destination. St Francis of Assisi was born here in 1182 into a wealthy family of cloth merchants and founded the mendicant Franciscan order in 1210. He was canonized in 1228, two years after his death, the same year that work began on the construction of the Basilica di San Francesco where he was buried in 1230. The church, which consists of an upper and lower

URBINO

Perched upon two hills in the Marche, Urbino enjoyed its heyday back in the 15th century, when important Renaissance artists and scholars made it Italy's center of culture and science. Under the Montefeltro dynasty the artists of the age created an architectural ensemble of Renaissance buildings here, the homogeneity of which is unique. The town's most important building is the Palazzo Ducale (above), which was transformed from an old castle into a complex Renaissance palace starting in 1444. The elevation, differing terrain, and the competition between the builders and the architects was decisive in the many distinct levels of the layout. Today it houses the Marche national gallery with works by Titian, Raphael, Piero della Francesca, Bellini and Botticelli.

basilica, is decorated with magnificent frescoes and is the town's most important attraction. It is considered to be Italy's largest church of artworks, and most of the famous painters of the age created significant works of art here: Cimabue, Giotto, Simone Martini and the Lorenzetti brothers. Giotto's *St Francis preaching before the Pope* fresco (below) from the end of the 13th century can be seen in the upper basilica.

Perugia, the capital of Umbria, is situated on a range of hills between the Tiber Valley and Lake Trasimeno. It was an important town even in Etruscan times and remains so today, a fact evidenced by the historical buildings that give Perugia's Old Town its very special flair, with narrow, often covered alleyways and splendid squares. Now a modern university city, the Piazza IV Novembre with the Palazzo dei Priori (above) still forms the center of the Old Town. The Fontana Maggiore (also above) has been in existence here since 1278, the fountain being fed with water from the hills around the town by means of a sophisticated system of pipes. The towering Gothic San Lorenzo Cathedral stands opposite the Palazzo dei Priori.

Inside the Cathedral of Orvieto is a fascinating blend of Romanesque architecture and Gothic window decoration (main picture). The Arab-Tuscan black and white bands on the upper section of the cathedral is only painted on.

When the crater of Mt Vesuvius exploded after centuries of tranquillity, hot magma rolled into the valley and covered Pompeii in lava and ash. A surprising number of wall paintings were preserved under the volcanic ash, as is the case with this depiction of two gods (main picture).

Vesuvius erupted on August 24 of the year AD 79, completely covering the Roman town of Pompeii under a layer of ash within roughly six hours. The neighboring town of Herculaneum was also smothered under glowing lava. After the eruption, the towns were not rebuilt and eventually forgotten. However, Pliny the Younger (ca. AD 61–113), whose uncle and adopted father were killed by the eruption, had described the event, which led the archaeologists in the right direction. The first excavations began in 1748, and today they provide an invaluable impression of life in antiquity. The remains of shops and the painted walls of splendid villas were still left standing; even petrified bread was found in the bakeries. Other discoveries included a mill, a latrine and some "graffiti" on the walls. The stepping stones that enabled passersby to cross the street without getting their feet are even still visible. The dead people are the most impressive, however, their bodies forming hollows of volcanic ash. Filled with plaster, the human figures are now visible again as silent witnesses of the eruption.

The portrait of Paquius Proculus and his wife (top) also survived and can be seen in the National Museum in Naples, as is the case with the delicate angel (middle). One of the loveliest wall paintings can be found in the Triclinium of the Villa dei Misteri (above), depicting the initiation of a young woman in the cult of Dionysus.

Around 15 km (9 mi) outside of Naples, Mt Vesuvius (left) is mainland Europe's only active volcano. Since the 18th century, excavations beneath the volcano's crater have been revealing remains of settlement in the lava layer, which is up to 7 m (23 ft) deep in places.

Excavations in Pompeii began in 1748, and since then entire streets including the buildings and the Forum (above) have been exposed. Today archeologists are primarily focused on preventing the deterioration of the ruins.

AMALFITANA

The small town of Amalfi on the Gulf of Salerno was once one of Italy's leading seafaring republics. Today the name is associated with one of the loveliest stretches of Mediterranean coastline. Cut straight into the cliffs in places, the Amalfitana coastal road connects the villages between Nerano and Salerno. It follows winding stretches of the shoreline for around 45 km (30 mi), continually providing spectacular panorama views of the azure-blue ocean and the Costiera Amalfitana. The view from the garden of the Villa Cimbrone is especially lovely, as is that from the Villa Rufulo, both in Ravello (above). The villages are strung together like pearls with lemon groves and vineyards scattered between them. The charming houses are built in precarious positions along the steep cliffs and cling to the slopes to create a picturesque scene.

AMALFI

The world's oldest maritime law – the Tavole Amalfitane – has its origins in Amalfi (main picture), the most important town along this stretch of coast. The 9th-century cathedral, which can be reached by a magnificent flight of steps from the Piazza Duomo (above), is a source of local pride. The Piazza Flavio Gioia is the ideal starting point for a tour.

POSITANO

"I have the feeling," wrote John Steinbeck of this seafaring town founded in the Middle Ages, "that the world is vertical in Positano. An unimaginably blue and green ocean washes up on the fine pebble beach in the bay." There are crossings to Capri from this splendid town.

The view from the sea of the impressive architectural enclosure carved into the cliffs at the end of the Valle dei Mulini gives an indication of the dangers that Amalfi used to face (main picture). The high storm tides of the Tyrrhenian Sea did in fact demolish parts of Amalfi in the 11th and 14th centuries, while severe landslides caused major damage in the 19th century. Amalfi has nevertheless survived as a medieval gem among the resorts along the Amalfi coast, set between groves of lemon trees and dramatic cliffs.

CAPRI

Capri is made up of pure limestone and the island's geological landmark, the three Faraglioni in the south-east, is the result of erosion of that limestone. The island is relatively small, just 6 km (4 mi) long and a maximum of 2.5 km (1.5 mi) wide. Ferries from the mainland dock at the Marina Grande. Sights include the villages of Capri and Anacapri on the slopes of Monte Solaro, as well as the cliffs of the Arco Naturale in the east. The Blue Grotto, a karst cave that is thought to have been known to Emperor Tiberius, is 54 m (175 ft) long, 15 m (50 ft) wide and up to 30 m (98 ft) high can be accessed through an entrance located just above water level. It owes its name to the mysterious blue color of the water – sunlight enters through the water creating a reflection that lights the cave.

PALERMO

Palermo was the main base for the Carthaginian fleet in the First Punic War and went on to enjoy exceptional periods of cultural prosperity under the Moors, Normans and the Hohenstaufens of Germany. Thankfully, a tremendous number of historic buildings have survived from all of these epochs. In the Old Town, Byzantine churches stand next to Moorish mosques and baroque and Catalan palaces are juxtaposed with classical barracks and Arabian-style pleasure palaces. Highlights here include the splendid cathedral (above right); the Norman Palace with the mosaic-embellished Cappella Palatina (main picture), and the 16th-century Piazza Pretoria with the mannerism-style Fontana Pretoria (below). The San Cataldo, La Martorana (right) and San Giovanni degli Eremiti churches, the La Zisa Palace, the Teatro Massimo, the

catacombs of the Capuchin monastery, and the National Gallery and the Archaeological Museum are all worth seeing as well.

The lively Vucciria market (above left) on the Piazza Caracciolo is nicknamed the "belly of Palermo". It is the town's best-known market and one of the oldest in Europe. The kiosks and shops selling fish, meat, fruits and vegetables are all strung together like an oriental souk along the narrow alleyways.

MONREALE

Situated around 8 km (5 mi) from Palermo is the small episcopal town of Monreale. Monte Caputo provides fabulous views of the Sicilian capital with its bay that looks like it was drawn with a compass, the Conca d'Oro. The main sightseeing attraction here, however, is the world-famous cathedral. William II, King of Sicily, was the original benefactor of a Benedictine abbey that was built on these lofty heights in 1172, which sooned formed into a town. Seeing the growth, he had a cathedral built at its center – a basilica intended to symbolize the triumph of the Christians over the Moors. With a length of 102 m (112 ft) and a width of 40 m 140 ft, Sicily's largest church is supported by eighteen antique columns. It houses the sarcophaguses of Kings William I and II and has a magnificent bronze portal and marble floors. The mosaics (above) in the cathedral cover 6,300 sq m (67,788 sq ft) and depict stories from the Bible in incomparable splendor. The cloister – the only surviving section of the monastery – is also worth seeing with its many differently designed column pairs.

The Cappella Palatina in the Palazzo Reale (Norman Palace) was added to the palace complex between 1132 and 1240 as Roger II's court chapel. Rather modest in its outward appearance, the interior is overwhelming with its marble pillars and luminescent mosaics on a golden background. All of this is crowned with a richly decorated wooden stalactite ceiling featuring Arab ornamentation and picture stories (main picture).

MOUNT ETNA

Unlike the highly explosive Vesuvius near Naples, Mt Etna (above and main picture) is a "good mountain": it erupts consistently and calmly instead of unexpectedly and intensely, and its lava contains little in the way of gases, making the volcano less explosive. Provided one sticks to the sign-posted paths, it is safe to make an excursion up to the 3,000 m (9,843 ft) peak – an unforgettable experience. Anyone looking to keep more of a distance can enjoy a wonderful hike around its lower slopes. The region was declared a national park in 1981.

TAORMINA

The whole east coast of Sicily is dominated by the silhouette of Etna, and the town of Taormina (above), the most frequently visited hamlet on the island. Its idyllic location on a cliff high above the ocean and its ancient amphi-

theater ensured that Taormina was to become a popular destination as far back as the 19th century. Founded in the 4th century BC, Taormina was Greek for more than 200 years before ultimately falling to Rome in 215 BC. From the Teatro Greco, built in the 2nd century BC on the foundations of

an existing Hellenistic structure, the view extends as far as Etna – easily one of the loveliest theater settings in the world (left). The terrace of the Piazza IX Aprile (above) situated 200 m (656 ft) above the sea provides a very good viewing area.

Mongibello, the "mountain of mountains", is what the Sicilians call Mount Etna, one of the last active volcanoes in Europe (main picture, during one of its nocturnal eruptions).

SARDINIA

Capo Caccia, the westernmost point of Sardinia, offers magnificent views of the sea and coast.

Sardinia is the second-largest island in the Mediterranean after Sicily and has a tremendous cultural heritage to match its magnificent natural splendor. Over thousands of years, the Phoenicians, Romans, Vandals, Byzantines, Moors, Pisanese, Genoese, Aragonese, Spanish and naturally mainland Italians have all left their mark here. Nevertheless, Sardinia was able to maintain its own language and culture.

The north is the most popular region with magnificent diving and sailing options. It features quaint villages with ancient, labyrinthine town centers, good infrastructure, and a romantic landscape with granite cliffs and dark maquis shrub land in the interior. The "Costa Smeralda", the Emerald Coast where the Aga Khan created an exclusive holiday resort in the early 1960s, is of course legendary.

COSTA SMERALDA

The Capo d'Orso rock formations (top) are one of the landmarks of the Costa Smeralda, with its clear blue bays and idyllic landscape.

CAPO TESTA

The granite cliffs on the Capo Testa Peninsula in the north-east of Sardinia have been formed into bizarre shapes by the wind and the weather, and worn by the constant motion of the waves.

MADDALENA

The Maddalena Archipelago in north-eastern Sardinia has been a national park since 1996 and comprises four main islands: Maddalena (above), Santo Stefano, Caprera and Spargi.

GROTTA DI NETTUNO

This stalactite cave on the rocky Capo Caccia Peninsula can be reached via a staircase comprising 656 steps cut into the cliffs (Escala del Cabirol), or by boat from Porta a Mare.

St. John's Co-Cathedral (main picture) is Valletta's main church. It has very elaborate interior decor (right, an image of the Madonna).

Control over the town of Valletta changed hands for centuries starting with the Phoenicians and moving on to the Greeks, the Carthaginians, the Romans, Byzantium, and the Moors until it was finally handed over to the Order of St John following the Turkish siege of 1565. It then grew into a fortified town that was characteristic of the 16th century. The Order of St John pro-ceeded to construct a series of Renaissance and baroque palaces, churches and hospices within its walls, the Order's newly-found confidence and wealth being expressed in the magnificent décor of the Grand Master's palace and its two courtyards. The baroque church of Our Lady of Victory was built as a sign of gratitude for the endurance during the siege of 1567. St. John's Co-Cathedral, built between 1573 and 1578 as a burial place for the knights of the Order, was decorated with ceiling frescoes and magnificent side chapels. The library founded by the order in 1555 houses valuable manuscripts. The Manoel Theatre dating from 1731 can be found within the labyrinth of alleys and steps and is one of the oldest stages in Europe.

Surrounded by the sea on three sides, Valletta (far left and left) is situated on a 60-m-high (199-ft) cliff on Malta's north coast. The large dome of the Carmelite church dominates the town.

GDANSK, TORUN, FROMBORK, MALBORK

GDANSK

Gdansk has a history going back more than 1,000 years, when it maintained close trade relations with Flanders, Russia and Byzantium continuing into the 12th and 13th centuries. Gdansk was a member of the Hanseatic League from 1361 and was assigned to the Polish crown in 1466. With ninety-five percent of the city in ruins at the end of World War II, Gdansk has since become a model of reconstruction work.

The most important attractions are naturally in the city center. St Mary's Church, for example, is the largest medieval brick church in Europe, its most striking feature being the 82-m-high (269-ft) bell tower. The city's Old Town comprises Long Street and the streets

adjoining it. Influential patricians built magnificent palaces like the 17th-century Hans von Eden House for themselves in the heart of the Old Town. The 15th-century Arthur's Court is among the finest examples of late-Gothic architecture in Northern Europe; the town hall, the Golden House and the Torture House are also worth seeing. One city gate from the Middle Ages has been converted into a port crane. In the northern part of the Old Town there is a series of churches, the Old Town Hall, the Small and the Large Mill and the Old Castle, which are worth visiting. The Vistula Spit, on the delta, is south of Gdansk. You can reach Malbork by crossing the spit to the south-east.

TORUN

The knights of the Teutonic Order once built a castle here, at the foot of which a town developed that went on to become a thriving commercial center in the 14th century. It even maintained its own merchant fleet for the purposes of trading with the Netherlands. The First and the Second Peace of Torun were concluded here in 1411 and 1466 between the Teu-

tonic Order and Poland. In 1454 the Teutonic Order castle was burnt down by the citizens of Torun (only remnants survive to this day) and the town became an independent city-state under the sovereignty of the Polish king. The town continued to change in appearance over the centuries, as is evidenced by the Gothic patricians' houses, the baroque and classic town houses and the opulent palaces of the 19th century. Construction of the Old Town Hall was begun in 1259, and Copernicus's birthplace dating from the 15th century has remained intact. The Cathedral of St John the Evangelist and John the Baptist as well as St Mary's Church (above left) are also worth seeing.

FROMBORK

The small town of Frombork in Warmia is culturally the most interesting town in the region with its historic complex on the cathedral hill (above). The museum next to the cathedral is dedicated to the important work of astronomist Nicholas Copernicus, who studied here. The water tower provides lovely views of the Vistula Lagoon and the port.

MALBORK

A white cloak with a black cross was the uniform of the Teutonic Knights, an order of knights that formed in the Holy Land during the Third Crusade (1189–1192). The knights then turned their attention to Europe just a few decades later and Prussia, along with Livonia and Courland, were subordinated and Christianized in the name of the black cross. Given sovereign powers as landlords by the emperor, the order founded towns, built castles, brought in German farmers as colonists, and promoted the arts and science. At the head of the order was the Grand Master, who was elected for life and whose seat and main fortress after 1309 was here in

Malbork Castle (main picture) on the Nogat River. It was here that all of the threads of the order's states came together, its territories already extending far into the Baltic States as well as into southern and central Germany.

The missionary work had long since become a minor priority by the time their secular rule began to crumble. The costly Battle of Tannenberg in 1410 against the more superior Poles and Lithuanians is seen to represent their beginning of the end. Held with some effort until 1457, Malbork Castle finally fell into Polish hands in 1466 with the Peace of Torun. The story of the holy state came to a definitive end in 1525 when

it became the secular Duchy of Prussia with Albrecht von Brandenburg-Ansbach as its first duke. This then became a hereditary duchy under Polish sovereignty during the Reformation.

Malbork Castle served as a barracks and a granary during the 18th century, and fell into visible disrepair during that time. The castle underwent thorough restoration in the 19th century and following the destruction of World War II it was rebuilt during the 1960s and 1970s based on original drawings.

Today the halls, chapels, corridors and courtyards house extensive museums with valuable medieval treasures.

Mighty walls and bastions encircle the Malbork Castle complex, residence of the Grand Master of the Teutonic Knights between 1309 and 1457 (main picture). The middle castle with the Grand Master's palace (left half of the image) is architecturally unique and a gem of northern German brick Gothic construction. The high castle (center of the image) housed assembly, living, and dining rooms as well as sleeping quarters and the castle church (the highest tower in the complex in the background). The Dankerts Tower (front right) was both a defensive tower and a lavatory.

Early morning in the Masurian Lake District. This idyllic landscape of eastern Poland is also referred to as the "Land of a Thousand Lakes."

THE MASURIAN LAKE DISTRICT

There is no denying the magic of this landscape. Hikers, cyclists and canoeists alike can all enjoy the thoroughly fascinating water landscape here. More than 3,000 lakes are linked via rivers and canals, all mingling with wonderful forests. Gnarled trees shade cobblestone alleys that are still traveled by horse-drawn carts, while storks build their nests in the tops of the steeple. A visit to Masuria is like taking a journey back in time to the early 20th century.

Olsztyn is the main center of the Masuria region as well as the perfect starting point for excursions to a number of different sightseeing attractions, including Lidzbark Warminskj with its mighty castle that used to be the seat of the Warmia bishops. Reszel Castle nearby dates back to the 13th century.

The powerful Teutonic Knights built a castle in Kętrzyn in 1329. Beyond Kętrzyn there is a sign pointing to the north-east indicating the "Wolfsschanze" (Wolf's Lair), which Hitler built in 1939, as his headquarters. The pilgrimage church of Święta Lipka is a baroque gem.

The Masurian Lake District is a refuge for more than 350 bird species including Steppe Eagles, Mute Swans and the Common Merganser (from top).

Top to bottom: The collegiate church in Dobre Miasto north of Olsztyn; the pilgrimage church Święta Lipka; and a panje horse cart.

BIAŁOWIEŻA

Despite the extreme temperatures here, which often sink well below the freezing point in winter, this cross-border national park possesses an astounding level of biodiversity. There are some 3,000 types of mushrooms and more than a dozen species of orchids. The heavily protected central zone of the park is home to the highest trees in all of Europe: 55-m-high (180-ft) spruces and 40-m-high (131-ft) ash trees. The Polish government began using zoo animals to breed European bison (left, also known as wisents) in the 1920s, with a scheduled program of reintroducing them to the wild as of 1952. Hunting had made these primeval oxen almost extinct by the end of the 19th century, but today there are around 300 of them wandering the vast forest areas again. They are the largest species of big game in Europe.

The wild horses that used to be found throughout Eurasia and which no longer exist in the wild have also found a refuge in this protected area. In addition to rare mammals such as bears, moose, lynxes and wolves, the area is also home to more than 220 different bird species.

KRAKOW

The 13th-century textile halls stand in the center of the Rynek, Krakow's market square (main picture). The ensemble originally comprised just a double row of small cloth merchants' shops, which were then amalgamated into a hall in the 14th century.

THE MARKET SQUARE, JEWISH QUARTER

Krakow was the capital of the Polish kings until 1596, and their coronation venue from the 11th to the 18th centuries. Wawel Hill with its royal castle and cathedral remains testimony to this bygone era. The Old Town here was designed by master builders and artists from throughout Europe from the 12th to the 17th centuries. The market square, one of Europe's largest medieval town squares, is the site of the textile halls and the Gothic St Mary's Church, converted in the 14th century. The famous high altar by Veit Stoss, who created his most important works in Krakow between 1477 and 1496, can be found here. Pivotal medieval intellectuals taught at the university, founded in the 14th century. A number of Gothic, Renaissance and baroque buildings including many churches and monasteries testifying to the city's rich history. The Kazimierz Quarter was once home to a thriving Jewish community where the Old Synagogue is worthy of special mention.

St Mary's Church opposite the main market square has an especially impressive interior with magnificent wall paintings and stained glass windows (far left). Corpus Christi Church in the former Jewish Quarter of Kazimierz (left) is one of the loveliest churches in Krakow.

The Charles Bridge is 500 m (547 ft) long and its sixteen arches are supported by fifteen pillars.

VYŠEHRAD HILL

Vyšehrad Hill with St Veit's Cathedral towers over Prague. It is a castle complex that has been the country's political, intellectual and cultural center for more than 1,000 years. Formerly the royal residence, it is now the official residence of the Czech president. Access to the complex is via the first of the inner wards (above).

ST VEIT'S CATHEDRAL

Emperor Charles IV commissioned St Veit's Cathedral on the grounds of Prague Castle in 1344, as Prague was being made into an archbishopric. The nave and the choir are supported by twenty-eight pillars. The largest church in the Czech Republic, it is the burial place of emperors and kings as well as the repository for the crown jewels.

THE GOLDEN ALLEY

Franz Kafka lived for a number of years in one of these cottages in Golden Alley on the castle grounds. The cottages were built along the castle walls in the 16th century to provide lodging for watchmen and tradesmen. The assertion that alchemists were at work here under Rudolf II has not been historically proven.

The unique beauty of the historic buildings in the "Golden City", combined with centuries as a European intellectual and cultural capital have made Prague a truly wonderful place to visit. Despite having been spared much of the reckless destruction of World War II, the ravages of time have nevertheless left a definite mark on the city. Thankfully, however, competent renovations have seen this more than 1,000-year-old city on the banks of the Vltava River restored to its former glory. Indeed, the Czechs have every reason to be proud of their lovely capital city, which was formerly a grand residence of the Bohemian kings and seat of the Habsburg emperors. Their former place of residence, Vyšehrad, also provides the best views of this marvel of historical urban development.

CHARLES BRIDGE

Construction on the grand Charles Bridge began in 1357. It was later embellished with its masterful baroque statues between 1707 and 1714. the bridge takes you from the Lesser Quarter, the area beneath Vyšehrad Hill, over the Vltava River to the Old Town. Its decor is based on the baroque figures of the saints on the Ponte Sant'Angelo in Rome, the most famous of which is the bronze statue of St John of Nepomuk from 1683. It honors the preacher and saint, John Nepomuk, whom King Wenceslas IV had thrown from the bridge into the Vltava River at this spot. The bridge is named after King Charles IV (1316–1378).

LESSER QUARTER

Prague's Lesser Quarter, which was legally an independent town from 1257 to 1784, is reached via the Lesser Quarter gate on the Charles Bridge. This area beneath the Prague Castle is dominated by the baroque St Nicholas Church with its 75-m-high (246-ft) dome that was built between 1702 and 1756. The Lesser Quarter was initially inhabited mainly by artisans because the rents were very low. It was only in the 17th century that this area of the city enjoyed an upswing, with new churches, monasteries and 200 aristocrats' palaces being built here under Hapsburg rule.

The Old Town Square (main picture) was originally established as a central marketplace and a part of the traditional coronation route for the Bohemian kings. It was also a place of execution.

THE OLD TOWN SQUARE

The Old Town Square, a market-place dating from the 12th century, is one of Prague's central attractions and is a key focal point for both visitors and locals with its cafés, street performers and musicians. It is dominated by the towers of the Gothic Tyn Church, which also houses the tomb of the Danish astronomer Tycho Brahe.

Today street performers turn the Old Town Square into an open-air stage.

THE ASTRONOMICAL CLOCK

The astronomical clock on the south side of the old city hall is the third-oldest of its kind. The Twelve Apostles appear in its windows every hour and the clock shows the phases of the moon, the position of the sun and the planet constellations – and of course the time.

Prague's astronomical clock is decorated with wooden figures, one of which symbolizes Death.

THE OLD JEWISH CEMETERY

The Old Jewish Cemetery was established in the 15th century, the oldest tombstone belonging to the scholar and writer Avigdor Karo, who wrote an elegy on the occasion of the 1389 pogrom and who died in 1439. The most recent grave is from 1787, that of Moses Beck. Since then, no further burials have taken place here.

In total, there are some 12,000 Gothic, Renaissance and baroque tombstones to be seen here under the elder trees. The fact that the Jewish faith does not allow the destruction of grave sites means that there are up to nine burial levels on top on one another in some places.

The most famous is the grave of Rabbi Loew (ca. 1525–1609), the creator of the "Golem" (in Hebrew, "Klumpen"), a homunculus formed of clay and brought to life by means of Cabbalistic rituals. Loew was a Jewish theologian and Cabbalist whose real name was Juda ben Bezalel. He was the regional rabbi of Moravia from 1553 to 1573 and rabbi in Prague from 1597.

Small stones are traditionally laid on Jewish graves instead of flowers (left, Old Jewish Cemetery in Prague). The custom is said to date back to the era of desert migrations when the dead were covered with stones in order to protect them from wild animals.

THE OLD NEW SYNAGOGUE

The Old New Synagogue was built in 1270. Its name derives from the legend of the angels said to have brought stones from the ruins of the destroyed temple in Jerusalem to Prague for its construction, albeit only "on condition that the stones be taken back to Jerusalem some day" for the coming of the Messiah in order to then rebuild his temple. "Altnai" is the Hebrew term for "on condition that" and from which "old new" is derived.

The Old New Synagogue in Prague is the only one from this era in Europe where Jewish services are still held.

THE CLEMENTINUM

The Clementinum, built between 1578 and 1726, was once a Jesuit college. A colossal complex of buildings surrounding five large courtyards, it is now home to the national library, among other things, whose priceless inventory includes historic globes and incunabula.

With its wonderful long galleries, the Clementinum's library has one of the loveliest baroque halls in Prague.

Medieval Spiš Castle (Spišský hrad), one of the largest of its kind in Central Europe, was built on the site of an earlier Slavic fortress in Spiš, a scenic region and historic administrative district in the foothills of the High Tatras. Following its sudden collapse, the 13th century tower house was replaced by a two-story Romanesque palace with a new round tower.

The castle chapel also dates back to the 13th century, when the castle survived an attack from the Mongolians almost without damage. Another fortress was built beneath the castle in the 15th century and both complexes underwent a Renaissance makeover in 1540. Spiš Castle declined in importance after its capture by Habsburg troops in 1710.

It was from the castle that Spišský Podhrahie ("church on top") and the Spišská Kapitula ("The Spiš Chapter", provost's residence), were founded. Located just a few miles away, they boast a number of buildings under historic protection including churches, a baroque monastery, a Renaissance town hall and some manor houses. The early-Gothic Church of the Holy Spirit in Žehra is also worth seeing.

Spiš Castle, one of the largest castle complexes in Europe, towers over the Spiš basin in north-eastern Slovakia (main picture).

BUDAPEST

BUDA, ÓBUDA, PEST

Buda, Óbuda (Old Buda) and Pest were all joined in 1872 to form "BudaPest," the new capital of the former Kingdom of Hungary. The royal castle town of Buda has largely retained its medieval character, with numerous Gothic and baroque buildings lining the narrow streets. Trinity Square lies at the center of the castle hill, which has been a municipality since the 17th century, and is dominated by the Church of Our Lady. Originally built in 1250, the church underwent a neo-Gothic conversion in the 19th century. Its south portal now features a tympanum relief comprised of original pieces from the high-Gothic building.

The royal castle, built on the site of a structure that was destroyed in the great siege of 1686, was begun in 1749 and is located just to the south of the castle hill. The excavation sites of the Roman settlement of Aquincum, with its large amphitheater that accommodated some 13,000 spectators, can be found in Óbuda. The monumental, classical-style synagogue was erected in 1820 and is also worth visiting.

Pest is situated on the other side of the Danube. This commercial town was a center of middle-class and intellectual life in the 19th century. The buildings around the city ring are especially impressive.

PARLIAMENT

The parliament building with its magnificent staircase is based on its counterpart in London and was built between 1885 and 1904 according to plans by Imre Steindl.

ST MATTHEW'S CHURCH

Construction of St Matthew's (below and inset right) took place between 1255 and 1269 and was commissioned by King Béla IV. King Louis the Great converted it into a Gothic hall church with a nave and two side aisles at the turn of the 15th century. King Matthias Corvinus then expanded the church with a five-floor tower and the royal oratorio in 1470.

THE GELLÉRT BATHS

Built in the Secessionist (Art Nouveau) style and opened in 1918, the Gellért Hotel and the Gellért Baths are the most famous in Budapest. The men's baths, the outdoor pools, and the thermal and steam baths for women are opulent in their design and decorated with lovely mosaics. Above the baths on the hill is a monument commemorating the baths' namesake, the martyred Bishop Gellért who, according to legend, was rolled into the Danube in a sealed barrel at this site.

FISHERMEN'S BASTION

The Fishermen's Bastion was built between 1895 and 1902 on the site of the old fish market in Buda. The architect Frigyes Schulek, who was also responsible for the neo-Gothic conversion of St Matthew's Church, based the building's conical towers on the tents of the Magyar people.

THE CHAIN BRIDGE

ST STEPHEN'S, OPERA HOUSE

The oldest of the nine bridges in Budapest is the Chain Bridge. Preparations for the first piers began on July 28, 1840, with wooden pickets first being driven into the bank to cordon off the construction site. The neoclassical construction is still supported by two triumphal arch-like buttresses that contain the iron chains of the bridge body, which measures a total of 375 m (1,237 ft).

The impressive dimensions of this magnificent church, which can accommodate around 8,500 people, become apparent with a glance at the almost 100-m-high (328-ft) dome with its wonderful mosaic decoration. The Hungarian state opera is a popular venue for extravagant musical productions (above).

Today there are nine bridges linking the districts of Buda (with Old Buda) and Pest (main picture; the Elizabeth Bridge in the foreground, with the Chain Bridge directly behind it).

Bled's landmark is the truly idyllic church island with the ancient Church of the Assumption in the middle (main picture).

THE JULIAN AND KAMNIK ALPS

The massive limestone pinnacles of this beautiful region appear as if out of nowhere during the winding journey over the Carinthian border passes. It is immediaetly clear that the Julian and Kamnik Alps are still very much a part of the High Alps, their peaks simply bearing more exotic names such as Skrlatica, Jalovec or Prisojnik. Almost all of the roads here lead directly into the wilderness and to Triglav National Park, which encompasses almost all of the Julian Alps. Parts of the Kamnik Alps (Grintovec, at 2,558 m/8,393 ft) north of the Slovenian capital Ljubljana are also now protected by parks.

BLED

The Karawanken Tunnel, roughly 8 km (5 mi) long, provides easy access from Carinthia (Austria) to Slovenia, where the spa resort of Bled on the shores of the lake of the same name is worth a quick first stop. It is a well visited spot, but almost unbeatably charming: an island with the baroque Church of the Assumption, the Karavanke Mountains towering in the background, the castle perched on a bare rock face, and white sailboats

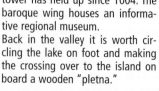

Bled is at the foot of the Julian Alps. The stately Bled Castle towers above the spa resort.

scattered around the blue waters of this idyllic alpine lake.

The island has been a popular Christian cult and pilgrimage destination for more than 1,000 years. It also became a beloved spot for those seeking rest and recuperation in the late-19th century when a resourceful Swiss spa physician set up shop here. By about 1900 it had become a fashionable meeting place for high society types. Bled's most prominent attraction is the castle, whose Romanesque tower has held up since 1004. The baroque wing houses an informative regional museum.

Back in the valley it is worth circling the lake on foot and making the crossing over to the island on board a wooden "pletna."

The mightiest of the peaks in the Julian Alps is the Triglav at 2,865 m (9,400 ft). Its name means "three-headed" (left and far left). It is situated in the national park of the same name and towers almost 2 km (1.2 mi) above the Vrata Valley. It was climbed for the first time in 1776.

LJUBLJANA

Although it has less than 300,000 residents, Slovenia's capital boasts all of the structural symbols of national sovereignty: the parliament building, various ministries and embassies as well as the national museum, gallery and library. Indeed, Ljubljana enjoys a very vibrant cultural ambience but it is the city's charm and grace that really make it special. Like Salzburg, the historical center is dominated by a castle from which the imperial Austrian governors administered the Duchy of Carniola for centuries.

To be certain, there is no denying the influence of the imperial Habsburgs on the overall appearance and character of Ljubljana, a city that is often still underestimated by many visitors:

Like Salzburg, Ljubljana has a pedestrian zone in its historic center on the Ljubljanica River. "Salzburg of the South" is one of the town's other names. Above: A view from the west bank of the river towards the three bridges and the old market).

pastel-colored baroque palaces, Wilhelminian buildings, Art Nouveau edifices, as well as older structures with quarry stone walls and shingled roofs. In many places it gives the impression of an accomplished miniature combination of Budapest and Vienna. The promenades along the Ljubljanica River and the alleyways lined with boutiques, souvenir and handicraft shops in the Old Town have something of a southern European flair. When the tables are set out in the open in front of the bistros and cafés, pivnicas and restavracijas, when the town's more than 50,000 students take a break from studying and go out on the town, the pedestrian zone is transformed into a Mediterranean parade.

THE PLITVICE LAKES

The sixteen lakes of Plitvice Lakes National Park, close to the border with Bosnia-Herzegovina, are connected by terraces, cascades and waterfalls and are testimony to the constantly changing yet pristine natural panorama of Croatian limestone. The chain of lakes extends over about 7 km (4 mi) and owes its existence to calcification and sinkholes.

Over several thousand years the limestone sinter has formed barriers and dams behind which the water pools up: algae and mosses are the reason for the shimmering blue and green hues of the twelve larger lakes.

The most impressive waterfalls, with drops of up to 76 m (249 ft), are near the four lower lakes. The lime-enriched water plunges over numerous terraces, themselves constantly collapsing and reforming, into the tiny ponds (left and main picture). The Korana is the end of the lakes where the Plitvica flows out.

The region at the foot of the mountain range known as the Small Kapela was declared a national park in 1949 and boasts rich flora and fauna. The dense forests are home to about 120 bird species as well as to deer, wolves and brown bears.

KORČULA, TROGIR, SPLIT, SIBENIK, HVAR

KORČULA

The capital of the island of the same name is proud of the fact that it is Marco Polo's birthplace. The idyllic, outstandingly well-preserved Old Town (main picture) is situated on a small peninsula. The late-Gothic Sv. Marko cathedral boasts modern sculptures that contrast with the Gothic tracery. The bishop's palace and treasury are home to valuable artifacts relating to the town's eventful history. Renaissance and baroque palaces line the alleyways of the Old Town and the Marco Polo House documents the life of the legendary sea voyager. The residents of the island put on a display of their famous Kumpanija dance during the sword dance festival at the beginning of July.

TROGIR

Trogir's beach promenade and Old Town are dominated by the St Nicholas tower of the Benedictine monastery and the clock tower of the St Laurence Cathedral (above). The Dalmatian port dates back to a Greek colony founded in 385 BC. The town, built on an island, fell under Byzantine control in the 6th century (until 1000), after which the Croats, Bosnians, Hungarians and Venetians then disputed its possession, with the Republic of Venice ultimately gaining the upper hand from 1420 to 1797.

The Benedictine monastery is home to reliefs and inscriptions dating from the 3rd to 1st centuries BC. The St Laurence Cathedral, a Romanesque-Gothic work, houses masterpieces of medieval painting and its West portal, built in around 1240 by master builder Radovan from Trogir, is one of the most important stone works in Croatia. The town hall and the loggia with the clock tower date from the 15th century.

Camerlengo Castle and the Markus Tower are part of the Venetian fortifications from the 15th and 16th centuries. Numerous Late Gothic as well as Renaissance and Baroque palaces and townhouses have also been preserved.

SPLIT

In just ten years the Roman Emperor Diocletian had a palace built for the period following his abdication in 305. His design was based on the example of a Roman castrum. His retirement home near the Roman town of Salona covers an area of about 215 by 180 m (705 by 591 ft) and was fortified with battlement walls. Following the Avar and Slav incursion (615) some of the residents of Salona fled into the ruins of the ancient Roman palace, the grounds of which came to form the core of what is now Split (above, seafront promenade; right

the imperial palace). Diocletian's octagonal mausoleum was turned into a Christian cathedral through the addition of an entrance hall and a bell tower, but the tomb's priceless decoration remained untouched. The Jupiter Temple was converted into the baptistery. There are vaults, columns, arches and frescoes dating back to the Roman palace complex all over town. The late-Gothic Papaliç Palace, the Cindro, the Agubio Palaces, and the loveliest baroque palaces in Split all date back to the golden age of this medieval trading town.

SIBENIK

This attractive port is dominated by the white St Jacob's Cathedral (above). The low side aisles extend all the way to the crown height thanks to the Dalmatian master builder and sculptor Juraj Dalmatinac, who also built the baptistery and the apses in 1441. Niccolò di Giovanni Fiorentino completed the side aisles starting in 1477 and fitted the roof with a self-supporting barrel vault made of stone slabs that also support the exterior: a technical masterpiece at the time. Construction was completed as of 1505 by Bartolomeo and Giacomo dal Mestre.

HVAR

This long, narrow island is a sight to behold in the summer, in particular when the lavender is in bloom. The main road leads to Hvar, a truly romantic town with a main square lined with Venetian and Classical buildings such as the loggia, the cathedral and the arsenal. The 16th-century Croatian poet Petar Hektoroviç lived in an attractive Renaissance castle in Stari Grad, the island's second town. This "old castle", Stari Grad, is the main attraction in the peaceful little hamlet.

DUBROVNIK

Dubrovnik was one of the most important centers of trade with the Eastern Mediterranean (the Levant) during the Middle Ages. Known at the time as Ragusa – Dubrovnik being its official name only since 1919 –, the town successfully fended off claims to power in the 14th century by the Venetians and the Hungarians. Officially under Turkish rule as of 1525, it determined its own fate as a free republic up until the annexation of Dalmatia by Napoleon in 1809. Its mighty fortresses, with walls up to 6 m (20 ft) thick and 25 m (82 ft) high remain a testimony to its strength.

Ragusa was a bastion of Humanism in its time and had a tremendous influence on Slavic literature and painting. It was here that Croatian developed as a literary language between the 15th and 17th centuries. The town was almost entirely destroyed by an earthquake in 1667, but the large medieval buildings like the Rector's Palace and the monastery have been renovated. Most of the structure, some of the interior decor, and the imposing cathedral were rebuilt in the baroque style.

The bay of Kotor resembles a fjord cutting deep into the Montenegrin coast. The limestone slopes rise 2,000 m (6,562 ft) out of the sea here. The Church of Our Lady of the Rock was built on the island of Gospa od Skrpjela in the early 17th century.

KOTOR

BUDVA

SVETI STEFAN

Founded by ancient Greek co-lonists, Kotor with its large natural port was on a par with Venice in the 13th and 14th centuries as a seafaring power and trading cen-ter. The town retains its historical character today, enclosed by 5 km (3 mi) of mighty walls with cov-ered battlements, situated 260 m (853 ft) up on the cliff, and guarded by the Sveti Ivan fortress.

According to a Greek legend, the city of Budva was founded more than 2,500 years ago by Kadmos, son of the Phoenician King Agenor and brother of Europa. Originally situated on an island, today Budva is con-nected to the mainland via a causeway. The picturesque his-toric Old Town is surrounded by an imposing fortress.

Sveti Stefan lies in the middle sec-tion of the Budvanska Riviera. Today, the medieval fishing village, which dates back to the 15th cen-tury and was initially built on an island to afford protection against pirates, is a comfortable hotel town with around 250 beds. Its facilities also include a casino, which is why Sveti Stefan is often referred to as "Monaco on the Adriatic".

OHRID

This unusual fresco is in a side cupola of the Naum monastery church in Ohrid and is thought to depict Jesus as world ruler with a child in his arms (main picture). He is surrounded by two angels and by saints of the Orthodox Church.

Founded by the Illyrians as Lychnidos, the Romans were also quick to recognize the strategic position of the town that later would be called Ohrid. Situated on the Via Egnatia, the main arterial road between Byzantium and the Adriatic, the town quickly developed into an important staging post. Klement and Naum, followers of the Slavic apostles Kyrill and Method, then founded several monasteries here in the late 9th century. The town became a Greek Orthodox bishop's see at the end of the 10th century as well as the imperial capital of the Bulgarian Czar Samuil for a spell. Subsequent Serbian rule under the auspices of Dushan was ended by the Ottomans in 1394, who then remained in Ohrid until 1913.

The Church of St Sophia was built by Archbishop Leo in the 11th century. It was converted to a mosque by the Ottomans and lost its dome, bell tower and interior galleries. The Church of St Clement houses the region's most valuable collection of icons. The historically protected Old Town boasts numerous Macedonian-style buildings of particular appeal.

Lake Ohrid is considered one of the oldest and deepest lakes in the world and is home to a number of endemic fish species. The Church of St John at Kaneo (left) was built on its steep shores in the 13th century, the octagonal tower being easily visible from the lake.

The ornate Late Byzantine outer façades of the monastery churches in Moldova (main picture, Voronet) were more than just decoration – they were a "Bible for the Poor".

During the 15th and 16th centuries, Moldovan Prince Stephen III (Stephen the Great, 1457-1504), his successors and other high-ranking dignitaries founded some forty monasteries and churches in the north of the country around the capital Suceava. The exterior walls of the religious buildings in Humor, Voronet, Moldovita, Sucevita and Arbore were painted up to their overhanging eaves. The tradition, which began in Humor after 1530, came to an end with the ornamental painting in Sucevita in around 1600. The probable intention was to provide an object of worship for the faithful for whom there was no room in the church. The images also brought the Christian content to ordinary people, who may not have understand the official Slavic language of the church. The images included legends of the saints, scenes from the Bible such as The Last Judgment, the genealogy of Jesus and the Hymn to the Mother of God. There are also references to political events such as the siege of Constantinople by the "non-believers". The paintings in the church in Arbore date back to 1541 and are of particular artistic value.

VORONEȚ

Voronet, the oldest of Moldova's monasteries, was built in 1488 by Stephen the Great. The image above (a copy of Voronet in the Royal Palace, Bucharest) depicts the founder with his family. The artistic quality and vibrant display of what are still the original outside frescoes have earned the church the title of the "Sistine Chapel of the East".

HUMOR

Hardly a centimeter in Moldovan monasteries remained unpainted. The southern façade of the Humor monastery (top), for example, is a vivid interpretation of the Akathist Hymn, one of the oldest Eastern Orthodox hymns dedicated to the Virgin Mary. The interior is a blaze of bright hues (above).

The interiors of Moldova's monasteries (far left Voronet, left Sucevita) also reveal an overwhelming grandeur and a wealth of images. These were places for the faithful to pray and to receive religious instruction.

SUCEVIŢA

The Moldovan monasteries were not just places of pious contemplation and higher education, they were also safe havens against the Turks. The magnificent painted church in Sucevita has a distinctly fortified character.

MOLDOVIŢA

The Moldovita monastery was founded by Prince Petru Rares (1532-1546). The images depicted in the frescoes on the southern façade (above, the south-east side) include the genealogy of Jesus (the "Jesse Tree") and the rescue of the besieged Constantinople by the Mother of God, the teaching being that orthodoxy brings victory.

One of the highlights of a trip to Romania is an excursion through the Danube Delta. This mighty river divides into three main arms close to Tulcea, more than 2,800 km (1,740 mi) from its source in Germany and almost 80 km (50 mi) before its estuary on the Black Sea coast. The three broad waterways encompass a wetland of around 4,500 sq km (1,737 sq mi), a unique ecosystem that is home to the world's largest cohesive reed cluster (over 800 sq km/309 sq mi). This vast network of waterways, backwaters, canals, lakes, islands, floodplain forests and marshes is also home to a huge diversity of animals and plants. The mighty gallery forests of oaks, willows and poplars are overgrown with lianas and creepers, an especially impressive sight. Water lilies and floating reed islands (Plaurs) cover vast expanses of the water. The diversity of the bird life is also particularly striking, with huge flocks of pelicans and cormorants, for example, and fish eagles and egrets – so rare elsewhere.

Gliding slowly through the narrow channels in a boat or crossing one of the lakes is a wonderful experience in this seemingly forgotten natural paradise. Only seldom do you get a glimpse of the reed-covered huts, which serve as seasonal homes for the fishermen, beekeepers and reed cutters. A fishing village will occasionally crop up, typically inhabited by Romanians as well as Ukrainians and Lipovans, the descendants of 17th-century Russian immigrants. The impression of a fully intact wilderness is deceptive, however. Now protected as a biosphere reserve, the natural equilibrium of the delta also suffered massive disruption, particularly in the 1980s, as a result of haphazard tree felling, irresponsible drainage practices, hunting and livestock farming.

The floodplain forest along the Danube estuary on the Black Sea coast is flooded in the spring (main picture); water chestnuts cover large areas of its surface (right).

The bird life of the Danube Delta
includes members of the egret family
such as the Squacco Heron (right,
a courting display). This is also the
main breeding ground for the endangered White Pelican (far right).

The Church of the Virgin Mary at the centre of the Rila Monastery is in complete harmony with the buildings around it (main picture).

RILA

The hermit Ivan withdrew to the inaccessible forests of the Rila Mountains in the 9th century. The monks who followed him soon

began construction of a monastery in the vicinity of his cave, a monastery that was later awarded extensive privileges by the Bulgarian czars and which enjoyed a golden age in the 14th century. The Rila monastery fell into disrepair following Bulgaria's conquest by the Ottoman Empire, however, and after being restored to its former glory between 1816 and 1862, it once again became an important cultural center and even a "national sanctuary". The pride of the complex is the Nativity of the Virgin Church, a domed basilica with three naves that is surrounded by an open colonnade (left and main picture).

PIRIN

The craggy, rugged landscape of the Pirin Mountains in southwestern Bulgaria, which is home to forty-five peaks above the 2,600 m (8,531 ft) mark, is also home to a sizable national park of the same name. The name Pirin

comes from the Slavic god of thunder and lightning. The park is dominated by Wichren, the third-highest mountain on the Balkan

Peninsula at 2,914 m (9,561 ft). Characteristic of this limestone soil region are the roughly seventy glacial lakes – remnants of the last ice age – and numerous waterfalls and caves. The diverse flora includes conifers such as the red-listed Black Pine and the Silver Fir. This pristine landscape is also home to the protected Eurasian Brown Bear (left) as well as some endangered wolves and a number of rare bird species.

ACROPOLIS

Settlement on the fortress hill in Athens can be traced back to the New Stone Age. The former royal fort was converted into a religious site as far back as the 6th century BC. After being destroyed by the Persians, the sanctuaries were quickly rebuilt in the second half of the 5th century BC. The image of Athens' Acropolis is now dominated by the Parthenon.

This temple, built between 447 and 422 BC, was dedicated to the goddess of the city, Pallas Athene. The structure is flanked by a series of mighty columns with eight across the ends and seventeen along the sides. The cult image of Athena once adorned the interior of the temple, the so-called Cella. The inside and outside of the building were decorated with elaborate, three-dimensional marble statues, of which only part still exist today. The gable reliefs in the west, for example, depict Athena's birth, while those in the east illustrate her epic battle with Poseidon.

The Erechtheion, named after the mythical king of Athens, was built between 421 and 406 BC. It is home to several cult sites,

which explains the unusual layout of the complex. The structure is surrounded by three large porches; the roof of the Caryatid Porch is supported by columns in the shape of young women (left and below). The Propylaea are the monumental gate complexes of the walls surrounding the Acropolis. They are considered the masterpiece of architect Mnesikles and were built between 437 and 432 BC. The variety of column arrangements here are remarkable. While the entire façade is Doric, the slender Ionic columns rise up in the central passage. Kallikrates' temple of Athena Nike was built between 425 and 421 BC, and is one of the oldest remaining buildings in Ionic style. The small but elegant temple has porches on both the eastern and western side.

Athens is the capital of Greece and a fast-paced international metropolis of five million people overlooking the Aegean. The sea of white houses is surrounded on three sides by mountains up to 1,413 m (4,636 ft) and scattered with bare cliffs poking up like islands. One of these rises bears the heart of ancient European culture, the Acropolis. At its feet, modern life pulsates, stretching as far as Piraeus, the port city on the Saronic Gulf.

PLÁKA UND PSIRRÍ

DIMOTIKÍ AGORÁ

Athens' most beautiful historic quarter is the Pláka, right below the Acropolis. You'll find eateries, small hotels and of course a slew of souvenir stores here among the stately neoclassical villas from the 19th century. Folklore is the focus in the music taverns of the steep "Odós Mnisikléous" alleyway. Hollywood stars act on the screen of the "Cine Paris" rooftop garden cinema, flanked by the illuminated backdrop of the Acropolis, while priests purchase their liturgical accesories and robes at Athens' Orthodox cathedral. The adjacent merchant and handicrafts quarter, Psirrí, has become the hip place to be, but many artisans and merchants still pursue their trade here during the day.

The "Dimotikí Agorá" market is over 100 years old and still the best address for fresh meat and fish. Although the products are now displayed in glass freezers and include everything from hen and sheep tongues to cow hearts and lamb cutlets, they are always artistically organized on their various shelves. The market halls are also a popular meeting place for both night owls and early risers – the market's taverns are open around the clock. Cheese, nut and olive dealers have their stalls outside while fruit, vegetable, sausages and stockfish are traded on the opposite side of the road.

View of the Acropolis from the south, with the mighty Parthenon in the center of the complex. Lykabettos Hill is in the background on the right.

MOUNT ATHOS

Moní Esfigménou Monastery (main picture) is located on the north-eastern coast of the Athos Peninsula. The chapel is home to an icon of a supposedly miraculous disposition, and the monastery library is located in the watchtower.

The first monastery was built on Mt Athos in 963, a holy mountain at the southern tip of the Chalcidice Peninsula. The monks' republic proclaimed here was declared autonomous as early as Byzantine times. Men under the age of twenty-one and women are still forbidden from entering. The monastery's quarters are currently inhabited by some 1,400 monks.

Athos has been an important center of Orthodox Christianity since 1054. Over the centuries, its scope of activities also included some 3,000 farmers working for the monastery in the 14th century; at its height, the republic's estate covered around 20,000 hectares (49,420 acres). The Athos school of icon painting had a significant influence on Orthodox art history, and

the typical monastery architecture left its mark in regions as far away as Russia. Each of the twenty main monasteries – seventeen Greek, one Russian, one Serbian and one Bulgarian – has a cross-in-square church in the center of the courtyard, with apses on three arms of the cross. Other buildings as well as the residential cells are located around the courtyard.

The autonomous monastic republic of Mount Athos, one of the most important centers of Orthodox Christianity, covers a total of twenty main monasteries (far left Vatopediou; left Hilandari) and twenty-two sketes (monastic villages). The minster of the Romanian skete Prodromou (center) is lavishly decorated.

METEORA

The Meteora monasteries (main picture; insets, Roussanou and Varlaam) were previously only accessible by makeshift rope ladders or simple cable pulls, but today they can be reached more easily by bridges, paths and steps hewn into the rock.

The name Meteora means "floating", which is a good description of the location where these monasteries are perched: the seemingly impossible Meteora formations soar out of the glacial valley of the Pínios like bizarre bowling pins. Hermits settled on the pillars in the 11th century, and a monk from Mount Athos founded the first of these rock monasteries in the 14th century. A total of twenty-four were eventually built. The Megalo Meteoro was founded by St Athanasios, Bishop of Alexandria, around 1360 and is the highest, and other monasteries were subordinate to it after 1490. The walls of the St Nikolas Anapavsas Monastery, founded around 1388, rise up on one of the other high cliffs. The Varlaam Monastery, named after the hermit who had built a church here back in the 14th century, was completed in 1517. The Roussanou Monastery has recently been re-inhabited by nuns and looks like a smaller version of Varlaam with its octagonal church. Agia Triada, or Holy Trinity, was established as early as 1438 and is accessed via 130 steps. It also featured in James Bond's *For Your Eyes Only*.

The Orthodox frescoes on the church dome (far left, the Meteora monastery of Varlaam) are always dedicated to Jesus, often depicted as a world ruler. The frescoes (left) in Meteora's Monastery of the Holy Trinity were created between 1692 and 1741.

The Poseidon Temple, built on Cape Soúnio between 444 and 440 BC, is visible from great distances rising up at the southern tip of the Attic Peninsula.

DELPHI

From the 8th century BC, Delphi was one of the most important sanctuaries of ancient times. In the center of the holy district was a temple for Apollo (below)

where Pythia, a divine priestess, presided over the famous Oracle of Delphi. The Pythic Games were held every four years, with the musical and literary competitions held in the now well-preserved theater, and the athletic disciplines were held in the stadium, located at the highest part of the sanctuary perched above the Corinthian Gulf. A large monastery was built east of Delphi in the 10th century. Its church is one of three places of worship in Greece whose magnificent mosaic decorations were largely preserved from the time around the year 1100.

OLYMPIA

An ancient document registers the name of the first winner of a track race in the Sanctuary of Zeus in Olympia in the year 776 BC, a date that has since been considered the date of the first Olympic Games. They were held every four years for over 1,350 years until a Byzantine emperor

forbade them as heathen practices. Near the village of Olimbía, German archaeologists have been excavating the stately remains of this ancient cult district, including its sporting sites, for more than 100 years; the Olympic flame for the modern Olympic Games is always lit here at the Temple of Hera. Three museums display masterpieces of ancient art and sporting aspects of the Olympic Games in both ancient and modern times. The Nike of Paionios (top) is one of the things to be admired there.

EPIDAUROS

The complex of Epidauros, located in a narrow valley in the far eastern reaches of the Peloponnese, spans several levels. It is of key importance to the Asklepios cult, which spread throughout all of Greece in the 5th century BC. In Greek mythology, the god of medicine was the son of Apollo, whose powers of healing were also channeled through him.

Epidauros was an important cult town and health resort at that time. The complex included a spa, clinic and even hospitals. Aside from the Temple of Asklepios, the most important monuments are the Temple of Artemis, the Tholos, the Enkoimeterion, and the Propylaea. The most impressive example of classic Greek architecture in Epidauros is the theater (above), dating back to the early 3rd century BC. It is the best preserved building of its kind in Greece, and is particularly remarkable because of its excellent acoustics.

MYCENAE

The Mycenaean culture, which dominated the entire eastern Mediterranean from the 15th to the 12th centuries BC, played an invaluable role in the development of classical Greece. Its name was taken from the Bronze Age fort, Mycenae, in the eastern Peloponnese. The region had already been settled since

4,000 BC, but greater development did not start until the late Bronze Age. According to Greek tradition, the ancestral seat of the Atrides family was established by Perseus, son of the god Zeus. The main gate, commonly known as the "Lion's Gate", is impressive with a relief of two mighty – but now headless – lions (top). Just behind that is the royal graves district where German archaeologist Heinrich Schliemann found the gold funeral mask of Agamemnon, who led the Greeks against Troy.

SOÚNIO

The Temple of Poseidon in Soúnio, whose sixteen remaining Doric marble columns still support the epistyle on which the temple's roof once rested. The location marks the southern border of Attika, which starts in the north near Egósthena at the Corinthian Gulf and Skála Oropoú at the Southern Euboean Gulf. In ancient times, Attika was basically the bread basket of Athens' agricultural hinterland. Slaves originally laid the foundations for Athens' wealth in the silver mines of Lávrio near Soúnio. In the Demeter Sanctuary of the present-day industrial city of Elefsína, free citizens wanted to demand better conditions for the afterlife by participating in this mysterious cult. In ancient times, the crews of Athenian war and trading ships thanked the temperamental god of the sea for their safe return at the Temple of Poseidon, partly decorated in gaudy colors. People hoped to be healed of illnesses in the Amphiáreion, while pregnant women made pilgrimages to Brauron to ask for assistance from the Goddess Artemis.

ZÁKYNTHOS

The southernmost of the Ionic islands was once called "the Flower of the Levant" by the Venetians. With its cobbled streets and squares, arcades and the free-standing church spires, the island capital still bears clear Venetian traces, although it had to be completely rebuilt after a severe earthquake in 1953. At that time, only a bank and the main church had withstood the fierce seismic shocks and subsequent fires. The wide Bay of Laganás has been declared a marine national park where giant sea turtles lay their eggs on the beaches. Near Kerí, liquid pitch, which was used to caulk boats until very recently, still springs up from underground sources. The main tourist attraction here is the Blue Grotto, whose light effects are equally as impressive as those of the Blue Grotto of Capri.

Shipwreck Beach near Anafonítria in the north-west of the island of Zákynthos can only be reached by boat.

The isle of Vlakherna, with its small convent, is located off Corfu and can be reached via a bridge. In the background is the small island of Pontikonissi, the so-called "Mouse Island".

KORFU

Corfu, with more than 100,000 inhabitants, is the most densely populated island of the Ionic Archipelago. Referred to as Kérkira by the Greeks, it is a charmingly green island characterized by rolling hills and beautiful coastlines (right, Cape Drástis). Its more than 100 villages have managed to retain much of their historic flair, and the island's capital is considered one of the most beautiful towns in Greece. Its Old Town quarter (top) is towered over by the Old Fort and the spire of the Spyrídon Church. On the eastern side of Corfu, facing the Albanian and Greek mainland, the beaches are long, narrow and pebbly. Long sandy beaches line the northern coast. Closer to the open sea, the shore is rockier, but many sandy beaches sprawl below the bluffs here, or are nestled between bizarre rock formations. Archaeological sites are scarce, but Corfu has two small castles: British prince consort Philip was born in Mon Repos Castle, while Empress Sissi of Bavaria and later Emperor Wilhelm II spent many holidays in Achillío Castle.

SANTORINI

Filigree bell holders and blue church cupolas are characteristic of Greek island architecture while the windmills and stray cats are simply an omnipresent feature. Santorini is also known to the Greeks as Thíra and is unique in the world. A mighty volcano once towered out of the ocean here until about 3,600 years ago and when it exploded only the rim of the island remained. The Aegean Sea flooded the resulting crater and people later built white villages on the over 300-m-high (984-ft) crater rims, villages that extend far down the steep lava slope using every bit of available space for small terraces. Anybody staying here for a few days or even just to enjoy a sundowner can get a feeling for how special it really is. Santorini had already been settled prior to the volcanic eruption as well. A town close to present-day Akrotíri was home to merchants and seafarers who had their houses decorated with accomplished wall paintings. Archaeologists have found evidence of this beneath a thick layer of ash and lava.

With its white and blue painted houses, Santorini, the southernmost island of the Cyclades symbolizes the dream of Greek island life (main picture). Born of fire and ash and perched on the edge of a volcano crater, this island is lapped continuously by the waters of the Aegean Sea and boasts some unforgettable sunsets.

The mosaic floor of a house on the island of Delos depicts Dionysus (main picture), the Greek god of wine, inebriation and plentifulness riding a leopard.

MYKONOS

One hundred years ago, admirers of Greek antiquities stopped on the Cyclades island of Mykonos to visit the sites of Apollo's cult on nearby Delos. They also had eyes for the hamlet of Chora, with its Old Town quarter. Artists and bohemians soon moved in. For fifty years now, the rich and beautiful of Europe have been frequenting Mykonos and, although the long beaches near town as well as those on the southern and southeastern coast are often quite crowded, the largely treeless coasts and bays still boast long sections where you can still find yourself all alone. There are at least four museums worth visiting here as well: the Nautiko Moussio (seafaring since Minoan times), the Archaeological Museum, the Folklore Museum and the House of Lena (civilian life in the 19th century). The most unusual architectural gem on Mykonos is the Panagia Paraportiani church. Additions have been made since the Middle Ages, merging oddly with one another under a constantly re-applied coat of whitewash.

DELOS

Settled since the 3rd century BC, the island of Delos first appeared in historical texts in the 14th century BC. It then became an important cult center and pilgrimage destination in the 7th century BC as the "birthplace" of the god Apollo. In the 5th century BC, the island was the focal point of the First Delian League, and later became an important trading site deemed useful even by the Romans in the 2nd century BC.

The emergence of new trading centers, pirate raids and attacks by the soldiers of Mithridates of Pontos in the 1st century BC finally

Marble lions, which guard the mythical birthplace of Apollo, are the symbol of Delos. Two headless statues stand in the House of Cleopatra.

resulted in Delos' collapse, but excavation work has unearthed the ruins of numerous houses whose inhabitants had laid mosaics in their interior courtyards depicting different images such as dolphins, tigers and a variety of religious idols. The three temples of Apollo, reached via the holy road, are probably the simplest of all the sanctuaries dedicated to this god. To the west is the Artemision, the temple to Apollo's sister.

Cyclades means circular islands, from the ancient Greek word "kyklos" (cycle or circle). Náxos is the largest island of the Cyclades. Delos is a lesser-known island gem, and Mykonos (left, the island's capital of the same name) is considered a particularly chic jet-set isle.

NÁXOS

The Portara, a monumental marble gate on the Palateia Peninsula north of the port, is the symbol of Náxos and the only remains of a giant temple project that had been planned to honor the god Apollo in the 6th century BC. Also revered in Náxos is a mountain grotto beneath Mt Zas ("Zas" is Modern Greek for Zeus), where Crete-born Zeus is said to have grown up. The "local god" on Náxos is considered to be Dionysus, god of wine. The Bronze Age culture of the Cyclades in the 3rd millennium BC saw the emergence of a special form of marble idols. The slender, usually female and often creatively abstract

Spectacular in both morning and evening light: the Portara marble gate on Náxos.

figures range from a few centimeters to life-size and were an earlier highlight of European art. The collection in the Náxos Museum is the second largest after that in the Museum for Cycladic Art in Athens. Until it was destroyed by the Persians in 490 BC, Náxos was the power center of the Aegean. Thereafter, the island had to conform to Athenian rule. Náxos did not experience another boom until the arrival of the Venetians, who made it into the center of the "Duchy of Náxos" and built the fort, which can still be seen today. The Catholic cathedral in the highest part of the fort quarter was also built at this time. To the north, in the Bourgos quarter, are more than forty Greek Orthodox churches and chapels.

Particularly worth seeing is the approximately 6-m-long (20-ft) sculpture of the "Kouros of Flerio" in Melanes, and the Panagia Drossiani church in the mountain village of Moni, which is home to some of the oldest Byzantine wall paintings.

RHODES

Greece's fourth-largest island (bottom, Mandraki Harbor) was once considered a possession of the sun god Helios. In ancient times, Rhodes was home to four important cities and, for a short time, even one of the seven world wonders: the Colossus of Rhodes.

The main island of the Dodecanese group, which belongs to the Southern Sporades, has seen many a ruler come and go. The island, which was settled early on, fell under Macedonian hegemony during the time of Alexander the Great before a spell of independence and later rule by Byzantium. From 1310, Rhodes fell under the rule of the Order of St John, and then in 1523 under Ottoman control. The Turkish rule lasted until 1912, when Italy conquered the island and held on to it until 1943. It was not until 1948 that the island became part of Greece. Rhodes City owes its present-day look to the Crusaders. Knights Road is a well-preserved example of a road in the 15th century. Around it are the "hostels", the hospices of the knights' regional associations. The road begins at the Byzantine cathedral and leads to the residence of the Grand Master of the Order of St John, which was rebuilt by the Italians according to old engravings. The knights' hospital, built between 1440 and 1489, is today an archaeological museum.

The minaret of the Ibrahim Pasha Mosque, built in 1581, towers over the city wall of historic Rhodes (far left). Knights Road, with its cobblestones and two-story houses built from natural stone on either side, transports you back to the Middle Ages (left).

KARPATHOS

The second-largest island of the Dodecanese is still very pristine. The white-washed and pastel-colored houses, churches and windmills of what is arguably Greece's most beautiful mountain village are nestled tightly onto a steep slope. The town of Olymbos was founded in 1420 by inhabitants of the now orphaned neighboring island of Saria, and the ancient Vrykos, who sought protection from pirates in the mountains.

Nowhere else in Greece has retained so much of its original culture as

None of the islands of the Dodecanese celebrates Easter with as much verve and color as the village of Olymbos on Karpathos.

Karpathos – thanks to its isolation, which the village maintained until well into the 1980s. The houses are built in the traditional style, the ancient Doric dialect is still spoken here and, particularly charming, the women still wear their traditional garb. Bread is also still baked in collective stone ovens, and centuries-old customs are maintained. Naturally, tourism motivates these traditions as visitors expect that rustic ambience from the locals. Indeed, the main source of income today apart from cattle breeding is tourism. All the same, the festivals in Olymbos are colorful and celebrated with gusto, particularly the traditional Easter festival.

CRETE

KNOSSOS

Knossos (main picture, northern wing of the palace) is one of Crete's most important Minoan sites. Only copies remain of the most precious findings – the originals can be seen at the Archeological Museum in the island capital of Heraklion.

Crete is roughly 260 km (162 mi) long and 60 km (37 mi) wide and situated between the Aegean and the Libyan Sea. Three mighty mountains, each of them over 2,000 m (6,562 ft), cut through the island and represent a continuation of the mountain range of the Peloponnese towards Asia Minor. This was where Europe's first civilization was created 4,000 years ago. Those enigmatic Minoans were, for over 500 years, able to pacify the eastern Mediterranean and operate a flourishing trade with Egypt and the kingdoms of the Middle East. From 1900 to 1941, English archaeologist Sir Arthur Evans excavated the economic and religious center of the Minoans some 5 km (3 mi) south-east of the island capital of Heraklion: Knossos, a building complex up to four stories high with 1,400 rooms and covering 20,000 sq m (215,200 sq ft). Many of the corridors and halls in Knossos were adorned with artistic frescoes. Drinking and sewage problems were solved with clever pipe systems. The Minoans also already had their own script.

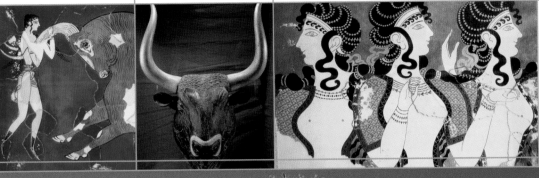

The Bull Leaper (far left, an excerpt) and the three Ladies in Blue (left) are famous Minoan frescoes found in Knossos along with the Rhython (center), a drinking vessel in the shape of a bull's head made from soapstone, gold and quartz.

GOLDEN HORN, GALATA BRIDGE, YENI CAMI MOSQUE

This city with three names – Byzantium, Constantinople and Istanbul – has experienced two empires in its history that significantly shaped the success of the Mediterranean for almost 2,000 years: the East Roman, or Byzantine, Empire and its direct successor, the Ottoman Empire. According to legend, the Byzantines fleeing the Ottomans threw so many treasures into the port basin that the water glistened gold. The "Golden Horn" (main picture with the Galata Bridge and the Yeni Cami Mosque, completed in 1663) was born. Istanbul has a unique relationship with the sea. The waters flow from the Black Sea through the Bosporus Strait, into the Sea of Marmara and the Dardanelles and out into the Aegean Sea. Indeed, a sought-after piece of real estate.

BLUE MOSQUE

The foundations of the Sultan Ahmed or "Blue" Mosque were laid in 1609, and the massive project was completed relatively quickly by 1616. Sultan Ahmed I, its sponsor, died one year after the mosque was finished. The colossal mosque, whose interior is decorated with predominantly blue Iznik tiles – hence its name – owes its spaciousness to the 43-m-high (141-ft) dome. It rests on four striking pillars, as well as four ascending half-domes, and has a diameter of 23.5 m (77 ft). The Mihrab, the prayer room, is made of marble and adorned with precious stones.

The Golden Horn (main picture, with the Galata Bridge and the Yeni Cami mosque from 1663) is one of the world's best natural ports.

The most imposing component of the almost 1,500-year-old Hagia Sophia, which is now a museum (main picture). The 55-m (180-ft) cupola (main picture). The wooden signs bearing the names of Mohammed and the first four caliphs in Arabic script testify to its interim use as a mosque.

HAGIA SOPHIA

The Hagia Sophia was built in the 6th century in a remarkable five years during the reign of Emperor Justinian I. The main Orthodox church in the Byzantine Empire as well as the coronation site of its emperors, it was converted to a mosque by the Ottomans in 1453 after their conquest of Constantinople. Today it is a museum (main picture).

The highlights at Hagia Sophia include mosaics such as the one from in the 10th century (bottom right) in the southern vestibule. It depicts the Virgin Mary with her child. She is enthroned between Emperors Justinian I and Constantine the Great. Justinian rightfully presents her with a church, the Hagia Sophia, while Constantine gave her his city, Constantinople. Another splendid mosaic, no longer fully preserved, is the Great Deesis, an image of intercession with Jesus raising his hand in blessing (top right) in the southern gallery of the Hagia Sophia. The mosaic is from the 13th century.

TOPKAPI PALACE

GRAND BAZAAR

EGYPTIAN BAZAAR

After a fire in the Old Palace in 1540/1541, Sultan Süleyman had his residence moved to the Topkapi Saray, which had been built on the site of the old Acropolis in the 15th century and provided a stunning view over the Bosporus. The complex stretches over an area of 6 hectares (15 acres) and is made up of numerous pavilions grouped around four spacious interior courtyards. The roof also forms a varied landscape (above). The Harem is made up of 300 rooms in a maze-like arrangement, at the centre of which is the festival room of the Padishah (below).

The Grand Bazaar, where visitors can haggle for whatever their hearts desire, stretches over more than 32 hectares (79 acres) in the Beyazit district. There are over 4,000 stalls in some sixty malls. Built as a wooden structure under Sultan Mehmed II in 1461, it was rebuilt in stone in the 17th century following several fires.

Also worth seeing is the covered Egyptian Bazaar, located in the Eminönü district near the Galata Bridge and the Yeni Cami Mosque. More than 100 merchants trade their goods there. The sites, sounds and smells are beguiling: nowhere else in the city will you find a richer selection of spices, sweets, dried fruit and tea.

PERGAMON

The cliffs, soaring to heights of over 300 m (984 ft), were used by the rulers of Pergamon for their capital city's acropolis (main picture). The awe-inspiring Altar of Zeus is now actually housed in the the Pergamon Museum in Berlin, but extensive remains of the royal city can also be seen on the original site and in the modern city of Bergama at the foot of the castle hill. The Temple of Emperor Trajan was completed by his successor, Hadrian, at the highest point of the ancient royal city of Pergamon – on the castle hill of modern-day Bergama.

MILETUS

Along with Ephesus and Priene, the ancient city of Miletus owes its wealth to sea trade, but had to be relocated several times due to the threat of silt buildup in the port. The old Lions Harbor is hardly recognizable among the ruins, which largely disappears in the wetlands of the Büyük Menderes river. A field of ruins, with the mighty theater building, the agora, and the walls of the thermal baths has been preserved. Today, frogs and storks make their home in the compound, which was formerly the largest city in ancient Greece, a region that comprised some eighty daughter cities and was where Thales, Anaximander and Anaximenes developed the basics of philosophy and mathematics. Miletus was famous for the woolen materials dyed with purple from the murex snail.

The ancient theater of Miletus (top) once seated up to 15,000 spectators. Bottom: The Temple to Athena in Priene.

PRIENE

Just like Miletus and Ephesus, the ancient city of Priene, located on the spectacular southern slope of the Mycale Mountain, was also a member of the mighty Ionian League, which was made up of twelve city-states and presumably founded by Greek colonists sometime before the year 1000 BC. The city was created around 450 BC by master builder Hippodamus of Miletus. The Temple of Athena, built in the 4th century BC to honor the city's tutelary goddess, is considered a masterpiece of Ionian architecture, and Alexander the Great continued to fund the construction after capturing the city. As Priene had already lost importance during Roman times, and had been uninhabited since the Middle Ages, the ruins provide an authentic picture of Hellenic city culture.

Originating as a mountain fortress, the town of Pergamon, capital of the Pergamon empire founded by Philetairos in around 280 BC, extended to the foot of the mountain, the remains of which can still be seen on the slopes today.

EPHESUS

This ancient city of ruins lies not far from the town of Selçuk. Long before Greek merchants and settlers arrived here on the Ionian coast, the Carians and Lydians considered it a holy place for the Great Mother Goddess Kybele. Its Temple of Artemis was part of the long tradition of the mother cult. In around AD 129, Ephesus became the capital of the Roman province of Asia and was home to an astounding 200,000 inhabitants at the time. Archaeologists have been able to reconstruct more of this ancient city's temples, grand boulevards, baths and residential dwelllings than any other site in Turkey. Only the port has disappeared through centuries of silt deposits – the sea is actually several miles away from the city today.

Modern library buildings can hardly compete with the grand pillared architecture of the Celsus Library (left). Originally built as a memorial tomb for the Roman proconsul Tiberius Julius Celsus in the 2nd century AD (his sarcophagus is under the library), it is probably the most intact library from ancient times. Some 12,000 scrolls were stored within its walls back in the day. The Temple of Hadrian (right) was built in AD 123, on the occasion of a visit by the Emperor himself.

PAMUKKALE

In addition to the remains of ancient buildings erected here until well into the 4th century, Pamukkale also has a magnificent and unusual natural spectacle to offer: hot springs rise to a height of roughly 100 m (328 ft) from a ledge in the Çökelez Mountains and flow down into the valley. Over time, the sediments (sinter) of the water, which was very rich in minerals, formed petrified waterfalls, forests of lime stalactites, and terrace-like basins, transforming Pamukkale into the surreal landscape you see today.

HIERAPOLIS

There have been settlements in the hot springs district of Pamukkale for thousands of years. The area was part of the Roman province of Asia in the 2nd century BC, and King Eumenes II of Pergamon had the city of Hierapolis built here in 190 BC. It was mainly planned as a fort complex. Along with the town came the first construction of thermal baths. Residential buildings, temples, a theater, as well as other Hellenic buildings. Some early Christian churches, whose ruins can still be seen today, were built in the area around the baths.

Pamukkale means "Cotton Fort" or "Cotton Castle" – a name that aptly describes the natural wonder of sinter lime created here from a hot spring. The warm healing waters pour from one limestone basin into another, leaving bizarre formations between the steps.

GÖREME, KONYA

The Karanlik Kilise (11th century), the "Dark Church", is famous for its biblical frescoes (main picture). The painting here was done by the best artists of the time, who came to Cappadocia from Constantinople. With one main and two small apses, it is one of the most important churches of the Late Byzantine.

Göreme, meaning "you should not see", is a volcanic tuff landscape extending from Kizilirmak (the "Red River") in the north to the subterranean settlements of Kaymakli and Derinkuyu in the south. It is hardly conceivable nowadays that more than 1,000 years ago the people of this region were busy carving passageways and cave dwellings out of the brittle rock, floor by floor, to depths of up to 85 m (279 ft) or more, in order to find refuge from attacks by the Ottomans. Giant millstones closed the entrances to each floor, air came in through long, narrow shafts, and the inhabitants drew their water from reservoirs. Visitors can explore Cappadocia's underworld through the same narrow passageways but Cappadocia has interesting things to discover aboveground as well: the abandoned rock-hewn churches of Christian hermits and monks in the broad, leafy valleys, for example. Using brick churches as models, they laboriously carved vaults and domes, arches and column capitals straight out of the tuff – around 150 in all.

The landscape of Cappadocia is characterized by bizarrely shaped tuff into which numerous cave dwellings and churches have been hewn. The rock formations (left) are known as "fairy chimneys" and are covered with "little hats" made of harder tuff.

KONYA

Modern Konya boasts wide boulevards and has more parking spaces than the other towns of Inner Anatolia, but fans of historic architecture and sculpture will find precious stonemasonry in the mosques and madrassahs of the former Seljuk capital. The Dervish monastery (Mevlânâ Tekkesi) has been a center of Mevlana worship for many centuries. Visitors wanting to

Konya is the home of the Order of the Whirling Dervishes. The dancers are known for their bell-shaped white skirts (both pictures, the Mevlana Monastery), with which they whirl themselves into a state of ecstasy in order to be nearer to God. They hold up their right hands in order to receive God's blessing, while the left hand pointing down "shares" the blessing with the world.

touch the sarcophagus of Jalal ad-Din Rumi and his closest followers with their hands and lips throng into the hall known as the "Huzuri Pir", which means "in the presence of the saint"). The order's founder originally came from Persia and lived in Konya for almost half a century where he ultimately died in 1273.

KYKKOS

Kykkos Monastery (main picture, the spacious cloister) near the town of Pedoulas is the most famous and mightiest monastery on Cyprus. It was founded at the end of the 11th century by Alexios Komnenos, the Byzantine emperor who donated his most precious treasure to the church, the icon of St Mary painted by the Apostle Luke. Cyprus' first president, Archbishop Marakios III, was a neophyte here in his younger years. Though the complex burned down several times and the current buildings are not original, the ancient findings and liturgical devices here are priceless antiques.

ASINOU

The Church of Our Lady of Asinou (top), or "Pangia Forviotissa", stands alone on a wooded hill near Nikitari. From the outside, it appears to be a simple and basic facility, but inside it is home to what is probably the most beautiful Byzantine fresco on the island. The Last Supper, Annunciation and Nativity, the Vita Jesu and the dozens of pictures of martyrs display the complete spectrum of exhilarating imagery from the Orthodox faith. Most of the murals date back to the 11th century. Despite having never been restored, they still look amazingly fresh.

PAPHOS

Close to the village of Kuklia, south-east of the modern city of Paphos, are the ruins of this town first settled by the Phoenicians in the 13th century BC. The sanctuary of Aphrodite was built here during the Mycenaean age in the 12th century. In the fourth century BC the ancient city of New Paphos was founded on the site of the present-day town; there was a sanctuary of Aphrodite here too. The remains of the fortifying walls or tombs, as well as the elaborate mosaics (above), are testimony to the importance of the ancient city of Paphos as a trading center up until Roman times.

The cloister of the Kykkos Monastery have been destroyed repeatedly by fire, making a great many of the lovely gold mosaics around 30 years old – still they are splendid.

The Kremlin panorama in Moscow (main picture with the promenade along the Moskva River) is characterized by an entire ensemble of fortress and church towers. The present-day design of Russia's center of power dates from its reconstruction after Napoleon destroyed it in 1812.

THE KREMLIN

Russia's capital lies on the Moskva River, a tributary of the Volga. First mention was made of it in 1147, and by 1325 it had become a grand ducal residence. During the reign of Czar Peter the Great, Moscow lost its capital city status in 1713 to newly founded St Petersburg. It was the Bolsheviks who made Moscow the political center of Russia again in 1918. Over the course of its history the city has been plundered repeatedly as well as suffering devastating fires. At the beginning of the 20th century Moscow boasted 450 churches, twenty-five monasteries, and 800 charitable institutions. After the disintegration of the USSR, the metropolis (with more than 10 million residents) still has an impressive cultural complement. With over sixty theaters, seventy-five museums, 100 colleges and about 2,300 historic buildings, Moscow maintains a leading position among the world's cities.

For centuries, historical and political events in Russia have been inextricably linked to the Moscow Kremlin, seat of the czars and the metropolitan bishops since the 13th century. Architecturally speaking, the Kremlin had already attained its current size at the time of Grand Prince Ivan IV, known as Ivan the Terrible, who had himself crowned as czar in 1547. First mention of the city's defensive wall was documented in 1147; it was still a wooden construction until the 14th century. Ivan the Terrible gradually had the city walls and the numerous churches almost entirely rebuilt by the leading Italian and Russian master builders of the time, preferring instead to have more ostentatious buildings constructed in their place. These grand edifices were continuously expanded and remodeled until well into the 20th century. They now house priceless works of art. The Kremlin is still Russia's seat of government, for which the term "Kremlin" is synonymous. Within its walls are magnificent palaces, armories, senate buildings, as well as cathedrals and churches with characteristic gilded domes. The Church of the Deposition (Zerkov Rispoloscheniya) was constructed by Russian builders in 1485 and is the seat of the Russian patriarchs and metropolitan bishops. The name derives from a Byzantine feast day celebrating the arrival of the Mother of God's robes in Constantinople. The valuable interior decor includes a 17th-century icon wall (above left).

RED SQUARE, ST BASIL'S CATHEDRAL

Red Square (below) is roughly 500 x 150 m (1,640 x 492 ft) and was built at the end of the 15th century as a market and gathering place, in addition to its use as a place of execution. The famous St Basil's Cathedral (right) was built by Ivan the Terrible after his victory over the Mongol Golden Horde. The cathedral, consecrated in 1561, is considered an

outstanding masterpiece of Old Russian construction. The central, steepled church is surrounded by eight chapels on a single foundation and arranged in the shape of a cross. It was the addition of the St Basil's Chapel that gave the whole complex its name. The central building with the pavilion roof is dominated by the nine differently designed chapels.

At the time of its completion in 1893, GUM, which was designed as a marketplace and today one of the largest department stores in the world, was considered one of the most advanced buildings in Russia with its steel and glass roof. Architect Pomeranzev combined both Renaissance and traditional Russian architectural elements in the building, designing it as a shopping center with the shops strung together.

THE GOLDEN RING

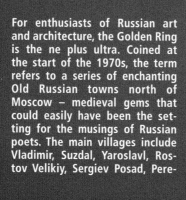

For enthusiasts of Russian art and architecture, the Golden Ring is the ne plus ultra. Coined at the start of the 1970s, the term refers to a series of enchanting Old Russian towns north of Moscow – medieval gems that could easily have been the setting for the musings of Russian poets. The main villages include Vladimir, Suzdal, Yaroslavl, Rostov Velikiy, Sergiev Posad, Pere-slavl-Zalesskiy and Kostroma. These Old Russian centers originally developed from the medieval fortresses built to protect against the Mongolians. Their mighty Kremlins, sturdy defensive monasteries and lovely churches are endowed with magnificent mosaics, icons and valuable treasures that were in stark contrast to the misery of everyday life in these rural towns.

SERGIEV POSAD

The Monastery of the Holy Trinity and St Sergius (above) is without doubt one of Russia's most important religious sites. The monastery complex, dating back to 1340, is a significant pilgrimage destination for Orthodox Christians. Enclosed by a mighty defensive wall that is 1600 m (1,750 yds) long, the complex was besieged in vain by Polish troops for sixteen months between 1608 and 1610. Sergiev Posad, referred to as Sagorsk between 1931 and 1991, was a national sanctuary even during the czarist era, enjoying support from the rulers who had had their own residence, the Chertogi Palace (17th century). The Russian state closed the monastery in 1920 and declared it a museum.

PERESLAVL-ZALESSKY

Founded in the 10th/11th centuries as a trading town on the shores of Lake Pleshcheye, Pereslavel-Zalessky is one of the oldest towns in Russia and has a wealth of churches and pretty wooden houses. The walls of the white cathedral (1152) on the Red Square inside the Kremlin are decorated with semicircular ornaments. One of the few older surviving Kremlin buildings is the Church of the Metropolitan Peter from 1585. The Annunciation Church (mid-17th century) boasts a spacious nave. The Goritsky Monastery (above) dates from the first half of the 14th century, and the Danilov Monastery, located in the south-western part of the town, is from the 16th century.

ROSTOV VELIKY

A panorama of rare beauty: the city with its cathedral of seven silver roofs, the walls of the Kremlin and the towers of the Monastery of Our Saviour and St Jacob as they rise up beyond picturesque Lake Nero. The name Rostov Veliky has a special significance in the colorful history of Old Russia. In Czarist times, only Novgorod and Rostov were entitled to use the adjunct "veliky" – meaning great. This town, established in 862, had already become a flourishing trading center by the Middle Ages. The Kremlin is protected by a wall over 1 km (0.6 mi) in length that features eleven towers. Domes decorated in silver and gold crown the Metropolitan's residence.

JAROSLAVL'

Prince Yaroslav founded this fortified town at the confluence of the Kotorosl and Volga rivers in 1010. Despite its age, many of the original historical buildings have actually survived the destruction of numerous wars. Having enjoyed its golden age in the 17th century, the buildings from this era are among the loveliest in Russia. The Monastery of Our Saviour (12th century) houses the 16th-century Cathedral of the Resurrection of Christ (above). The town's most magnificent church bears the name of the Prophet Elias. It was built in the 17th century, is decorated with wonderful frescoes and is located on the central town square, where the roads radiate out in a star pattern.

The term "golden" refers to the gilded domes of the medieval churches (main picture), while the word "ring" denotes the close cultural and historic links between the individual towns. Today they still stand as testimony to the "Old Russia", which existed up until the October Revolution and which was a deeply religious nation.

KOSTROMA

Kostroma represents the northern-most point on the Golden Ring and is a classic drawingboard town. It was built in its current manifestation following a devastating fire in 1773. A number of significant monasteries such as the Ipatiev Monastery, as well as the Resurrection Church, are among the few surviving witnesses to the period prior to that unfortunate year. A collection of wooden buildings typical of the region are on display in the Museum of Wooden Architecture, including a windmill, a farmhouse and some churches. The museum is located in the Monastery of St Hypathius, which is dominated by the Holy Trinity Cathedral with its golden towers.

SUZDAL

This unique museum town with over 100 historic buildings is the most intact Old Russian town. The monastery became the religious center of medieval Russia after the fall of Kiev. In the 11th century the small town housed the residence of the most powerful principality in Russia, before being destroyed by the Mongolians in 1238. The Kremlin, the market square, the open-air museum of wooden architecture, the monasteries and the traditional wooden houses stand out among the attractions. Some of the 18th- and 19th-century houses are adorned with wood or stone carvings. The 600-year-old Spaso-Yevfimiev monastery in the east of town is the largest in Suzdal.

VLADIMIR

This town on the Klyazma River was founded in 1108 by Vladimir Monomakh, the Grand Prince of Kiev, and was also named after him. The earthen walls and the Golden Gate from the 12th century have managed to survive and the magnificent churches here are well able to compete even with those of Kiev. Prince Andrei Bogolyubsky had the town's most famous landmark built in 1160, the Assumption Cathedral, with its three grandiose domes. A two-floor gallery, crowned with four golden domes, was later erected around the main building. The St Demetrius Cathedral is also worth visiting. Above: A large Easter procession with Russian Orthodox dignitaries.

ST PETERSBURG

After Czar Peter the Great had forced the Swedish King Karl XII to part with a strip of coastline along the Gulf of Finland, he finally gained his long-awaited access to the Baltic Sea, and thus to the West. He then built his new capital there, St Petersburg, which was intended to outmatch the splendor of other European cities. A great number of master architects and builders from Western and Central Europe such as Bartolomeo Rastrelli, Domenico Trezzini and Andreas Schlüter were involved in the construction of St Petersburg, a city that is particularly impressive with regard to the harmony created between its baroque and classical styles, grandiose squares, and numerous canals with more than 400 bridges. Nevsky Prospekt, St Petersburg's magnificent promenade, is lined with ostentatious buildings such as the Anitchkov and Stroganov Palaces.

THE WINTER PALACE

The Winter Palace (main picture and above: the splendid Jordan Staircase) is one of the most significant buildings in Russian baroque style. Begun in 1754 based on plans drawn up by Bartolomeo Rastrelli, it was intended as be an imperial residence directly alongside the Neva River. The Winter Palace is the largest component of the Hermitage complex.

THE HERMITAGE

The Hermitage is one of the most important art museums in the world. It comprises the Winter Palace, the Small, the New and the Old Hermitage, as well as the Hermitage Theater. The Hermitage art collection, which was started by Catherine the Great, is a museum of superlatives (right). The more than 1,000 magnificently designed rooms display around 60,000 exhibits, while the archive encompasses three million items. In addition to the archaeological section with exhibits dating back to antiquity, visitors can also enjoy a massive collection of classical European art.

Today the former Winter Palace (main picture, from the banks of the Neva), main residence of the czars in St Petersburg, houses one of the most famous art museums in the world.

PALACE SQUARE

The Winter Palace owes its current design to Peter the Great's successor, Empress Elizabeth. In fact, the building where the Emperor died in 1725 – on the site that is now occupied by the Hermitage Theater – was torn down completely to make way for the new palace. The square in front of the Winter Palace with the Alexander Column (right) has been the scene of key historical events. It was here that more than 1,000 demonstrators were murdered by czarist troops in 1905, and it was here that the October Revolution began in 1917, when the Bolsheviks stormed the grounds.

THE SMOLNY MONASTERY

The baroque Smolny Cathedral with its central dome and four corner towers was designed by Bartolomeo Rastrelliand and completed in about 1835 by Vasily Stasov. Nowadays it used as a concert hall.

PETER AND PAUL FORTRESS

The orthodox Peter and Paul Cathedral with its distinctive golden spires was built on the grounds of the Peter and Paul Fortress between 1712 and 1733. This imposing cathedral is also the burial place of members of the Russian royal family (above).

THE NEVSKY PROSPECT

The Nevsky Prospect is the main boulevard in St Petersburg, lined with magnificent palatial build- ings from the 18th and 19th centuries, one of which has housed the Art Nouveau-style Grand Hotel Europe since 1875. Extending over a distance of 5 km (3 mi), the road links the Admiralty with the Alexander Nevsky Monastery, crossing several bridges that span the rivers and canals of St Petersburg, the "Venice of the East". Left, the Anitshkov Bridge over the Fontanka.

THE ADMIRALTY, ST ISAAC'S CATHEDRAL

The Peter and Paul Fortress (main picture), built in 1703 on an island in the Neva River estuary, is considered to be the nucleus of the city of St Petersburg. Acquired following the victory over Sweden, it was originally intended to secure Russia's access to the Baltic Sea but was later used as a prison in which Dostoevsky was also incarcerated. It is mainly used as a museum today.

Shortly after construction of the city began, between 1704 and 1705, Peter the Great had a shipyard built on the southern bank of the Neva River. He also built the first Admiralty building, enclosed by ramparts (above middle) and which already had its tower with the narrow steeple back then. Today's late-neoclassical building with its massive,

406-m-long (1,340-ft) façade facing Alexander Park was designed by architect Andrei Dmitrievich Sakharov. The splendid tower with its needle-like steeple crowned by a golden weather vane in the shape of a caravel (St Petersburg's symbol) forms the building's focal point. The magnificent Admiralty complex is decorated with a wealth of sculptures

(above left) and has housed a navy college since 1925; it is meant to symbolize Russia's significance as a seafaring nation. The 19th-century St Isaac's Cathedral (above right) rises behind the Admiralty on Senate Square. It is 111 m (340 ft) long, 97 m (300 ft) wide and 101.5 m (333 ft) high, making it one of the largest domed churches in the world.

THE CATHEDRAL OF THE RESURRECTION OF CHRIST, THE KAZAN CATHEDRAL

After being converted into secular buildings during the Soviet era, orthodox churches are once again

being used for religious services. With the exception of the Cathedral of the Resurrection of Christ (left), the typical onion domes are missing – Peter the Great explicitly forbade "Russian towers". The Cathedral of the Resurrection of Christ was built on the site of an assassination attempt on Czar Alexander II. It is meant to emulate St Basil's Cathedral in Moscow. The Kazan Cathedral, meanwhile, with

its colonnade (above, a church service), is based on St Peter's Basilica in Rome.

PETERHOF

The Peterhof residence (main picture) was built in 1714. It has an ornately designed garden and is indubitably the most elegant of the imperial residences around St Petersburg. Particular attention was paid during its planning to sophisticated water features including decadent fountains for which special wells were built (above, the Samson Fountain). A canal runs from the Golden Cascade, underneath the terrace used for musical and ballet performances, out to the Baltic Sea.

LOMONOSSOV

The suburb of Lomonossov, once referred to as Oranienbaum, is home to an extensive complex of palaces and parks built for Prince Alexander Menshikov in the 18th century by Italian and German architects. It was later converted into a summer residence. The interior of this rococo palace boasts magnificent decor: furniture and parquet flooring of the finest wood, silk wall hangings, embroidery, porcelain vases and lacquer work as well as wall and ceiling paintings.

PAVLOVSK

Just 5 km (3 mi) away from Tsarskoe Selo is another imperial palace in the midst of Europe's largest landscaped park: Pavlovsk Palace. The name goes back to Czar Paul I, who commissioned Scottish architect Charles Cameron with this classic summer residence in 1780. Above: Czar Paul I's four-poster bed.

TSARSKOE SELO

The colossal Catherine Palace, based on plans by Bartolomeo Rastrelli, has a 300-m-long (984-ft) baroque façade and forms the heart of the Tsarskoe Selo (Pushkin) palace and park complex about 25 km (16 mi) outside of St Petersburg.

Johann Braunstein, Jean Baptiste Leblond, Nicolo Michetti, the Rastrellis (both father and son) as well as possibly Andreas Schlüter all worked as architects on the Peterhof residence (main picture). The greatest architectural influence is attributed to the Le Nôtre student, Leblond, whom Peter the Great had met in Paris and engaged as Schlüter's successor. Leblond was also a very skilled landscape architect, which is why Peterhof is more of a "park with a palace and pavilions" than a "palace with a park".

THE AMBER ROOM

This gift to Peter the Great simply had to be monumental. At that time, the Prussians were keen to garner Russia as an ally in the costly war against Sweden. To this end Emperor Frederick Wilhelm I made the decision to sacrifice his extravagant Amber Room. After all, the czar had been very impressed by the chamber during his visit to the city palace in Berlin.

This truly imperial gift – with magnificent amber paneling shimmering in shades of warm gold – was ultimately brought to St Petersburg in 1716 and initially installed in the Winter Palace. Later, it was moved to the Catherine Palace in Tsarskoe Selo, the imperial summer residence south of St Petersburg. The brilliance of the amber room was dazzling, having been built in 1701 in Danzig and Königsberg by the best amber cutters and turners in Europe. The design was originally drafted by German sculptor Andreas Schlüter, but it was only after World War II that the Amber Room achieved real international fame – when it disappeared. In the hope of saving it from the ravages of war, German soldiers actually dismantled the panels in 1941 and stashed them away in Königsberg. The unique work of art remains at large to this day. In 1997, a commode and a mosaic were found in Germany – the only original parts of the now reconstructed Amber Room. They form the key attraction in the Catherine Palace. The painstaking reconstruction work began in 1979, and was finally completed in 2003. The newly created Amber Room was then presented to the international public in the presence of President Vladimir Putin and German Chancellor Gerhard Schröder.

The world's highest mountains, vast shimmering deserts and dense misty rainforests are all hallmarks of Asia, the largest continent on earth. The cultures from the Euphrates and Tigris rivers were the cradle of human civilizations. The empires of the ancient Orient, of Islam, Hinduism, and Buddhism all generated an immeasurably rich cultural heritage. One example are the rice terraces built into steep mountain slopes on Bali (main picture), a testament to skills developed over centuries.

The Geghard monastery comprises a number of smaller buildings that are mostly carved from the rock. The central Church of the Blessed Virgin Mary (main pictures) sits in front of the caves. The larger building attached to it was hewn from the rock as well.

The monastery complex of Geghard, situated some 50 km (31 mi) west of Yerevan, owes its extraordinary character to its cave churches and the tombs that have been painstakingly cut out of the living rock. In the early 13th century the monastery belonged to the Zakarians, who had the main cathedral built in 1215. Only a few decades later, it became the property of the aristocratic Proshian family, who used it mainly as a burial site. Many of the buildings are grouped together in the monastic complex, most of them carved straight from the rock. The main cathedral (Katoghike) – a cross-vaulted church with a high dome and pointed steeple cone – rises on the outside of the rock on a small plateau immediately in front of the caves while the adjacent, larger building, the vestry, was hewn into the granite formation. Four round pilasters and pointed arches divide the space to create harmony. The ceiling's central section is a stalactite dome that indicates Islamic influences. Four further sacral chambers were hewn from the rock; the largest of these served as a sepulcher for the princes.

The churches and monks' chambers here are only sparingly illuminated with natural light (far left). One of the churches was a burial site for the Proshian family and features their family crest above the entrance (middle). Left is an Easter mass in the main Church of our Dear Lady.

ALEPPO, DAMASCUS

ALEPPO

The north-western part of what is now Syria has been a cultural hotbed for thousands of years and Aleppo, a town situated at the crossroads of ancient trading routes, possesses many well preserved examples of this history. Excavations on Citadel Hill prove that it is in fact one of the oldest continuously inhabited places in the world – settled in the third millennium BC. Two monuments stand out in Aleppo's Old Town, which is richly endowed with medieval madrassas, palaces, caravanserais and bath houses: the Citadel (main picture) and the Friday Mosque, built in 715 by the Omayyads and rebuilt in 1190.

Until its conversion in the year 705, the Omayyad Friday Mosque in Damascus also served as a Christian church. Colonnaded walkways decorated with Byzantine mosaics enclose the larger inner courtyard and several pavilions (main picture). Left: An arched bridge leads to the upper gatehouse of Aleppo's Citadel, built in 1211.

DAMASCUS

While the façades of the Sayyida Ruqayya Mosque, the main Shiite mosque in the Old Town of Damascus, are fairly plain, its interior decoration counts as one of the most beautiful examples of Persian interior architecture. The mosque was completed in 1985 with financial support from Iran, and houses the mausoleum of Ruqayya bint al-Hussein ash-Shaheed bi-Kerbala, a grand-daughter in-law of the Prophet Mohammed and the daughter of the martyr, Hussein of Kerbala (above). The shrine is decorated with solid gold plates, and the walls are adorned with poly-chrome mosaics.

Mohammed himself is said to have refused to visit the city of Damascus because he did not wish to enter any paradise other than that awaiting him in Heaven. Today the city still does justice to its poetic name, "Diamond of the Desert". The cityscape has been marked by Islam since the eighth century. The Great Mosque was built on the foundations of a Christian church in 705, at the zenith of Omayyad rule. It is one of the oldest Islamic prayer houses and a trend-setter in Islamic architecture. In the immediate vicinity of the Omayyad Mosque are the city's famous markets (souks), including the roofed Souk al-Hamidiyya (below), and other treasures of Islamic architecture such as Maristan Nureddin, a hospital built in 1154; the Nureddin Madrassa; and the tomb of Saladin from the year 1193.

PALMYRA

Monumental ruins in the Syrian Desert testify to the former political and economic power of the Roman colony of Palmyra and the subsequent splinter empire under Zenobia, the legendary queen of Syria. Located between Damascus and the Euphrates River, this merchant city was already of great importance in pre-Roman times, acting as a trading hub between East and West. However, the greatest period of prosperity for Palmyra, the present-day city of Tadmur, actually came at the time when Rome dominated Asia Minor. The oasis city was a crossroads for north-south and east-west caravan routes, and attained its zenith of economic significance when Emperor Caracalla raised it to the status of a Roman colony. Profiting from its location on the Silk Road, Palmyra quickly accumulated great wealth. Queen Zenobia, who ruled the Palmyrene Empire from 267, expanded the city into a magnificent royal residence based on Roman models, and in the process mingled the cultures of the Hellenic Orient with that of the Parthians and Romans. The Baal Temple of Palmyra, a wide columned road, a grand amphitheater (left), an agora, the tower graves and the subterranean cemeteries in the "Valley of the Tombs" are all testimony to the highly developed art of the time.

CHEVALIERS AND SALADDIN

Syria's medieval castles are among the best-preserved fortification complexes from the time of the Crusades in the Near East. The Crac des Chevaliers fortress (Qala'at al-Hosn, above) dominates the 755-m-high (2,477-ft) Djebel Khalil in the southern foothills of the Ansariye Mountains and is visible from great distances. It dominates the Hims Gap. Because of its position and construction, this mighty 12th-century crusader fortress was virtually impregnable.

Qal'at Salah El-Din (Citadel of Saladin), a short way to the east of Latakia, is located on a ridge surrounded by gorges and forest on three sides. On the fourth, accessible side, the builders carved a 130-m-long (400-ft), 28-m-deep (92-ft) ditch into the rock, leaving the top of a rock standing as an abutment for the drawbridge. The first fortified complex was built in the 10th century. Crusaders resided there during the 12th century, until Sultan Saladin conquered the castle in 1188.

The decumanus, a great colonnaded street and one of the most prestigious boulevards in ancient Syria, once began at the Arch of Triumph in Palmyra, a monument erected in honor of the Roman Emperor Hadrian. In the background beyond the ruins is a 16th-century Arab castle sitting high up on a hill (main picture).

BAALBEK

According to the Bible, Adam, the original man, lived near Baalbek. Cain, Noah and Abraham are allegedly linked with this place as well. The name Baalbek goes back to the Phoenician period, when the town was founded. It means "Lord of the Bekaa Plain". In the third and second centuries BC, the settlement was known as Heliopolis, the "City of the Sun". Various rock graves are preserved from that time. As is often the case, however, it owes its most important remains to the Romans, who conquered Syria in the year 64 BC and proceeded to construct one of the largest and most interesting temple complexes of the ancient world. In the year AD 14, during the reign of Emperor Augustus, construction began on the enormous Temple of Jupiter (main picture), which was built on the ruins of existing Phoenician houses of worship. It took some fifty years to complete. From the same period are the Temple of Bacchus (left), a masterpiece of Greco-Roman architecture that is considered the best-preserved ancient temple complex in the entire Middle East. Baalbek is also famous for its giant stone foundation blocks used in constructing the temple town. The "largest building block in the world" weighs 1,500 metric tons.

The vast size of the Temple of Jupiter in the former Roman city of Baalbek in Lebanon can still be deduced from the 22-m-high (72-ft) Corinthian columns (main picture).

JERUSALEM

THE OLD CITY

There are few other places in the world that are as intertwined with world history as Jerusalem. The city offers a multifaceted journey through time, with the great monuments of Judaism, Christianity and Islam clearly visible to all – and most are located within the Old City of Jerusalem and its fortified walls. The main sites include the Citadel with the Tower of David; the Armenian Quarter with the St James Cathedral; the Jewish Quarter with the Ha'ari and Ramban synagogues; the ruins of the Hurva Synagogue; the "Burnt House"; and the Western Wall, the most important Jewish sanctuary. Nearly one-sixth of the Old City is taken up by the Temple Mount where, according to the Old Testament, Abraham sacrificed his son Isaac. The Via Dolorosa, the "Road of Pain" along which Jesus carried his crucifix in the New Testament, leads via the fourteen Stations of the Cross up to Calvary with the Church of the Holy Sepulcher on Temple Mount. In the middle of the Temple Mount area stands the mosaic-adorned Dome of the Rock.

THE WESTERN WALL

The Western or Wailing Wall is a 48-m (130-ft) section of a wall dating back to the Second Temple. Built on the site of the Holy Temple, it is one of the most sacred sites in Judaism, a pilgrimage destination where slips of paper containing prayers, wishes and thanks can be placed into cracks in the wall.

JEWISH QUARTER

This neighborhood below the Western Wall has been settled by Jews since the eighth century BC but their presence grew through the 13th century when they began building Talmud Torah schools and synagogues. In 1701, construction of the Hurva Synagogue began under Rabbi Yehuda Hassid. When the Jewish cleric died, however, construction was halted and the synagogue was not completed until 150 years later. It was then destroyed by the Jordanians during the 1948 Arab-Israeli War. The ruins have been preserved as a memorial (above).

According to the Jewish faith, the Messiah will one day sit in the Last Judgment in the Kidron Valley below the Mount of Olives. A Jewish cemetery with a memorial was therefore built on this hill north-east of the Old Town (left).

DOME OF THE ROCK

At the end of the seventh century, during the reign of Caliph Abd al-Malik, Byzantine and Arab architects built the Dome of the Rock on the Temple Mount, the oldest of all sacred Islamic buildings. Stained-glass windows allow soft light to flood the interior of the cupola, which is supported by colonnaded arcades.

THE HOLY SEPULCHER

Six Christian denominations share the Church of the Holy Sepulcher on Temple Mount (top). It marks the location of the Resurrection of Christ (right). The Roman Catholic Chapel of the Invention of the Holy Cross is said to be on the spot where the True Cross of Christ was found (above).

The most important archeological relic of the Nabataeans is hidden in the Jebel Haroun Mountains, midway between the Gulf of Aqqaba and the Dead Sea: Petra. The "Rock city" is Petra's most famous building and was known to the Bedouins as the "Pharaoh's Treasure House".

PETRA

In 169 BC the Nabataeans chose for their capital a place that enjoyed perfect natural protection: the bottom of the Wadi Musa valley behind the narrow Siq Gorge, which is only a few meters wide but 200 m (656 ft) deep and thus virtually inaccessible to would-be invaders. The most impressive structures of Petra are giant rock graves that were hewn into the rock, their splendid façades presenting an impressive interplay of traditional Arab construction methods and Hellenic architecture featuring mighty columns, cornices and gables. Richly adorned tombs with interesting names make it apparent that the Nabataeans believed in life after death.

WADI RUM

The roughly 50-km-long (31-mi) valley is one of Jordan's most fascinating destinations (above) where for centuries Howeitat Bedouins (right) have lived with their camels and goats. Today, many of them work as guides in the desert valley and the protected nature reserve. People have made use of the favorable conditions here since prehistoric times as countless wells can be found at the dividing line between the bizarre sandstone formations and the much deeper impermeable granite plinth. Less known is the fact that the Wadi Rum is a rich source of phosphate, which is mined here and constitutes an important source of income for Jordan.

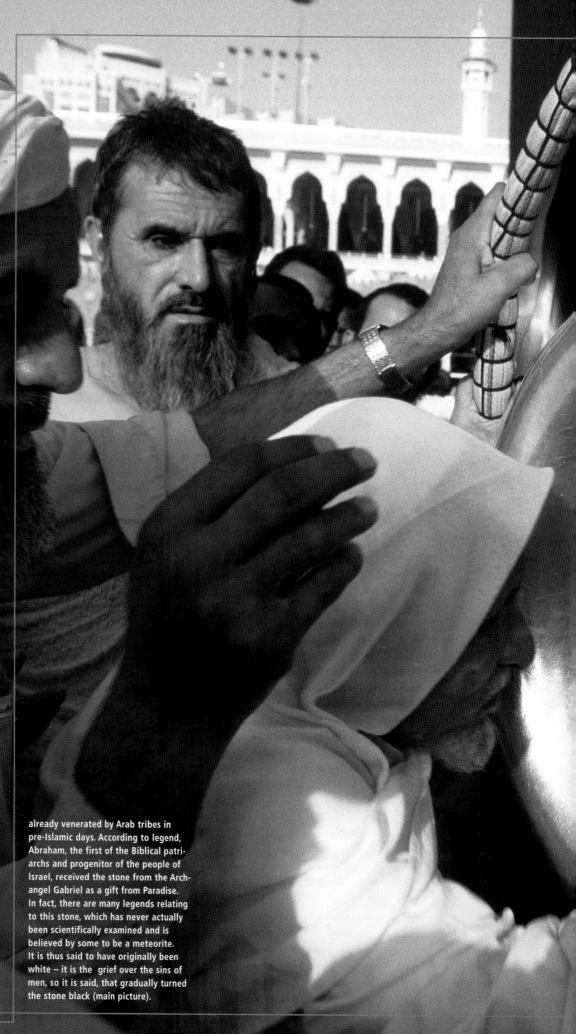

According to Islam, every Muslim should visit the Kaaba (Arabic for "cube") in Mecca at least once in his life, to shout there like Abraham and Mohammed: "Labaik Allahumma labaik!" ("Here I am, oh God, here I am!"). The Kaaba, in the courtyard of the main mosque, Masjid al-Haram, is a windowless, cube-shaped building covered by a black silk and golden curtain (kiswah) that is replaced every year. The main picture here shows a pilgrim touching the Ruknu l-Aswad or "Black Stone", on the eastern corner of the otherwise empty Kaaba. It was already venerated by Arab tribes in pre-Islamic days. According to legend, Abraham, the first of the Biblical patriarchs and progenitor of the people of Israel, received the stone from the Archangel Gabriel as a gift from Paradise. In fact, there are many legends relating to this stone, which has never actually been scientifically examined and is believed by some to be a meteorite. It is thus said to have originally been white – it is the grief over the sins of men, so it is said, that gradually turned the stone black (main picture).

MECCA

MEDINA

As the birthplace of the Prophet Mohammed (c. 570–632), Mecca, situated in western Saudi Arabia, is the holiest and most important sacred site in Islam. Every year millions of worshippers make the pilgrimage to the town, forbidden to non-Muslims. In the courtyard of the mosque with its seven minarets (above) is the Kaaba, a cube-shaped building that is said to date back to Abraham.

Medina is the second most important pilgrimage destination in Islam, and is also closed to non-Muslims. Mohammed and his daughter Fatima are buried in the Great Mosque (above).

SANA'A

The town of Sana'a dates back to a fortress from Sabaean days. It prospered under the rule of the Himyarite kings after 520. In 628 present-day Yemen became part of an Islamic caliphate; Mohammed himself is believed to have supervised the building of the first mosque in Sana'a. The Great Mosque from that time is certainly impressive, yet it is undisputedly the Old Town which possesses the most historic significance. Ancient "skyscrapers" that are up to 1,000 years old were built in Sana'a, some of them boasting up to eight floors. The lower floors were built in traditional style using natural stone while the upper floors were constructed using mud bricks. The look of the façades of these tower houses is especially remarkable. Decorative elements adorn the houses, which have white trim and stucco friezes that indicate the height of each floor. The most common features are the mostly semicircular skylight openings that are framed by stucco carvings with floral or geometric designs and decorated with stained glass.

SHIBAM

The impressive high-rise houses built from air-dried bricks and rammed clay are characteristic of the well-preserved historic center of the desert town of Shibam in the Hadramaut region. The Old Town and its 500 homes, some of them rising to eight or nine floors – nearly 30 m (98 ft) high – is the earliest example of vertical urban planning.

Mud-brick tower blocks with artfully
decorated façades litter the Old Town of
Sana'a (main picture), capital of Yemen
and once among the most beautiful
places on the Incense Route.

MUSCAT, HAJAR, BAT, AL-KHUTM AND AL-AYN

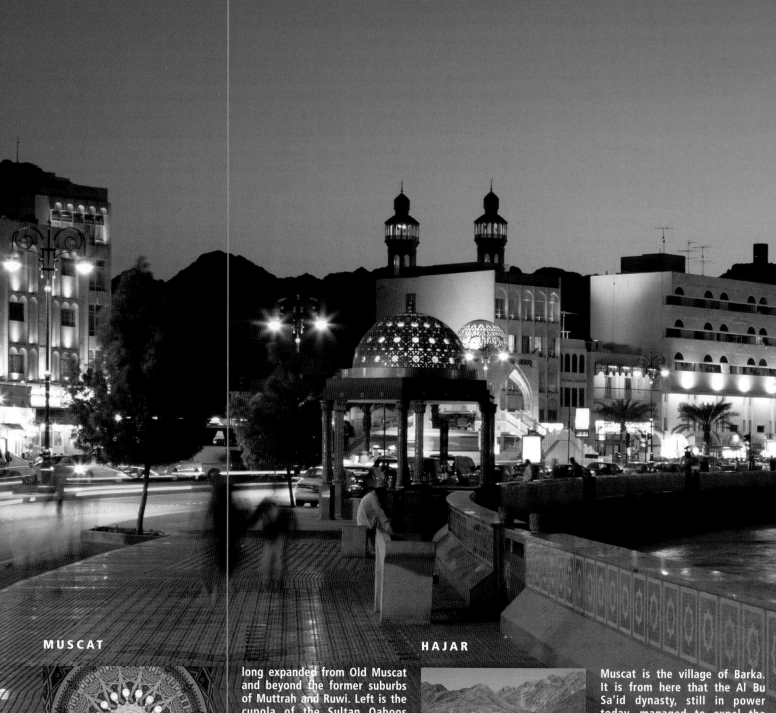

MUSCAT

The capital of the Sultanate of Oman is surrounde by the mountains of the Al Hajar range, directly by the sea. The Portuguese conquered the town in the early 16th century but were forced to withdraw 150 years later. The two fortresses Al Mirani and Al Jalali (right) were further developed by subsequent rulers. Today, lovingly cared for parks characterize the city, which has

long expanded from Old Muscat and beyond the former suburbs of Muttrah and Ruwi. Left is the cupola of the Sultan Qaboos Grand Mosque, completed in 2001. Despite modernization, the "Capital Area" has preserved its unique charm. A modern port was built in Muttrah with a corniche lined by beautifully painted merchants' homes that were built there in the 18th century.

HAJAR

From Muscat it is worth taking a detour into the Al Hajar Mountains, which rise to 3,000 m (9,843 ft) and stretch in a gentle S-shape along the coast from the Musandam Peninsula in the north to the south-eastern corner of the Arabian Peninsula. Farmers still irrigate the narrow terraced fields on the slopes here using the ancient falaj tunnel system. About 80 km (50 mi) outside of

Muscat is the village of Barka. It is from here that the Al Bu Sa'id dynasty, still in power today, managed to expel the Persians from the coastal towns of Oman in the 18th century. The old fortress towers above the city. The Bait Na'aman Palace nearby was built in the 18th century as a residence in an extensive palm grove. South of Barka, at the foot of the Al Hajar Range is the start of the eastern end of the Al Batinah Plain where the village of Nakhal ("palm tree") is dominated by one of the largest clay castles in Oman (left). It sits atop a rock outcropping and was built to protect the entire Al Batinah region. In the nearby palm groves are the hot springs of Ath-Thawarah.

BAT, AL-KHUTM AND AL-AYN

The historic site of Bat (above) and the nearby excavation sites of Al-Khutm and Al-Ayn are deep in the interior of the Sultanate of Oman, near the Bat Oasis. The remains of four towers and a settlement as well as interesting necropolises were found here. In front of the steep walls of the western Al Hajar Range you can see beehive-shaped tomb structures made from the local brown-

ish limestone, which disintegrates into tile-like blocks when cut and which was ritually piled up here to a height of 8 m (26 ft).
The sheer number of buildings and tombs indicates that this region on the ancient copper trade routes to Mesopotamia was once densely populated. For unknown reasons, however, the area was abandoned at the end of the third millennium BC.

Muttrah, a former suburb that has been absorbed into Muscat, still has some of the brightly painted merchants' homes from the 18th century along the corniche, or harbor promenade (main picture).

"Las Vegas on the Gulf" attracted seafarers from Great Britain and India back at the beginning of the 20th century, at a time when the trade in gold was already an important pillar of the economy. Indeed, the rulers of Dubai do not simply rely on oil when planning for the future. Aside from the Jebel Ali Free Zone and the international airport, tourism is adding increasing amounts of money to the state's coffers. Luxury hotels are built in neo-Oriental style and new beaches are created using the finest white sand. One of the most recent and most impressive examples of making seemingly utopian dreams come true are the Palm Islands (below), the new icon of Dubai locatednext to the Burj Al Arab Hotel (main picture), which is shaped like the sail of a *dhow*, and the Burj Dubai (far left), completed in 2009 – at 818 m (2,684 ft) the highest skyscraper in the world. Next to them, the old houses with their wind towers are quite modest. Divided in two by Dubai Creek (al-Khor), the emirate markets itself is as

"the most beautiful shopping paradise in the world" with lively bazaars, or *souks*, arranged in covered shopping alleys (above). In the south-west is Bur Dubai with the Dubai Museum in the old Al-Fahidi Fortress and the oldest district, Bastakiah. On the other side of the Creek, in the Deira port district, you can still get an idea of life in the Emirates before the oil boom. This is where the *dhows* anchor, merchant boats with triangular sails that were in use in pre-Islamic days.

The Burj Al Arab in Dubai, built as a stylized sail, is the only 7-star hotel in the world.

In the 16th and 17th centuries, Isfahan, about 350 km (217 mi) south of Tehran in the foothills of the Zagros Mountains, developed as a center of Islamic architecture and scholarship. Shah Abbas I (1587–1629) was obsessed with construction and made extensive changes to his residence. During his reign, Isfahan became one of the most important cities in the Orient as far as culture and art are concerned. His most important building project was the vast Naghsh-e Jahan Square (the "Design of the World"), later renamed Meidan-e-Shah ("Royal Square"), and since the revolution known as Meidan-e Imam (Imam Square).

Surrounded by two-story arcades and extending over a length of 500 m (1,600 ft), it is among the largest squares in the world. The square is framed in by four remarkable building complexes: the former royal mosque known as Imam Mosque on the south side; the Sheikh Lotfollah Mosque (left) on the east side; the royal Ali Qapu Palace ("High Gate", below) on the west side; and the main portal to the Royal Qeisarieh Bazaar on the north side. The most important edifice on the grand square is the Imam Mosque (main picture and opposite page) with its four tall iwans typical of Iranian-Islamic four-iwan architecture.

The four 27-m-high (89-ft) entrance portals to the Imam Mosque feature magnificent decorations. *Muqarnas*, which fill the niche above the main portal with a stalactite-type ornamentation, are one of the typical style elements (main picture). The mosque has a separate area for women (left) as well as superb tiles and mosaics.

PERSEPOLIS

The Achaemenid King Darius I, the most important ruler of the Achaemenid dynasty, laid the foundation stone for the royal palace of Persepolis in 520 BC. Although he already had two capitals at the time – Pasargadae and Susa – he wished to present the world with an outstanding residence that would reflect the size of his empire. The result was the most magnificent work of Achaemenidic Persian art, built on an artificial terrace covering 125,000 sq m (1,345,000 sq ft). The royal buildings took almost sixty years to complete. A relief in the treasure house of Persepolis depicts Great King Darius I receiving a delegation of Medeans who had been subjugated by a predecessor of his, Cyrus II.

Darius I himself only lived to see the completion of the palace, the treasury and the colonnaded hall (Apadana) with its thirty-six columns measuring nearly 20 m (66 ft) and featuring superb reliefs (above and main picture). It was his son Xerxes who continued with the ambitious plans. The main entrance to the royal residence (top) that he had built was known as the "Gate of all Nations". Everyone had to be registered there upon arrival in order to be considered for an audience with the king. However, the "Dream of Darius" was laid to waste as early as the year 330 BC by Alexander the Great. The last Shah of Iran, Reza Pahlavi, had some parts of the town rebuilt in 1971.

The 70-m-long (77-yd) relief on the eastern ascent of the colonnaded hall of Persepolis depicts the delegates of twenty-eight nations from the Achaemenid Empire who had come to pay tribute for the New Year. They are sporting traditional attire and hairstyles from their regions (main picture).

The first documented mention of Samarkand dates back to the year 329 BC when Alexander the Great conquered the former Marakanda. Even at that time, trade, artisanship and culture flourished in this oasis city nestled in the valley of the Zarafshan River. Once the Silk Route had finally connected China with the Mediterranean in the first century BC, Samarkand became a lively hub of culture and

The Tilla-Kari Madrassa, its name meaning "covered in gold", was built in the 17th century and served as both a Qur'anic school and the main mosque of Samarkand. Restoration of the prayer hall began in 1970. Today the iwans and arches as well as the dome once again shine with their former golden splendor (above left). The cupolas of the Sher-Dor Madrassa are flanked by decorative minarets (above right).

civilization. The prosperous trading town has been conquered by a number of empires and dynasties including led by the Chinese, Arabs, Samanids and Seljuks – and was finally destroyed in 1220 by the hordes of Genghis Khan. In 1369, Mongol ruler Timur Leng (Tamerlane) made Samarkand the capital of his empire, ultimately commissioning the most eminent artists, architects and scientists

Samarkand was ideally situated on the Silk Route, making it a melting pot of Eurasian culture. Today the oasis town still shines with its masterpieces of Islamic art and architecture. Registan Square, for example, is surrounded by the magnificent Ulughbek, Tilla Kari and Sher-Dor madrassas (main picture, from left to right).

of the day to build a city of unsurpassed splendor. His grandson Ulughbek, ruler of the Timurid Dynasty from 1447, continued Timur's work. Ulughbek himself was also known as an outstanding astronomer. His three-story observatory and its brick sextant were excavated in Samarkand in the 20th century. Some other masterpieces of medieval Islamic architecture date from this Timurid

After his successful India campaign, the Mongol conqueror Timur ordered construction of the Bibi-Khanym Mosque (above left, one of the two domed buildings of the transverse axis), allegedly named after his favorite wife. It was completed in 1404. Legend has it that the cousin of the Prophet Mohammed is buried in the Shah-i-Sinda necropolis with its mosques, mausoleums and other tomb structures (above right).

period in Samarkand, such as the Bibi-Khanym Mosque with its 44-m-high (144-ft) domed central building. One of the most splendid squares in all of Central Asia is the Registan, which is surrounded by three madrassas. On the Samarkand city limits is the impressive Shah-i-Zinda necropolis, a pilgrimage destination with a large number of mausoleums from Timur's period.

JAM

The Minaret of Jam, tapered towards the top, rises into the sky from an octagonal base. On the outside it is decorated with geometric patterns in stucco and relief tiles, with strips of writing in blue ceramic that repeat the 19th Sura of the Qur'an (left).

The second-highest minaret in the world (after the 210-m (689-ft) minaret of the Hassan II Mosque in Casablanca) is situated in the narrow Hari Rud Valley, west of Chaghcharan in the desolate mountain landscape of the Hindu Kush. The 65-m (213-ft) Minaret of Jam, built in 1194, is a lavishly decorated brick structure with floral and geometric ornamentation as well as tiled inscriptions. Thanks to its enormous size and the artistic decoration, this slim brick tower marks a highpoint not only of Islamic architecture in the Middle Ages, but also illuminates the period of the Ghorids, who ruled in this region in the 12th and 13th centuries. Their sphere of influence extended all the way to the Indian subcontinent – the Minaret of Jam actually became the model for the Qutb Minar in Delhi, which of course considerably better known today.

After the decline of the Ghorid Dynasty, Jam was long forgotten until it was rediscovered during an archeological expedition in 1957. Less spectacular, but also of great historic interest, are the ruins of a fortress, a palace, a Jewish cemetery and a bazaar as well as a fortification wall near the minaret.

HERAT

One of the most beautiful towns in Afghanistan is Herat, founded by Alexander the Great. Its beauty earned it mention in ancient Persian inscriptions as the "Pearl of Persia". Located in the west of the country in the Hari Rud Valley, the city features a citadel dating back to the 10th/11th centuries, and the Masjid-i-Jami Mosque, built in about 1175 and an especially worthy sight (above).

BAMIYAN VALLEY

As a result of Indian influences, the Bamiyan Valley, around 200 km (124 mi) north-west of Kabul, developed into a center of Buddhism. Under Kanishka, the great Kushan King who ruled in Bamiyan during the 1st century BC, work was begun on caves in the cliffs of the Bamiyan Valley, which were then decorated with religious frescoes and stucco details. Later, probably during the 6th century, giant Buddha statues were chiseled out of the rock. These were tragically destroyed in March 2001 by the Taliban, who considered them idolatry, which is prohibited by Sharia Law.

On the hills surrounding the Minaret of Jam are the ruins of a medieval fortress (main picture).

KARAKORAM

small area. The tallest peak in the range – K2, at 8,614 m (28,263 ft) – is also the second-highest on earth. The Karakoram Highway, a combined project between Pakistan and China that was completed in 1978 after about twenty years of construction, is 1,284 km (798 mi) long and connects Havelian in north-west Pakistan with Kashgar in the western Chinese province of Xinjiang. Snaking its way past 8,000-m (25,000-ft) peaks such as Nanga Parbat, the Karakoram Highway – the highest road in the world – reaches its highest point on the 4,733-m (15,529-ft) Khunjerab Pass, which also marks the border between Pakistan and China. The architec-

tural style of the 600-year-old Baltit Fort, former residence of the commander of Hunza, also reveals Tibetan influences. In 1979, German ethnographer Karl Jettner discovered some 30,000 rock paintings and inscriptions in the Hunza and Indus valleys (below), the oldest of which are from the Early Bronze Age. Left: The Hunza Valley after a storm.

Northern Pakistan is dominated by enormous mountain ranges that continue into China to the east. The Karakoram, as they are called, join the Himalayas here in the Hindu Kush and boast some of the highest peaks on earth. In fact, about half of the world's one hundred highest summits are in the Karakoram, all within a very

The Baltoro Glacier (main picture) is 57 km (35 mi) long and covers an area of 754 sq km (291 sq mi), making it one of the largest glaciers outside the polar regions.

Spacious halls with finely decorated vaults, columns and windows are typical of the structures of the Red Fort (main picture). The shapes and patterns combine Persian and Central Asian elements with Indian and Hindu architectural styles.

THE RED FORT COMPLEX

Shah Jahan (Persian for "King of the World") was the fifth in a notable series of Mughal rulers in India and was an energetic commissioner of buildings, including the Taj Mahal in Agra. Begun in 1639, it took just nine years to complete the Red Fort next to the Salimgarh Fort, which had been built by Islam Shah Suri back in 1546.

With magnificent portals (top: Lahore Gate), opulent watchtowers and defiant walls, the Red Fort was a clear symbol of Mughal power. The monumental complex comprises numerous palaces.

Together, these two grand edifices form the complex of the Red Fort in Old Delhi. This impressive structure, which was plundered twice during its colored history – once in 1739 by Persian forces and then in 1857 by British troops –, owes its name to the imposing, 16-m-high (52-ft) sandstone walls that surround the complex. During sunset the red hues of the stone create a dazzling spectacle.

QUTB MINAR

At the end of the 12th century, Muslims under Qutb-ud-din Aybak conquered northern India and the Rajput fortress of Lal Kot, a settlement that preceded the foundation of Delhi. When they erected their first mosque there, Qutb-ud-din's subjects relied primarily on local architects and traditions, which is why the Quwwat ul-Islam (Might of Islam) Mosque was built in the reddish-yellow sandstone typical of the area on the site of a columned hall characteristic of earlier Jain sanctuaries. Only the decoration and the bands of calligraphic script along the walls and façades are actually traditional Islamic features. From the ruins of the large mosque rises the 72-m-high (236-ft) Qutb Minar, the tallest brick minaret in the world. Its base is around 15 m (49 ft) in diameter while the tip is just under 3 m (10 ft). Known for its red sandstone fluting, used here for the first time in India as a stylistic feature, the top two floors of Qutb Minar were destroyed by lightning in the 14th century and rebuilt later in white marble.

The famous Qutb Minar tower (left, in background) is the first Islamic building ever constructed on Indian soil. It is a stunning amalgamation of Indian-Hindu elements and Islamic architectural styles.

HUMAYUN'S TOMB

The works of Humayun, son of Babur, founder of the Mughal dynasty in India, were pivotal in the history of Mughal architecture. Although the security of his empire in India – he ruled between 1531 and 1556 – was initially less than ideal, the result was a boon. The young regent spent fifteen years in exile in Persia before returning, this time not just with a mighty army, but a host of master

Humayun's tomb was built on the initiative of his widow, Hamida Banu Begam, also known as Haji Begum. The Mughal ruler's final resting place (bottom) was not begun until 1570, some fourteen years after his death in 1556.

builders and artisans as well. His decision proved to be of great benefit to the architectural milieu on the Indian subcontinent, which flourished in the flood of new inspiration.

The Persian influence of his court is exemplified by the dome atop the high tambour, the gracefully arched alcoves and the spacious corridors of the tomb. The white marble and red sandstone façade also recalls Persian tradition.

AGRA

One of the most beautiful Islamic buildings in the world, the Taj Mahal (main picture) was constructed in Agra by the great Mughal emperor Shah Jahan as a tomb for his favorite wife, Mumtaz Mahal, who died in 1631. The complex is surrounded by an 18-hectare park.

THE RED FORT

Agra, situated on the west bank of the Yamuna River, owes its importance to the Mughal emperors, who built the Red Fort here (right, 2nd picture). The complex offers stunning views all the way to the Taj Mahal (right) and is named for the red sandstone from which it was constructed.

Begun in the year 1565 by Mughal Emperor Akbar, the Red Fort was later enlarged by Akbar's grandson, Shah Jahan. The buildings clearly demonstrate the different aesthetic preferences of the two rulers. Indicative of Akbar's imperial style are the Amar Singh Gate and the entire outer wall (below), while Shah Jahan preferred white marble.

TAJ MAHAL

The name of this famous white-marble architectural gem derives from Mumtaz Mahal, the endearing name of Shah Jahan's beloved wife, Arjumand Banu Begum, who lies buried there. The name means "Diadem Palace", or "Pearl of the Palace", and the edifice represents the zenith of a style that was initially developed in the architecture of the tomb of Humayun, one of Jahan's predecessors. At the end of long, terraced gardens and surrounded by grand water fountains, the perfectly symmetrical mausoleum

In the Taj Mahal's main chamber stand the two empty cenotaphs of Shah Jahan and his wife (top), adorned with passages from the Qur'an and decorative inlay work. Their actual tombs are found in the crypt below (bottom).

rises elegantly from a massive square plinth (right). The central domed tower sits on a high tambour in the Persian style and is surrounded by other domed pavilions. The wonderful façades, which are also designed in the Persian style, are oriented toward the four points of the compass while the four minarets accentuate the four corners of the plinth. The obvious Persian influence is thought to be the work of the lead archtiect, Isa Afandi, from Shiraz in the south-west of what is now Iran.

Agra is on the western bank of the Yamuna river and was the center of power for the Mughal emperors who build the Red Fort here. It is one of the largest in the world and provides fantastic views of the Taj Mahal (far left).

FATEHPUR SIKRI

In building Fatehpur Sikri, or "City of Victory", the illustrious Mughal Emperor Akbar not only bequeathed upon the world a Mughal town that remains intact in its original state, but he also honored a vow he had made. The story tells of the Sufi saint and advisor to the emperor, Salim Chishti, who once lived not far from Agra. When Salim's prophecy came true that the Mughal emperor would be borne three sons, Akbar pledged to build a town

near the wise man's camp. The foundation stone was laid in 1569, and after just three years the Royal Mosque (above left: the inner courtyard) and the tomb of Sheikh Salim Chishti (above) had

already been completed. Followers of Sufism also pray inside the mausoleum (above), as Salim was an important Sufi mystic.
All told, it took roughly ten years to build the entire city of Fatehpur

Sikri, a fairytale capital built in the idyllic rolling countryside and featuring several palaces and terraces. Ultimately, the court was forced to abandon the town in 1585 due to drought.

Keoladeo National Park is particularly busy after the monsoon rains when flocks of migrant birds join the indigenous aquatic species. Purple herons (main picture) feel at home here as well.

KEOLADEO

Keoladeo National Park is a vast, man-made wetland region (below) that was originally created by the maharajas of Bharatpur, who once enjoyed hunting the plentiful duck population. The marshy area was so abundant with the water-fowl they coveted that several thousand birds could be rounded up in a single day.

In order to make an even larger marshland area for hunting, the

maharajas built artificial canals and dams in the 19th century. This allowed a region to develop that soon became a popular breeding ground for other birds due to the very dry surrounding country.

Today, the protected area provides a permanent sanctuary for about 120 bird species (above, left to right: Indian roller, rose-ringed or Alexandrine parakeet, and river kingfisher). It is also home to one of the largest populations of herons in the world. In the winter months some 240 species of migratory birds make their way here including the rare Siberian crane (or snow crane) and the fal-cated duck. The Siberian cranes used to be one of Keoladeo's main attractions – more than 100 birds were still coming to spend winter in the swamps in 1976. Now they are unfortunately all but extinct.

AMBER FORT

The fortified Palace of Amber was the seat of the Kachhawaha Dynasty until 1727 – all proud Rajput families, all of them Hindus and all of them belonging to the second-highest Indian caste, the Kshatriya caste, which is reserved for warriors, princes and kings.

The fortress was built by Man Singh I in the year 1592 on the remains of a fort from the 12th century. The magnificent building in the center of the complex was built on the orders of Jai Singh I. Visitors can ride elephants up the serpentine path to the structure on the ridge (above), entering through the Suraj Pol, or Sun Gate. The Ganesh Pol, a three-story gate from the year 1640 (above left), leads into the private chambers of the fortress. Women lived on the first level behind mesh-like windows (main picture).

JAL MAHAL

Roughly five miles north of Jaipur, the capital of Rajasthan, you come upon yet another Mughal landmark, the Jal Mahal "Water Palace", built in the 18th century by King Madho Singh I. For much of the year Mansagar Lake is dry, but during the monsoon rains water levels rises dramatically and the palace looks as if it's floating (above), hence the idyllic palace's name. The building was based on the lake palace in Udaipur, where the king grew up. The garden is enclosed by wonderful arched gates.

From the bay windows of the Hawa Mahal ("Palace of Winds") the ladies of the court were able to watch everyday life in the street through stone grillwork without being seen themselves (main picture).

CITY PALACE

The complex of the town palace of Jaipur comprises several buildings and courtyards, all dominated by the multistory Chandra Mahal ("Moon Palace") from the 18th century. The former Mubarak Mahal ("Auspicious Palace") was built of sandstone in 1900 as a guesthouse and houses an exhibit of precious textiles including the finest silk and gold-embroidered brocade.

Large parts of the City Palace (top and center; bottom: the Hall of Private Audience, which the Maharaja still uses today) are open to the public, much like a museum.

Sileh Khana, a collection from the former arsenal, is one of the most valuable in India. In the Diwan-e-Khas ("Hall of Private Audience"), which the Maharaja still uses for receptions today, are two silver urns the Guinness Book of Records says are the largest silver vessels in the world. Also worth seeing is the royal collection of miniatures in the City Palace's Diwan-e-Aam (the former "Hall of Public Audience"). The Silver Throne is also here.

TRIPOLIA AND JOHARI BAZAARS

It was the pink façades of the buildings that gave Jaipur its other name, the "Pink City". The capital of Rajasthan, Jaipur was founded in 1727 by Maharaja Sawai Jai Singh II, the 30th ruler of the Kachwaha dynasty and a man with a prominent place in his country's history books as a brilliant statesman, scholar and promoter of the arts. "Sawai" (meaning "One and a Quarter") is an honorary title for exceptional people that was bestowed on Jai Singh II early in his 43-year rule. In line with Hindu architectural tradition, Jaipur is laid out in a strict geometric plan. The residential blocks are aligned with the points of the compass while taking to consideration caste as well as astral constellations.

Aside from the tourist attractions you should also visit the bustling bazaars of the city, such as the Tripolia and the Johari bazaars, with everything from snake charmers, spices and vegetable merchants, and even precious stone traders in the jeweler's market at the end of Johari.

Jaipur is a feast for the senses, especially at the bazaars. Snake charmers invite spectators to an ancient dance while festively adorned elephants are proudly paraded through the lanes – in Jaipur tradition and modernity create a fascinating synthesis (left).

JANTAR MANTAR

Maharaja Sawai Jai Singh II built an observatory near the City Palace that was equipped with highly complicated astronomical instruments. The complex was constructed according to his own calculations. At first glance the huge sundials and measuring instruments seem futuristic even now, but Sawai Jai Singh II was a passionate mathematician, astronomer and astrologer. Having ascended to the throne

Jai Singh was of the opinion that the larger the instruments, the more accurate the results would be. Aside from the observatory in Jaipur (above) he had four more built in Delhi, Ujjain, Mathura and Varanasi.

at the tender age of eleven, he devoted himself to scholarship and knew all the current writings of his day. He read the works of Mirza Ulug Begh, for example, the famous astronomer and king of Samarkand. He studied Copernicus and Kepler and then wrote his own scientific compendium based on the measurements he made in his observatory. Astrologists even used some of his instruments when compiling horoscopes.

JODHPUR

Jodhpur, located in the south-eastern corner of the so-called "Golden Desert Triangle", is Rajasthan's second-largest city and forms a stark contrast to the rural areas on either side of the road that takes you there. Hectic traffic and lively trading in the bazaar characterize life in the center of the city while museums, markets, arts and crafts, and wonderful antiques await visitors in the small alleyways. Jodhpur is also known as the "Blue City" after the color of its houses (main picture and below).

Blue is the divine color of Hinduism. The most popular Hindu god, Krishna (Sanskrit for "the dark one"), is typically depicted with blue skin. This is why in the past only the Brahmin, the members of the highest Hindu caste, were allowed to paint their houses blue in Jodhpur. The walls of the Old Town are surrounded by roughly 10 km (6 mi) of fortified walls.

MEHRANGARH FORT

Mighty Mehrangarh Fort (above and below) towers majestically over the town of Jodhpur. It is home to magnificent buildings from the 16th to 19th centuries including the Pearl Palace (Moti Mahal) and the Palace of Flowers (Phool Mahal) with its lavish murals, attractive stained-glass windows (right) and carefully executed mirror works. The complex recalls the opulent lifestyle of the maharajas of the Rathore clan. In 1459, King Rao Jodha selected the nearly 120-m-high (39-ft)

promontory as the site for the fortress. Jodhpur, the city at the foot of the ridge, was named after him and is famous for its blue Brahmin houses.

PUSHKAR

The name Pushkar means "lotus flower" and the tiny lake of the same name is said to have sprung from just such a flower dropped by Lord Brahma here. The legend has transformed the small town of Pushkar into one of the holiest places in the country. It features modest white houses and fresh green oasis vegetation, and is surrounded by an arc of mountains that gives it a truly majestic beauty (above).

"Little Varanasi" on Pushkar Lake is best visited in the early morning. The Savitri Temple on top of the hill is dedicated to Brahma's wife and affords superb views of the surrounding area. It takes about thirty minutes to reach the shrine on foot. In autumn, visitors come for the Pushkar Mela, a camel and cattle market (below) that is reminiscent of *One Thousand and One Nights* – a very special experience.

VARANASI

Varanasi (formerly called Benares) has been a documented Hindu pilgrimage site since as early as the 7th century. Most of the temples were built between the 16th and the 18th centuries and are dedicated to Shiva. Every day, pilgrims from around the world flock here to take a ritual cleansing bath in the Ganga River (or "Mother Ganga"), trek from temple to temple and pour the water from the Ganga over the lingam, Shiva's phallus symbol. Every Hindu is supposed to make a pilgrimage to Varanasi once in his or her life in order to achieve a better reincarnation or perhaps even the release of the soul from the circle of transmigrations. Life on the *ghats* is particularly lively in the early morning, when the sun lifts above the horizon. Stone staircases with a hundred steps each lead down to the river, religious tunes can be heard from the temples, and the faithful submerge themselves in the murky waters while muttering prayers and setting adrift sacrificial orange garlands of marigolds and oil lamps on the holy river.

Varanasi is also known as Kashi in India, meaning "City of Light" or the "Shining One". It is the holiest place in Hinduism as Shiva is said to have risen to heaven as a column of light after cleansing himself of his sins here. Many believers come not just to wash away their sins in the Ganga but also to die. Shiva, it is said, whispers into the ears of the dying and whoever dies in Varanasi is guaranteed salvation.

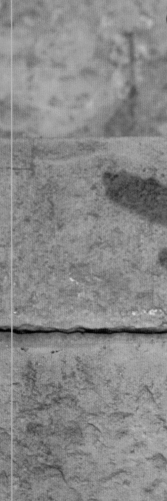

A sadhu on a *ghat* (step) in Varanasi: People who have devoted their lives to religion express their veneration of a divinity by wearing the tilaka or prayer marks on their forehead. The forehead, which is not soiled by any excretions, is considered by Hindus to be a particularly pure part of the body. The ritual forehead marks as well as the skin color of the main Hindu gods are deeply symbolic.

The temples of Khajuraho are lavishly decorated with reliefs and sculptures that are famous for their erotic and sexual themes (main pictures).

ELEPHANTA

The rock sanctuary of Elephanta is located on an island out in a bay near Mumbai (formerly Bombay) and is dedicated to the Hindu god Shiva. The refuge is famous for its exquisite stone reliefs that depict the powerful deity in his many incarnations. The sculptures in this 7th-century rock temple are among the best examples of early Hindu art. The 6-m-tall (20-ft) bust of Shiva Mahadeva is especially impressive, showing the god with three faces and wearing a splendid head decoration. Its dimensions are truly monumental.

Shiva, who, along with Brahma and Vishnu, is one of the most important gods in the Hindu pantheon, is known among other things as the god of creativity. He is worshipped in the form of the lingam (phallus), but is also known as the cosmic dancer, or Shiva Nataraja. He often appears with an entourage of creatures that are half divine and half demonic in nature. Like Shiva, these various figures are also represented in the sculptures at Elephanta.

SANCHI

The stupa or pilgrimage site of Sanchi includes some of the oldest Buddhist buildings in India. Legend has it that the complex was originally founded by Ashoka the Great (ruled 268–233 BC), an emperor who converted to Buddhism and then actively propagated the religion on the subcontinent. It is certain that at least some of the buildings were commissioned by him. The ruins were excavated and restored between 1912 and 1919.

The oldest Buddhist sanctuary in India, located north-east of Bhopal in Madhya Pradesh, was an important religious center up until the 12th century.

Highlights of the artisanship here can be seen in the magnificent masonry works around Stupa 1, which was built in the middle of the 3rd century BC. It is said to have been built over the bones of the Buddha himself.

The sanctuary is shaped like a semicircle and surrounded by a palisade through which access is gained via four mighty stone gates or torana, each facing one of the four directions of the compass. Built in the 1st century BC, they are decorated with reliefs that vividly illustrate scenes from the life of the Buddha. Aside from two more recent stupas, remains of several monasteries and other temple complexes have also been preserved.

The easterly shrine to Shiva was cut directly into the rock on Elephanta (left). He is depicted in several poses and with different expressions that represent his three faces as the Creator, the Preserver and the Destroyer.

KHAJURAHO

Khajuraho, in present-day Madhya Pradesh, is famous for the erotic motifs on the outside walls of its temples. The scenes of sexual intercourse that are depicted here symbolize fertility and the re-creation of the world.
Khajuraho is divided into distinct areas. In the village itself stands a group of Brahma, Vamana and Jawari temples while east of the village are Jain temples that are today still centers of an active cult.

Close attention to detail and liveliness mark the temple scenes of Khajuraho. The erotic and sexual themes symbolize the eternal cycle of birth and death.

In the 10th to 11th centuries, Khajuraho was the capital of the Chandela dynasty, a fact that is evident in the ensemble of Lakhshman, Kandariya, Vishvanath and Chitragupta temples. All the temples are built according to similar principles of construction, with their main axis oriented from east to west. In the west is the entrance gateway followed by a porch, main chamber, a vestibule and the sanctuary, or cella. The roof rises like a series of towers above the individual sections of the buildings, getting steadily higher toward the cella. The latter symbolizes the world mountain of Meru, the seat of the deity, and it holds the god's image, which faces east.

BODH GAYA

The first great empire in India's history was founded by Emperor Ashoka (272–231 BC). After converting to Buddhism, he built a temple on the very site where the Buddha had supposedly attained supreme enlightenment under a Bodhi tree. The present-day circular Mahabodhi Temple, a structure that was built later, measures about 50 m (164 ft) in height and was erected during the Gupta Dynasty (AD 320–540), when Buddhism was being promoted as the state

The Mahabodhi temple complex in the Indian state of Bihar is closely linked with the life of the Buddha and with the religious history of the country. Ten thousand pilgrims visit each year to celebrate there.

religion. Yet the Mahabodhi Temple is more than merely a great spiritual and national symbol. One of the oldest brick temple towers on the subcontinent, the structure also ranks as a significant feature in Indian architectural history. The elaborate stone reliefs and the delicately decorated balustrades are particularly impressive.
Even in its early days the temple was a popular pilgrimage destination, but when Hinduism slowly but surely began to displace Buddhism after the Gupta period, the sanctuary went into slow decline. The complex was first restored in the 19th century and a modern, scientifically methodical restoration began in February 2002.

Remains were found of Vijayanagara (main picture), the last capital of the Indian Hindu Empire before Islam prevailed, near Hampi, a little town in the federal state of Karnataka. The site abounds with opulently decorated buildings.

PATTADAKAL

In addition to the historical tolerance of Chalukya rulers, it is the inland location in the federal state of Karnataka in the border region between northern and southern India that has made Pattadakal into a melting pot of very diverse architectural styles. The northern Indian style, for example, is represented by the small Kashi Vishwanath Temple whose special feature is the structural unity of the shikhara tower and the cella, which is preceded by an entrance hall. The main cult image in the cella can only be walked around outside the building.

The southern Indian style, which was promoted as early as the 7th century among the Pallava rulers, is characterized by a corridor that was built around the cella. The temple room with its cult cell and the spacious entry hall open up toward each other across nearly the full width of the building. The best example of this is the Virupaksha Temple, the largest structure in Pattadakal and dedicated to the god Shiva. It is lavishly decorated with masterpieces of masonry.

HAMPI

This former capital, founded in the 14th century, is akin to an open-air museum of southern Indian architecture. It is surrounded by circular walls and includes a number of palaces and temples of the Dravidian princes.

The Vittala Temple, begun in the first half of the 16th century but never completed, is impressive thanks to a number of sculptures standing in front of the pillars and an 8-m-high (26-ft) temple chariot

All the temples and palaces feature ornamental elements, such as this frieze with figures (top). Particularly famous is the chariot (bottom) cut from a single block of granite in the temple district of Vijayanagar.

cut from a single block of stone. The highlight of the Virupaksha Temple, aside from its lavish figurative decoration, is the more than 50-m-high (164-ft) gopura (the gate tower typical of southern Indian architecture). Dedicated to the god Shiva, Virupaksha was built on a former place of worship from as early as the 9th century. While the temples are concentrated in the northern half of the town, the palaces are mostly concentrated in the southern half. It is here that Hindu princes had the walls of their palaces covered with impressive reliefs telling epic Indian tales such as the famous *Ramayana*.

The temples of Pattadakal are covered with lavish sculptural details (left). The largest sanctuary is the Virupaksha Temple (far left), which was built around 745 – twelve years before the demise of the Chalukya Dynasty.

KERALA (KOCHI)

The evergreen federal state of Kerala stretches for 550 km (342 mi) along the Malabar Coast where the Apostle Thomas is said to have gone ashore at Muziris in the year AD 52. In 1498, Portuguese navigator Vasco da Gama landed in Calicut, officially discovering the sea route to India for the Europeans. In around 1500, Cochin (now called Kochi) became the first European settlement in India. The harbor town is spread across several islands off the coast of its mainland sister city,

During the Theyyam Festival in Kochi, temple dancers from Kerala perform wearing colorful robes and artistic face paintings (top). Middle: A Keralan thali – an Indian meal – served on a banana leaf. Bottom: Fishing nets on the coast at Kochi.

Ernakulam. On the isle of Mattancherry, the St Francis Church was the first Christian church in India, built in 1510. Mattancherry Palace was built by the Portuguese in 1567. In 1663, the Dutch renovated the palace, which has been known as the "Dutch Palace" ever since. The adjoining Jewish quarter is usually very lively.

SUNDARBARNS NATIONAL PARK

Two exceptionally large rivers, the Ganges and the Brahmaputra, as well as their combined estuary region, the Meghna, form the natural basis for the Sundarbans. This rich wetland ecosystem is a transitional zone between salt-water and freshwater that offers an ideal habitat for a wide range of animals including the common otter, water snakes, tortoises, water monitors and crocodiles. It is also home to migratory birds such as storks, herons, cormorants, curlews, seagulls and terns. The surviving 250 Bengal tigers, smaller and with a more reddish coat than other tigers in India, kill chital deer and wild boar for prey – as well as the occasional human.

The Sundarbans in the Ganga-Brahmaputra Delta are the largest mangrove forest in the world and a sanctuary for the endangered Bengal tiger.

MANAS

This reservation in Assam, in the foothills of the Himalayas and close to the border with Bhutan, is named after the raging Manas River. Grassland makes up about sixty percent of the territory and it is home to, among other species, wild buffalo and the pygmy hog, considered extinct in Assam but then rediscovered in Manas. The swamp deer, or barasingha, the leopard cat and pangolins also find refuge here.

Grass savanna, forests and rivers also offer a habitat to a diverse range of bird species such as blue-breasted quail, drongo cuckoo and forest eagle owl. The park borders Royal Manas National Park in Bhutan.

Manas Game Reserve has populations of both golden langurs (inset, above left) and capped langurs, both leaf monkeys. After the elk and the red stag, the sambar is the largest deer species. During the day, it prefers to hide in the dense undergrowth, like here in the Kaziringa National Park (main picture).

KAZIRANGA NATIONAL PARK

The Kaziranga National Park in Assam is a veritable nature paradise. Its principal attractions are the Indian rhinoceroses that roam the grassland, but elephants and water buffalo are also at home here.

Kaziranga National Park is defined by the boisterous fluctuations of the Brahmaputra River. During the monsoon rains in July and August, two-thirds of the park are flooded on a regular basis. The animals are forced to escape to higher ground, sometimes outside the park.

Protection of the Indian rhinoceros has always been at the heart of animal conservation efforts here. As early as the early 19th century, its population was so severely decimated that no further hunting licenses were issued. In 1908, the area was declared a forest preserve. In 1950, it became a game reserve, and in 1974 a national park. Today, there are an estimated 1,500 rhinos. Animals from the park were recently resettled in the nearby Manas Game Reserve in order to renew the population there, but the park also boasts numerous elephants, buffalo and various types of deer. Gibbons, tigers and wild boar as well as rare birds such as Bengal floricans and spot-billed pelican also call it home. American black bears and sloth bears have also established a sanctuary for themselves here.

The Descent of Ganga (also known as *Arjuna's Penance*) is a massive bas-relief in the temple district of Mahabalipuram (main picture) that tells of the origins of the river Ganga. Shiva, who lets the river flow through his hair, is depicted in a rock crevice.

THANJAVUR

Southern India was ruled by the Chola dynasty from the 9th until about the 12th century. Thanjavur, which is roughly 350 km (217 mi) south of Chennai (Madras), was the capital of the Chola empire from 907 until the early 11th century. The Chola rulers built the town in the southern Indian style following the model of the Pallava princes from Mahabalipuram. The Brihadeeswarar Temple of Thanjavur, built by King RajaRaja Chola I and completed around 1010, is one of the most colossal building achievements of its day.

The temple tower above the cella, which was built from granite as a 13-story stepped pyramid and topped by a large headstone, rises to a height of more than 60 m (197 ft) and once boasted a gilded copper roof.

Like so many temples, the complex is dedicated to Shiva, the god of creation and destruction, obvious from the abundance of phallus symbols, the countless images of him, and the numerous depictions of Nandi, the bull and Shiva's personal mount.

MAHABALIPURAM

Unlike most conquerors, the Pallavan Prince Narasimhavarman I, who reigned from 625 to 645, also had quite a thirst for knowledge and scholarly pursuits. During the conquest of neighboring cities in the area, he became acquainted with the breathtaking architecture of the Chalukya rulers, and subsequently ordered that his own town, Mahabalipuram, be similarly beautified. Some of the most attractive structures of Dravidian archi-

One of the most impressive archeological sites in southern India is located some 50 km (31 mi) south of Chennai (Madras).

tecture were created at his behest, and their forms became the standard for architecture all over southern India.

As part of his experimentation with the different possibilities for cult worship architecture, Narasimhavarman had five rathas built. They were not temples in the true sense, but rather colossal sculptures cut straight from the bedrock. Ratha No. 1 still looked fairly plain, but Ratha No. 5 ultimately became the prototype for a number of Dravidian temples. It was in his wake that Narasimhavarman's successor had the coastal temple of Mahabalipuram built along the lines of the ratha model.

Impressively realistic stone sculptures greet visitors at Brihadishvara Temple in Thanjavur (left). The complex comprises a whole series of temples and halls, and is completely enclosed by a wall.

KONARAK

Surya, the sun god, together with Agni, the god of fire, and Indra, the god of thunder, formed a divine trinity as early as the Vedic period. Surya, for his part, has always been highly worshipped by Hindus as the giver of life, steering a chariot in heaven pulled by seven horses – much like Apollo in Greek mythology.

The temple in Konarak, with its 75-m-high (246-ft) pyramid-like Shikhara Tower and the cella below it, is an image of the chariot-turned-stone,

The gigantic sun wheel with its detailed decorations is one of the emblems of Konarak. Gods and female musicians also feature in the stories.

which the god drives across the firmament every day. The twelve wheels on the sides of the plinth symbolize the sun in two senses: the roundness of the wheels represents the basic shape of the sun, while the number of wheels symbolizes the twelve months needed for earth to orbit our central star.

While the walls of the temple were adorned with figures, the surfaces of the high plinth and the wheels are covered with detailed reliefs and artistic masonry right into the center of the wheel. Completed in the 13th century, the complex was abandoned shortly after for reasons unknown to science and history.

No other federal state in India has as many temples as Tamil Nadu (above: the Meenakshi Sundareshvara Temple in Madurai), and nowhere else do the gods reside in such splendor as here. Compared with this thousand-year-old cultural landscape, the old capital Chennai (formerly Madras) still seems relatively young. Near the sea is Fort St George, the first British fortification dating back to the year 1644. The Cauvery Delta is considered the rice bowl of India.

The tall towers of the Shri Meenakshi Temple in Madurai are visible from afar (main picture) and covered with colorful paintings of gods and demons.

The Temple of the Dancing Shiva in Chidambaram (above left) is said to have been founded as early as the year 500 by Brahmans from Kashmir. The present building, however, was not erected until 1000. The Sri Meenakshi Temple in Madurai (above right) is one of the largest temple complexes in India.

ANURADHAPURA, DAMBULLA, POLONNARUWA

ANURADHAPURA

The establishment of Anuradhapura as the first capital of the Singhalese kingdoms is linked to the story of a holy tree: In the year 244 BC, Sanghamitta, a Buddhist nun, brought to Sri Lanka the branch of a tree under which the Buddha once meditated on his path to enlightenment. The tree is now 2,200 years old and the oldest known Bodhi tree in the world.

The Isurumuniya rock temple also dates back to the original Bodhi branch. The laypeople who founded the sanctuary were so in awe of the miracles that took place during the planting of the branch that they had themselves ordained as monks. The temple houses one of the most beautiful reliefs in the country and the dome of the Ruwanveli Dagoba (2nd C. BC) is over 110 m (361 ft) high. The Abhayagiri Monastery dates back the first century BC while the Jetavana Dagoba goes back to the 4th century. The latter is the largest stupa in the world – just under 130 m (427 ft) high. Another lovely statue of the Samadhi Buddha is also from that period.

The five cave temples of Dambulla in central Sri Lanka date back to the origins of Lankan Buddhism and feature hundreds of statues and frescoes (main picture).

DAMBULLA

The first of three documented periods of construction on the slopes of the "Black Rock" began in the early 1st century BC under King Vattagamani Abhaya, who had fled Anuradhapura before the second large influx of Tamil people. During his fourteen years in exile, he found refuge in Dambulla in the granite rock caves where a number of temples were built. The sanctuary was then forgotten and not rediscovered until the 12th century, when it was expanded during the second period of construction.

No fewer than 154 Buddha statues have been counted in the richly adorned cave temples of Dambulla, including some meditating and some reclining Buddhas.

The third period came during the reign of King Sri Kirti Rajasinha in the late 18th century.

The first cave, the "Cave of the Divine King" (Devaraja Vihara), has a stunning, 14-m-long (46-ft) reclining Buddha. The largest cave, the "Temple of the Great Kings" (Maharaja Vihara), boasts a number of statues and paintings of outstanding quality. The "Great New Monastery" (Maha Alut Vihara) is the third cave and was commissioned by King Sri Kirti Rajasinha. The fourth is the oldest, dating back to the 1st century BC, and the fifth temple was more recently renovated in the style of 1820.

The "*Reclining Buddha*" at Isurumuniya Monastery was probably created in the 7th or 8th century (left).

POLONNARUVA

The medieval royal residence in northern central Sri Lanka is home to some important buildings and excellent examples of Singhalese sculpture. Polonnaruwa first became the seat of the government in the 8th century. Then, in 1017, when Anuradhapura was destroyed, it was declared the permanent capital, after which it was ruled by both Indian and Singhalese kings. The most important Singhalese ruler was Parakramabahu I (1153–86) during whose reign temples, schools, hospitals, irrigation systems and a magnificent palace were built. The

The former royal city of Polonnaruwa features some outstanding examples of Singhalese sculpture, inlcuding the impressive monumental statues of the Buddha (above). The reclining Buddha (top) here is 14 m (46 ft) long and a masterpiece of stone masonry.

city was ultimately abandoned in the 13th century.

The palace complex was also built during the golden age of Polonnaruwa, under Parakramabahu I, and includes the King's Council Chamber, the Royal Bathing Pool, the Vatadage (a circular relic house), the "Moonstone" (a half-moon-shaped stone slab), the Atadage or "House of Eight Relics", the 55-m-high (9-ft) Ruwanveli Seya, and the Thuparama Dagoba. Four large figures of the Buddha have been preserved in the Gal Vihara rock shrine – they are were carved straight out of the granite wall.

The fortress of the kings of Anuradhapura rests high upon on the Sigiriya, or "Lion's Rock", which rises straight out of the tropical vegetation. As can be seen from the majestic and impressively well-preserved frescoes that line the path leading up the steep hill, it was built as both a defensive structure and a royal pleasure palace. The scenes depict divine nymphs, women with fashionable haircuts and opulent jewelry.

The path to the summit originally began at the Lion's Gate, of which today only the gigantic paws remain. The citadel itself is but a ruin these days, but it is still easy to make out what is left of the chambers, baths, bridges, gardens and fountains that once adorned the complex. Planned in the 5th century by King Dhatusena, Sigiriya was actually inhabited by his son Kassapa, who usurped the royal throne by killing his father and expelling his half-brother Moggallana. The return of Moggallana eighteen years later led to a decisive battle during which Kassapa took his own life.

The kings of Anuradhapura built their mountain fortress and capital city atop the "Lion's Rock", the entrance to which was adorned with awe-inspiring lion paws. The path that leads up to the island fortress features numerous depictions of elegantly adorned, bare-breasted women and represents the apex of ancient Indian painting. These Apsaras, or divine nymphs, are shown emerging from the clouds scattering flowers to greet the mighty king.

The fortress is situated on top of a 200-m-high (656-ft), heavily weathered and degraded volcano (main picture). The path to the top leads through crags and along catwalks and staircases (above).

KANDY

The upper floor of the two-story "Temple of the Tooth" (main picture) houses a shrine with a very important relic – one of Buddha's teeth. According to legend, four teeth and a collarbone were saved from the ashes when the body of the religious leader Siddhartha Gautama was cremated in 480 BC. Many myths are woven around the subsequent odyssey these relics experienced. The tooth in Kandy, for example, is said to have been taken to Sri Lanka concealed in the hair of a Buddhist nun.

The highpoint of the Perahara Kandy, a two-week celebration that takes place every year in July/August in honor of the relic, features a great festival procession with musicians and dancers, whip crackers, acrobats and torchbearers as well as many splendidly caparisone elephants (left).

KATHMANDU

From left to right: Six Buddha figures, their right hands touching the earth, sitting at the entrance to the Temple of Swayambunath; the Golden Temple in Patan, founded in the 11th century; Durbar Square, bordered by the Archeological Museum and the Degutale Temple.

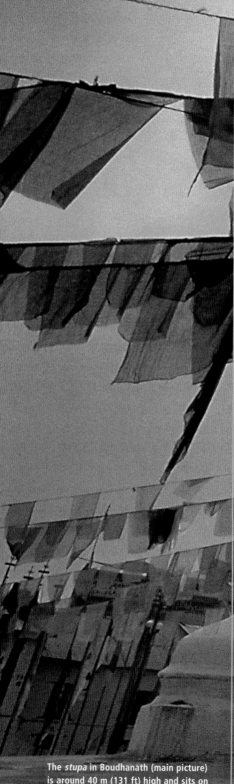

The *stupa* in Boudhanath (main picture) is around 40 m (131 ft) high and sits on a dome that in turn stands on three accessible plinths.

356 **Asia** | Nepal

The fascinating ambience of the Kathmandu Valley is difficult to describe, but the pagoda-like roofs of the palaces, temples and houses, the wealth of exquisite carvings, and the opulence of the golden treasures in the temples all contribute greatly to the place. It is the whole package here that is so stunning, manifested in an atmosphere created by the inhabitants long before the first capital was founded in 723. Nepal's capital, the royal city of Kathmandu, is at an elevation of 1,300 m (4,265 ft) and is the focal point of the valley. Situated at the confluence of the Bagmati and Vishnumati rivers, Kathmandu was an important trading center as early as the 10th century and one which, in competition with Patan and Bhaktapur, developed into one of Nepal's religious, cultural and political hubs before ultimately becoming the sole royal city.

The heart of the city is formed by Durbar Square, which the Nepalese call "Hanuman Dhoka". It is the site of Buddhist and Hindu temples and shrines as well as the home of the former royal palace. The Malla kings and the kings of the Shah Dynasty resided here for centuries. The Boudhanath stupa, the largest sanctuary for Tibetan Nepalese people, is about 5 km (3 mi) outside of the heart of the city. The fascinating Swayambuna temple complex is situated in the north-west of the Old Town and is well worth a visit.

The highest mountain on earth is known to the Nepalese as Sagarmatha, or "Goddess of the Skies". The Tibetans call the mountain Chomolungma, "Mother Goddess of the Universe". Sagarmatha National Park, founded in 1976, not only contains three of the world's 8,000-m (26,000-ft) peaks (Mount Everest, Lhotse and Cho Oyu), but also has a number of 7,000-m (22,000-ft) and 6,000-m (19,0006-ft) summits.

The mountain's southern slopes are only snow-free for a short period in summer, a time when a variety of carnations, gentians and cruciferous plants blossom at elevations of up to 6,000 m (19,686 ft). Only very undemanding soil fungi are able to survive in the higher zones, while alpine plants such as edelweiss, irises and shrubs flourish in the lower regions. Deciduous and coniferous forests reach elevations of up to 4,000 m (13,124 ft). The national park is inhabited by some thirty mammal species and the skies are ruled by majestic raptors. The existence of the Yeti, however, still remains to be proven.

A breathtaking mountain landscape greets visitors in Sagarmatha National Park (main picture). In addition to the well-used southern route, a northern route from China takes mountaineers via the Rongbuk Valley to the top of Mount Everest (left) at 8,850 m (29,037 ft). Right: A view of Mount Everest and Lhotse from the Khumbu Valley.

MANDALAY

Buddha himself is said to have predicted that Mandalay would one day become a hub not only of Burmese culture but also of Buddhism. Legend has it that he and his student, Ananda, once visited Mandalay Hill where they encountered a female demon upon whom the Enlightened One made such an impression that she cut off her breasts with the intention of giving them to Buddha. The latter is alleged to have smiled and, pointing to the foot of the hill, said: "There, one day, 2,400 years after my death, a descendant of this demon will found a city that will blossom into a center of my teaching". In accordance with this prophecy, King Mindon laid the foundation stone for a new city, Mandalay, in February 1857, and it was to be the capital of the Burmese kingdom until 1885. The city was largely destroyed during World War II and though parts of the former royal palace were later restored, they were not entirely true to the original (above).

Main picture: A reclining Buddha in the Shwesandaw Pagoda in Bagan. As a neighbor of India, the territory of present-day Myanmar fell under Buddhist influence early on.

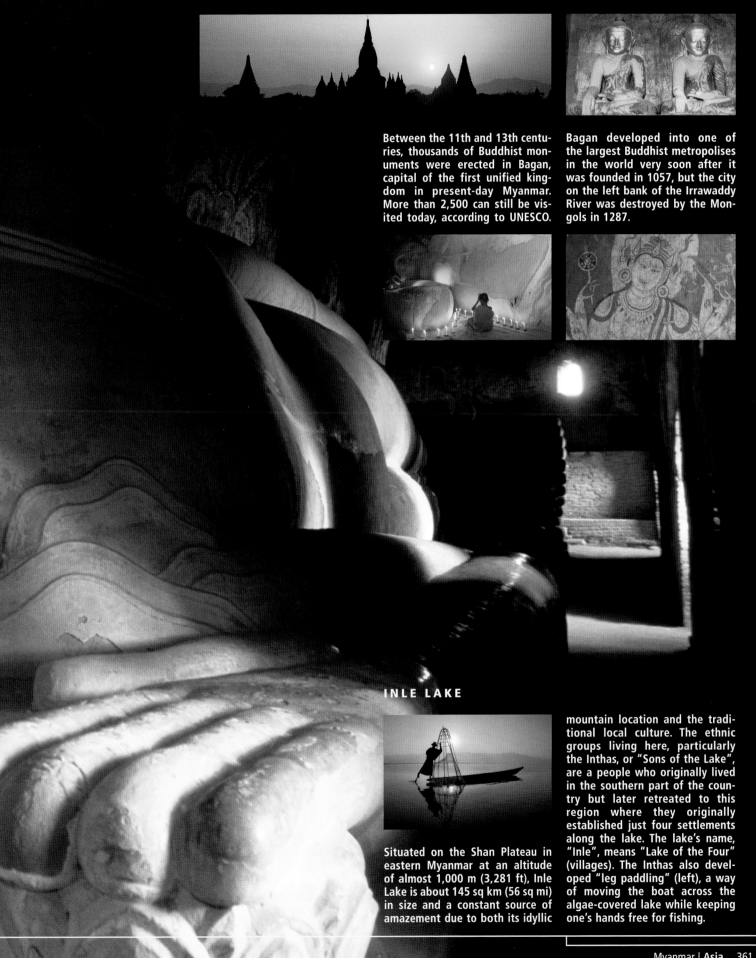

Between the 11th and 13th centuries, thousands of Buddhist monuments were erected in Bagan, capital of the first unified kingdom in present-day Myanmar. More than 2,500 can still be visited today, according to UNESCO.

Bagan developed into one of the largest Buddhist metropolises in the world very soon after it was founded in 1057, but the city on the left bank of the Irrawaddy River was destroyed by the Mongols in 1287.

INLE LAKE

Situated on the Shan Plateau in eastern Myanmar at an altitude of almost 1,000 m (3,281 ft), Inle Lake is about 145 sq km (56 sq mi) in size and a constant source of amazement due to both its idyllic

mountain location and the traditional local culture. The ethnic groups living here, particularly the Inthas, or "Sons of the Lake", are a people who originally lived in the southern part of the country but later retreated to this region where they originally established just four settlements along the lake. The lake's name, "Inle", means "Lake of the Four" (villages). The Inthas also developed "leg paddling" (left), a way of moving the boat across the algae-covered lake while keeping one's hands free for fishing.

KYAIKTIYO PAGODA

The small town of Kyaiktiyo in southern Myanmar is perched precariously atop Golden Rock Mountain at a height of 1,100 m (3,609 ft). Legend has it that a reliquary in the pagoda on top of the gilded granite formation (above) contains one hair of Buddha and it is this single hair that ensures the necessary balance to keep the rock from falling. Buddha himself is said to have given the reliquary containing the hair to a hermit who once lived in the mountains here and allegedly kept it in a topknot on his head. The hair was later placed in the pagoda on the rock, which is reminiscent of a human skull. In the Mon language "Kyaiktiyo Pagoda" means "the pagoda on the hermit's head" and designates what is today one of the country's most important Buddhist pilgrimage destinations.

SHWEDAGON PAGODA

The most important religious site in Myanmar is the Shwedagon Pagoda in Yangon, built on a hill north of the historical heart of the former capital. The origins of the 116-m-high (381-ft) structure, which has been decorated time and again with gold and precious stones over the centuries, are said to go back to the era of the Buddha, Siddhartha Gautama (ca. 560 to 480 BC). Apparently, the pagoda contains eight hairs from his head. The building stands on a marble platform measuring 60,000 sq m (645,600 sq ft), with numerous small pagodas scattered around its octagonal base, which has a circumference of 413 m (4,445 sq ft). Its canopied roof is made of gilded mesh decorated with thousands of precious stones, at the top of which is a 76-carat diamond symbolizing enlightenment.

Burmese writer Khin Myo Chit claimed that it is impossible to stand near the Kyaiktiyo Pagoda and not be moved. Pilgrims visiting the site bring small leaves of gold with them, which they then paste onto the holy Golden Rock (main picture).

Lake Baikal can make many claims: It is the planet's deepest freshwater lake, has the greatest volume of water, and is the oldest lake in the world, created around 25 million years ago. Main picture: Peschanaya Bay.

ALTAI

Russia's Altai Republic in southern Siberia is part of a mountain system in Asia that also includes the Mongolian and the Gobi Altai Mountains. A total of three separate Altai regions have been joined together to make a UNESCO World Heritage site within the republic: the Altai Nature Reserve, which forms a buffer zone around Lake Teletskoye, which is 80 km long (50 mi); the Katunski Nature Reserve which contains Mount Belukha; and the Ukok Plateau.

From the steppes up to the alpine zone, Altai boasts the most comprehensive sequence of vegetation zones in all of Central Siberia. The plant diversity is enormous, with more than 2,000 genera having been identified, including 212 endemic plant species. The diverse animal world is characteristic of the Siberian forest fauna with over seventy mammal, 300 bird, eleven reptile and amphibian, and more than twenty fish species. Some of the indigenous mammals and many of the bird species are listed as endangered in Russia.

LAKE BAIKAL

Baikal, with a length of almost 650 km (404 mi) and an average width of almost 50 km (31 mi), is situated in southern Siberia near the city of Irkutsk. This seismically active zone experiences frequent earthquakes but also features some splendid resorts around the hot springs that rise from fissures on the lakeshore.

In Buryat, Baikal means "Rich lake", a name that aptly describes

Lena National Park (top) and Peschanaya Bay (middle) on Lake Baikal offer a tranquil and largely untouched natural environment. The rose variety Sibbaldia altaica (bottom) is one of the flowers that blossoms here.

the diverse plant and animal world both in and around the body of water. More than 1,200 animal species have been identified in the lake alone. The majority of the diverse fauna is endemic, such as the Baikal Seal and the Golomyanka, a fish that gives birth to live offspring. Some 600 plant species grow in the area and on the shores of Lake Baikal.

The magnificently remote region around the 4,506-m-high (14,784-ft) Mount Belukha on the Russian-Kazakh border (left) has pristine lakes such as Ak-Kam (far left).

Kamchatka lies in a subduction zone where the Pacific Plate pushes under the Eurasian Plate, a region that is part of the volcanic chain known as the Pacific Ring of Fire. It is home to a number of active stratovolcanoes such as Avachinsky (main picture).

KAMCHATKA

The Kamchatka Peninsula extends over a length of 1,200 km (746 mi) and is up to 480 km (298 mi) wide. It is situated between the Sea of Okhotsk in the west and the Pacific Ocean and the Bering Sea in the east, and is traversed by two parallel mountain ranges that are divided by the Kamchatka River Valley. The west or central range is dominated by extinct volcanoes, while the east range transforms into a plateau with a number of active volcanoes. Above: Karymsky volcano. Above right: Kronotsky volcano.

The west coast features expansive marshlands while the east is characterized by steep cliffs. The lower-lying zones are mostly covered with deciduous forest, the region providing a habitat for many primeval indigenous plants. Its geographic location across the Pacific from the Americas meant that Kamchatka was a prohibited area until the end of the Cold War in 1990. This period provided ideal conditions for the local animal population to thrive relatively undisturbed. Its most spectacular representative is the Kamchatka brown bear (below, both photos), a subspecies of the brown bear that thoroughly enjoys the plentiful berries and fresh salmon on the peninsula.

WRANGEL ISLAND

them unique. Its mountainous terrain meant that it was never entirely covered in glaciers during the Ice Age, the result of which is that many plant and animal species exist here where elsewhere they have become extinct. Wrangel Island consequently has more than 400 species and subspecies of vascular plants alone, twice as many as in any other tundra region of comparable size. These also include twenty-three indigenous species that are the result of recent hybridization. The island is home to the world's largest population of Pacific walrus, numbering up to 100,000 specimens, and boasts the greatest density of polar bear caves in the world. Musk oxen also graze in the Arctic tundra landscape. Gray whales come here from Mexico to feed in these rich waters, and around 100 migrant bird species come here to breed. The large number of lemmings exhibit behavioral patterns that set them apart from other Arctic populations, while the reindeer have also adapted to the environmental conditions.

Wrangel Island – named after the Baltic German admiral and Siberian explorer Ferdinand von Wrangel – is situated well north of the Arctic Circle on the western edge of Chukchi Sea. It boasts a great diversity of geological formations and habitats, each with differing microclimates that make

ORCHON VALLEY

This valley lies in the Changai Mountains, the so-called cradle of the Mongolian nation. During the 13th and 14th centuries, Kharkhorin (Karakorum in English) was the capital of the Mongolian empire, from which the khans who descended from Genghis Khan (1155–1227) once ruled over a vast world empire. The Orkhon Valley had actually been settled much earlier, however, and is said to have been a political hub for large parts of Central Asia since the sixth century, during which time symbiotic relationships developed between the nomadic tribes and the political, religious and cultural centers. The region is still inhabited by nomads.

Nomads with their animals move from place to place across the Uvs Nuur Basin (main picture), a region named after the Uvs Nuur salt lake in northern Mongolia.

UVS NUUR BASIN

The Uvs Nuur region extends as far as the autonomous Republic of Tuva in Russia. It measures over 600 km (373 mi) from west to east and over 160 km (99 mi) from north to south. What makes it so extraordinary is the fact that all of Central Asia's major ecosystems are represented in this comparatively small area: wetlands, desert, various steppe formations and forest types, rivers, freshwater lakes, alpine habitats

The *berkutchi* (Kazakh "eagle men") in western Mongolia hunt with female golden eagles (top) that are larger and more aggressive than their male counterparts. They capture the females as young chicks in order to tame them as they grow to full size, when they weigh up to 7 kg (15 lbs). Their eyesight is about eight times stronger than that of humans. Nomads live in traditional yurts (bottom) when they are on the move.

and permafrost. The national park also includes bizarre, often pillow-shaped, weathered mountains, cliffs and granite rocks.
The region's grasslands have been used for thousands of years by nomads living in yurts. Due to its ecological consistency the Uvs Nuur Basin is also used for monitoring global warming and climate change. The different ecosystems include many indigenous plants and invertebrate animals.

The Orchon (far left) is Mongolia's lifeline. Archaeologists have excavated decorative artifacts such as these stone tortoises (left) as well as golden adornments and various seals (center). The Erdene Zuu monastery (opposite page), begun in 1586, is also in the Orchon Valley.

BEIJING

The Chinese empire was ruled from Beijing's Forbidden City for nearly 400 years until 1911 when republican opposition movements triggered the demise of the monarchy. The emperor once occupied the Dragon Throne in the Hall of Supreme Harmony (main picture). The last emperor had to leave the palace in 1924, which now serves as a museum.

Beijing, which means "northern capital", was founded during the Jin Dynasty (1115–1234) before being laid to waste and rebuilt by the Mongols. The city was then once again built up by the Ming emperors between 1368 and 1420 based on plans from the original city. The town was to be a mirror image of the cosmos, whose laws were reflected in the city's layout. The old city center is formed by the Forbidden City, which straddles Beijing's main north-south axis. The modern center of Beijing is dominated by the vast Square of Heavenly Peace, named after the Gate of Heavenly Peace

(Tiananmen), and is just to the south. It was here that Mao Zedong proclaimed the People's Republic of China in 1949. On the square stand the Monument to the People's Heroes and the Mao Zedong Memorial Hall. On the western side it is bordered by the Great Hall of the People, and on the eastern side by the Museum of Chinese History and the Museum of the Chinese Revolution. When the square was built in 1958, it gave the capital city a socialist heart, a sort of "state cathedral".
Outside the Forbidden City is Chang'an Avenue, which runs

from east to west across the city. The 40-km (25-mi) road is roughly 120 m (394 ft) wide at Tiananmen Square and was another of Mao Zedong's projects from the 1950s. Today, the glamorous boulevard is lined with government buildings, multinational company headquarters and modern hotels.
The inner-city districts essentially make up the historic center. So-called "hutong", houses built around courtyards and narrow alleyways, once characterized the older neighborhoods. Now only a few of them remain, for example around the Drum Tower, and these have been fully restored. Most

were demolished to make room for new roads and massive residential blocks. At the beginning of the socialist era, many inner-city districts were also peppered with iron and steel works, car and machine manufacturing facilities, locomotive and train car plants, and factories for the production of electronics and agricultural machines. These dramatic construction projects were meant to transform the bourgeois consumer town of the imperial age into a productive modern city. The result was that Beijing developed into the largest industrial center in China.

The historic ring of fortifications around the center was sacrificed for the enlargement of the city and construction of new roads, but the main axes of the road network follow the wall's former course, giving you an idea of the extent of the old imperial plan. Beijing also boasts a number of large parks. One of the best-known and largest – covering an area of 270 ha (667 acres) – is the park that houses the Temple of Heaven (Tian Tan), which contains the Hall of Prayer for Good Harvest and the Altar of Heaven. Both were built at the beginning of the 15th century.

For the Summer Olympic Games in 2008, the city's infrastructure was once again dramatically transformed, the most prominent new architectural feature being the national stadium. Designed by Swiss architects Herzog & de Meuron, it is 330 m (1,083 ft) long, 220 m (722 ft) wide, 69 m (227 ft) tall and has capacity for around 80,000 spectators. The stadium is north of the city about 9 km (6 mi) along the extension of the Forbidden City's northern axis in the Olympic Park, which was also newly constructed for the Games and covers an area of 800 ha (1,977 acres).

Insets, from left to right: The Imperial Palace, protected by a moat; the Gate of Heavenly Peace that led to the palace; the Hall of Prayer for Good Harvest, in the Temple of Heaven; the Zhichun Pavilion in Empress Cixi's Summer Palace, located on an island in Kunming Lake – a masterpiece of Chinese garden and landscape architecture near Beijing.

THE GREAT WALL OF CHINA

The original Great Wall – Wanli Chang Cheng – was built in the 5th century BC and largely made of clay. The brick reinforcement came later (main picture).

First mention of the building of a "long wall" on China's northern border was made in 214 BC. The territory had been united shortly before that by the Emperor Qin Shi Huang and the wall was intended to keep the nomadic people of the north at bay. Indeed, the problem of protecting Chinese interests became a recurring theme over the 1,900 years that followed.

The fortifications eventually fell into disrepair and were rebuilt on several occasions over the centuries. During the Ming Dynasty, in the 15th and 16th centuries, the wall was not only repaired but expanded to become a larger and more solid construction than ever before. The result is what we see today: a 6,000-km (3,728-mi) colossus, 2,000 km (1,243 mi) of

which are an average of 7-10 m (23-26 ft) high and 6 m (6.5 yds) wide between the Bohai Sea and the Yellow River. The watchtowers also served as soldiers' quarters and enabled the rapid communication of messages by means of beacons. The best-preserved and/or restored section of the wall is to be found near Badaling, north-west of Beijing.

With a length of more than 6,000 km (3,728 mi), the Great Wall (left near Jinshanling) is the largest structure on Earth. It was modified repeatedly for nearly 2,000 years. Ironically, the wall was never really able to protect the empire from attack.

The impressive temple inside the imperial summer palace grounds near Chengde is the Temple of Sumeru, Happiness and Longevity (main picture). It was built by Emperor Qianlong in 1780 as a copy of the ancestral seat of the sixth Panchen Lama in Tibet.

PING YAO

Originally founded in pre-Christian times, Ping Yao's real rise to dominance and major expansion took place in the 14th century. Today it is considered a prime example of Chinese architecture from the Ming and Qing eras, with the urban developments of more than six centuries clearly visible.

The historical heart of Ping Yao was enclosed in 1370 by an imposing, 12-m-high (39-ft) city wall that averages a width of 5 m (16 ft). Forming a gigantic square with an overall length of more than 6 km (4 mi), it contains an elaborate ensemble of established shopping streets with well-preserved commercial and banking buildings that provide an insight into everyday life and commerce in ancient China.

Ping Yao owed its wealth to these merchants and banks and consequently declined in significance when the trading routes were altered towards the end of the 19th century. The Old Town and the walls were fortunately spared the destructive effects of modernization.

CHENGDE

It was in Chengde – on the way to the imperial hunting grounds – that the Manchu emperors found refuge from the summer heat in Beijing. The abundance of water allowed them to build an extravagant garden landscape to offset the palace buildings, which were of a more modest design than those in Beijing.

Magnificent Buddhist temples and monasteries were later built outside the roughly 5 sq km (2 sq mi) of walled palace grounds. The central hall of the Temple of Universal Peace houses a 22-m (72-ft) statue with 42 arms depicting Guanyin, the Goddess of Mercy (above).

YUNGANG

The emperors of the Wei Dynasty established Buddhism as the official religion, but Emperor Tai Wudi suddenly banned it in 446 for fear of it threatening his authority. He died unexpectedly shortly thereafter. His grandson, Wen Chengdi, saw this as a sign from heaven and had the Yungang Grottoes carved out of the rocks in the Wuzhou Mountains. Today the 252 Yungang Grottoes are the largest man-made caves in the world. Some of the statues of Buddha (above) even bear the facial features of the Wei emperors.

Black brick buildings characterize the Old Town in Ping Yao (far left), once one of China's most important financial centers. A sentinel statue (left) protects the Shuangli Temple about 5 km (3 mi) outside of town where a number of vibrant Buddha, warrior and monk sculptures are on display.

MOGAO

For more than a thousand years, merchants, generals, wealthy widows and simple monks alike gathered in the prosperous oasis of Dunhuang to convey their prayers, gratitude, and hopes of salvation to the deities of the day by carving grottoes into a nearby cliff and decorating them with scenes from the life of Buddha Gautama. Their offerings included images of paradise, worldly scenes and elaborate ornaments. The result of their efforts has today become the largest collection of Buddhist imagery in the world. In 1900 a Taoist monk discovered a walled-up library in grotto No. 17 with more than 50,000 manuscripts dating from the 4th to the 10th centuries.

YIN XU

Yin Xu was the capital of the late Shang Dynasty from around 1300 to 1066 BC. Yin went into rapid decline following the dynasty's demise and became Yin Xu, the ruined city, where jade workshops, bronze foundries, palaces, tombs as well as countless labelled bones have been found. The area measures around 30 sq km (12 sq mi) and encompasses sections to the north and south of the Yellow River. The most significant find is the grave of Fu Hao, the only one of the Shang dynasty to have been preserved in its entirety.

The most impressive tomb in China was only discovered in 1974, that of Emperor Qin Shi Huang, who was buried there more than 2,000 years ago surrounded by thousands of individually designed terracotta statues depicting a mighty army and his royal court (main picture).

THE TOMB OF CHINA'S FIRST EMPEROR

LONGMEN

Immediately after having united the territory, China's first emperor, Qin Shi Huang, began construction of his own burial site. It was to be one befitting of his station and located some 30 km (19 mi) north-east of Xi'an, then the imperial capital and a major center on the Silk Route. The fact that the tomb comprised more than just the prominent burial mound became evident only in 1974, when farmers digging for water came across fragments of the larger of the warrior statues. They form just part of a still unfinished excavation of an army of about 7,600 soldiers. Arranged in underground chambers, the army was intended to protect both the tomb and empire of the deceased emperor from evil forces in the afterlife, as well as document the emperor's elevated status.

Over 2,000 grottoes and niches line the steep slopes of Dragon Mountain above the Yi River in Hénán Province. Covering a distance of about 1 km (0.6 mi), the grottoes served as a cult worship site and contain a number of valuable inscriptions as well as more than 100,000 stone Buddhist statues and elaborately carved ceilings and wall decorations.

Construction of the grotto sanctuaries was begun by the rulers of the Northern Wei Dynasty in 494, after they had officially made the ancient Buddhist seat of Luoyang their capital. The early Guyang Caves, which date from 495 to 499, and the Binyang Caves from 500 to 532, have also been nicely preserved. In the centuries that followed, the cave complex was further expanded under the rulers of the Sui and Tang Dynasties in what is now considered the golden age of Buddhism. The Fengxian Grotto, which is the largest of the caves, is located in the western portion of the site and was built by the later Empress Wu between 672 and 675.

The enchanting Wudang Mountains with their glorious 72 peaks have been referred to as some of the holiest mountains on earth. The numerous temples, monasteries, shrines, grottoes and hermitages include the Monastery of Supreme Harmony (main picture).

IMPERIAL BURIAL SITES OF THE MING AND QING DYNASTIES

The royal burial sites of the Ming and Qing dynasties, from 1368–1644 and 1644–1911, respectively, represent more than five hundred years of feudal Chinese rule, the prevailing world view of those times, and the overwhelming power of the emperors. The Xianling Mausoleum in Hubei Province, for example, is the largest single Ming tomb and contains both the old and new burial chambers. Emperor Jiajing, who ruled from 1521–1567, had his father's grave converted into a large tomb complex comprising a total of thirty buildings. The imposing Qing dynasty tombs are located at two sites, each about 100 km (62 mi) from Beijing. The eastern group of Qing Dynasty tombs near Zunhua were consecrated in 1663 and consist of fifteen graves. The western portion was built in 1723 south-west of Beijing, near Baoding. The actual sites, chosen by Feng Shui masters, are situated in remote and very picturesque mountain regions.

WUDANG

Taoist hermits began retreating to this remote but not inhospitable mountain region in north-west Hubei Province at the latest during the Eastern Han Era, (AD 25–220). During the Tang Era, from 618 to 907, legends that the Emperor of the Northern Heaven had once lived here inspired the monks to establish the monasteries that ultimately transformed the Wudang Mountains into a popular pilgrimage destination.

In 1214, motivated by political aims, the third emperor of the Ming dynasty, Yongle, began building new monasteries of palatial

Pilgrims typically head to the monastery town on the summit of Tianzhu at 1,612 m (5,289 ft) (top) with the Golden Hall (bottom), which houses the statues of the warrior king Zhen Wun as well as sculptures of the Taoist immortals.

proportions. They were elaborately decorated and required the efforts of some 300,000 workers. A total of 129 of the religious sites survived, albeit mostly as ruins, including ten imperial palaces, another eight main monasteries, twenty cliff temples and twenty-three stone bridges. Visitors and pilgrims head for the summit of Tianzhu at 1,612 m (5,289 ft), the region's highest mountain, and the Golden Hall, a 14-sq-m (151-sq-ft) structure built entirely of bronze.

Only three tombs of Ming Dynasty emperors are open to visitors, including the Changling complex (left) with the 15th-century tomb of Emperor Yongle, which took eighteen years to complete. The most compact Ming grave complex in China (far left) lies in a valley of the Tianshou Mountains near Beijing.

The Huangshan Mountains comprise one of the most famous regions in China. The bizarre cliff shapes and gnarled pines (main picture) embody the traditional Chinese landscape.

SUZHOU

Situated just to the west of Shanghai, Suzhou owes much of its prosperity to the Grand Canal, the longest artificial river in the world. The numerous waterways, some spanned by old stone bridges, are still an important means of transport within the city today. Suzhou is primarily known for its gardens, however, which help to preserve some of the atmosphere of the old city with their ponds, creative rock formations and highly symbolic yet sparing vegetation. The Garden of the Surging Wave on the Canglang Canal, for example, dates from 1044 and its name is a literary allusion to the prevailing corruption. The Humble Administrator's Garden, built in 1509, is considered the most representative garden of the Ming Era and extends over some 4 ha (10 acres). The Lion Grove (ca. 1342) owes its name to the bizarre stone shapes that are found there. The Lingering Garden, built in 1522 and redesigned in about 1770, is just half a hectare (1.2 acres) in size but is one of Suzhou's most popular destinations.

HUANGSHAN

"Anyone who has ever seen Huangshan will never need to regret not seeing another mountain range," says a Chinese proverb referring to the mountains that have inspired painters and poets throughout the ages. Covering a surprisingly small area of less than 150 sq km (58 sq mi), the Huangshan Range (or Yellow Mountain) in Anui Province boasts seventy-seven peaks from 1,000 to 1,849 m (3,281 to 6,067 ft).

The Huangshan Mountains include the Capital of Heaven Peak (above) and the Lotus Peak, reached via the Hundred-Steps-to-the-Clouds (top).

The mist that fills the steep canyons on around 250 days of the year is so thick that from above the landscape looks like a sea spotted with islands. Over the centuries, a number of pavilions have been built in order to enjoy the beautiful scenery that has come to embody the Chinese landscape ideal. The Huangshan aesthetic, which had a strong influence on China's classic scholarly culture, is perfected by the ancient pines growing out of the rock crevasses.

With its many canals and bridges, Suzhou is also known as the Venice of the East (middle). Numerous pagodas have been built in the many famous gardens, the loveliest of which include The Humble Administrator's Garden (far left) and the Garden of the North Temple (left).

LUSHAN

Few mountains have had their praises sung as often as Lushan. Almost all important Chinese poets have revered it with a visit, leaving behind inscriptions alongside those of philosophers, painters, monks and politicians. The "mountain of the supernatural being" has also long been a popular pilgrimage site for Taoists and Buddhists. Its lakes, waterfalls, forests and cliffs meant it was predestined for summer breaks. Often shrouded in mist, the mountain influenced the

The enchanting beauty of Lushan Mountain (bottom) with its temples and pagodas high above the Yangtze is considered to be the birthplace of Chinese landscape painting.

Chinese landscape aesthetic early on, much like Huangshan. It was here in the 12th century that Zhu Xi (1130–1200), the most influential supporter of Neo-Confucian philosophy, taught at the Bailudong Academy, an important institution in China's feudal culture for hundreds of years. The temple monasteries at the base of the 1,400-m (4,593-ft) peak include the Donglin Monastery, which was founded in 384 by the monk Huiyuan as the seat of the Buddhist Jing Tu School.

The Bund, an embankment in the old city center, offers a view of the Pudong skyscrapers (main picture). Not only is Shanghai growing horizontally, engulfing the Yangtze Kiang Delta; it is also expanding vertically, with the number of high-rise buildings and skyscrapers increasing on a daily basis.

Shanghai roughly means "up or above the sea" due to its position at the confluence of two rivers at the coast. The Bund (above) is the embankment in the historical center of Shanghai. The city is home to China's most famous shopping mile, Nanjing Lu (left), and was once no more than a mooring place for junks that was then enclosed by a protective wall in the 16th century. Today a ring road still follows the oval outline of the wall. The Yu Garden in the northern part of the Old Town Nanshi is worth a visit. Modern Shanghai dates back to the Treaty of Nanjing (1842), which granted the right of domicile to Europeans. Below is one of the spectacular flyover constructions on the Huangpu River meant to cope with ever increasing traffic from the Old Town to new Shanghai. Shanghai has become an important port town with multinational companies, banks, villas, factories and artisan quarters. The Huangpu District is on the north side of the Old Town and contains a number of interesting historical colonial buildings along the Bund. Above is the façade of the city museum.

WUYI

WULINGYUAN

The biodiversity of the ancient subtropical forests in the Wuyi region makes it a paradise for rare plants and animals. The steep cliffs and crystal clear rivers (above: the Jiuquxi River, which rises in the western part of the Wuyi) also give it a special aesthetic appeal. Almost 2,500 plant species as well as around 5,000 insects and 475 vertebrate species have been counted here, with the Wuyishan providing an important sanctuary in densely populated China. The average altitude is no more than 350 m (1,148 ft) above sea level and consequently the temperatures here are relatively mild, even in winter.

More than 3,000 overgrown sandstone pillars rise majestically out of the valleys in this stunning nature park. They were shaped by erosion from a 500-m-thick (1,641-ft) layer of sediment. The canyons between them are so narrow that agriculture is impossible, a fact that has made the region virtually uninhabitable. Almost all of the prominent formations have floral names. The region is known for its dense vegetation, many rivers and the 3,000 plant species that have been counted here. The world's highest natural bridge is also here: 40 m (44 yds) long and 350 m (1,148 ft) above the valley.

Writers and scholars often retreated to the remote, mountainous Wuyi region (main picture). Around 95 percent of the land is covered with forest – a paradise for birds and snakes.

Beneath the stone reliefs in Dazu are numerous images of Buddha and a giant demon holding the Wheel of Life in his fangs (main pictures).

DAZU

The various cliff faces here, which range in height from about 7 to 30 m (30 and 98 ft) and are up to 500 m (55 yds) in length, offer a kaleidoscope of Buddhist sculptures going back some 1,000 years. Unlike the large, ancient cliff temple complexes in northern China, which were mainly built in man-made grottoes, a majority of the vibrant Dazu sculptures and reliefs are actually outside. The figure of Buddha, for example, which is recognizable by the simple monk's attire, is an especially common motif along with the Bodhisattvas, who sacrificed their entry to Nirvana in order to help man and to save him from the earthly Vale of Tears.

Scenes from Buddhist version of paradise illustrate the happiness that awaits pious believers. Sentinel deities, scenes of hell and even secular motifs are also to be found. The latter provide an insight into the modes of dress and everyday life at the time the works were created. The roughly 10,000 sculptures on Treasure Peak were created by a single monk.

HUANGLONG

In addition to the fascinating mountain and glacial landscape, visitors to Huanglong Scenic and Historic Interest Area will find a long series of limestone terraces extending roughly 4 km (2.5 mi) through a beautiful forested valley. The terraced pools (above) were formed during the Ice Age when the region was covered by a glacier. Rich in minerals, the glacial water eroded basins and caves into the soft limestone cliffs, in which water now collects, flowing from one basin to the next as the water continues to fall.

JIUZHAIGOU

A unique abundance of natural wonders awaits you in the high-altitude valleys here, including crystal clear ponds, amazing cataracts, rare animals and dense vegetation. The name of this national scenic area means "valley of nine villages", a reference to the nine Tibetan villages located here. Nearly 120 lakes (top) shimmer with different colors depending on the time of year. They feed waterfalls (above) that crash down into basins and create new lakes.

Many of the temple grottoes carved into the rock at Dazu with their numerous sculptures and inscriptions are more than 1,000 years old. Dazu is an important religious site for Taoists, Buddhists and Confucians alike. Far left: A reclining Buddha. Left: Sentinels.

Black Dragon Pond Park lies at the foot of Xianshan Mountain north of Lijiang and affords wonderful views of Jade Dragon Snow Mountain. A man-made waterfall thunders beyond the Shuocui Bridge (main picture).

GUILIN

The six-hour boat trip from Canton to Guilin on the Li River passes through one of China's most recognizable landscapes, a virtual forest of karst towers whose characteristic irregular shapes are produced by carbonic acid reactions here in China's tropical south.

The names of the mountains on both sides of the river resonate with the poetry of this unusual region (Mountain of the Waiting Wife; Old Man at the Mill Stone; Climbing Tortoise; Green Lotus Peak) while groves of Phoenix tail bamboo grow on the river banks, water buffalo doze in the shallow water along the shores and cormorants go about their fishing.

LIJANG

Lijiang is situated in the strategically important transition zone between central and south Asia, not far from the border with Myanmar, and was once a remote outpost of the Chinese Empire. The historic Old Town (above) with its narrow streets and buildings is considered one of the most well-preserved in China. For centuries Lijiang has boasted a unique irrigation system fed by three canals, the result being that a babbling brook flows past almost every building in the city.

SANQINGSHAN

This national park in south-eastern China boasts a landscape of fascinating beauty that is characterized by dense forests and bizarre rock formations. The silhouettes of many of these cliffs are even reminiscent of living creatures. They attract amateur and expert geologists, the great age of the mountains making them an important site for research. The oldest rock layers date from the Mesoproterozoic Era around 1.6 billion years ago and provide important indicators of the Earth's geological development.

The romantic landscape along the Li River with its striking karst formations is what makes Guilin so appealing (left, far left). Cormorant fishermen on bamboo rafts attract the fish using lanterns and the birds dive after them – they are kept from swallowing their prey by means of a neck ring (left page).

FUJIAN TULOU

The Hakka settlements are situated in the midst of rice, tobacco and tea plantations in Fujian Province, a mountainous region of south-western China. The large round or square mud houses (above), known as Tulou, illustrate the Hakka's ability to adapt their way of life and their building methods to the conditions in the region, in particular to the threat of hostile attacks during the Ming and Qing dynasties. Between two and five floors in height, the houses with their walls of unbaked mud form several rings enclosing a lively courtyard.

KAIPING

The residential towers of the city of Kaiping and the surrounding villages (above) present a bizarre sight in this rural area. Chinese nationals returning from abroad combined European, American and other elements with local traditions in building the residential towers. Three types of towers can be distinguished: communal towers inhabited by several families, more ostentatious towers owned by individual families, and watchtowers. The majority of them were built of reinforced concrete during the 1920s.

HONG KONG

The name Hong Kong means "Fragrant Harbor". Right is the seat of the Legislative Council in front of the Bank of China tower. The rocky island at the mouth of the Pearl River was named as such on account of the incense sticks produced there. On the other side of the river is the Kowloon Peninsula which owes its name of "Nine Dragons" to the hilly landscape. Hong Kong became a British colony in 1842 and it was from here that the British ran their profit-

able opium trade, encroaching on Kowloon in 1860. The so-called Unequal Treaties of 1898 gave the British a 99-year lease on the New

Territories along with 235 islands. The Crown Colony at the gateway to China eventually developed into one of the most densely populated and financially powerful trading hubs in the world. It has been a Special Administrative Region of China since July 1, 1997, a status that will last for 50 years, with its own currency, own economy and left-hand driving. "One nation – two systems" has since been the new order of things for Hong Kong.

Breathtaking: the view of Hong Kong's skyline in the nighttime sea of lights (main picture).

MACAU

Macau, situated in the Pearl River Delta, can be reached via speedboat from Hong Kong. After living under Portuguese rule for almost 500 years it was handed back to the People's Republic of China in December 1999.

The peninsula receives around six million visitors annually, mainly from Hong Kong, most of whom enjoy a stroll through the Old Town "where Portugal meets China". The central square Largo do Senado (above) with its wavy mosaic pavement is reminiscent of Portuguese towns.

Sightseeing attractions include Chinese temples juxtaposed with Christian churches and European-style palaces scattered among Chinese cemeteries. Some tourists come in search of rest and recuperation on the fine beaches of the islands of Taipe and Coloane, but the majority of visitors typically head straight for the multitude of floating casinos that constitute Macau's main source of income.

LHASA

Lhasa, meaning "place of the gods" and is capital of the Tibet Autonomous Region (TAR), lies on the Kyichu River at an altitude of almost 3,700 m (12,140 ft). Originally founded in the 7th century as the residential seat of the Tibetan kings (7th to 9th centuries), it later became the seat of government of the Lamaist theocracy in the

15th century, ruled by the Dalai Lamas. For hundreds of years, Lhasa was a "forbidden city" for foreigners.

The two-floor Jokhang Temple (above) dates from the 7th century and is situated in the heart of the Old Town. It is the oldest Buddhist

monastery in Tibet as well as a sort of Tibetan national sanctuary. All of the roads in Lhasa therefore lead to it. The temple is incidentally once again inhabited by practicing monks.

Almost as old as the Jokhang Temple is the Ramoche Temple (right) of the Chinese Princess Wencheng with its mighty outer walls. Unfortunately, the temple's many statues were either destroyed or confiscated by the Red Guards during the Cultural Revolution. With thirteen floors it rises 110 m (362 ft) above the city. Its façade alone is 360 m (1,000 ft) long, behind which are said to be 999 rooms

covering an area of 130,000 sq m (1,398,800 sq ft). Opposite is the grotto temple Drolha Lubuk with images of Buddhist deities alleged to have been created on their own. The Dalai Lama's summer palace, Norbulingka, in the west of Lhasa, is even larger.

KAILASH

"On seeing this snow-capped jewel our people leapt down from their saddles and bowed down on the ground," noted Sven Hedin after an excursion to Mount Kailash on Lake Manasarovar. The 6,714-m (22,029-ft) peak in Gangdisê Shan, the western section of the Tibetan Transhimalaya range, is believed to be the residence or throne of the gods – it is the holiest mountain in the world for Hindus, Buddhists, followers of the Ancient Tibetan Bön religion as well as those of the Ancient Indian Jain religion. Its summit may not be ascended and the 55-km (34-mi) circular route ("kora") is one of the most difficult pilgrimage paths in the world because of its altitude (around 5,000m/16,500 ft). It generally takes three to four days to complete. A kora corresponds to one revolution of the Wheel of Life and, according to the Tibetan faith, redeems all of the sins that the pilgrim has committed in his life to date. Especially pious Tibetans continually throw themselves onto the ground during the pilgrimage and measure the route with their own body length.

Main picture: The whitewashed section of the palace houses the administrative offices and storerooms, while the red section was the residence of the Dalai Lama until he fled in 1959. The entire complex has been a museum since then.

HAEINSA

Haeinsa, situated on Mount Kaya in the province of South Kyongsang, is home to an artifact venerated in the Buddhist world: the Tripitaka Koreana ("Teaching of the three baskets"), 81,258 wooden blocks that make up the most comprehensive collection of Buddhist texts. They are stored on the shelves of two depositories called Changgyong Pango. The blocks are carved on both sides, creating a total of 162,516 pages. Each page features twenty-two lines of fourteen Chinese characters each – Chinese because the Koreans did not yet have their own alphabet at the time. Two hundred monks spent twelve years working on the blocks, finishing them in 1248.

The treatment of the wood was an achievement in its own right, an unusual process intended to preserve it for eternity. It was stored for three years at a time in seawater, fresh water, in the ground and in the open air. Only at the end of this process were the blocks then carved. The air circulation and humidity in the ancient storerooms are controlled as well.

The Haeinsa Monastery (main picture, carvings on the temple roof) houses Korea's most comprehensive collection of Buddhist documents dating from the 13th century.

SOKKURAM, PULGUKSA

Together with the adjacent Seokguram grotto, Pulguksa, South Korea's most frequently visited temple, is located to the east of Kyongju and is a masterpiece of Buddhist Silla Dynasty art (from 668–935). Above: Carvings on the beams of the temple roof (top), and the white granite Shakyamuni Buddha housed in one of the grotto's rotundas (bottom).

KYONGJU

As the "Golden City" (Kumsong) of the Unified Silla realm, Kyongju was the hub of the first centralized Korean state from the 7th to the 10th centuries. Situated in south-eastern South Korea, it is now the focal point of a beautiful national park. The historic Kyongju region also includes the area around Namsan Mountain with its monumental carvings of the Buddha (above). This is allegedly the birthplace of Hyokkose, the founder of the Silla Dynasty.

Haeinsa, the "Temple of Reflection on a Smooth Sea" , dates back to 802. The microclimate in the "library depositary" – built in 1488 – Changgyong Pango (left) is perfectly adapted its contents: 81,258 blocks of Chinese script. Far left: A door painted with sentinel figures.

HWASONG

At the end of the 18th century, Emperor Cheongju had a residence built around 50 km (31 mi) from the capital, Seoul. Hwasong is an example of contemporary military architecture that combines the finest expertise from both East and West. Above: Changanmun, one of the fortress' four gates.

CHONGMYO

Korea's oldest royal Confucian shrine was commissioned by the founder of the Choson Dynasty (1392–1910) for the purposes of ancestral worship. Traditional ceremonies featuring instruments, song and dance have been performed here virtually unchanged since the 15th century.

CHANGDOK

Emperor Taejong had a "getaway residence" built near the Chongmyo shrine in Seoul (above, the throne room or reception hall of the Changdok Palace). It represents a type of palace architecture that blends harmoniously with the surrounding landscape.

TOKYO

Roughly eight million people live in the Japanese capital and more than twelve million live in the greater prefecture. Tokyo is not only Japan's largest city, but also its most important economic and cultural center. This expansive metropolis is littered with skyscrapers that are visible from far and wide. Tokyo Tower, for example, (lit up in the main picture) is 333 m (1,093 ft) high, even taller than its role model, the Eiffel Tower in Paris.
Insets, left to right: the Shinjuku shopping district and the neon jungle of the main business and entertainment district, Ginza.

Main picture: The Rainbow Bridge
spanning Tokyo Bay was completed in
1993 and measures 798 m (2,600 ft) in
length – 570 m of which are between
the two towers.

BANDAI-ASAHI, SHIRAKAMI-SANCHI, SHIRAKAWA-GO AND GOKAYAMA

Shirakama-Sanchi is home to red-faced macaques (main picture), a species endemic to Japan that lives farther north than any other monkey species in the world. They live in socially structured groups of thirty to sixty animals, each group having its own territory.

BANDAI-ASAHI

Honshu, the largest of Japan's four main islands, possesses many of the country's most beautiful natural features, and the important elements of its biodiversity are protected in a series of truly stunning parks. Bandai-Asahi National Park is divided into separate sections: to the west is Mount Iide at 2,105 m (6,907 ft); to the north is the Asahi Range with the holy Dewa Sanzan mountain shrines; to the east are the Bandai Azuma mountains; and to the south is Lake Inawashiro. Japan's fourth-largest lake, Inawashiro-ko was dammed by masses of lava from Bandai Volcano. The park is accessible via panoramic toll roads including the Bandai Azuma Skyline, which is open from April to November and is one of the busiest routes. Like many other regions on Honshu there are hot springs in the park, Tsuchiyu-Onsen being one of the most popular. The Tsuchiyu Pass, on the access road between Inawashiro-ko and Fukushima provides an enchanting view.

SHIRAKAMI-SANCHI

Almost all of Japan was once covered with primeval forests in which Siebold's beech was the predominant species of tree. Sadly, most of these forests have been badly decimated by logging over the centuries, but prolonged deliberations in the 1980s ultimately saved the remaining clusters in the north of Honshu by creating nature preserves and national parks. The heart of Shirakami-Sanchi covers about 100 sq km (39 sq mi).

The waters of the Anmongawa River plunge over the Shadow Gate Falls into the Meya Valley.

The largest primeval beech forest in East Asia is an important refuge for the world's most northerly monkey population, the Asian black bear, the Japanese serow (a goat species) and eighty-seven bird species including the endangered black woodpecker.
More than 500 plant species also flourish in the Shirakami Fforest, including rare orchids. The mountain landscape, which rises to an elevation of 1,243 m (4,078 ft) and is the origin of fifteen rivers, is largely impassable and in the past it was only the occasional herb gatherer that was likely to have strayed into this region.

The Japanese landscape is very fragmented, and the national parks are therefore often split into several sections that are not directly connected with one another. This is true of Bandai-Asahi National Park, for instance. Left: An autumn scene at Lake Hibara.

SHIRAKAWA-GO AND GOKAYAMA

The unusual timber-frame houses in the villages of Shirakawa-go and Gokayama on the north side of the main island of Honshu all feature the Gassho style of steeply pitched thatched roofs. The pitch enables the houses to withstand the weight of the heavy snow during the long, hard winters here – snowfalls of 2 to 4 m (7 to 13 ft) are not uncommon. Silkworm breeding is another important reason for the traditional architecture

Almost all of the thatched, timber-frame houses in the village of Shirakawa-go are surrounded by gardens and fields (top). One of the houses is a museum displaying equipment for mulberry tree cultivation and silkworm breeding (bottom).

that is still common in this remote region. It requires a covered space that is provided beneath the high roofs on what are usually two to four, and sometimes even five floors. The houses are large enough to accommodate forty to fifty people.

The villages of Shirakawa-go and Gokayama are testimony to a preservation of tradition that is unique within Japan. Elsewhere in the country, economic progress and the accompanying social change have largely led to the disappearance of this type of architecture. Even more conservative Japanese farmers now adapt their houses to modern styles.

MOUNT FUJI

Japan's holy mountain (main picture) last erupted on December 16, 1707. The eruption lasted two weeks, forming an additional crater about halfway up as well as a second peak.

The islands of Japan form part of the so-called Ring of Fire, a string of seismically and volcanically active regions that encircles the Pacific Ocean. One of the many manifestations of this frequent activity is earthquakes, and Japan gets plenty of them. Although the Japanese use state-of-the-art technology in the construction of their buildings and transport network, even they are not able to combat the forces at work below the earth's surface.

Mount Fuji, a glorious result of the Ring of Fire's powers, rises up from the island in stoic silence. It is not only Japan's highest mountain, but also the country's undisputed icon – the pride of an entire nation. At a towering 3,776 m (12,38 ft), Fuji is crowned by a massive crater 600 m (1,900 ft) across and 150 m (492 ft) deep, with temples, cabins, a weather station and a radar station on its rim. Every year up to 400,000 people make the ascent in the summer season (July and August). There are five lakes – Motosu-ko, Shoji-ko, Sai-ko, Kawaguchi-ko and Ymanaka-ko – on the north side of the mountain.

The Fushimi Shrine, built in 711, is one of the most important buildings in the former imperial city of Kyoto. It is dedicated to the goddess of rice growing and features a 4-km-long (2.5-mi) avenue of red Shinto gates (torii) leading to the inner complex (main picture).

KYOTO

Many Japanese people are of the opinion that their country can only really be understood by strolling through the alleyways of the former imperial city of Kyoto, capital of Japan for more than 1,000 years from 794 to 1868 – and almost without interruption. The administrative seat permanently moved to Tokyo at that point. Despite the loss of central political power, however, Kyoto went on to remain the cultural and spiritual hub of Japan, renowned for its architecture and its theaters, its handicrafts and kimono collections, and

Kiyomizu-dera temple (top) is situated high above the city and has been visited by pilgrims for more than 1,000 years. The Heian Shrine (bottom) is a scaled-down copy of the first imperial palace from 794 and was built in 1894 to mark the 1,100th anniversary of the founding of Kyoto.

traditional fan manufacturing and festivals. No other city displays Japan's cultural wealth as well as Kyoto, where architecture, sculpture and painting flourished for centuries. The city boasts nearly 2,000 magnificent palaces, temples and shrines that give entire districts of the city an absolutely wonderful ambience. Particularly stunning examples include the Kiyomizu-dera temple, the Heian Shrine and the Fushimi Shrine.

HORYU-JI

Horyu-ji, 10 km (6 mi) south-west of the former imperial city of Nara, dates back to the very beginning of Japanese Buddhism, which was declared the national religion at the start of the 7th century. Construction began in 607 on the orders of Prince Regent Shotoku (573–621).

The original Chinese-style temple burned almost completely to the ground in 670, but the buildings here today are still considered the oldest wooden constructions in the world and were built by about 710, the start of the Nara Period. They include the main hall (Golden Hall), the five-floor pagoda, the middle gate and the adjoining gallery. Six of the figures in the main hall are thought to date back to the previous building, which went down with the fire. This would make them the oldest surviving sculptures of this kind in Japan. The most important place of worship in the Buddhist temple complex is the Golden Hall. The pagoda was built next to it, a deliberate rejection of the symmetrical specifications observed previously.

平成記念
月吉日建之
平成二年六月吉日建之
平成元年二月吉日建之
平成六年四月吉日建之
平成三年十月吉日建之
平成元年四月吉日建之
十周年記念再建

The treasures of Horyu-ji include fierce guardian figures, or gamu, (far left) in the middle gate (Chunon), which leads to the Inner Sanctuary, as well as gilded wooden sculptures depicting Buddha (left) and protective spirits.

NARA

The temple and shrines of the first permanent imperial residence mark the beginning of the aristocratic period and the first peak of Japanese Buddhist art. Based on the Chinese Tang city of Chang'an, the new Japanese capital of Nara was built in just four years and features a grid pattern.

To the north of the city is a magnificent imperial palace that hosted seven emperors up until the end of the Nara period (710–784). From there a wide arterial road leading south divides the city into two equal rectangles. The Buddhist schools that had only been introduced to Japan shortly before that

The 16-m-high (52-ft) Daibutsu (Big Buddha) in Nara's Todai-ji Temple is the world's largest gilded bronze statue of Buddha (above). It is made of 437 tons of bronze to which 130 kg (287 lbs) of pure gold were added.

time then set up temples and monasteries in the new capital.

The main hall of the Toshodai-ji temple from 759 was part of the imperial palace and is considered the most important building in Nara. One of the world's largest wooden buildings is located near the Todai-ji temple (728), seat of the influential Kegon sect. The dimensions of the Great Buddha Hall (Daibutsu) are colossal: 58 m (180 ft) long, 51 m (160 ft) wide and 49 m (161 ft) high. The building, which was reconstructed in 1708, is smaller than the original, however.

ITSUKUSHIMA

The vermilion shrine complex of Itsukushima is situated in one of the loveliest coastal locations in Japan and perfectly embodies the Shinto worship of nature. Just off the island of Miyajima in the Seto Inland Sea close to Hiroshima, the shrine appears to be hovering over the water. The legend that this building was built in 593 and dedicated to the three daughters of the storm god may indeed be true because the island of Miyajima, or Itsukushima, was a holy site very early on and could only be accessed by priests up until the 11th century. There is no cemetery on the island to this

day, a measure to ensure that the purity of the religious site is preserved. Although the main buildings date from the period 1556 to 1571, the overall complex with its glistening red paintwork retains the distinct style of the Heian Period, from the 8th to the

12th centuries, when a similar version was first built.

Eight larger and several smaller buildings were built on stilts in the shallow water and connected to one another via covered passageways. More buildings on the mainland complete the complex. The 16-m-tall (52-ft) Torii, the gate to the sacred site, was built in 1875. This eighth gate of the Itsukushima Shrine, standing in the water 175 m (191 yds) offshore, perfects the sense of harmony radiated by the scene. This reason alone makes the Torii the most famous construction in all of Japan.

The red camphor wood Torii off the island of Miyajima was based on an older gate of wooden beams. It is submerged at high tide (main picture).

HIROSHIMA

"It was a black, sticky rain. It stuck to absolutely everything. When it fell on trees and leaves it just stayed there, and everything turned black. When it fell on your clothes, all your clothes turned black. It even stuck to your hands and feet and you couldn't wash it off. I couldn't get it off of me."

(Isao Kita, witness)

August 6, 1945, was a day that changed the world. During World War II, the United States made the fateful decision to use a newly developed weapon to force the Japanese Empire into unconditional surrender. The first atom bomb, somewhat ironically named Little Boy, was dropped by the B29 bomber Enola Gay and exploded 570 m (1,870 ft) above the heart of the port city of Hiroshima. Every form of life within a radius of 4 km (2.5 mi) was destroyed in an instant. Between 90,000 and 200,000 civilians were killed including thousands of Koreans who were

in Japan as forced laborers. The second atom bomb was dropped on Japan in Nagasaki just three days later, on August 9, killing 25,000 to 75,000 people. The torment of the survivors (hibakusha) affected by the radioactive outfall was immeasurable. There are still people dying from the long-term consequences.

As far as the buildings are concerned, it seems not a single one was left standing after the devastating explosion. Only one Western-style brick building built in 1914/15 managed to tower up out of the rubble of Hiroshima: the former Chamber of Trade and Industry. With its burnt-out dome (above) it has since become a symbol for the city and the world of the horror of modern warfare, which reached entirely new proportions of terror through the unleashing of nuclear energy. Atomic weapons wiped out two complete cities with just one bomb. Each killed hundreds of thousands of people and rendered large areas uninhabitable for generations.

The Peace Memorial Museum is near the ruins and documents in great detail the effects and consequences of the Hiroshima bomb. The Genbakudomu itself is intended to be a plea to create a world without atomic weapons and one that values freedom above all else. Hiroshima was rebuilt after 1949.

"Atom bombs do not discriminate. Atom bombs kill everything in their path, from tiny babies to the elderly. And it is no easy death. It is a gruelling and very painful way to die. I think it must never be allowed to happen again, anywhere in the world." (Isao Kita)

The marine landscape in Halong Bay – in the Gulf of Tonkin in northern Vietnam – comprises around 2,000 islands and features bizarre limestone cliffs. The wind, the weather and the tides have created an alluring natural work of art here (main picture).

The limestone cliffs in Halong can be up to 100 m (328 ft) high and most of them are covered with dense vegetation. Reminiscent of Chinese landscape paintings, these cliffs and mountains come in a wide variety of shapes ranging from broad-based pyramids and high, arched "elephant backs" to thin, towering needles of rock. The island landscape has often been perceived as more of a mythical spectacle than as a natural phenomenon: A dragon (Ha Long) descended from the mountains (or from heaven) is said to have created this natural wonder when it destroyed an army of enemy invaders with blows from its mighty tail – or was it that the dragon had been disturbed and therefore angered? The water displaced by the dragon as it dived under the sea then spilled into the resulting channels and canyons. The geological reality is somewhat more down-to-earth: Following the last Ice Age the coastal landscape forming part of the south-west Chinese limestone plateau sank and was flooded. It was erosion which ultimately formed the bizarre-shaped cones of rock.

Halong Bay is usually dominated by brisk shipping traffic (far left). Almost every one of the countless islands has its own name (left). Many of the grottoes and stalactite caves are only accessible at low tide (left).

Main picture: This elaborately decorated gate is the entrance to the main Thien Mu temple, or "Pagoda of the heavenly lady", with its seven-story Phuoc Duyen tower. Only very few of the more than fifty buildings destroyed in Hue during the Vietnam War have been rebuilt.

HOI AN

The port city of Hoi An was an important trading hub from the 15th to the 19th centuries. Both Asian and European influences overlap in the city's layout, buildings and temples. The first Portuguese landed on the coast of Vietnam in 1516, followed soon after by Jesuit missionaries. The Portuguese quickly established a trading post in Hoi An in 1535, developing it into a vibrant city. Chinese, Japanese and later other Europeans, especially the Dutch, then settled as traders in the city, also known as Phai Fu, each nationality taking over its own district within the city. Even when the Vietnamese Empire, fragmented after fifty years of civil war, lost interest in trading with Europe at the end of the 17th century, Hoi An remained an important gateway to the West. Large parts of the city were destroyed during the Tay Son uprising at the end of the 18th century, and the increased silting up of the Thu Bon River meant that Hoi An slowly lost its position to Da Nang in the 19th century as Vietnam's most important port city.

HUE

Vietnam's capital from 1802 until 1945, Hue is still one of the country's cultural, religious, political and intellectual centers. Nguyen Anh, who reunited a fragmented Vietnam in 1802 and ascended the throne as Emperor Gia Long, commissioned a fortified residence in the city center that reflects Chinese palatial styles. His desire to emulate Chinese imperial architecture is exemplified by details such as the design of the roof decoration. The royal household and the servants lived in the imperial town (Da Noi)

Built on a hill overlooking the Song Huong, or "Perfume River", the Thien Mu Pagoda in Hue is one of Vietnam's most famous sights. The 21-m (70-ft) octagonal tower was built in 1844, and each of the seven floors is dedicated to a Buddha who appeared in human likeness.

to the south of the citadel. The "Forbidden City", in the center, was reserved for the ruling family only. It was also known as the "Purple City": Purple symbolizes the North Star, what many consider the pivotal point of the universe, which is then in turn being personified by the emperor. The southern Midday Gate (Ngo Mon) is the residence's most complex structure. Seven of the Nguyen emperors had their tombs built outside Hue.

The Japanese Bridge (left) connected the Chinese and Japanese districts in Hoi San. The altar was intended to mollify the river spirit. Stone figures of apes and dogs indicate the beginning (1539) and the end (1595) of the bridge's construction.

MY SON

The kingdom of the Champa or Cham, a Malayo-Indonesian people, dates back to the year 192 when, following the collapse of the Han dynasty in China, the local Han governor founded his own kingdom in the area around the present-day city of Hue. Starting in 400, an empire initially comprising four and then later two states developed under Indian cultural influences against a backdrop of constant disputes between the local tribes and the Chinese colonies.

The first wooden temple was built in My Son during the reign of Prince

At the foot of the "Beautiful Mountain" (My Son) the Hindu god Shiva was an object of particular veneration by the Cham. The temple towers (top) stand on a square plinth and taper towards the top. Their exteriors feature pilasters, friezes and statues of the gods (bottom).

Bhadravarman. The first brick temple was built by a successor in the seventh century, and was the beginning of an architectural tradition that continued into the 13th century. The Hindu Cham kingdom was organized according to castes and gave itself over to Chinese protection as of the sixth century. Conflicts with the Confucian Vietnamese in the north worsened from the 10th century and the increasingly influential Khmer began their rise in present-day Cambodia. The Cham vanished from history after the conquest of their capital Vijaya by the Vietnamese in 1471.

HO CHI MINH CITY

While Hanoi is the country's political hub, Ho Chi Min City (in Vietnamese: Thanh Pho Ho Chi Minh, and formerly Saigon), is considered to be the industrial and economic heart of Vietnam. Modernization has indeed left its traces on the urban look and feel here, but the past still manages to shine through in some places. The colonial-style buildings, for example, and the roadside kiosks selling baguettes add a touch of the French colonial atmosphere to some of the city's neighborhoods. There are still oases of tradition in this vibrant metropolis, with monks praying in tranquil pagodas and puppeteers putting on shows in the parks. Like no other in Vietnam, Ho Chi Minh City embodies the dawning of a new era in the country. Above: City Hall, built in the French colonial style at the beginning of the 20th century.

One of the largest river deltas on earth is situated in southern Vietnam: the approximately 70,000-sq-km- (27,020-sq mile-) wide mouth of the Mekong River. The lotus flowers growing here (main picture) are seen as a symbol of purity because, although they flourish in muddy waters, their unique surface structure makes them appear completely clean. The pure blossoms growing out of the mud are the Buddhist symbol for the enlightened soul.

MEKONG DELTA

South of Ho Chi Minh City is a series of rolling hills that gives way to an almost perfectly flat expanse – the Mekong Delta. Rice paddy after rice paddy stretches between the countless channels where much of the daily activity takes place. Above: A farmer tends to his ducks. The delta is formed by the accumulated sedimentary deposits of the Mekong River, a process that is ongoing. The coastline along the river mouth extends further into the sea by around 80 m (262 ft) every year. This fertile land is used intensively for agriculture, making the region Vietnam's undisputed rice bowl (right).

This area is also one of the most densely populated in the country. The constant danger of flooding means that almost all of the houses here are built on stilts. Trading takes to the water during periods of flooding, when the river markets take place (left).

Wat Xieng Thong got its name from a Bodhi tree (thong), which is depicted in a glass mosaic on the rear of the Sim. The walls and columns inside, where monks pray in front of a giant Buddha statue (main picture), are also decorated with vibrant glass mosaics.

WAT PHU AND CHAMPASAK

The Wat Phu temple complex represents an important historical legacy going back to the first century, harmonizing beautifully with the ancient cultural landscape of Champasak in the south-west of Laos. In the fifth century this was the site of the capital of a pre-Angkorian kingdom. Between the 10th and 13th centuries, Champasak formed part of the Khmer kingdom of Angkor, the territory under its control extending up the Mekong as far as Viang Chan (present-day Vientiane). At that time the region between the holy mountain Kao and the plain was used for organized rice farming, with irrigation systems, temple complexes and two cities on the banks of the Mekong. All of this still reflects the pre-Angkorian Hindu worldview of the unity between the universe, nature and man. The Wat Phu temple complex, comprising "landscape pyramids" of temples, shrines, canals, roads and water pools built in the 10th century under the Angkor ruler Jayavarman IV, forms an additional part of this legacy.

LUANG PRABANG

More than any other city, Luang Prabang is the embodiment of traditional Laos. Even though political power has been based in Vientiane (Wiang Chan) since the French colonial era, Luang Prabang remains the country's cultural hub. This city at the mouth of the Nam Khan on the upper reaches of the Mekong got its name at the end of the 15th century from the popular, almost 1-m-high (3-ft) Phra Bang Buddha statue dating from the 14th century and for which a separate temple was built. At that

King Setthathirat founded the Wat Xieng Thong temple with its gilded carvings (bottom) in around 1560. The steeply pitched roof (top) of the main building, known as the Sim in Laos, is especially impressive.

time, as Muong Swa, Luang Prabang had already been the center of one of three Lao kingdoms, the "Land of a million elephants" (Lan Chang), for over a century. The former royal city still boasts numerous Buddhist temples and monasteries with magnificent art treasures. The most imposing of these complexes is the 16th-century royal temple Wat Xieng Thong. The temples are built of stone and the secular buildings of wood. The Old Town beneath Phu Si hill is characterized by traditional buildings and French colonial architecture.

From the temple ruins at the foot of Phu Kao, the path takes you up more than ninety steep steps to the former Shiva sanctuary on the mountain (second from right, the main temple). Today the formerly Hindu Wat Phu is a Buddhist temple, as is indicated by the seventh-century statues clad in monks' robes.

ANGKOR

Angkor Wat is the largest temple complex in Angkor, the former Khmer capital (main picture). The impressive ensemble with its distinctive prangs (temple towers) is approached from the main entrance along a stone embankment that is several hundred yards long.

The Khmer culture was strongly influenced by the Indian peoples that migrated to Southeast Asia in the first half of the first millennium. They prospered particularly after shaking off the domination of the Funan Empire (second to sixth centuries), which was also heavily influenced by Indian culture. The founder of the Khmer empire was Jayavarman II, who ascended the throne in 802. As the god king of Angkor with absolute religious and secular power, he acted as intermediary between heaven and earth. As a human being he lived in a palace and was venerated as a god in the temple. The Khmer rulers were Hindu-orientated until the beginning of the 13th century and were venerated in the form of Linga (the phallus of Shiva, creator and destroyer of the world), then later as an incarnation of Bodhisattva. Since the temple became the tomb of the god king after his death, every Khmer king built a sanctuary for himself. The most impressive complex is that of Angkor Wat, the temple of Suryavarman II (1113–50), under whom the Khmer culture reached its zenith.

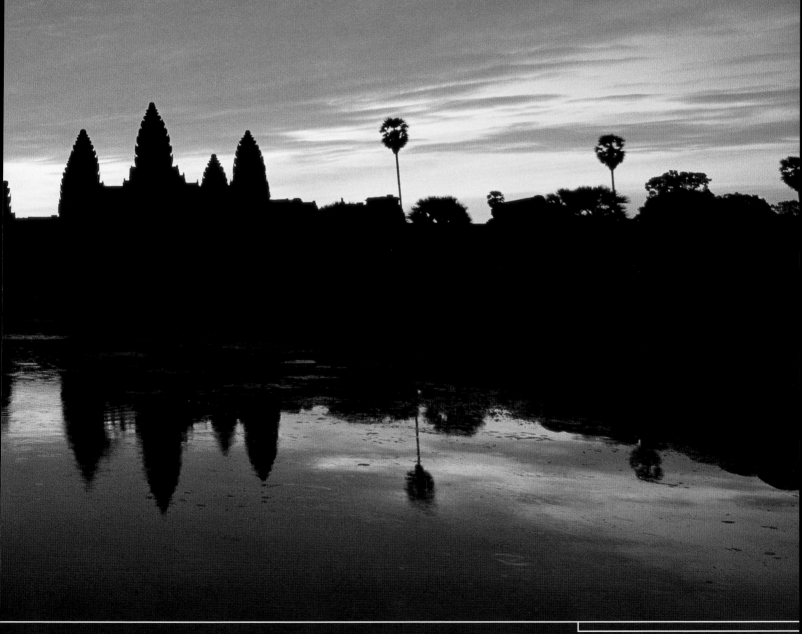

Bangkok's Grand Palace (main picture) used to be a city in itself. The wealth of shades and shapes represented by the more than 100 buildings on the historical site continues to overwhelm visitors to this day.

GRAND PALACE UND WAT PHRA KAEO

The Siamese withdrew to Thonburi (now a district of Bangkok) after the destruction of their former capital Ayutthaya by the Burmese in 1767. It was here that Chao Phaya Chakri ascended to the throne in 1782 as King Rama I, thus founding the Chakri Dynasty, which is still the royal house of Thailand. It was in the first year of his regency that Rama I moved the seat of government to the opposite (east) bank of the river where the grounds of the Grand

The Grand Palace grounds feature mythical creatures, demons and giants with "protective powers".

Palace now cover an area of 218,400 sq m (2,349,984 sq ft), enclosed on all four sides by a wall measuring 1,900 m (6,000 ft). Also on the east bank of the river was the village of Baan Makok, then largely inhabited by Chinese people, and from which the name conventionally used in the West, Bangkok, derives. The abbreviated form of the extended official name, Krung Thep, means "City of Angels". The most important sanctuary in the Grand Palace is the Wat Phra Kaeo Temple. Its architecture is based on the royal palace of Ayutthaya, a temple reserved solely for the king and his Buddhist ceremonies and which houses the most highly venerated Buddha statue in Thailand, the Emerald Buddha.

CHINATOWN

Bangkok is vibrant, bustling, loud, chaotic and dazzling. More than ten million people live in the greater city and it is from here that the country is governed. The king lives here and all of the major companies are based here. It is also a city that never sleeps. Skyscrapers, luxury hotels and shopping malls make up modern Bangkok while the traditional monks, fortune-tellers and healers can be found in the temples along the river. The Chinese community in Bangkok has been here longer than Bangkok has been the Thai capital. The present-day Grand Palace grounds were home to a number of Chinese traders even before King Rama I moved his capital from Thonburi to the opposite bank of the Chao Praya River in 1782. Forced to make way for the king's plans, the community withdrew to what is now Chinatown. A gate at Odeon Circle marks the entrance to Yaowarat Road (with an express boat you can reach Chinatown from Ratchawong Pier) where it is best to continue on foot to explore the neighborhood.

A kaleidoscope of Chinese culture in Bangkok (from far left): a calligrapher waits for customers; fresh piglet on a spit; shops sell their wares at street stalls.

WAT PHO

Not far from the Grand Palace is Wat Pho, the largest and oldest (16th century) temple complex in Bangkok with Thailand's largest statue of Buddha. The 45-m-long (150-ft) and 15-m-high (49-ft) statue (above) depicts Buddha shortly before his entry into Nirvana – a state of enlightenment (bodhi) in which the cycle of life (death, life and rebirth: samsara) is left behind. The historical Buddha achieved this state at the age of thirty-five and taught for another forty-five years thereafter.

WAT ARUN

The Temple of Wat Arun with its impressive tower and central sanctuary in which a seated Buddha invites the faithful to pray is one of the capital's most recognizable landmarks. The temple acquired its current name, the Temple of the Dawn, after King Taksin was rowed along the river one morning. It was Rama II, however, who then had an 86-m-high (282-ft) Khmer-style tower built over the original building. The main tower is flanked by four smaller towers. Thousands of Chinese pottery fragments were used to decorate the façade and while the result from up close tends to be somewhat dizzying, from a distance the details create a unique optical effect.

SUKHOTHAI

"May the land of Sukhothai thrive and prosper" – that is the stone inscription on the tomb of King Ramkhamhaeng the Great (ruled 1279–98) that is now housed in the National Museum in Bangkok. Sukhothai was the Siamese kingdom's first capital and it indeed enjoyed its greatest period of prosperity under him. The first independent kingdom of Siam expanded as far as present-day Laos and, for a few decades, to the Malay Peninsula after the retreat of the Khmer around 1238. A "golden age" prevailed until the end of the 14th century, one that saw the development of the Thai alphabet as well as the creation of the loveliest Siamese works of art. Following its decline in the 14th century, however, it was largely forgotten until restoration work on the ruins began in 1977 and the Sukhothai National Historical Park

was opened. The Sukhothai Historical Park includes several dozen temples both inside and outside the original Sukhothai city walls. Monumental Buddha statues look over Wat Sra Sri, with its bell-

shaped, Sri Lankan-style *chedi* (above). Wat Sorasak, with its bell-shaped *chedi* surrounded by twenty-five stone elephants is a special highlight in Sukhothai (right).

Wat Mahathat (main picture) with its some 200 *chedis* was the religious hub of old Sukhothai. The dimensions of the historical town were about 2 by 1.5 km (0.9 mi) and it is surrounded by earthworks and moats.

SI SATCHANALAI

Si Satchanalai was built in around 1250, at about the same time as Sukhothai. It became the second seat of the first king of Thailand as well as the seat of the viceroy after two Thai princes from the surrounding area had defeated the Khmer governor of Sukhothai in a bloody battle. In the 17th century Si Satchanalai became part of the kingdom of Ayutthaya, which was abandoned by its inhabitants when the Burmese reached the city gates in the 18th century.

Today the more than 100 ruins making up the Si Satchanalai Historical Park about 60 km (37 mi) north of Sukhothai remain a testimony to a rich past. Chaliang – the oldest Khmer town with Wat Phra Si Ratana Mahathat (left, a detail from the east gate) lies on a bend in the river in the southeastern section of the park.

KAMPHAENG PHET

Around 80 km (50 mi) south-west of Sukhothai is Kamphaeng Phet, once one of the capitals of the Sukhothai realm. The Wat Phra Kaeo – Temple of the Emerald Buddha – is located in the Historical Park in the center of the city. The weathered, Uthong-style Buddha statues (above) with their angular faces and continuous eyebrows also belong to the treasures found in the park.

THUNG YAI, HUAI KHA KHAENG, KHAO YAI

Khao Yai National Park is the most easily accessible of the four national parks that form the Dong Phayayen-Khao Yai forest, a UNESCO World Natural Heritage site. Main picture: The Nam Tok Haeo Suwat waterfall.

KHAO YAI

Khao Yai National Park is part of the Dong Phayayen-Khao Yai forest, protected as a UNESCO World Heritage site with the Thap Lan, Pang Sida, Ta Phraya national parks and the Dong Yai Wildlife Reserve. It covers a vast area of 2,168 sq km (837 sq mi) at the edge of the Khorat Plateau and is considered to be the most populous wildlife reserve in Thailand. The park is traversed by a total of around

The park's rainforest is a refuge for wildlife. Top: A great hornbill. Bottom: Rhesus monkeys.

40 km (25 mi) of hiking trails and is mainly accessible between December and June. In the dense evergreen mountain forests, however, it is often only the sounds of the primeval forest that are perceptible – the humming of the cicadas, for example, or the characteristic sound of the great hornbill concealed in the tree tops. Waterfalls such as the Nam Tok Haeo Suwat, where parts of the film *The Beach* were shot, are another popular attraction.

THUNG YAI, HUAI KHA KHAENG

The Thung Yai and Huai Kha Khaeng nature reserves in western Thailand make up one of the largest wildlife sanctuaries in South-East Asia, with a total area of around 6,100 sq km (2,355 sq mi). These splendid highlands on the border with Myanmar are traversed by rivers and streams and alternate between savannah-like plateaus (Thung Yai) and dense forests that are largely comprised of bamboo but also contain tropical woods such as teak. There is hardly any species of plant on the South-East Asian mainland that is not represented in this region. The fauna comprises around 120 mammal, 400 bird, more than 100 freshwater fish, almost fifty amphibian and some 100 reptile species. The two reserves are accessible only for small groups with permits. This has meant that even large mammals such as tigers, leopards, elephants and bears have been given the chance to survive, carefully watched over by rangers and largely undisturbed by people.

The reserve's grasslands and evergreen forests are home to animals as diverse as the clouded leopard (left) and the hog deer (far left), so called because it runs through the undergrowth with its head down instead of leaping over obstacles like other deer.

AYUTTHAYA

The Buddha statues at the ruins of Wat Mahathat temple in Ayutthaya add a unique element to the typical corn cob-like *prangs* and bell-shaped *chedis*. Main picture, opposite page: A Buddha head entwined in the roots of a Bodhi tree.

The Siamese empire's second capital was founded in 1350 by King U-Thong (Thibodi I) on the east bank of the Chao Phraya River. Today it has been converted into a magnificent open-air museum of ancient Buddhist culture. The monasteries, *chedis*, *prangs* (the Thai version of the Khmer temple towers) as well as the numerous monumental sculptures are testimony to its former glory. At the height of its power, "The Invincible" – as the name Ayutthaya translates – was a cosmopolitan city with one million inhabitants, 375 monasteries and temples, ninety-four city gates and twenty-nine fortresses. The city was not ultimately invincible, however, and fell to the Burmese in 1767. Up until that point Ayutthaya had been the political and, more importantly, the cultural hub of a kingdom that had inherited the spectacular legacy of Angkor under thirty-three kings for more than 400 years. Excavated in 1956, the former royal city was restored with UNESCO support and the most important monuments are now assembled in the ruins of a city where Buddha is, as expected, omnipresent.

In Ayutthaya, Buddha is venerated in the form of countless statues (left) that are distinguished by the four classic Asana postures: standing, walking, sitting and reclining. The sitting Buddha statues in Ayutthaya are clad in orange monks' robes. Far left: Wat Chai Wattanaram.

Nail Island in Ao Phang-nga National Park was made famous by the James Bond film *The Man with the Golden Gun* (main picture).

KO SAMUI

Where holiday dreams come true: miles of immaculate white-sand beaches and idyllic bays (above Coral Cove Bay on "Coconut Island", as Ko Samui is also called); crystal-clear, turquoise water; palms waving in the warm breeze; rainforests and waterfalls; picturesque cliffs; and unspoilt fishing villages. These are the things that make Ko Samui, Thai-

land's third-largest island after Phuket and Ko Chang, one of the country's most popular travel destinations. Swimming, snorkelling and diving are usually at the top of the list of activities with visitors who land at the regional airport situated almost at the foot of the "Big Buddha" (below) built in 1972.

PHUKET

Phuket is Thailand's largest island and one of the most popular holiday destinations in East Asia. It is connected to the mainland in the north by a 700-m-long (2,475-ft) bridge. Both the town and the island offer a wealth of nature, culture and folklore to explore. Phuket's original wealth derived from tin mining and the still magnificent vil-

las in the Chinese-Portuguese heart of Phuket recall that time. The Vegetarian Festival is also of Chinese origin (left, the dragon parade). Setting sail on the Andaman Sea from Phuket in a longtail boat (below) is an unforgettable experience. The boats are steered by means of a propeller shaft (longtail) with a motor attached to it.

KRABI

The bays (below, Hat Tham Phra Nang Beach on the Phra Nang Peninsula) around the port of Krabi boast some of Thailand's finest beaches and clearest waters. Once a sleepy fishing village, Krabi has become the administrative heart of the province of the same name. It lies at the mouth of the Krabi River where it flows into the Andaman Sea.

AO PHANG-NGA

The bizarre rock formations, cones and pyramids tower out of the water in Phang Nga Bay like the backs of prehistoric dragons. These visible peaks of limestone reef in the Andaman Sea, which once extended from northern Malaysia as far as Central China, were formed over the course of 100 million years. An area covering roughly 400 sq km (154 sq mi)

was used to create Ao Phang-nga National Park in 1981 and was primarily intended to protect the mangroves in the northern part of the bay – the largest in Thailand. The Nail Island cliff formations (main picture) were made famous by the James Bond film *The Man with the Golden Gun*. Many of the islands abound with karst caves (below).

KO PHI PHI

Smooth sandy beaches, rocky bays, caves and a magnificent underwater world are all at your disposal south of Krabi in Hat Noppharat Thara – Mu Ko Phi Phi National Park. The most famous island group in the park is Ko Phi Phi (above) thanks to Danny Boyle's filming of Alex Garland's cult novel *The Beach* with Leonardo di Caprio.

At 452 m (1,483 ft), the Petronas Towers (main picture and inset) are among the highest buildings in the world, not to mention Kuala Lumpur's most recognizable landmark. The 58-m (175-ft) Sky Bridge links the two towers at a height of 170 m (558 ft). The building was conceived by Cesar Pelli and officially opened in 1998.

KUALA LUMPUR

Malaysia's largest city is also the political and economic center of this Southeast Asian country. At this point, however, there is nothing about the capital today that is reminiscent of a "muddy estuary", which is what the name means. No other city in the country manifests so consistently the will of Malaysia to present itself internationally as an up-and-coming industrial nation, and it does so impressively with modern high-rise complexes such as the Petronas Towers (main picture and inset left), the administrative offices of multinational companies, banks and institutions as well as the numerous hotels.

Kuala Lumpur's appeal derives primarily from its vibrant ambience, the plentiful green spaces in the city center, the relaxing parks on the periphery, and particularly from the multicultural population mix – Chinese, Malay and Indian being the main ethnic groups – with their different cultures, traditions and ways of life.

The modern skyline is interspersed with the older parts of the city: the administrative buildings of the former British colonial powers and the villas of the tin barons as well as the traditional residential areas of the Indians and Chinese who live here.

BATU CAVES

The Batu Caves are around 15 km (9 mi) north of the capital on the road to Kuantan and are among the most frequently visited attractions in the Kuala Lumpur area. The enormous limestone caves form part of a labyrinth of rock openings and passageways that stretch over 1 km (0.6 mi).

The shrine (above) that was set up in the main cave back in 1892 has made this one of the most important pilgrimage destinations in the country for Malaysia's Hindu population.

Thousands of visitors travel to the Batu Caves in January and February every year when the two-day long Thaipusam Festival takes place. The highlight of the festivities is a procession of penitents who have metal hooks pushed into their backs and their chests (above).

Covering an area of 754,770 sq km (291,341 sq mi), the world's third-largest island – after Greenland and New Guinea – is one of the Greater Sunda Islands. Mount Kinabalu (main picture) is the highest peak in this very fragmented mountain region.

KINABALU

Kinabalu Park is situated in the Malaysian province of Sabah, at the northern end of the island of Borneo. It is known mainly for its primeval vegetation and for the highest mountain in Southeast Asia, Mount Kinabalu, which forms the impressive focal point of the park and – at 4,095 m (13,436 ft) – the highest mountain between the Himalayas and New Guinea. It is characterized by very diverse plant life that constantly changes between the different zones and

The rare flora and fauna on the island are protected by national parks. Top: Rainforest in Kinabalu Park. Middle and bottom: A ginger and a pitcher plant, respectively.

extends as far as the barren, rocky summit region. The tropical rainforest in the lowlands has more than 1,200 wild orchid species and many rhododendrons. The flowers range in hue from deep red to pale pink and white, followed at higher altitudes by montane forest with forty different types of oak overgrown with moss and ferns, coniferous forests and an alpine meadow and bush zone.

GUNUNG MULU

The largest cave complex on earth is tucked away in the spectacular mountain range of Gunung Mulu National Park, in the Malaysian province of Sarawak on Borneo. The formation of this craggy landscape began around thirty million years ago when pulverized volcanic rock formed the sand and sediment that made up what was then still a seabed. Coral and other marine fauna then formed the limestone over millions of years. Uplifting and a drop in sea levels about five million years ago then led to the creation of the mountain range that is today part of the protected national park territory and boasts stunning limestone formations like the 1,750-m-high (5,742-ft) Gunung Api. Directly adjacent to that limestone is a sandstone massif that makes up the highest peak, Gunung Mulu at 2,377 m (7,799 ft), after which the national park is named. The magnificent cave system, inhabited by a multitude of bats and insect species, was carved out by river erosion over the course of millions of years.

Gunung Mulu National Park, with its jagged limestone formations (left) and the gigantic cave complex (center: the Wind Cave) forms part of an impressive karst landscape. The Melinau River flows through the canyon of the same name (far left) in the park.

SINGAPORE

Singapore's financial district (main picture) boasts one futuristic skyscraper after the other; the airport is one of the largest in Asia; and the container port is the largest in the world. In addition to this, however, there are a multitude of historic buildings that keep the old Singapore alive.

The city-state of Singapore is on a small island at the south end of the Malaysi Peninsula on the Strait of Malacca. The city was founded in 1819 as a trading post and rose to become Southeast Asia's most important transportation, financial and economical hub within just a few decades. It is here that modernity and the future co-exist peacefully with history and tradition.

Singapore (above: Orchard Road) is considered the cleanest of Asian cities, with the best air quality of any city in the world. This is ensured by high penalties for littering, for instance, as well as high road charges, extreme vehicle taxes and severely limited licensing regulations for new vehicles. This seemingly draconian range of measures has managed to keep cars away from the city for many years, however, and the outstanding public transport system means that any point within the city is easily and quickly accessible.

The population is composed of two-thirds Chinese together with a mix of Indians and Malays. In colonial times, each ethnic group had their own district, all of which have undergone extensive renovations in recent years. Their markets, shops and restaurants are full of atmosphere, particularly in the evenings, the most vibrant of which can be found in Little India.

IFUGAO (LUZÓN)

The rice terraces in the Philippine Cordillera are one of those "Eighth wonders of the world" (main picture near Banaue). To work each hectare (2.5 acres) requires around 1,000 hours as the steep slopes prohibit the use of machines and the terraces are harvested just once a year.

Deepwater rice cultivation is one of the most important cultural accomplishments in Asian history and the Ifugao – an indigenous mountain people living in the province of the same name in the Philippine Cordillera – are especially gifted in this ancient skill. There are five areas on the island of Luzón that are particularly worth seeing: two in Banaue (Battad and Bangaan), as well as one each in the municipalities of Mayoyao, Kiangan (Nacadan) and Hungduan. They are all located in the around 20-km-long (12-mi) Banaue Valley where the rice terraces, laboriously built by hand, literally cling to the steep slopes. The paddies are about 3 m (10 ft) wide, separated by stone walls comprising multiple layers of rubble 10 to 15 m (33 to 49 ft) high, and are built to adapt to the shape of the mountain. Irrigation is provided by a sophisticated system of bamboo pipes, canals and small sluices that ensures every single terrace from the very top down to the valley has enough water.

The Ifugao, who belong to the Igorot tribe, have been cultivating rice on the emerald-green terraces of northern Luzón (left) for around 2,000 years.

PUERTO PRINCESA SUBTERRANEAN RIVER NATIONAL PARK (PALAWAN)

This national park is located about 80 km (50 mi) north-west of Puerto Princesa, the capital of the island of Palawan. Among its most impressive features are the limestone formations of the St Paul Mountain Range. The 1,027-m-high (3,370-ft) Mount St Paul

The national park's karst limestone landscape (top and bottom) is traversed by an underground river that rises about 2 km (1.2 mi) south-west of Mount St Paul and then reappears again near St Paul's Bay after flowing underground for almost its entire distance.

is the highest peak in a crest of eroded limestone mountains that runs north-south along the slender island.
The main scenic attraction is provided by the longest navigable underground river on earth, which extends over a distance of around 8 km (5 mi), more than 4 km (2.5 mi) of which are navigable, creating a cave complex of enormous dimensions.

TROPICAL RAIN FORESTS OF SUMATRA

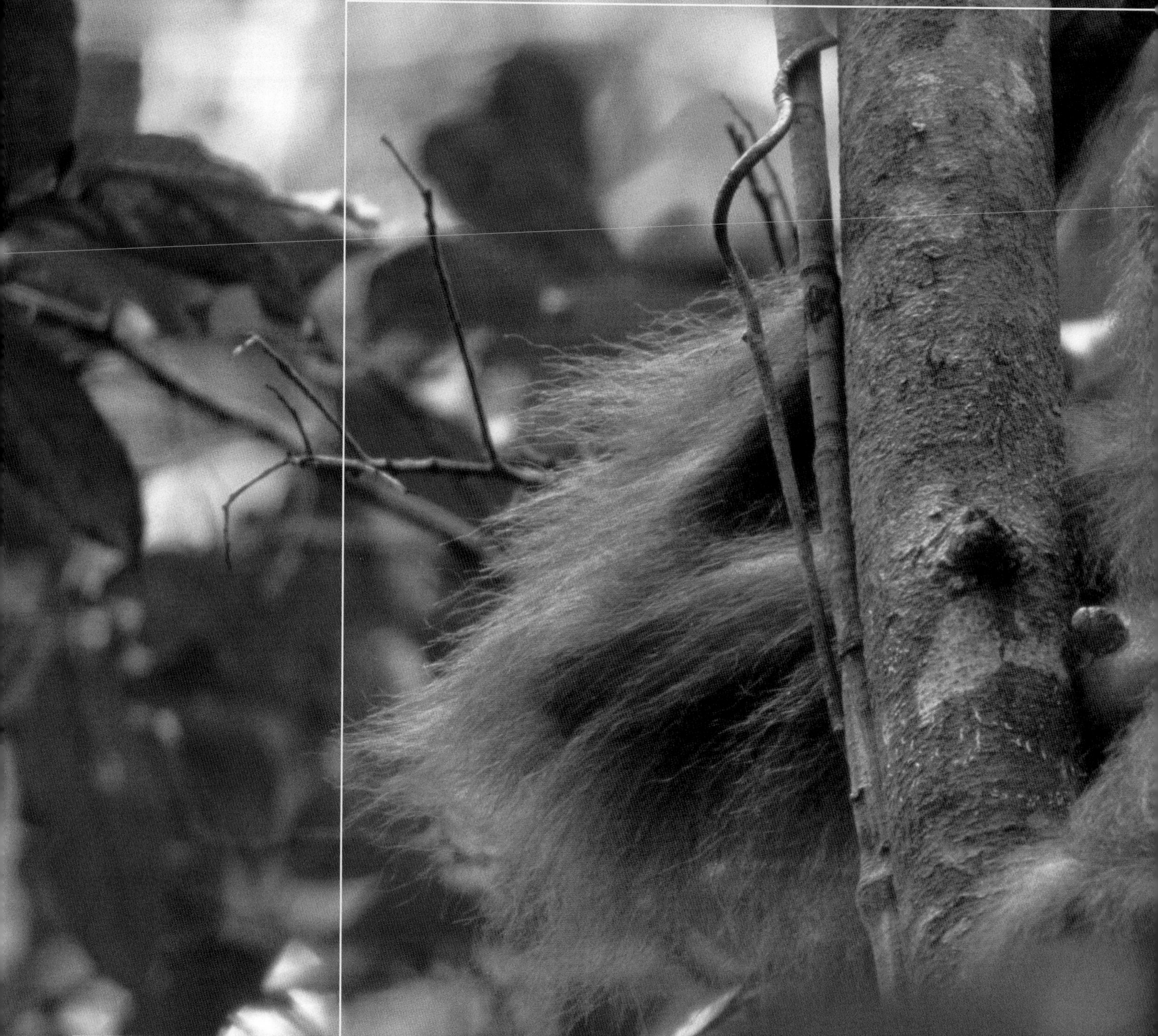

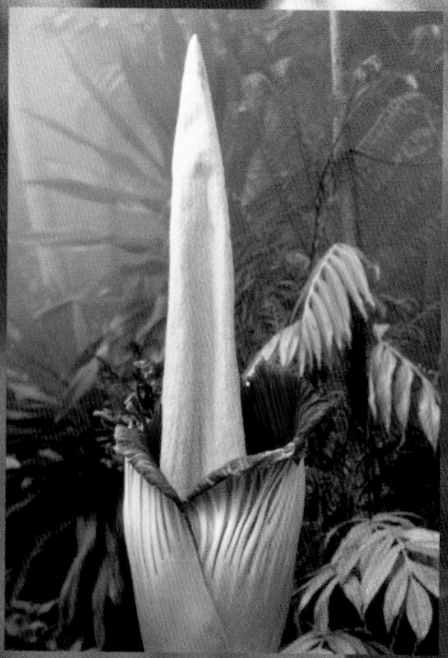

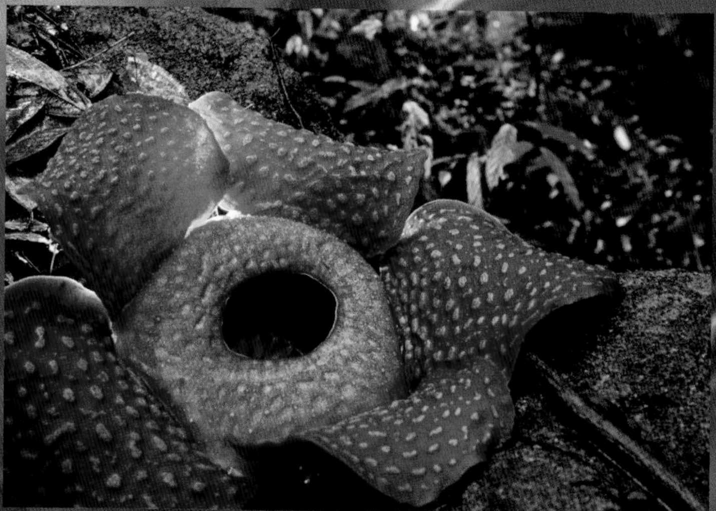

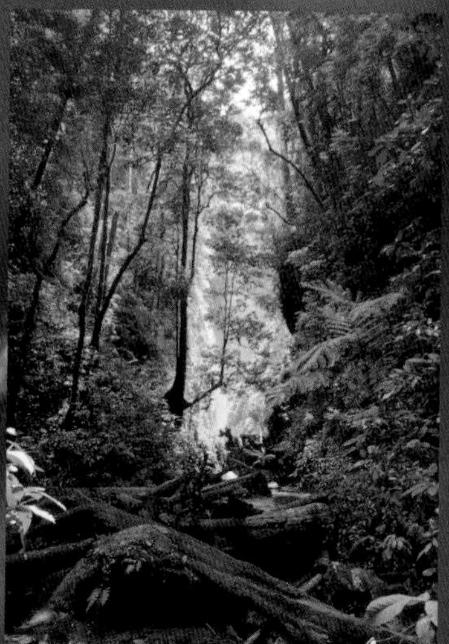

One of the last continuous rain forest areas on earth is protected by three national parks on the island of Sumatra: Gunung Leuser in the north, Kerinci Seblat in the center and Bukit Barisan Selatan further to the south. Some 10,000 plant species flourish in this region, including seventeen endemic genera. The flowering plants here comprise more than fifty percent of the species on Sumatra, which is famous for its populations of the world's largest flower, Rafflesia arnoldii, and the flower with the highest inflorescence in the world, the titan arum (Amorphophallus titanum). Also enormously diverse, the animal world has until now only been partially researched by scientists. Over 580 bird species alone have been discovered, twenty-one of which are endemic. The most spectacular of the local animal species are the orangutans, tigers, rhinos, elephants, serow, tapirs and the clouded leopard. This high level of biodiversity is matched only by the wealth of geological formations and habitats.

Among the myriad flora and fauna in the rainforests of Sumatra and Borneo, the endangered orangutan is the most famous inhabitant (main picture). The males of this great ape species can weigh up to 80 kg (176 lbs), making them the largest tree dwellers on earth. Opposite page, from left: A titan arum, the plant with the largest inflorescence in the world – 3 m (10 ft); a giant rafflesia, its five red petals reaching up to a diameter of 1 m (3.3 ft); and the rain forest in Gunung Leuser National Park.

BOROBUDUR

This temple complex built in the eighth century on the Indonesian island of Java is the most important Buddhist sanctuary outside India. Buddha himself is said to have determined the design of the stupa here by folding his mendicant robes into a mound, placing his alms bowl on the top, and then crowning it with a staff. The art historian Karl With once described the whole temple complex of Borobudur as embodying "a monument to the godly in which the universe flows together and appears as a sanctuary before your very eyes" – a truly magical place.

PRAMBANAN

What was once the most important Hindu religious site on Java was originally dedicated to the gods Brahma, Vishnu and Shiva. Construction on the complex's high temple towers, known as *prangs*, began in the eighth century, but the main temple, Loro Jonggrang, is said to have been completed only in around 915. It is dedicated to Shiva, the Indian god of virility and called "Maha Deva" here. He is the most powerful of the three deities, signalled by the omnipresence of his symbol here, the phallus (lingam). Brahma and Vishnu each have their own smaller temples.

The temple complex at Borobudur (main picture) symbolizes the cosmic notion of Mount Meru emerging from the heart of the world with its various elevations: the "world of desires", the "world of names and shapes" and the "formless world". The faithful who ritually paced around the temple complex situated on a round, 30-m-high (98-ft) hill in central Java also underwent Buddhist instruction while here.

BROMO-TENGGER-SEMERU

Gunung Bromo in Bromo-Tengger-Semeru National Park (above, left and right) is 2,392 m (7,848 ft) high and the most frequently visited volcano on Java due to its unique setting. The country's highest volcano, Semeru, at a gigantic 3,676 m (12,061 ft), also towers above the park, which covers an area of about 58,000 ha (143,318 acres). Climbing the mountain surrounded by picturesque lakes is not for the faint-hearted, however: A 1,300 m (4,265 ft) difference in altitude awaits takers, with half of the route taking you over steep, open lava scree beneath the crater. This remote region is inhabited by the Tengger people, who retreated to these mountains when Islam spread across Java. They have managed to maintain their Hindu traditions to this day.

The Indonesian holiday paradise of Bali continues to fascinate visitors from all over the world. While the north and west are dominated by narrow, dark beaches, the south of the island boasts magnificent sandy beaches near Denpasar, picturesque bays and an overwhelmingly beautiful underwater world. The rice terraces in the center of the island are the work of generations of farmers who made the steep slopes arable. Tanah Lot, one of the island's most scenic temples, is located on an offshore rocky outcrop. The romantic Pura Ulun Danu Bratan temple complex (above right with traditional carved deity masks), is situated on the southwestern shores of Bali's Lake

Bratan and, founded in the 17th century, is dedicated to the water goddess Dewi Danu. The "Mother of all Balinese temples", Pura Besakih, is situated atop the 3,142-m (10,309-ft) active volcano, Gunung Agung. Every clan and every professional category is represented by its own temple here. The holiest of complexes, it is accessible only to Hindus. The

summit of Gunung Agung offers a magnificent view of the adjacent island of Lombok. Visitors will find temples and palaces on the west coast of Lombok that are similar to Bali as well as picture-postcard sandy palm beaches. There are impressive coral reefs around the island as well, making snorkelling or diving trips here a unique experience.

Main picture: Balinese dancers wear elaborate makeup for their "Homage to the gods" dance.

The solitude of the sand desert, the fires of the Virunga volcanoes, the raging waters of Victoria Falls, the majesty of Mount Kilimanjaro, the pyramids of Egypt, the palaces of Morocco, and the monasteries of Ethiopia. The Serengeti, Masai Mara, Okavango Delta, Chobe. Tuareg, Nuba, Samburu, Zulus. The diversity in Africa is hard to beat. Main picture: Quiver trees, endemic aloe plants in the southern Namibian desert.

RABAT

Together with its twin city, Salé, the capital of Morocco has some 1.5 million inhabitants. Rabat, or "Ribat el-Ftah", was originally built in the 12th century by the Almohad dynasty as a fortress before buccaneers later settled there. In 1956, it became the capital of independent Morocco with its historic center built around the casbah of the Udayas on a hill above the Bou Regreg River. The 12th-century Bab Al-Oudayas gate, with magnificent stone carvings, leads into a maze of partly covered alleyways that end at the "platform", where you get a view of neighboring Salé. East of the casbah stand 200 column stumps and the Hassan Tower, the minaret (above) of the Mosque of Hassan, which was planned by Ya'qub al-Mansour but never completed after the sultan died in 1199.

TETOUAN

The largest town in the Rif Mountains, a folded range in the northwest of Morocco that resembles the Alps, was under Spanish rule until Morocco gained its independence in 1956. The medina, completely surrounded by fortified walls, has countless vaulted alleyways and houses with windows with wrought-iron grilles. Tétouan's medina is the fourth-largest in Morocco. On market days, farmers come from the Rif Mountains to sell their produce in town (below).

CASABLANCA

EL JADIDA

A visit to this city of three million inhabitants is worthwhile especially to see the Hassan II Mosque (above and main picture). Dedicated by the king in 1993, more than 3,000 artisans from all over the country were involved in adorning it with traditional majolica mosaics, stucco, delicate inlay work as well as dark-cedar wood carvings. The prayer hall can accommodate 25,000l, and 80,000 can fit the forecourt under the shade of the 200-m-high (656-ft) minaret. A laser beam at the top of the minaret points toward Mecca at all times and the mosque is the only house of god in Morocco that may be visited by non-Muslims (every day apart from Friday).
Also worth seeing is the center of Casablanca with its neo-Moorish buildings dating from Morocco's time as a French colony.

The story of El Jadida (above and below) began around the year 1500, when the Portuguese set up their fortress there on the Atlantic coast just 100 km (62 mi) south of present-day Casablanca. Over the centuries it was transformed into a defensive post to ward off attacks and occupations.
It was not until the end of the 18th century that the Moroccans managed to conquer and burn down the Mazagan fortress. Arab tribes and the Jewish community then settled there. Over time, a

new town emerged, El Jadida, "the new one". Especially worth seeing here are the Church of the Assumption built in the Manueline style and the Portuguese Cistern (below), a complex of three chambers and four towers. The cross-vaulting of the main chamber rests on twelve round columns and thirteen pillars. Synagogues, mosques, churches and the 19th-century mansions of European merchants bear witness to the earlier cosmopolitan ambience in the town.

The Hassan II Mosque in Casablanca (main picture) was built on a man-made platform in the ocean and appears to float over the water.

In 809, Idris II made Fez an imperial town. The city has since grown into a modern metropolis, but in the Old Town (main picture: Bab Bou Jeloud Gate), time seems to have stood still.

THE OLD TOWN

Fez was founded by the Idrisid rulers as a twin city on an important trading route from the Sahara Desert to the Mediterranean Sea. The oldest part of the town, Fes el-Bali, was settled by Andalusian refugees from the Moorish region of Spain as well as by families from present-day Kairouan in Tunisia. The Kairaouine Mosque, which goes back to these settlers, provides room for more than 20,000 worshippers. It is also the center of the highly regarded university that was founded in the year 959. Andalusia Mosque also dates back to the early days of the town. Fes el-Bali is surrounded by impressive city walls featuring twelve unique gates.

Fez experienced a time of great prosperity in the 14th century under the Marinid rulers. The Royal Palace, the Bou Inania Medersa and the Mellah (the Jewish Quarter) all date from that time. Qur'anic schools, mosques and the tombs of the Marinids testify to the importance of this part of town, Fès el-Djedid. The French conquered the city in 1911.

KAIRAOUINE MOSQUE

The green-tiled roofs of Kairaouine Mosque (above) can clearly be made out in the sea of houses in Fez el-Bali's medina. Morocco's second-largest sacred building, it was constructed in Moorish style, with 270 supporting columns.

TANNERY QUARTER

Visitors here can get a glimpse of the densely packed vats filled with natural tannins and dyes (above) as well as of the hard physical labor of the tanners. The animal hides are cleaned, soaked, hung up to dry and then dyed.

ROYAL PALACE

The gate to the Royal Palace in "New Fez", founded by the Marinid sultans to the south-east of Fez el-Bali, features seven beautifully gilded brass doors that are framed by zellij polychrome tiles and stucco (above).

Although it is not the capital city, Fez is still considered the spiritual and cultural center of Morocco. The Old Town features partly covered alleyways and a number of stylish minarets (left).

NEJJARINE SQUARE

Nejjarine Square, near the carpenters' souk, has one of the most beautiful fountains in the city (above). To the left you enter the Nejjarine Foundouk, the former Inn of the Carpenters and today the Nejjarine Museum of Wood Arts & Crafts.

TOMB OF MOULAY IDRISS II

The Zaouia (shrine) of Moulay Idriss II in Fez is still one of the most important pilgrimage sites in Morocco. The complex of buildings includes a delightful mosque and a courtyard. Precious materials were used in the ornamentation (above).

MADRASSA ES-SHARIJ

The Marinids are responsible for some of Morocco's most famous madrassas – religious schools. One, the Madrassa es-Sharij, was named after the large fountain shaped like a water basin in the middle of its magnificent inner courtyard (above).

ESSAOUIRA

The fortification walls that completely surround the Old Town of Essaouira, which dates back to the Portuguese fortress of Mogador, are greatly influenced by European military architecture. The Phoenicians had used this location on the central Atlantic coast of Morocco as a trading station. They were followed in the first century BC by the Romans, who established an important purple-dye factory here.

The Portuguese later built what was initially a military, then a commercial port for the trade in sugar, salt and ostrich feathers. Mogador was rebuilt in the middle of the 18th century during the reign of Sultan Sidi Mohammed Ben Abdallah, who entrusted the work to architect Théodore Cornut, who based his design on the French town of Saint-Malo, which explains the European look of the center. Built on a rectangular grid,

it features arcades and white houses with blue doors and window frames.

The majestic gates lead to the Old Town, which comprises the original fort, known as the casbah, the mellah, or Jewish quarter, and the medina, the actual center with the souks, or markets. The harbor fortifications are also very well preserved. The city was renamed Essaouira in 1956, the year of Moroccan independence.

VOLUBILIS

Volubilis, situated to the north of Meknès, was once the most important Roman settlement in what is now Morocco. Founded during the rule of Carthage, the city was officially incorporated into the Roman Empire in AD 44. In the years that followed, magnificent secular and religious buildings were erected here. A particularly active period of construction took place during the reign of Emperor Septimius Severus, who ruled from 193 to 211 and bequeathed many architectural treasures upon North Africa. Since 1887, these structures have been methodically excavated by archaeologists.

The main road, the Decumanus Maximus, stretches nearly 1 km (0.5 mi) through the town (above), which during its heyday boasted more than 10,000 inhabitants. The magnificent Caracalla Arch was built in AD 217 in honor of Septimius Severus' eldest son. The 2nd-century basilica originally had five aisles and served as a court and administrative building. Residences such as the enormous Gordian Palace and private mansions such as the "House of the Cortège of Venus", with its beautiful mosaic floors (below), give insight into the everyday life of the Roman governor and the inhabitants of Volubilis.

MEKNÈS

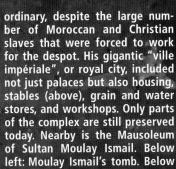

Meknès, which developed around a former Berber fortress, was conquered a number of times by Almoravid, Almohad and Marinid rulers. It enjoyed its greatest prosperity under the Alaouite Sultan Moulay Ismail (1672 to 1727) who turned Meknès (above left, the Bab el-Mans Gate) into a "Moroccan Versailles". Even his European contemporaries were impressed. Moulay Ismail's architectural legacy is indeed extraordinary, despite the large number of Moroccan and Christian slaves that were forced to work for the despot. His gigantic "ville impériale", or royal city, included not just palaces but also housing, stables (above), grain and water stores, and workshops. Only parts of the complex are still preserved today. Nearby is the Mausoleum of Sultan Moulay Ismail. Below left: Moulay Ismail's tomb. Below right: The antechamber.

Main picture: A street scene in Essaouira. The port with its massive walls and the Scala fortress might look Portuguese, but it was not founded until 1760 by Sultan Mohammed Ben Abdallah.

MARRAKESH

The minaret of the Koutoubia Mosque is the best-known landmark in Marrakesh, the southernmost of Morocco's four former imperial cities. The oasis city was once an important center for trans-Saharan trade and served as a capital for the rulers of several dynasties.

Among the structures dating from the early period of the medina, the town walls have been very well preserved. Overall, they cover roughly 10 km (6 mi) and contain ten gates and more than 200 towers, some of which were added later. The mosque and its minaret, built in the year 1153 by the Almohad sultans, is one of the most attractive buildings in the city. Together with the Giralda of Seville and the Hassan Tower of Rabat, the nearly 80-m (262-ft) masterpiece is a mixture of Spanish and Moorish architecture that quickly became a model for min-

arets all around the country. Just behind the beautiful mosque is the tomb of the city's founder, Yusuf ibn Tashfin.

Visitors enter the ancient fortified town of the Almohads, referred to as a casbah, via the 12th-century Bab Agnaou, Marrakesh's most beautiful city gate. Another architectural gem is the Ben Youssef Madrassa, built in the 14th century under the "Black Sultan" – a Marinid ruler. The 16th century was another period of great building activity. Dating back to this period are the elaborate Saad tombs (above). The inner rooms of the necropolis are splendidly decorated with cedar, stuccowork and mosaics. In addition to several palaces – the Royal Palace, Bahia Palace (top left), the ruins of El Badi – the souks (insets, opposite page) and the main market square, Djemaa el Fna (main picture), with its traveling entertainers are among the top attractions in Marrakesh. The Agdal and Menara Gardens outside the city (above) are also worth seeing.

Located in the heart of Marrakesh is Djemaa el Fna, the "Square of the Beheaded". After sunset, hundreds of people crowd around the food stalls, snake charmers, storytellers and acrobats (main picture).

THE HIGH ATLAS, CASBAH TRAIL

Main picture: A panoramic view of the Todra River Valley, which rises in the High Atlas. In the language of the Berbers, "ouzuoud" means "olives", after which the 110-m (361-ft) Ouzoud Waterfalls were named (opposite page).

THE HIGH ATLAS

Rising up between Middle Atlas and Anti-Atlas, the High Atlas range forms the border between fertile Morocco and the desert. Its highest mountain is Jbel Toubkal (4,167 m/13,672ft). The Cascades d'Ouzoud are a spectacle of incomparable beauty and Morocco's most impressive waterfalls.

In the deep, narrow Todra and Dades Gorges of the High Atlas, farmers make use of every tiny scrap of fertile land. The Todra River cuts its course through steep rock faces and extends from the High Atlas down to the Dades Valley, where its banks are lined by thousands of palm trees. The cool canyon is popular among rock climbers and hikers.

THE CASBAH TRAIL

Thanks to its many clay fortresses, the Dades Valley is also known as the "Route of 1,000 Casbahs". At the turn of the 20th century, it was El Glaoui in particular, the infamous pasha of Marrakesh, who secured his sphere of influence by commissioning such casbahs to billet his troops.

The summits of the High Atlas are covered with snow until well into the spring (far left). In the deep ravines (left, a meandering river) near the "Route of 1,000 Casbahs", farmers make use of every available scrap of fertile land to grow tomatoes, alfalfa and millet in their tiny fields.

M'ZAB VALLEY, ALGIERS, GRAND ERG OCCIDENTAL

The oasis region in M'zab Valley has existed for thousands of years, with the first traces of settlement stemming from Neolithic times. The towns there today (main picture, Ghardaïa with the towering minaret) were founded at the beginning of the 11th century.

M'ZAB VALLEY

Five fortified settlements (*ksour*) were built by the Mozabites of the Ibadi community in the valley of the Oued M'zab, which carries water only once a year. They include El Atteuf, Bou Noura, the holy town of Beni Isguen, Melika and Ghardaïa. The last and largest of these is Ghardaïa. Like the other settlements, it was built around a mosque on top of a hill and encircled by walls. The mosque's minaret was also a watchtower. The mosque itself was conceived as an independent entity, with grain storage silos and an arsenal of weapons.

The earth-colored buildings and traditional family structures are perfectly adapted for the desert climate, often windowless with a small opening in the roof as their only light source. Gardens and palm groves here are kept alive with the help of clever irrigation systems developed over centuries. The unique architecture of the M'zab Valley knows virtually no corners and edges. It is said to have served as the inspiration for the architect Le Corbusier.

ALGIERS

Originally founded by the Phoenicians and later known as "Icosium" during the days of Roman rule, the settlement that is now Algiers only developed into an important trading post after the Arab conquest. It repeatedly attracted foreign powers, however. In the 16th century the Spanish conquered the town, which in response called upon the pirate Khair ad-Din, aka Barbarossa, an Ottoman admiral. When he had reconquered Algiers, Khair ad-Din then submitted to the Ottoman

The lovingly detailed doors are especially impressive on a walk through the maze of narrow alleyways in the Old Town of Algiers.

Sultan. For a long time, Algiers remained a haven of piracy but by 1830 the French had occupied the strategically important city and would remain until 1962. Not until the end of the 19th century did Algiers grow beyond the confines of the city walls that enclosed the original casbah and citadel.

Most of the buildings in the casbah are from the Ottoman period. Only the Djemaa el-Kebir, or Great Mosque, is older – it was built on the site of a Christian basilica in the Almoravid style. The minbar, built in 1097, boasts splendid carvings, and the minaret is from 1323. The New Mosque from 1660 is another important monument.

The minaret of the central mosque stands tall amongst houses arranged in concentric circles. Traditional garb is common here, and only unmarried women appear without the veil. Married women are completely covered except for small slits for the eyes.

GRAND ERG OCCIDENTAL

"Erg", or Arabic "irq", is the name for those parts of the Sahara that are covered by sand dunes, the classic image of the desert, although in fact they are relatively rare. In the Sahara only about twenty percent of the desert surface consists of ergs. In the Central Sahara these are the Grand Erg Oriental in eastern Algeria and western Libya, and the Grand Erg Occidental, which begins west of the road from Algiers to Tamanrasset and stretches all the way up to Morocco, Mali and Mauritania.

Shaped by the elements, the dune landscapes of the Western Sahara are the most beautiful of many landscapes in the region.

In fact, the geological formations of the Sahara are remarkably diverse. Having been flooded several times over the last few million years, vast sedimentary deposits were left in the many shallow basins that are now covered in stone deserts (hammada) or coarse gravel plains (reg) and are fringed by ridges where the often-crystalline Sahara Basement rises to the surface. In the central Sahara, these ridges are especially pronounced and have been further uplifted by volcanic activity. An example is the Hoggar Mountains where the transition from the basins to the ridges is formed by layers of terraced folds and plateaus such as the eroded sandstones of Tassili n'Ajjer.

TASSILI N'AJJER, HOGGAR MOUNTAINS

TASSILI N'AJJER

In one of the most inhospitable areas of the Sahara Desert, close to the borders with Libya and Niger, the Tassili-n'Ajjer Plateau extends over an area about the size of England. The region most accurately resembles a lunar landscape, with eroded rocks rising from the sands like giant stalagmites. In 1933, a major discovery was made in this grand setting: more than 15,000 rock paintings and engravings, and not all of them have been documented yet.

The images, which were produced during different periods beginning around 6000 BC, record significant phases of human cultural development at a time when the present-day desert still enjoyed a humid tropical climate. The paintings, which were done in naturally protective crevasses and caves, depict hunters chasing herds of elephants, giraffes and buffalo. Humans then also seem to have kept domestic herds: the images show shepherds grazing their animals in the savannah.

Different styles and periods can be clearly discerned in the hunting and cult scenes as well. The oldest images show only little realism and are schematic in style, while the scenes that were produced in subsequent periods are characterized by vitality, movement and elegance. In some depictions, the people are shown wearing elaborate ornaments and jewelry (left).

Main picture: The Tassili-n'Ajjer Plateau is also known as the "Louvre of the Sahara". The rock paintings produced thousands of years ago tell of the hunters, gatherers and herdsmen at a time when the climate and landscape resembled that of a savannah. The main picture dates back to the so-called Cattle Period (4000–1500 BC.).

HOGGAR MOUNTAINS

The Sahara, which covers virtually the entire northern portion of the African continent (roughly 8.7 million sq km / 3.4 million sq mi) boasts a rich diversity of landscapes in its central regions where the national boundaries of Algeria, Libya, Chad, Niger and Mali come together. A number of mountain ranges – the Hoggar Mountains in southern Algeria, the Tassili n'Ajjer Plateau farther to the east, which continues as the Libyan Jebel Akakus, the Aïr Mountains in northern Niger and the Tibesti Mountains in Chad – all make up the desert plateaus of the central Sahara.

The landscape here is mostly bedrock consisting of crystalline slate, gneiss, granite and quartzite that was formed during the Pre- cambrian and subsequently "denuded". Later, they were further affected by volcanic activity after which erosion finally shaped them into the bizarre formations that they display now. In the Hoggar Mountains (above and below) erosion exposed the basalt vents of the now dormant volcanoes – they now stand like silhouettes of black chimneys amidst the bright gravel plains.

KAIROUAN

The town of Kairouan, around 150 km (230 mi) south of Tunis, was founded in about 670 by the Uqba ibn Nafi of the Omayyad Dynasty as an outpost for the conquering Arab army. The mosque named after him is the oldest in North Africa and one of the most attractive religious structures in Tunisia (above). The town experienced its heyday in the ninth century during the rule of the Aghlabids Dynasty of emirs.

TUNIS

Around two million people live in greater Tunis where the suburbs spread like the tentacles of an octopus along the Bay of Tunis, from Bou Kornine Mountain to the saline lakes of the lagoon. The history of the city goes back to the ninth century BC. When the Phoenicians founded Carthage, a settlement established by the indigenous Numidians and originally known as Tunes already existed there. It wasn't until 894, however, that Tunis finally became an important capital during Aghlabid rule. A walk through the medina – the largest preserved

Old Town in North Africa – takes visitors past whitewashed houses with splendidly mosaic and tiled façades (below), past mosques and minarets and through the expansive colonnaded *souks*, or bazaars. The Zitouna Mosque (left) in the heart of the city is surpassed in size and importance only by the Great Mosque in Kairouan. It owes its name to an olive tree that once stood there and is supposed to have had miraculous healing powers.

Kairouan is still one of the most important Islamic centers in North Africa. Especially worth seeing is the Great Mosque in the Old Town whose prayer hall is structured by Roman columns (main picture).

EL DJEM

The Roman amphitheater of El Djem in Central Tunisia was built in about AD 230 and remodeled as a fortress after the withdrawal of the Romans. During the seventh century it served as a sanctuary for the female Berber leader Dahia al-Kahina in her futile battle against the Arab conquerors. Measuring 148 by 122 m (450 by 375 ft) and a good 40 m (131 ft) high, the massive oval building can accommodate 30,000 spectators and is still one of the largest and best-preserved amphitheaters in the entire former Roman Empire.

A guest entering one of the traditional houses in the oasis town of Ghadames in Libya is greeted by a riot of colors. Planned to the minutest of details, rooms inside are decorated with bright murals (main picture).

GHADAMES

The ancient city of Cydamus was originally founded by the Romans as a garrison before becoming a bishop's see during the Byzantine Empire and finally being converted to Islam by Arab conquerors in the 8th century. In its heyday, this town at the crossroads of the Saharan caravan routes had trading relations from Timbuktu to the coast of Morocco. Today, most people live in the new city, but they take good care of the old adobe town as well. Many in fact live in the Old Town during the hot summer months as the brick, two-story constructions are better suited to the climate here. Traditionally, before their weddings, women are given the option of deco-rating the whitewashed rooms of the house with red ornaments and there is one special room in these houses – the *kouba* – that is used only two times during the lives of its inhabitants: on the wedding day and when the husband dies, in order to receive grieving guests. The alleys between the houses are often covered with mats in order to keep the neighborhood cool.

CYRENE

The former Greek colony of Cyrene on the Mediterranean coast is the origin of Cyrenaica, now Libya. Until the 4th century it was one of the largest cities in Africa with an agora (marketplace) featuring a round temple with statues of the gods Demeter and Kore (top). Valuable mosaics such as the detail with nymph and satyr above are now housed in the Cyrene Museum with other art of the period.

LEPTIS MAGNA

Founded by the Phoenicians, Leptis Magna was one of the most beautiful cities in the Roman Empire. This fact is made obvious by its splendid ruins, which include the impressive market building (top) and the vast Forum of Severus, whose arcades were once decorated by Medusa heads (above).

The high walls on either side of the road in Ghadames seem like protective barriers (far left, middle). Some are only partly covered, however, in order to allow in sufficient light. Wandering through the covered alleyways can be as disorienting as a labyrinth (left).

SABRATHA

After the fall of Carthage and a brief interlude as part of the Numidian empire of King Massinissa, Tripolitania came under Roman rule. In the 3rd century, Sabratha became a bishop's see and in the middle of the 5th century it fell to Vandals before the Byzantines emperors conquered the town in the 6th century, only to cede it again to the Arabs in the 7th century. They were then replaced by the Ottomans in the 16th century.

The most impressive monument in Sabratha is the theater, which features a superb wall at the back of the stage (top) and beautiful carvings on its proscenium frieze. Other finds are similarly important, for example this splendid mosaic (above).

Sabratha, about 70 km (43 mi) west of the present-day Libyan city of Tripoli (the ancient Oea), still features many well-preserved remains from Roman times including the theater built around 200; the Forum which is surrounded by columns; the Temple of Antonius and Faustina; the Temple of Jupiter; the 1st-century Basilica; public baths; and fountains, latrines and various other secular and religious structures. In the early Christian period a church was built into the Roman law court basilica.

CAIRO

"He who has not seen Cairo has not seen the world," it says in the tales of One Thousand and One Nights. Today, nearly one in four of the just under 70 million Egyptians live Africa's largest city. The glitter of the metropolis on the Nile may have faded a little since the days of Scheherazade, but Cairo is much more than just the undisputed political, spiritual and economic heart of the country. It is also the epitome of an Oriental fairytale city and as such it continues to fascinate visitors.

Al Qahira – the "Triumphant One", a name that was later corrupted to Cairo by Italian merchants, was founded in the year 969 by Shiite rulers, the Fatimids, near the ancient Arabic settlement of Fustat. Initially it served as a palace city, but it was Saladin, founder of the Ayyubid dynasty, who finally opened the royal enclave to the public.

OLD CAIRO

The district of Old Cairo is primarily inhabited by Copts, the Christian descendants of the ancient Egyptians and boasts more than 2,000 years of history. During the reign of the emperors Hadrian and Trajan, a Roman fortress named Babylon already controlled transport on the Nile. In 642, the Muslim conqueror Amr Ibn el-As erected the encampment which eventually developed into the first Arabic capital. One slightly peculiar sight is the Al-Moallaqa Church, which is dedicated to the Madonna (left and right) and boasts more than 100

icons, some dating back more than a thousand years. It owes its epithet, "the Hanging One", to the fact that – at least visually – it appears "suspended" above the entrance to the historic Babylon.

AL-AZHAR

The Al-Azhar Mosque and University rise gloriously out of the heart of the Old Town. It was named after Fatima, the Prophet's daughter, who is said to have been so beautiful that she was known as al-Zahra, "the Most Flourishing and Shining". The intricate complex of buildings comprises a place of worship, a madrassa, or Qur'anic school, and students' hostels as well as five minarets. For more than 1,000 years it has been the intellectual and power center for the entire Arab and Muslim world; somewhat similar to the relationship Oxford and the Sorbonne have with the Vatican. A subdued bustle usually prevails in the interior courtyard here, which is encircled by alabaster columns. The adjoining prayer hall was once used for lectures.

KHAN EL-KHALILI

Khan el-Khalili, Cairo's vast *souk*, or market, is situated between Muski Street and the Hussein Mosque and attracts visitors like a giant magnet. It was named after a Mamluk stable master who some 600 years ago had a large trading estate built here. Nearby was the spice market where merchants from Arabia, Persia and India traded exotically scented goods. Today, the range of wares consists largely of trinkets for credit card-wielding tourists. As far as the overall atmosphere is concerned, however, the maze of narrow and mostly covered alleyways still conjures up the authentic atmosphere of a large bazaar.

MOHAMMED-ALI

The Mosque of Mohammed Ali (1824–57), with its slender minarets and mighty vaulted dome, stands out in all senses of the term. As the defining silhouette of the Old Town, it is perched high atop Citadel Hill. Its walls are covered in alabaster, a mar-

ble-like plaster that gave the mosque its other name – the Alabaster Mosque. Mohammed Ali (1769–1849), born in what is now Macedonia, is buried in the western corner of the domed Byzantine edifice. He is revered as the founder of modern Egypt.

Three thousand years and thirty-one dynasties are on display in the fifty rooms of the Egyptian Museum. Thousands of steles,

EGYPTIAN MUSEUM

reliefs and sarcophagi, jewelry, small houses, models of ships and other sacrificial offerings command respect and admiration from every visitor. The featured attractions are the death masks of the ancient Egyptian pharaohs (left: the mask of Tutankhamun).

Main picture: Cairo is also known as the "City of 1,000 Minarets": Here the towers of the 14th-century Sultan Hassan Mosque mingle with the adjacent Er Rifai Mosque dating back to 1912.

GIZA

Closely linked with Cairo is the provincial capital of Giza on the west bank of the Nile. On a limestone plateau above the town stand the three large pyramids of the pharaohs (kings) Khufu, Khafre and Menkaure (top). They were built in the 3rd millennium BC as tombs that were to survive for all eternity.

Each of the blocks used to build the vast mount of the Great (or Khufu) Pyramid weigh an average of two tons. It is a majestic and awe-inspiring sight, even without the finely polished casing originally used to enshroud the structure's core. After completion, the pyramid was nearly 147 m (482 ft)

tall, but today it is some 10 m (33 ft) shorter because Cairo builders during the Middle Ages felt justified in helping themselves to the free materials.

The adjacent Khafre Pyramid has preserved some of its outer casing. The pyramid of Menkaure is markedly smaller – about half the size – at only 65.5 m (215 ft) in height, a rather modest attempt when compared with the neighboring giants.

The Great Sphinx (above and main picture) lies to the east of the three monuments. Hewn from natural rock, it is a representation of the Sun God. The Sphinx Temple stands in front of statue's giant paws, a veneration temple also carved from rock. Beside it is a valley temple built and clad in rose granite and alabaster.

In the 1950s, a sensational discovery was made: On the southern side of the pyramid, more than 1,000 fragments of a cedar-wood boat was excavated and reconstructed in a pit. A museum next to the pyramid displays the "Solar Barque of Khufu" in its full splendor (left).

A sphinx – half human and half lion – crouches in a hollow in front of the Khafre Pyramid (main picture); over 70 m (77 yds) long and around 20 m (66 ft) tall, it is a colossal guardian depicting the Sun God.

MEMPHIS, SAKKARA

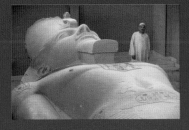

Memphis has played many roles in its long history: Egypt's first capital, administrative center, largest garrison town, and sanctuary of the God Ptah. Today, however, not a lot is left of this former metropolis. The palaces and mansions made from clay tiles have vanished and reverted to fertile agricultural land. Only the colossal figure of Ramses II (left) and an alabaster sphinx testify to its former heyday. They are located in the open-air museum in a palm grove close to the small village of Mitrahina on the south-western margins of Giza.

Much more impressive is the ancient cemetery of Sakkara, Ancient Egypt's largest necropolis. In the middle of this vast complex is the burial precinct of King Djoser, whose 4,600-year-old

step pyramid (above) is believed to be the oldest stone structure in the history of humankind.

With their fascinating relief pictures, the many mastabas (tombs) offer superb insight into the everyday life not only of high-ranking officials but also of farmers, artisans and fishermen. They also depict the fauna and flora of the time.

DAHSHUR

The burial field of Dahshur is located on the left bank of the Nile, a few miles south of Sakkara. It features the Bent Pyramid (above, in the background), which is 105 m (345 ft) tall and can only be viewed from the outside. It is assumed that the original angle of inclination of the pyramid proved too steep, and that it was therefore decided to continue building at a shallower angle, hence the slightly rounded peak.

The Red Pyramid (above, in the foreground) is 101 m (331 ft) tall and was named for the hue of the stone from which it was built. It is fully open to the public, right into its innermost burial chamber, and is considered the oldest structure in human history to have been built in pure pyramid shape. Both pyramids were erected over 4,500 years ago by King Snofru.

LUXOR

The temple city of Karnak, a necropolis on the west bank of the Nile, combines with the town of Luxor on the east bank to form a focal point of ancient Egyptian culture. They are the main attractions of any visit to Upper Egypt. The foundation stone for the central temple complex, which stands in the heart of the urban area right on the promenade, was laid as early as 1380 BC by Amenophis III (or Amenhotep III).

A symbol of power in the New Kingdom, the temple was dedicated to the trinity of gods in Thebes: Amun, Mut and Chons. Today it still presents an amazing wealth of giant statues, obelisks, pylons and papyrus columns all lined up over a length of 260 m (853 ft). The smaller artifacts from there and other excavation sites have all been taken to the local museum where they are expertly displayed.

KARNAK

For many centuries, the temple complex of Karnak (above), north of Luxor's city center, was Egypt's main spiritual sanctuary. It is dedicated to Amun, the "Hidden One", an ancient divinity mentioned as far back as the pyramid texts of the Old Kingdom but who did not become the imperial god Amun-Ra of Thebes until 2000 BC. The complex originally boasted ten entrance gates, known as pylons. Today, the main entrance to the compound of ruins leads

through an avenue lined with ram-headed sphinxes (below). From there to the Precinct of Mut, more than half a mile away, visitors are faced with one superlative after the other: the tallest obelisk at 30 m (98 ft) weighing 323 tons; the largest columned hall with 134 petrified umbels and papyrus plants, each up to 10 m (33 ft) in circumference; and the largest pylon at 113 m (3,652 ft) wide, 43 m (141 ft) tall and about 15m (49 ft) deep).

In ancient Egypt, a temple was a likeness of the world. Its columns symbolically carried the firmament. The inner sanctum, which even the king could only enter after he had observed strict purification rituals, was hidden in darkness. Main picture: The Great Hypostyle Hall in Karnak.

The Nile: lifeblood of Egypt. Few other countries are as strongly marked by a single river as Egypt. The classic image includes feluccas – sailing boats with one or two masts (main picture, near Aswan).

THE NILE

A cruise on the Nile in Upper Egypt reveals a seductively idyllic and constant world – despite the ships having to jostle for position between Luxor and Aswan in high season. The riverbanks are lined with children at play and women tending to their washing; with water buffalo, ibises, and the odd camel; with sand dunes and rock faces, deep green sugarcane fields and date palm groves; with villages with mud huts and thatched roofs, and the ever-fascinating tombs and temples all forming the backdrop for this picturesque scene. Right: A granite threshold cuts through the riverbed, shaping the landscape near Aswan, Egypt's most southerly town.

PHILAE

This temple complex – moved from Philae to the adjacent Nile island of Agilkia near Aswan – is dominated by the Ptolemaic Temple of Isis whose pylons are adorned with relief images. Inside is the sanctuary with a plinth for the Barque of Isis. Next to the Temple of Isis stands the Roman kiosk of Hadrian with its beautiful column capitals.

Tomb No. 62 in the Valley of the Kings, features Tutankhamun's sarcophagus made of red quartzite (main picture). The golden throne from his burial treasure (opposite page) shows the young pharaoh and his wife.

THEBES WEST

In the days of the pharaohs, the east bank of the Nile was the bank of life. It was in Thebes, the "City of a Hundred Towers", as it was known to the Greeks, where people established their settlements. It is also where the rulers' palaces and the monumental temples stood. The opposite bank belonged to the dead. Vast funerary sanctuaries and necropolises were erected there in Thebes West.

Among the multitude of temples, those of Ramses II (the Ramesseum), of Ramses III (Medinet Habu) and of Queen Hatshepsut (Deir el-Bahri) stand out. The latter, with its majestic ramps and three column-lined terraces, all in front of a backdrop of a 300-m-high (984-ft) rock face counts as one of the top attractions in Upper Egypt. Part of the same complex is also a small temple of Thutmosis III, Hatshepsut's son-in-law.

A fascinating sight on the journey to the complex are the two Memnon Colossuses – two seated statues just under 18 m (59 ft) tall that were built by Amenhotep III.

VALLEY OF THE KINGS

In the face of all the skepticism, Howard Carter firmly believed that there were still more treasures to be discovered in the Valley of the Kings. In 1922, the British archeologist was vindicated when he discovered the legendary treasure of Tutankhamun. Since then, researchers have uncovered more than sixty Pharaonic tombs in the shadowless rocky valley on the

The Valley of the Kings was once known as the "Place of Truths". After years of disappointment, on November 4, 1922, Howard Carter at last discovered a staircase that led into the depths.

northern fringes of the Nile's west bank. Only less than one-third is accessible to the general public, but one ticket entitles visitors to view three tombs, the interiors of which are truly amazing. The walls are covered in superb reliefs, some in surprisingly well-preserved colors. Measurements have shown that the visitor masses in high season perspired up to 27 liters (7 U.S. gallons) a day in a single chamber. No surprise then that the sheen of the frescoes has faded rapidly, even though glass plates now protect most of them – and that the authorities had to issue strict rules to regulate the visits.

Hatshepsut was the only female pharaoh of ancient Egypt, which was dominated by men in order to maintain power. Her burial temple (left) in the Deir el-Bahari Valley, extends across several levels linked by ramps and is visible from Karnak on a clear day.

They are certainly among the more lasting memories of any Nile cruise: The four 20-m-tall (66-ft) colossal statues of King Ramses II (main picture and above). Commissioned by the pharaoh to be hewn straight out of the rock formation on the west bank of the

Nile, between the First and the Second Cataract, these giant reliefs are at the gable end of the Great Temple dedicated to Amun-Ra and Re-Harakhte and were completed in the 13th century BC. Behind the entrance to the Great Temple is a hall of columns with giant figures of Ramses II (left). The smaller temple (above) was dedicated to the goddess Hathor and to his wife Nefertari.

When the two giants were in endangered by the future Lake Nasser in the 1960s, UNESCO had them moved 65 m (213 ft) higher up – a massive effort that took four years to complete.

The Great Temple of Ramses II (main picture) would have been submerged in Lake Nasser forever had it not been cut into stone blocks weighing 20 tons each and reassembled at a higher level.

St Catherine's Monastery (main picture) is tucked in behind fortress-like walls at the base of Mount Sinai. Its holiest place is the Chapel of the Burning Bush, built in 1216. It marks the spot where God called upon Moses: "...for the place whereon thou standest is holy ground".

THE RED SEA

The Sinai Peninsula is 60,000 sq km (23,160 sq mi) in size and forms a link between Asia and Africa. It is mostly shapeless and flat in the north, where it has served as a gateway for almost all of Egypt's invaders, from the Hyksos and Persians to the British. Toward the south, however, the scenery becomes more dramatic, culminating in the mountainous region around St Catherine's Monastery. The main attractions here are the fine beaches along the Red Sea and the fascinating underwater world. The reefs between Sharm el-Sheikh and the border town of Taba in the Gulf of Aqaba are among the most attractive diving areas on Earth.

ST CATHERINE'S MONASTERY

The St Catherine's Monastery is set between the steep rock faces of the Wadi Araba, a valley at 1,500 m (4,922 ft) where the Israelites are said to have danced around the Golden Calf. Covering 6,200 sq m (67,000 sq ft), it is the smallest diocese in the world as well as one of the oldest monasteries in all of Christendom. Its history goes back to the year 330, when Helena, the Empress of

As early as the 4th century AD, hermits settled at this place. Inside the walls of the St Catherine's Monastery, the scion of the legendary Burning Bush is hidden.

Byzantium, and her husband Justinian built a small chapel here. The monastery received its name later, in the Middle Ages, when rumors spread that the Orthodox Greek monks were keeping in their basilica the alleged body of Saint Catherine of Alexandria – the daughter of the King of Cyprus, who is said to have lived in Alexandria around the year 300.

Aside from its mountain ranges, the main attraction on the southern Sinai Peninsula is the underwater world of the Red Sea (left). Some 250 different types of coral and more than 1,000 fish species live along the 1,500 km (932 mi) of reef. The diving areas are right by the shore, and begin just under the surface.

MOUNT SINAI

St Catherine's Monastery receives around 50,000 visitors each year. More than half of these, it is estimated, climb the adjacent peak on which, according to the Bible, Yahweh is said to have given the Tablets of Law with their Ten Commandments to the Prophet. Several routes lead up the 2,285-m-high (7,497-ft) Mount Sinai, the most direct of which has a staircase with more than 3,000 stone steps. Legend has it that it was built by a single monk honoring a vow.

View from Mount Sinai. "For they ... were come to the desert of Sinai, and had pitched in the wilderness, Israel camped before the mount" – the Bible.

RÂS MUHAMMAD

An insignificant fishing village only one generation ago, the town of Sharm el-Sheikh, not far from the southern tip of the Sinai Peninsula, has developed into a popular seaside and diving resort. The islands and most of the coastline in the area around Râs Muhammad and Nabq are nature reserves that are guarded by game wardens. The underwater world enchants the senses – even a snorkeling trip gives a good impression of this.

Râs Muhammad National Park protects around 480 sq km (185 sq mi) of land and sea on the southern tip of the Sinai Peninsula. The park also includes the coastal strip off Sharm el-Sheikh.

KSOUR OF OUADANE, CHINGUETTI, TICHITT AND OUALATA

These four fortified towns, known as *ksar* (plural: *ksour*) on the caravan routes of the North African Sahara, are testimonies to a grandiose history. All of them have been partially preserved as ruins. Oualata in the south-east of the Mauritanian Sahel was an important trading city and, with its Qur'anic school and library, also a great center of Islamic scholarship. The classic one- and two-story houses here stand closely together and are built from stone before being plastered with reddish-brown clay. Following ancient traditions the façades, door frames, window niches and rooms are decorated with red-

dish-brown ornamentation on a white background. Among the ruins of Tichitt, an important trading city halfway between Timbuktu and the Atlantic that was founded in 1150, the traditional architecture captivates with its simplicity. Light and greenish sedimentary rocks are used here as a building material for residential homes.

Ouadane, also once an important post for the camel caravans that transported salt, dates and gold from West African countries to the north, is virtually a field of ruins nowadays. The Harmattan trade winds blowing from the north-east make their own contribution, gradually burying the ruins under desert sand (right). The oldest part of the settlement in the Adrar Massif in north-west Mauritania is formed by the Ksar el-Khali, a fortress complex.

Chinguetti (left, in the Friday Mosque) was founded in the 13th century and is also in the Adrar Massif. It is the most famous his-

toric desert settlement in the country's interior. A stopover on the camel caravans, Chinguetti was once a much-frequented gathering point for pilgrims on their way to Mecca, and was even one of the Seven Holy Cities of Islam. Amidst the medieval box-shaped stone houses with their ornamented niches stands the oldest mosque in the country. The minaret here is typical for the architecture of this region, assembled from stone plates with ornamental niches. The battlements were capped with ostrich egg finials. Some 1,300 historic manuscripts are kept in the central library of Chinguetti.

The privately-run manuscript libraries of Chinguetti, some of which are in traditional mud houses (main picture), are also open to students and visitors. Many of the manuscripts are editions of the Qur'an or collections of *hadiths*, sayings by the Prophet Muhammad.

DJENNÉ

For centuries Djenné, a town situated on a branch of the Bani River, a tributary of the Niger, maintained a very close trading relationship with Timbuktu, which could be reached on the river. Even after Djenné had been integrated into the Songhai Empire in the 15th century, it continued to flourish both economically and spiritually. A 2.5-km-long (1.5-mi) mud-brick forti-fication wall, multi-level palaces with defensive battlements, and magnificent portals as well as the Great Mosque were built here. In the 19th century a radical Islamist ruler, wishing to establish a theocratic state in Djenné, had this sacred building and the other mosques torn down. From 1907 to 1909 the Great Mosque was rebuilt according to the original plans in the traditional Sudano-Sahelian mud-brick style. The oldest city districts still have the classic houses of merchants and artisans from the 16th to the 19th centuries. Typical of the Djenné style in the one- or two-story flat-roofed buildings are window openings with ceramic crossbars, richly ornamented façades and doors with iron fittings.

In the Old Town, grain is still ground in the traditional fashion (far left and middle). Mud-brick buildings require regular maintenance, and so the inhabitants of Djenné repair the walls of their Great Mosque (left) every year during the "Fête de Crépissage" (plastering festival).

THE NIGER, TIMBUKTU

THE NIGER

The Niger, Africa's third-largest river, crosses the Sahel and Sahara regions of Mali and Niger on its way from the Guinea Highlands in the south-west to Nigeria. The river has taken the lives of many explorers and travelers, including the Scotsman Mungo Park, but it was not until the mid-19th century that the German geographer Heinrich Barth finally solved the riddle of the river's course. In Mali the Niger turns north in a large arc deep into the desert and then, north of the ancient royal town of Gao, it veers south and finally discharges itself into the sea in Nigeria. The river has always been an important trade route with major posts on both banks.

TIMBUKTU

By 1330, Timbuktu (or Tomboucto) had become one of the most important centers of trade and culture in West Africa. During its heyday in the 15th century, this town on the Niger was the main transshipment center for Saharan trade as well as a focal point for Islamic scholarship. The main points of interest in the northern districts are the medieval university and the Sankoré Mosque (above). It has a pyramid-shaped minaret and is built in traditional mud-brick and wood. It is the model for Islamic buildings in sub-Saharan Africa. The Djinguereber (below) is the oldest mosque and the Sidi Yahya mosque is the smallest.

In the Gao region the Niger runs through barren desert scenery (main picture). Partly navigable during high water, the river ends its journey in a vast delta that covers roughly 25,000 sq km (9,650 sq mi) in the Gulf of Guinea.

These masks are part of a tradition of highly developed carving among the Dogon. They are worn for the Sigi festival (an initiation ritual) as well as many other ceremonies to honor the dead, whose souls are said to be helped by the masks in their transit to a final resting place. The exact significance of the masks is only known to the members of the secret mask society.

East of Mopti is a rocky mountain range, the Cliff of Bandiagara, that extends for about 150 km (93 mi). It is the home of the Dogon, a people famous for their cliff buildings and creative masks. In the Dogon's worldview, all elements in the universe are linked with each other by a tight network of symbolic relationships. The construction style for their homes, cult buildings and gathering places reflects this and is characterized by religious and mythological notions. Similar patterns and structures can be found in the façades of the houses, villages, gardens, even in the fields or a shroud. The villages are laid out according to anthropomorphic shapes that are modeled on the mythical ancestor of the Dogon, while the architecture of the mud buildings reflects the duality of man and woman.

Most spectacular among the Dogon settlements are the villages that have been built into the steep rock cliffs (left and main picture) where mud box houses and storage silos with conical roofs are piled on top of each other over several levels. Men and women have separate silos where millet and even jewelry can be stored. In between the silos are binu sanctuaries, which are reminiscent of temples and feature round towers. There are also *togunas*, gathering places for elders with roofs made from millet straw. Closely linked with the local mythology of the Dogon is the use of masks, which play a pivotal role in their social life. There are around 100 different types of masks that are worn for a variety of festivals and rituals. The Dogon also excel in their artisanship when it comes to rock paintings. The paintings below (left and right) come from a cave near Songo, where three times a year the Dogon hold circumcision ceremonies. To create the paintings, red, white and black pigments are applied as finger paint. The subjects that are depicted represent mythical ancestors, masks, weapons, and animals, but also everyday objects as well as important cosmological and historical events.

The mud box houses of the Dogon are like birds' nests in the rocky precipices of the Cliff of Bandiagara (main picture). Many of them can only be reached by ladder. Even cemeteries have been built here.

This nature reserve is the largest in Africa and covers just under 80,000 sq km (30,880 sq mi). One of the most impressive landscapes to be experienced here is the transitional area between Aïr and Ténéré, where rock formations and sandy desert meet to create a fascinating contrast (left). The Aïr Mountains in north-western Niger stretch over 400 km (249 mi) from north to south. It is an eroded plateau punctuated by a series of flat granite peaks of volcanic origin that are on average 700 m (2,297 ft) high. They feature series of individual peaks that are separated from one other by dune valleys or *koris* that are at their highest up on Mont Gréboun. In the Ténéré Desert to the east, shallow gravel and sandy plains give way to a sea of dunes. Often there is no rainfall here for years, and the range of temperatures is extreme. The humid south-western slopes of the Aïr Mountains feature grassy plains, for example. The *koris* store groundwater allowing palm trees and acacia shrub to flourish, while wild olive trees and cypresses grow up in the mountains. Barbary sheep, wild asses and fennec foxes live here. In the northern parts of the mountains prehistoric humans created superb rock paintings (right: near Tiguidit). The oldest paintings here indicate a much wetter savannah climate and date from the Neolithic period when people began herding cattle. In the early Tertiary, some parts of the Ténéré were a shallow inland sea and it is this era that produced the many fossils here (dinosaurs, tortoises, crocodiles, extinct fishes). Arrowheads from 7000 to 3000 BC indicate hunting and farming cultures.

The Montagnes Bleues on the border of Aïr and Ténéré National Parks in Niger feature a bizarre world of sand and rock formations (main picture).

NIMBA

The Mount Nimba Strict Nature Reserve is located in the border triangle of Liberia, Guinea and Côte d'Ivoire. Its highest elevation and most distinctive landmark is the 1,752-m-high (5,748-ft) Mount Nimba Massif, which straddles the border of Côte d'Ivoire and Guinea. It is covered by a virtually uninterrupted blanket of forest. On the lower slopes it is mostly still deciduous, while above 1,000 m (3,281 ft) a montane forest dominates, and the summit is characterized by savannah. About forty indigenous plant and more than 200 animal species thrive here. Among the animals on the reserve are elephants, buffaloes, antelopes, lions, leopards, hyenas, old world monkeys and chimpanzees. In the waters, pygmy hippopotami und dwarf crocodiles (above) roam freely. Vultures, snakes and rare species of amphibians such as viviparous toads also live here.

COMOÉ

The largest most species-rich nature reserve in Côte d'Ivoire is Comoé National Park, in the north-east of the country straddling the transitional zone from savannah to rainforest. The park covers roughly 11,500 sq km (4,439 sq mi) and owes its name to the Comoé River, which is between 100 and 200 m (328 and 650 ft) wide and runs north-south through the park for over 230 km (143 mi). It carries sufficient water even during the dry season and is fringed by dense gallery forests. Near the water's edge you will find hippos, crocodiles and many species of birds. In the savannah, Cape buffalo, warthogs, monkeys – eleven species of monkey live here – and antelopes roam the wilderness. Elephants dominate the forests in the southern part of the park. Predators such as lions, leopards (above) and hyenas also prowl about here, but their populations are now quite small.

Main picture: Four subspecies of chimpanzee are common all over West and Central Africa. This likeable chap lives in Taï National Park in Côte d'Ivoire.

TAÏ

Taï National Park comprises a large part of Africa's remaining tropical rainforests that once covered the countries of Ghana, Côte d'Ivoire, Liberia and Sierra Leone. The dense tropical vegetation in this 3,300-sq-km (1,274-sq-mi) nature reserve in south-western Côte d'Ivoire is characterized by a number of endemic species and more than 50-m-tall (164-ft) trees whose dense foliage and vines allow little sunlight to penetrate down to the forest floor. In the northern and south-eastern areas, the soils are poor in nutrients while in the south-west the ground is damper. Aside from many bird species, this is also a habitat for forest elephants, pygmy hippopotami, leopards, antelopes, buffalo and more than ten species of apes, including chimpanzees (main picture). The tropical rainforest also provides a habitat for numerous reptiles such as the West African bush viper (above).

LOPÉ-OKANDA

The Lopé-Okanda Game Reserve in Gabon offers an unusual mix of tropical rainforest and savannah. Archaeological finds (above) show that West African tribes migrated through this area as far back as the Neolithic and Iron Ages.

VIRUNGA

Virunga National Park covers a vast expanse of just under 8,000 sq km (3,088 sq mi). It extends along the Great African Rift Valley, to the north and south of Lake Rutanzige (formerly Lake Edward) in the north-eastern section of the Democratic Republic of the Congo on the border with Uganda and Rwanda. Formerly known as Albert National Park, which was Africa's first national park founded in 1925, Virunga is home to leopards, okapis and several species of antelopes, a number of primates, and migratory birds from Siberia

and Europe who spend their winters here. Mountain gorillas, which are seriously endangered (right and main picture), have also found a last refuge in the Virunga Mountains. In 1967, U.S. zoologist Dian Fossey began her long-term study here, first on Congolese, then on Rwandan territory. Of the estimated global population of 700 great apes, a good fifty percent live in Virunga. The Democratic Republic of the Congo, Rwanda and Uganda employ special patrols in order to protect this close relative of humans from extinction.

There are only several hundred or so mountain gorillas left, and about half of them live in Virunga National Park in north-eastern Democratic Republic of the Congo (main picture).

AKSUM

The kingdom of Aksum in the heart of ancient Ethiopia existed in the first century and was converted to Christianity in the fourth century. The ruins of the capital of the same name were characterized by about 130 giant stele, obelisk-like monoliths made from trachyte. They were replicas of the up to nine-story "ghost homes" in the ancient Hadramaut region, where immigrants arrived in Ethiopia in the seventh century.

The Omo Valley southern Ethiopia is home to the Karo tribe who adorn their heads with particularly elaborate headdresses and bright paint (main picture).

SIMIEN

mountain range, offers a refuge to some extremely rare animal species. Among these are the Gelada baboon, the Simien fox and the Walia ibex. The rare Ethiopian wolf (below), a member of the wild dog family, also roams this beautiful national park.

Due to heavy erosion, the Simien Mountains developed into one of the most spectacular landscapes on earth. The peaks reach heights of 4,500 m (14,765 ft), while raging torrents course through rugged basalt gorges that are up to 1,500 m (4,922 ft) deep. Towering above all of this is the 4,620-m-high (15,158-ft) Ras Dashan (above), the fourth-highest mountain in Africe. Simien National Park, named after the

OMO

The Omo River (right) is roughly about 800 km (497 mi) long and carries water throughout the year to its final destination, Lake Turkana, on Ethiopia's southern border. Among the peoples who live here, the Karo tribe is well known for its body decorations (above). The lower reaches of the river have gained recognition as an archaeological excavation site for prehistoric remains. According to scientific research, Homo sapi-

ens has lived in East Africa for nearly 200,000 years. Two skulls and other skeletal remains ("Omo I" and "Omo II") that were found in 1967 by the U.S. paleoanthropologist Richard Leakey near Kibish in the Omo Valley are estimated to be 130,000 years old but may even be much older. An analysis of mineral crystals in the soil layers where the bones were found suggest a likely age of 195,000 years.

LALIBELA

King Lalibela is said to have been told directly by God himself, and in keeping with the apocalypse, to build a copy of "heavenly Jerusalem" on this spot – now named after the king. Heavenly assistance was said to have been forthcoming as well. The story continues that angels helped the architects and even got involved in the masonry and construction at night. Ultimately, the eleven churches of Lalibela were finished in just twenty-three years. Bete Giyorgis (main picture) is the most intact of them now. It was hewn from the surrounding rocks in the shape of a Greek cross.

Situated in the heart of the highlands of Ethiopia at an elevation of around 2,600 m (8,531 ft), the rock-hewn churches of Lalibela were built from the end of the 12th century during the reign of Gebre Mesqel Lalibela. He was the most important king of the Zagwe Dynasty, and Roha, as the capital was formerly known, was renamed in his honor. The eleven churches are architecturally among the most beautiful places of worship in Africa. They are monolithic churches, that is, they were cut from straight the vol-

canic rock over the course of several decades and linked by a maze of paths and tunnels that have been dug out of the rock. The most popular destination for pilgrims traveling to Lalibela is the Bete Maryam, or Saint Mary's Church. Bete Medhane Alem is the largest monolithic church in the world. The best-known is Bete Giyorgis (main picture), modeled after a Greek Orthodox cross. Inside Lalibela's churches (left) priests guard the art treasures that include valuable manuscripts, crucifixes and murals.

Measuring up to 4 m (13 ft) in height and weighing up to 8 tons, the African elephant (main picture, in Amboseli National Park) is the largest living land mammal. An elephant spends fifteen to twenty hours a day feeding and requires 200 to 300 kg (441 to 662 lbs) of food and 100 to 150 liters (22 to 33 gallons) of water.

AMBOSELI

Kenya's most frequented national park owes its popularity to the breathtaking beauty of Mount Kilimanjaro as a backdrop. The relatively small nature reserve, covering an area of only 392 sq km (151 sq mi), boasts an astonishing diversity of species, especially around Lake Amboseli, which attracts large herds with its juicy savannah grass. Black rhino, elephant, buffalo, leopard and lion sightings are often a daily occurrence in Amboseli National Park.

TSAVO

Covering an area of 20,800 sq km (8,029 sq mi), Kenya's largest national park is divided into an eastern and a western part by the parallel road and rail tracks that run through it. While sparse vegetation with thorn bushes and open scrubland predominate in Tsavo East, Tsavo West features denser vegetation. The rolling Taita Hills make the countryside in the west altogether more attractive, but they also make it more difficult to observe the wildlife (above, a leopard).

MASAI MARA

The Masai Mara Reserve consists of open, hilly grassland and is situated at an elevation of between 1,500 and 1,700 m (4,922 and 5,578 ft). The Mara and Talek rivers flow through the area year-round, providing an important habitat for hippopotamuses and crocodiles while Burchell's zebra, buffaloes, giraffes and hartebeest graze in the open savannah. From June to October they are joined by some 250,000 Burchell's zebra and 1.3 million wildebeests (above) migrating north from the Serengeti. In addition to the interior, which covers roughly 520 sq km (200 sq mi), the Masai Mara Reserve is not reserved for animals alone. The Masai (below), in whose traditional herding and grazing grounds the reserve has been established, are allowed to continue their semi-nomadic life on the perimeter of the national park. Leopards, cheetahs and the largest population of lions in Kenya are just as much at home here as elephants and a few rare black rhinos. The latter are virtually extinct and now under special protection. The guides in the lodges know the protected area well. It is best to join an organized safari to be sure you see the "big five" (elephants, rhinos, lions, leopards and buffalo) on your trip.

The montane forests and marshlands of the Rwenzori Mountains in Uganda provide a biosphere and sanctuary of vast dimensions for numerous endangered animal and plant species (main pictures).

BWINDI

Bwindi Impenetrable National Park is located in a remote transitional area between steppe and mountains. More than 100 species of ferns exist here, and no fewer than 160 tree species form the montane forest. Of the approximately 300 bird species that have been documented so far, the woodland birds make up about two-thirds and they are joined by about 200 types of butterflies. The nature reserve is famous for its mountain gorillas and the park's higher altitudes are home to about 300 of them – roughly half of the world population of this endangered species. They live in peaceful family communities led by an older male or silverback.

RUWENZORI

This roughly 120-km-long (75-mi) and 50-km-wide (31-mi) mountain range was created by movements in the earth's crust and is situated on the border between the Democratic Republic of the Congo and Uganda. Its highest peak is Mount Stanley at 5,109 m (16,763 ft). The national park comprises a mountain territory covering roughly 1,000 sq km (6,214 sq mi) in south-western Uganda and, aside from glaciers, lakes and waterfalls at the higher altitudes there are also vast marshes and swamps in the valleys and foothills of the Rwenzori Mountains, where tall plant species such as papyrus offer protection to the elephants. The volcanic craters are covered in

The giant lobelia grows in the alpine zone of the tropical high mountains.

lush grasses that provide food for gazelles, antelopes and buffaloes. Bamboo even grows at elevations of about 2,000 m (6,562 ft). This is the natural habitat of the leopard. At higher elevations, the montane forests are almost continuously shrouded in mist and feature flora of unusual sizes. Lobelias, which normally grow to a height of 30 cm (12 in), attain heights here of 7 m (23 ft). In protected places, ferns can grow to more than 10 m (33 ft) in height and some of the heather species grow to tree-like sizes. This gigantism can only be ascribed to a combination of mineral-rich soils, constant temperatures, high air humidity and the fact that the typically thick layer of mist reduces the high ultraviolet radiation of the upper altitudes that is harmful for plants.

Bwindi in the south-western corner of Uganda is known for its diversity of tree and fern species (left and far left) as well as its rare bird and butterfly species. The montane forests are also one of the last remaining refuges for the endangered mountain gorilla (opposite page).

SERENGETI

The Serengeti, a vast savannah east of Lake Victoria, extends from northwestern Tanzania all the way to neighboring Kenya. The "kopjes" (Dutch for "little heads") that rise everywhere from the otherwise flat grasslands (above) are gneiss and quartzite rocks that once lay below the surface of the soil. Laid open by erosion over thousands of years, they now serve as viewpoints for people as well as animals (right, from top to bottom: giraffes, elephants, zebras, lions), but they also provide protection from enemies and the often blazing hot sun. Around 15,000 sq km (5,790 sq mi) of Tanzanian territory have been turned into a national park which is now the setting for an annual mass migration of animals. Each year vast herds of Burchell's zebras, wildebeests and Thomson gazelles trek across the steppe and savannah landscapes of the Serengeti on their quest for water and food, often covering distances up to 1,500 km (932 mi).

NGORONGORO

The Ngorongoro Conservation Area covers 8,000 sq km (3,088 sq mi) of the Ngorongoro crater floor in northern Tanzania. Against the backdrop of an impressive natural landscape (above), thousands of wild animals roam freely, representing a cross-section of the biodiversity here. For a long time this area was part of the Serengeti, which had received its protected status as early as 1921 and was made a national park thirty years later. In 1974 it became an independent wildlife reserve. The floor of the crater, largely covered with grass, is the grazing land for large herds of Masai livestock.

"Siringitu", meaning "endless plain", is the Masai name for the large savannah in northern Tanzania. Twice a year, large herds of graminivores start here on their long migration in search of water and fresh grass, with wildebeests leading the way. Huge herds of Cape buffalo also trek across the Serengeti (main picture).

KILIMANJARO

The Kilimanjaro range rises majestically out of the savannah in northern Tanzania on the border with Kenya (main picture, in the morning light). A national park covering 750 sq km (290 sq mi) has been established here to protect the unique montane forest in the upper regions of the mountain.

Mount Kilimanjaro comprises three main cones and numerous smaller peaks of volcanic origin. In the west is the 4,000-m-high (13,124-ft) Shira; in the middle is Kibo at 5,895 m (19,341 ft), the highest point in Africa; and in the east is the 5,148-m (16,891-ft) Mawenzi. The lesser peaks are lined up along a crevasse that runs from south-east to north-west.

Although it is situated not far from the Equator, the peaks of Kilimanjaro are often covered with snow. The massif in the heart of the savannah features a great range of climate and vegetation zones. Above the savannah is a cultivated agricultural belt and former woodland savannah that today remains only on the northern slopes. This zone blends into the deciduous

montane forest that goes up to 3,000 m (9,843 ft). This is followed by an extensive ericaceous and alpine belt, which itself gives way to the ice-capped summit region. The national park provides a habitat for numerous animals including gazelles, rhinoceroses, Cape buffalo, elephants and leopards, some of them endangered species.

Africa's highest mountain can be climbed during a strenuous five-day trek starting in the Tanzanian village of Marangu. During the ascent, hikers cross into a new vegetation and climate zone every day all the way up to the snow-capped summit of the "Mountain of God" (left).

Victoria Falls are among the most spectacular waterfalls in the world. With ear-shattering force, the Zambezi River, which forms the border between Zambia and Zimbabwe, plunges about 110 m (361 ft) into the abyss, a natural spectacle reflected in the falls' local name: "Mosi-oa-Tunya", or "Smoke that thunders". During the spring floods in March and April, the falls grow into a nearly 2-km-wide (1.2-mi) wide curtain of water with up to 10,000 cu m (353,147 cu ft) of water plummeting over the edge every second. David Livingstone was the first European to see the falls, in 1855, and named them for Queen Victoria of England.

During the rainy season, Victoria Falls, comprising the Devil's Cataract, the Main Falls, Horseshoe Falls, Rainbow Falls and the Eastern Cataract, are considered the largest continuous curtain of water on the planet. Beyond the waterfall, the Zambezi squeezes through the Boiling Pot (above) before overcoming yet more rapids (main picture) and finally pouring itself into Lake Kariba.

Main picture: The deep gorge into which the Zambezi plunges from the crest line of the Victoria Falls was dug out over millions of years. The water continues to erode the soft rock – Victoria Falls are "on the move".

This hippopotamus is difficult to spot among the water hyacinths in Mana Pools National Park (main picture). During the rainy season the Zambezi and its tributaries flood their banks creating a landscape of lakes.

GREAT ZIMBABWE

In 1871, German explorer Karl Mauch discovered the ruins of Great Zimbabwe. For a long time it was believed that foreign peoples such as the Phoenicians or Arabic tribes might have been the founders of this former trading metropolis, but archeological research ultimately showed that the remains originate from the Shona culture. This ethnic group, belonging to the larger Bantu community, first settled the region in the 11th century. Around 200 years later, a ring of fortifications was begun around the town that then had nearly 20,000 inhabitants. The elliptical wall extends for 250 m (770 ft) with a height of more than 10 m (33 ft) in sections and boasts a width at the base of 5 m (16 ft), making it the largest structure in sub-Saharan Africa from pre-colonial days. Tools and pots prove that gold, copper and iron existed in Zimbabwe at the time, and there was a brisk trade with the Arabs on the east coast of Africa. The Shona culture experienced its heyday in the 14th and 15th centuries.

MANA POOLS

This national park on the southern shores of the Zambezi River and the two adjacent safari parks of Sapi and Chewore are a paradise for animals. The three parks in the border region between Zimbabwe, Zambia and Mozambique cover an area of just under 7,000 sq km (2,702 sq mi), with Chewore occupying about half of this. In the north the Zambezi forms the natural boundary of the national park and the river regularly floods the

Cape buffalo (top) live in family groups of three to ten animals, but they also band together in large herds of up to 2,000 animals. The leaves of the wild fig trees are highly prized by elephants (above).

grassland and the wooded areas of the reserves. Mana Pools is actually the name of four of the Zambezi's main basins. A large number of animals inhabit this fertile landscape including about 400 bird species living in the woods and thousands of elephants roaming the territory. Buffalo and zebra herds present rich prey for big cats such as leopards and cheetahs. The Chewore Safari Park, meanwhile, has become the habitat of one of the largest populations of massive white rhinoceroses. Hippos splash about in the calmer pools as well as on the banks of the river itself.

The best-preserved part of the settlement of Great Zimbabwe, which covered nearly 80 ha (198 acres) and is also known as "Africa's Acropolis", is "The Great Enclosure", an elliptical ring of fortification walls (left and far left). The defensive corridors between its walls were probably once covered in colored plaster (middle).

MAKGADIKGADI, OKAVANGO DELTA, CHOBE

MAKGADIKGADI

Saltpans of all sizes make up the core of the Makgadikgadi. In an area covering about 12,000 sq km (4,362 sq mi) they are not only the largest of their kind in the world but also the most recognizable feature of this part of the Kalahari Desert. Although they appear to be utterly hostile to any form of life, the saltpans are in fact a veritable paradise for certain creatures. Depending on the season, colonies of zebra and herds of antelope settle around their margins (main picture) along with pink flamingos and a number of other animals. During the rains the hard salt crust softens and turns into a treacherous sludge that is impassable for vehicles; the 165-km (103-mi) route across the Makgadikgadi Pan to Kubu Island is only open during the dry season. In the north it rejoins an asphalted road that continues eastward to Nata.

OKAVANGO DELTA

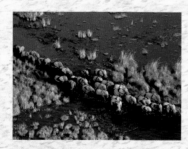

The Okavango Delta in Botswana is a unique natural habitat in the Kalahari Desert. The Okavango River rises in the Angolan highlands and ultimately flows through Namibia and northern Botswana before evaporating and seeping away in this inland delta. Covering a vast area of roughly 15,000 sq km (5,790 sq mi), the delta is a mostly flat terrain with only few high spots. It floods each year in June (above) when the waters of the Cuando River arrive after the rainy season.

CHOBE

Chobe National Park, which has existed in its present size since 1968, covers about 12,000 sq km (4,362 sq mi) of widely differing ecosystems ranging from the Chobe riverfront, which features dense vegetation, to open woodland savannah and barren desert-like terrain. Chobe's great treasures are its elephant herds and prides of lions (above). Aside from the banks of the Chobe River, the Savuti Marshes in the south-west of the park also offer a rich variety of wildlife and habitats.

Visitors at Etosha National Park can choose from three rest areas to view the incredible animal kingdom here, but only between sunrise and sunset. Main picture: Gazelles and zebras in a moment of leisure.

"Etosha" means "Great white place" and refers to the vast saltpans in Etosha National Park that provide sanctuary for the numerous animal species here. Elephants, which were nearly extinct in the area, have been able to reproduce here in great numbers, and the parl's population of black and white rhinoceroses is one of the largest in Africa. Cheetahs, lions, leop-ards, hyenas, bat-eared foxes and jackals find a gluttonous menu including vast herds of antelopes, gazelles, zebras and giraffes. Right: A Kudu calf falls prey to a lioness. The birds are similarly fascinating, ranging from bizarre marabou storks to yellow-beaked tokos. Flamingos even arrive after the rains. Visitors can enjoy the spectacle from safe viewing areas.

"Nature is relentless and unchangeable, and she is indifferent as to whether her hidden motivations and actions are understandable to humans or not" – Galileo Galilei. Left: Lions resting after a feed.

The main attraction of Namib Nau-kluft National Park is the Sossusvlei (main picture), home to a sensual dune landscape that stretches in gloriously shaped waves as far as the eye can see.

NAMIB NAUKLUFT

Covering a vast area of 50,000 sq km (19,300 sq mi), Namib Naukluft National Park is one of the largest nature reserves in the world. It comprises the Naukluft Range and a large portion of the Namib Desert, which goes straight down to the coast and is about 1,500 km (932 mi) long and 80 to 130 km (50 to 81 mi) wide. Although the area is nothing but subtropical desert landscape, it nevertheless boasts great species diversity. The geological features range from blackish gravel plains and regions of strangely eroded island mountains to dune seas in the Central Namib. The Naukluft Range has rugged peaks that reach nearly 2,000 m (6,562 ft) and dramatic valleys that together form a unique ecosystem. First and foremost, there is sufficient water here to provide for a diverse range of flora and fauna while mountain zebra, baboons, jackals and springboks coexist with a number of bird species including Nubian vultures, dune larks and Gray's larks. The latter two are indigenous to these gravel plains.

SOSSUSVLEI

The desert is alive – tracks on the mighty sand dunes of the Sossusvlei testify to the nighttime activities in what at first glance seems a totally inhospitable environment. Some of these small desert-dwellers include darkling beetles and some scorpion varieties, but even larger gerbils, jackals and Oryx antelopes – their bodies perfectly adapted to the arid climate – also manage to find sufficient food here. And when the rains are good, the Tsauchab River carries plenty of water in from the highlands and will even flood the so-called *vlei*, the depressions in the dunes.

KOKERBOOM FOREST

Quiver trees, part of the Aloe family, were given their name by the San, a Namibian people of hunters and gatherers who used its hollow branches as quivers for their arrows. The unassuming plant prefers a rocky ground and usually grows as a solitary tree making the forest of quiver trees growing near Keetmanshop in southern Namibia a rather unusual sight.

The Oryx antelope carefully takes up a scent (left). What it can smell is the humid air from the Atlantic whose precious moisture the animal needs in order to survive. To do so, it stands on the crest of a dune waiting for the mist banks to drift inland, then it licks the drops of water that condense on its nostrils.

FISH RIVER CANYON

With a length of 161 km (100 mi) and a depth of 450 to 550 m (1,476 to 1,805 ft), this is the second largest gorge in the world after the Grand Canyon. From above it is easy to make out the two different levels of the canyon. The first canyon, on a north-south axis, is a rift valley about 20 km (12 mi) wide that was created by tectonic shifting in the plateau during the Paleozoic about 500 million years ago. During an ice age some 200 million years later, the glaciers further deepened this valley. For the last 50 million years or so, since the Tertiary, the Fish River has carved its course into the canyon, further eroding it over time and in the process creating the second portion of the

Fish River Canyon in southern Namibia is the largest gorge in Africa.

canyon, which is also the narrowest and deepest section. From the vista point, a steep path takes visitors down to the valley floor. Hiking the Fish River Canyon is a challenge, however. The trail leads from Hikers' View to the Ai-Ais Hot Springs resort about 85 km (53 mi) away at the southern exit from the canyon. The trek lasts a good four days and takes you across the more or less dry riverbed several times. It passes the German Soldiers' Grave (the officers died during a skirmish between German soldiers and the South-West African Nama in 1905). Encounters with baboons, Hartmann's mountain zebras and klipspringers are not uncommon. The glorious conclusion to the hike, which is only permitted during the cool time of year, are the hot springs of Ai-Ais. The name comes from the Nama language and means "hot water" – the thermal springs have a surface temperature of 60 °C (140 °F).

TABLE MOUNTAIN, CAPE TOWN

For a long time the area around Cape Town's working port seemed to have been left to decay. At the end of the 1980s, however, following the model of Fisherman's Wharf in San Francisco, the elegant shopping and entertainment district of Victoria & Alfred Waterfront was created. The yachts and the fishing boats in the harbor add to the charm of the area (main picture).

TABLE MOUNTAIN

The Khoikhoï people native to the region called Table Mountain (right) "Hoeri 'kwaggo", meaning "sea mountain". It owes its present name to the first European man to ascend the mountain, the Portuguese Antonio da Saldanha, who christened it Taboa do Cabo, or Table of the Cape, in 1503.

Today no one has to climb Table Mountain on foot anymore: the tramway takes visitors from the valley station right to the top. Other peaks around Table Mountain and Cape Town include Lion's Head and Signal Hill in the north-west and the Twelve Apostles to the south-west.

CAPE TOWN

Framed in by Table Mountain and its auxiliary peaks (below: Lion's Head) on one side and the ocean on the other, Cape Town's historical and multicultural essence is plainly evidenced in the former colonial buildings on Long Street and the variety of people who have settled here. It is also considered one of the most attractive urban centers in the world. Since it was founded in 1652 by Jan van Riebeeck, the city has steadily increased in size and now has roughly 3.5 million people.

The Castle of Good Hope, built in around 1679 in the star fort style, reflects colonial history in its Victorian and Cape Dutch architecture. Former suburbs like Bo Kaap now have a distinctly Asian flair to them. The main attraction for night owls is the Victoria & Alfred Waterfront. Here, water lovers can choose between the beaches on the Atlantic side of the Cape peninsula and those in False Bay, which – although still on the Atlantic side, not the Indian Ocean side – is not affected by the cold waters of the Benguela current. This current originates in the Antarctic and cools the waters on South Africa's west coast to a chilly 12 to 15 °C (54 to 59 °F), while in False Bay the sea can reach a pleasantly warm 20 °C (68 °F) on hot summer days. Left: The traditional seaside resort of Muizenberg.

South Africa boasts one-tenth of all the flowering plant species in the world – more than all European countries put together! The most spectacular of all is the Giant or King Protea, South Africa's incredibly hardy, gloriously colorful national flower (main picture).

WINELANDS

Jan van Riebeeck, founder of Cape Town, was clever enough to order grapevines for his trading post and in 1654 tasted the first drops of locally produced Muscadet wine. The royal courts of Europe appreciated the South African libation at the time, but Cape wines did not really come into their own until the beginning of the 1990s, when the international trade embargo was lifted. South African vintners then began creating top wines, some in cooperation with renowned European vineyards. The idyllic wine-growing region north-east of Cape Town, which has a very European look about it, quickly became a popular travel destination.

GARDEN ROUTE

South Africa's most famous road, the Garden Route, runs for about 200 km (124 mi) from Mossel Bay to Storm River along the Indian Ocean coastline with its many charming bays and coves. Among the best-known sights along the way is Knysna Lagoon, which is best viewed from the rocky cliffs of Knysna Head. Knysna Forest nearby is South Africa's largest woodland, home to yellowwood

Mossel Bay (top) marks the beginning of the Garden Route with its abundant wildflowers (middle). The Outeniqua Choo-Tjoe Train (bottom) takes visitors up and down the coast.

trees that can grow to be 800 years old. It is also a haven for the nearly extinct African forest elephants. Plettenberg Bay is probably the most popular beach resort on the Garden Route, where upscale hotels and elegant beach villas belonging to wealthy South Africans line the powdery white beaches. During the winter months, whales come into the bay to calve. A section of the coast here is covered in dense primeval forest and protected within Tsitsi-kamma National Park.

The first vines were planted in South Africa in the 17th century. Vineyards such as Boschendal (opposite page) now enjoy worldwide recognition. Groot Constantia (far left) is South Africa's oldest vineyard. The Kooperatiewe Wijnbouwers Vereeniging is in Paarl. Left and center: Lanzerac Manor and Winery near Stellenbosch.

South Africa is a paradise for ornithologists. The country is home to more than 850 different species of bird. Main picture: The Northern Ground-Hornbill.

DRAKENSBERG RANGE

The Drakensberg Range forms a boundary between the South African interior plateau and the east coast over a distance of more than one thousand kilometers. Its northern section, the Transvaal Drakensberg, is protected by the Blyde River Canyon Nature Reserve while the southern region, known as Natal Drakensberg, features impressively high mountains that rise to 3,377 m (11,080 ft) amidst quaint lakes. Declared a national park known as uKhahlamba Drakensberg Park, the range's greatest treasures are the 4,000-year-old rock paintings (above) created by the San people. The center of their artistic activity is Giant's Castle Game Reserve. Blyde River Canyon (below) is in the northern part of the Drakensberg mountains. At 26 km (16 mi) in length and a depth of 800 m (2,625 ft), Blyde River Canyon is one of the largest gorges in the world.

GREATER ST LUCIA WETLAND

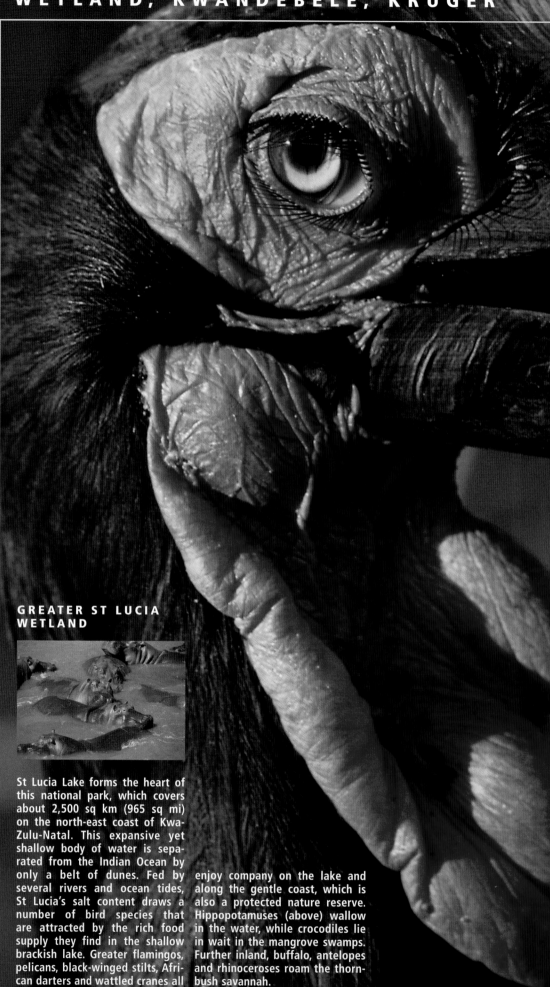

St Lucia Lake forms the heart of this national park, which covers about 2,500 sq km (965 sq mi) on the north-east coast of Kwa-Zulu-Natal. This expansive yet shallow body of water is separated from the Indian Ocean by only a belt of dunes. Fed by several rivers and ocean tides, St Lucia's salt content draws a number of bird species that are attracted by the rich food supply they find in the shallow brackish lake. Greater flamingos, pelicans, black-winged stilts, African darters and wattled cranes all enjoy company on the lake and along the gentle coast, which is also a protected nature reserve. Hippopotamuses (above) wallow in the water, while crocodiles lie in wait in the mangrove swamps. Further inland, buffalo, antelopes and rhinoceroses roam the thorn-bush savannah.

KWANDEBELE

The Ndebele people arrived in South Africa in about the 16th century. Under the lash of Apartheid they were assigned KwaNdebele as a "homeland" north of Pretoria, the capital. Many still live there. Despite numerous restrictions, the traditions of the Ndebele have still prevailed, especially their love of artistic body and wall painting and colorful clothing.

KRUGER NATIONAL PARK

What is now Kruger National Park was created around the turn of the 20th century. It now boasts the most animals of any African park, where even encounters with leopards (above) are not unusual. Covering 2,000 sq km (1,242 sq mi) of territory, Kruger is one of the largest national parks in the world and offers a wide variety of wilderness along with fifteen rest camps, from simple tents to a luxury lodge. As you move south from the thorny savannahs in the north vegetation becomes more plentiful, featuring Mopane woods, expansive, grass-covered plains and thick acacia forests that form a habitat for roughly 500 different species of birds, black and white rhinoceroses, elephants, antelopes and lions. Buffaloes roam the bush while giraffes nibble the leaves of umbrella thorns.

Madagascar's appeal lies in its exceptional world of flora and fauna, dazzling coral reefs, bizarre limestone formations, volcanic craters, endless sandy beaches and the relics of ancient civilizations. The island is tropical, with the exception of its very southern tip. Its length of 1,580 km (982 mi), means that the climate and vegetation zones differ greatly between the north and the south. The backbone of the landscape is formed by mountain ranges and volcanoes that run nearly the entire length of the island. The eastern highlands drop steeply down to the Indian Ocean coast while in the west they drop off into the coastal lowlands along the Mozambique Channel. The west coast is much drier and more fragmented with coves and promontories than the east coast and is dominated by a savannah landscape that features impressive, towering baobab trees (bottom left). Influenced by the south-easterly trade winds, the east side of Madagascar is covered with lush rainforest. In addition, there are a number of islands off Madagascar's nearly 5,000-km (3,107-mi) coast which, like Nosy Be in the north-west and Nosy Sainte-Marie in the east, for instance, are surrounded by coral reefs that make them prized swimming and diving territory.

Insets, clockwise from the top left: Lemurs on the razor-sharp rock needles in the Ankarana Reserve; the canyon systems; spectacular cliff formations of the Isalo Mountains; the peaks of the Andringitra National Park reflected in a lake; Baobab Alley, not far from Morondava; and the dramatic limestone landscape of Tsingy de Bemaraha National Park.

The world's fourth-largest island split off from the African continent about 130 million years ago. Its flora and fauna – today protected by several national parks – therefore developed completely independently ever since. There are now thirty-eight different species of chameleon on Madagascar, for example (main picture).

SEYCHELLES

The **Seychelles** are a tropical island paradise. The rocky **Anse Soleil beach** is on the main island of **Mahé** (main picture) whose urban center, **Victoria**, is often referred to as the smallest capital in the world.

This group of islands, "discovered" in the western Indian Ocean by Vasco da Gama in 1501, comprises more than one hundred individual islands, fewer than half of which are actually inhabited. While many of the islands are no more than coral reefs or atolls (covering a total surface area of about 210 sq km/81 sq mi), the main islands of Mahé, Praslin, Silhouette and La Digue are quite mountainous with the peaks on Mahé, the largest island at 158 sq km (61 sq mi), reaching an altitude of up to 905 m (2,969 ft) and featuring only very sparse vegetation. The tropical oceanic climate means that the year is divided into a dry, and relatively cool, season (from May to September) and a hot, rainy north-west monsoon season (from December to March). As far as religion is concerned, a large majority of the population is Roman Catholic. The ethnic breakdown is mixed including Asian, African and European (mainly French). The brisk tourist trade means that residents of the Seychelles have the highest per capita income of all African countries; about ninety percent of them live on Mahé.

Located about 6 km (4 mi) east of Praslin, the Seychelles island of La Digue is characterized by giant, smooth granite blocks that owe their pale red hue to embedded feldspar (left).

Discovered by the Portuguese mariner Pedro de Mascarenhas in about 1510, the island of Mauritius (main picture: Tamarin Bay) belongs to the group of islands called the Mascarene Islands, which are named after him and which include the now French island of Réunion.

The small islands of Mauritius and Réunion belong to the Mascarene Islands, a group of islands around 850 km (528 mi) east of Madagascar. The first European to discover the islands was a Portuguese mariner named Pedro Mascarenhas at the beginning of the 16th century. Both islands were formed by a hotspot in the earth's crust – at eight million years old Mauritius is the oldest island in the group while Réunion is only three million years old.

Réunion's mountainous landscape is dominated by the 3,070-m (10,073-ft) Piton de Neiges, with its wild yet dormant calderas (cirques), while its smaller neighbor, the 2,632-m (8,636-ft) Piton de la Fournaise (right), is one of the most active volcanoes in the world. A lovely trail to the Trois Bassins of St-Gilles-les-Hautes on the west coast of the island leads to the Bassin des Aigrettes, where several waterfalls cascade over the cliffs (below).

A ring of coral reefs has formed in the warm tropical waters of the Indian Ocean around the volcanic heart of Mauritius, producing ideal conditions for a rich underwater world. On land the original tropical vegetation is now only found in a few places in the south-west while most of the island, which otherwise features just a few imposing mountains (far left: the Trois Mamelles), is taken up with sugar cane fields.

AUSTRALIA / OCEANIA

The land of "Dreamtime"... and dreamy landscapes. From the azure blue Barrier Reef to the dark green rainforests of the Wet Tropics, from the glowing red rock monoliths of Uluru National Park to the yellow-gold sand dunes of Nambung National Park, the fifth continent mirrors the earth's fascinating variety. The view of the Caroline Islands (main picture), the largest group of islands in Micronesia, is also unforgettable. They comprise 963 islands and atolls, most of which are volcanic in origin. There is archeological evidence of early settlement here.

Main picture: Kangaroo offspring in Kakadu National Park. Usually only one joey – the colloquial Australian name for a young kangaroo – is born following a short gestation period (30 to 40 days), crawling by itself into the mother's pouch and attaching itself to a teat. The joey leaves the mother's pouch after several months. Kangaroos are herbivores, grow to between 25 and 165 cm (10 to 65 inches) in height, have a small head, weak front legs, a strong supportive tail and generally move by hopping on their long hind legs.

Situated about 250 km (155 mi) east of Darwin, Kakadu National Park, having been extended a number of times to its present size of around 20,000 sq km (7,720 sq mi), actually encompasses five different ecological zones. Mangrove trees with stilt-like roots have anchored themselves in the mud of tidal rivers and serve to protect the hinterland from the destructive effects of wave action. During the rainy season from November to April – known as "the Wet" in Australia – coastal areas are transformed into a vibrant carpet of lotuses, water lilies (left) and floating ferns. Rare waterfowl such as the brolga, jacana, white-faced heron, black-necked stork and darters are as much at home here as the up to 6-m-long (20-ft) estuarine crocodile. The adjacent hilly landscape with its diverse vegetation consists of open tropical forests, savannah and grassy plains and extends over most of the park. It provides a haven for endangered animal species such as dingoes and wallabies. A number of rare kangaroo species live on the sandstone plateau of Arnhem Land as well as on the Arnhem Escarpment, a steep bluff around 500 km (311 mi) long that traverses the park from the south-west to the north-east.

The national park became known on an international level in the middle of the 20th century when excavations revealed stone implements that were at least 30,000 years old. More than 5,000 Aborigine rock paintings (below, Nour-langie Rock) were also discovered here as well. The motifs, which were either scratched or painted depict episodes from what Aboriginals consider mythical primordial times. A special feature is the so called x-ray style which illustrates not only the visible body but also parts of the skeleton and the organs as well.

While Uluru (aka Ayer's Rock, main picture, top) is a single formation with a circumference of about 10 km (6 mi), Kata Tjuta comprises thirty-six smaller, rounded domes (main picture, bottom).

SIMPSON DESERT

Large, rusty-red sand dunes extend up to 300 km (186 mi) to the northwest and seem to glow in the evening light. They are the main feature of Simpson Desert National Park, which contains the longest parallel dunes in the world. It was only mapped from the air in 1929. The first non-vehicular crossing was undertaken forty-four years later, in 1973, and another four years later by writer Robin Davidson, who started in South Australia on camelback. He managed to find the Oodnadatta Track, a stretch of outback covering more than 615 km (382 mi) that was named after the tiny outpost of Oodnadatta on the southwestern edge of the Simpson Desert.

ULURU AND KATA TJUTA

The Uluru and Kata Tjuta National Park is situated in a vast area of sparse, dry savannah. The iconic red rocks were discovered almost simultaneously in October 1873 by the two explorers William Gosse and Ernest Giles. They named Ayers Rock after Henry Ayers, the prime minister of South Australia at the time – to which the Northern Territory then belonged.

The formation of Uluru (the Aboriginal name for Ayers Rock) began around 570 million years ago and is related to the geological crea-

Uluru – "shady place" – is what the Aborigines call their sacred mountain (top and bottom). The monument was returned to them in 1985 and forms the heart of a national park that also encompasses the rock formations of Kata Tjuta, meaning "many heads".

tion of the entire Australian continent. Unlike the surrounding rock, the cliffs are very resistant and weathered very slowly, today towering above the plain as magnificent petrified witnesses of the Paleozoic. Despite the inhospitable surroundings, the Anangu have been living in this area for thousands of years; for the Aborigines this is the meeting place of their mythical ancestors in Dreamtime.

Even a desert as seemingly inhospitable as the Simpson Desert (far left: a satellite image) is not lifeless. Pictures, from right to left: A python; a thorny devil, which eats mainly ants but can let the morning dew run into their mouths via grooves in their skin; and a collared lizard.

NITMILUK

The main attraction in this national park roughly 30 km (19 mi) north-east of the town of Katherine is the stunning system of canyons, commonly known as Katherine Gorge, formed by the river of the same name. Over millions of years the Katherine River has worked itself deep into the Arnhem Plateau over a stretch of 12 km (7 mi), creating canyons as deep as 13 to 100 m (43 to 328 ft). Some of the more spectactular spots can be viewed by boat or canoe but during the rainy season the Katherine River becomes a raging torrent and can therefore only really be negotiated

A canoe trip through Katherine Gorge (top) in Nitmiluk National Park is a unique experience. Inhabitants of the area include the Argus monitor (bottom). From the water you can get amazing views of the up to 100-m-high (328-ft) rock faces.

safely during the dry season (April to October). During this time, however, it is more a series of separate pools between which you will have to carry your canoes over the dried-out rapids. Anyone who goes to this trouble will be able to access a total of nine gorges and enjoy the wild beauty of the glorious red-rock walls. Tourist boats are limited to the first four gorges.

The structure of the Great Barrier Reef appears clearly in the satellite images of Princess Charlotte Bay and Cape Melville (right). The longest living coral reef on earth extends from the Tropic of Capricorn to the mouth of the Fly River (New Guinea). The reef, comprised of around 2,500 individual reefs and 500 coral islands, follows more than 2,000 km (1,243 mi) of the north-eastern coast of Australia at a distance from the mainland of 15 to 200 km (9 to 124 mi).

The masterbuilders of this natural wonder are coral polyps (below, middle) who live together with blue-green algae. The polyp larvae hatch in the spring and are already able to swim at birth. They then attach themselves to the reef close to the surface of the water, slowly developing their skeletons and forming colonies with other members of their species. After a short while they die off and their calcium carbonate tubes are ground into fine sand. The algae then "cake" the sand into a new reef layer on which new young polyps are able to settle the following year. This is how the reefs and islands have developed over thousands of years. Around 1,500 species of fish live in the waters around the reef, including the bright clownfish (below, left), made famous in the film *Finding Nemo*, the gray reef shark (below, right), pomacentrids, manta rays and stingrays. The reef is also home to thousands of bird, coral and invertebrate species.

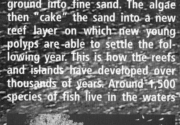

One of the loveliest sections of the Great
Barrier Reef is off the Whitsunday Islands
(main picture). Coral polyps have been
working on the earth's largest natural
"construction" for around 8,000 years.

GONDWANA, WET TROPICS, FRASER ISLAND

The rainforest in the Wet Tropics features tree ferns of up to 20 m (66 ft) in height (main picture, top). Main picture, bottom: Millaa Millaa Falls on the Atherton Tableland.

GONDWANA

The Gondwana Rainforests of Australia are a UNESCO World Heritage Site that essentially comprise fifteen national parks and various other protected zones in Queensland and New South Wales. The name refers to Gondwana, the former supercontinent in the southern hemisphere that broke up towards the end of the Mesozoic Period to form the continents as we know them today.

These combined protected areas are located in the ecological transition zones between a moist, tropical and a warm, temperate zone – a mixture that allows a very diverse range of vegetation to develop within a relatively small area. The south is an area of warm, temperate forest featuring southern beech trees, while upland moors with toon trees and eucalyptus species extend over the high plateaus. Tropical rainforest with strangler figs, orchids and ferns dominate further north and on the volcanic plateaus. Subalpine forest with eucalyptus trees is to be found at higher altitudes of up to 1,500 m (4,922 ft).

WET TROPICS

Large areas of Australia used to be covered with tropical rainforest, much of which has declined significantly due to climate change as well as human intervention. Today the most extensive tropical zone is protected by Wet Tropics National Park and no other rain-

The climbing palm (top) is a rattan species. Above: a giant tree frog

forest in Australia boasts the biodiversity of this area. It is home to about fifty endemic animal species including the rare musky rat-kangaroo and, though it is a relatively small area of around 900,000 ha (2,223,900 acres) – about one-thousandth of the Australian continent's total area – it contains around one-third of all marsupials, twenty-five percent of the frogs, many reptile species and two-thirds of all bats and butterflies in Australia. The largest concentration of primeval flowering plant families in the world is also to be found in the Wet Tropics – a virtual laboratory of evolution.

Insets, from left to right: Barrington Tops National Park (far left) is characterized by temperate rainforest on its valley floors; a waterfall plunges over a cliff edge in the Dandahra Gorge of Gibraltar Range National Park (middle); rainforest inhabitants include parrots such as these two rainbow lorikeets (left).

FRASER ISLAND

The surface of this 120-km-long (75-mi) long island at the southern end of the Great Barrier Reef has been in motion for more than 140,000 years. The crescent-shaped dunes are up to 250 m (820 ft) high – shaped by the continual south-easterly trade winds – and migrate up to 3 m (10 ft) to the north-west every year. Not long after the island was discovered in 1836, immigrants began plundering the extremely diverse tropical rainforest for its timber. In addition to the Queensland kauri, the araucaria, the tallow-wood and the blackbutt eucalyptus, the up to 70-m-high (230-ft)

K'gari – meaning "paradise" – is what the Aboriginals called Fraser Island, the largest sand island in the world (top). Bottom: A monitor on a paperbark tree. Although such monitors can become very large in size (up to 3 m/10 ft), they pose no threat to humans.

satinay tree was also frequently felled. Today only small areas in the interior of the island are still covered with rainforest. The rest of the landscape is also diverse and provides a haven for more than 240 bird species. The mangrove honeyeater lives in the mangroves along the coast while the ground parrot is found in the moors close to the sea. The red and green king parrot seeks out nectar in the tropical forests while the pectoral quail keeps to the humid moorlands.

SYDNEY

BLUE MOUNTAINS

MUNGO

The view of Sydney with the bridge and the opera house is famous throughout the world. In 1955, a largely unknown Danish architect named Jörn Utzon won the contest for the opera house design. He submitted no more than sketches as plans and it was only much later, in 1959, once the foundations had been built, that any thought was given to how the roof was actually to be structured. In the end it cost a total of 102 million Australian dollars instead of the intended seven million.

In 1836, a prominent witness to the beauty of the Blue Mountains, Charles Darwin, described the view from the rocky ledges as "fantastic". His opinion is likely to be confirmed by anyone venturing into Sydney's hinterland. Despite their low altitude of between 600 and 1,000 m (1,969 and 3,2181 ft), the mountains are very rugged, with much of the area still more or less untouched by humans. Above: A waterfall in the Valley of the Waters.

The landscape of Mungo National Park (above) was overgrazed by sheep in the 19th century, lumber was taken for houses and barns, and the loose soil was then carried away by the wind. But 15,000 years ago the entire area was under water and traces of settlements around 40,000 years old have now been found along the shores of the former lake – including petrified human remains. DNA analysis indicated they are the oldest traces of Homo sapiens in Australia.

Sydney Harbour Bridge (main picture) was built by around 1,400 laborers. Paul Hogan, alias Crocodile Dundee, was one of them. The view of the city from the bridge is well worth seeing.

Constantly pounded by the surf, the Twelve Apostles rock formations, up to 65 m (213 ft) in height and subject to unrelenting wind and waves, are the landmark of Port Campbell National Park along the idyllic Great Ocean Road.

GREAT OCEAN ROAD

MELBOURNE

The Great Ocean Road begins south of Geelong and heads westwards before joining the Princes Highway. The route covers around 300 km (186 mi), much of which is along the coast. The cold winds from the Antarctic can be felt here in autumn and winter – this is a region defined by prevailing westerlies and the Roaring Forties. The consistent waves are a big draw for surfers. The most spectacular section of this route takes you through Port Campbell National Park with the rusty-red sandstone cliffs known as the Twelve Apostles (main picture).

For a long time Melbourne was the largest and most important city in Australia, a status it developed during the area's gold rush in the mid-19th century. It was here that the first inner-city transportation services went into operation in 1869: initially a horse-drawn omnibus, then cable cars based on the example of San Francisco with miles of steel cable, and ultimately electric trams. The trams still give the city an appealing flair today and some of them have been in service for more than fifty years. Melbourne was actually Australia's capital for a quarter of a century,

before this role was given to Canberra as a compromise between Melbourne and Sydney. The bridge over the Yarra River (above) provides a view of the city center with Flinders Street Station (below), the railway station built in 1905.

Australia's largest island is also its smallest state. Typical for Tasmania are the steep steps, the so-called "tiers", tablelands which drop down to the coast (main picture: at South Cape). Large areas of the island remain largely untouched even today.

FLINDERS ISLAND

Flinders Island lies to the northeast of Tasmania in the Bass Strait and was named after surveyor Matthew Flinders who was here as a cartographer in 1797. It forms part of the Furneaux Group – thought to be the remains of a former land bridge between Tasmania and the Australian continent – and has something of a dark past. The indigenous inhabitants of Tasmania were exterminated within just a few decades of British colonial rule. Strzelecki National Park, which affords a view of Cape Barren Island, is situated in the south.

EAST COAST

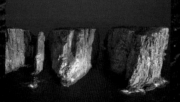

In contrast to the largely uninhabited west coast, Tasmania's east coast is more easily accessible and can be reached on the Tasman Highway. Part of the east coast is formed by the Tasman Peninsula, where the former Port Arthur prison camp is situated. There are five important protected areas along the east coast: Tasman National Park (above the dolerite cliffs off the coast), Maria Island National Park, Freycinet National Park with Wineglass Bay, Douglas Apsley National Park, and Mount William National Park, virtually on the northern tip of the island.

TASMANIAN WILDERNESS

This protected area essentially includes the national parks of Cradle Mountain–Lake St Clair, Southwest, Franklin Lower Gordon Wild Rivers as well as three smaller areas. The wild, romantic landscape was formed by glaciers during the last ice age and is characterized by a great many lakes and waterfalls. Abel Tasman, the first white man to set foot on the island on December 2, 1642, thought it too bleak for settlement. The island receives up to 2,500 mm (98 in) of annual rain, however, facilitating the growth of temperate rainforests (left). They look familiar from a distance and close up we recognize them: a place of sub-Antarctic and Australian shapes. Tasmania's most famous animals are the unique duck-billed platypus and the Tasmanian devil (above).

CAPE REINGA

Visitors and locals alike consider Cape Reinga to be New Zealand's northernmost point, but the claim in fact belongs to the Surville Cliffs to the north-east of the cape where the Tasman Sea and the Pacific converge. When the weather is right, it is possible to see the Three Kings Islands, which owe their name to Dutchman Abel Tasman who anchored there on Three Kings Day (the Twelfth Day of Christmas) in 1643. It was also here in 1902 that the Elingamite steamship sank with forty-three crew members and a hoard of gold. To this day, only a portion of the ship and its treasure have been recovered.

Nearby Spirits Bay is home to an ancient, weathered Pohutukawa tree. The Maori believe the souls of the dead slide down its roots into the ocean to begin their last journey to the mythical homeland of Hawaiki. Indeed, for Maori, life is a journey to and from Hawaiki.

BAY OF ISLANDS

The former Maori settlements around the Bay of Islands were a focal point of the early colonization of New Zealand and therefore considered the cradle of the nation. The idyllic Waitangi Peninsula is home to a monument (above, a detail from the boat house) where, in 1840, Maori chiefs signed the Treaty of Waitangi with delegates from England. It is considered the founding document of an independent New Zealand. The first white settlement was founded in Russell in 1809 and became New Zealand's first capital in 1840.

MURIWAI BEACH

Gannets (above and far right) are incredibly acrobatic birds who hunt fish with precision nosedive technique. They are able to spot their prey from a height of up to 45 m (148 ft) and reach speeds of up to 100 kph (60 mph) when diving. The impact when they hit the water is softened by inflatable air sacks under their plumage. Some 70,000 gannets nest on the islands off the coast of New Zealand between October and March. The females each lay just one bluish-white egg and both birds share the brooding.

Gannets are very aggressive defenders of the territory around their nests. Young birds become independent of their parents after just three months and the chicks are put to the test on their maiden flights, which take them over 2,000 km (1,243 mi) as far as Australia. The young birds only return to New Zealand when they are about four years old in order to then breed themselves. The Muriwai Beach colony (left) on the west coast north of Auckland expanded gradually from the islands off the coast to the cliffs on the mainland.

The Tasman Sea and the Pacific Ocean converge north of Cape Reinga (main picture). The return journey from the Cape can also be made with a four-wheel-drive vehicle along Ninety Mile Beach.

"Middle Earth" in New Zealand: Mount Ngauruhoe's mighty, flat volcanic cone (main picture) was the model for "Mount Doom" in Peter Jackson's internationally successful film adaptation of J.R.R Tolkien's "Lord of the Rings".

TONGARIRO

Tongariro, the oldest national park in New Zealand, was donated by New Zealand's original Polynesian population, the Maori. In 1887, Chief Te Heuheu Tukino gave the Maori's sacred land around the Tongariro volcano to the New Zealand government with the specific condition that it be protected for all humankind. Situated in the heart of New Zealand's North Island, the national park encompasses three active volcano systems within a total area of around 750 sq km (290 sq mi). Mount Tongariro, after which the park is named, is actually the smallest of the three volcanoes at a height of 1,968 m (6,457 ft). To the south of that is Mount Ngauruhoe at 2,290 m (7,513 ft), seen above with Tongariro in the background. It is the most active of the three volcanoes in this national park. The third, Ruapehu (left), comprises several cones and is the highest mountain on the North Island at 2,797 m (9,177 ft).

EGMONT

Egmont National Park encompasses the last primeval forest areas around the volcanic mountain Taranaki, which has been dormant for the last 300 years.

Asphalt roads bring visitors to rest points at an altitude of roughly 1,100 m (3,609 ft) above sea level, while short hiking trails provide access to fabulous, fairy-tale-like forests. For the Maori, the snow-covered peak of New Zealand's most famous mountain symbolizes the sacred heads of their ancestors. It was here that the bones of leaders who had fallen in battle were laid to rest while legends about murderous giants and wicked elves kept intruders out. Every Maori tribe had its "own" mountain and a volcanic eruption was seen as a sign of wrath or as a signal to take up arms. A victory could also cause the mountain to swell with pride. When two tribes made peace after battle their mountains were also symbolically wed.

The geothermal center of the North Island boasts geysers, bubbling mud pools, hot springs, ten lakes and an abundance of Maori folklore. Lake Tarawera (above) is one of the loveliest and most pristine lakes in the Rotorua area. Pohutu Geyser (below) is in the Maori center of Te Puia near Rotorua.

Main picture: The facial tattoos (often only painted these days) known as "moko" differ from person to person. In the past it was only the highest ranking of the Maori leaders who were allowed to sport a full facial tattoo; it was an accolade awarded like a medal. Sticking out the tongue is only common practice in dances. It is intended to deter evil spirits and symbolize fearlessness.

AORAKI/MOUNT COOK

Aoraki/Mount Cook National Park, which covers a vast area of about 700 sq km (270 sq m), is home to all of New Zealand's 3,000-m (9,843-ft) peaks, with the exception of Mount Aspiring. The highest of the peaks is Mount Cook at 3,754 m (12,317 ft), known to the Maori as "Aoraki", which can be roughly translated as "cloud piercer". A rock slide in 1991 reduced the height of Aoraki to 3,754 m (12,317 ft), but it still towers a few hundred meters over its number two, Mount Tasman, at 3,498 m (11,477 ft).

Once the training ground for Sir Edmund Hillary, the Auckland-born mountaineer who managed the first ascent of Mount Everest,

Mount Tasman is accessible from the east via a 60-km (37-mi) access road that takes you along the shores of Lake Pukaki. New Zealand's most formidable ice field, the Tasman Glacier, is 29 km (18 mi) long, up to 3 km (1.8 mi) wide and nearly 600 m (1,969 ft) thick in places.

In addition to the Kea mountain parrot, the flora and fauna in this national park include rare falcon and owl species, while the star amongst the plants is the Mount Cook Lily. The hiking trail through Hooker Valley takes you across the valley floor (below) and crosses the Hooker River glacier by means of two rope bridges. The routes over ice and snow are naturally more strenuous.

WESTLAND

Because the Fox and Franz Josef glaciers are easily accessible and draw around 350,000 visitors annually, most of the other routes in the Westland National Park (main picture: Lake Matheson) are usually deserted.

It is out on the bright sheets of ice that the mountain world of the Westland National Park reveals its full allure. Its magnificent main glaciers, Franz Josef in the north and Fox (above) in the south, flow down the steep valleys from the main alpine ridge around Mount Cook and end in the rainforests around 13 km (8 mi) from the coast. Both glaciers had been receding consistently for four decades before advancing once again in the 1980s when the weight of heavy snowfalls on the main plateau pushed the Franz Josef Glacier edge down the valley at an average of 6 m (20 ft) a week. The Fox Glacier only managed 1 m (3 ft) in the same period. Although both glaciers are again receding at present and are far removed from their historical peaks (indicated along the route with the dates), the Franz Josef Glacier today extends 600 m (1,969 ft) further into the valley than it did in 1982.

MOUNT ASPIRING, FIORDLAND

MOUNT ASPIRING

The northern border of Mount Aspiring National Park is formed by the mighty Haast River, which flows into the Tasman Sea close to the town of the same name. It then extends south as far as Fiordland National Park. The focal point of the park is of course Mount Aspiring at 3,027 m (9,932 ft) – the only 3,000-m (9,843-ft) peak outside of Mount Cook National Park.

The hiking routes here are generally very challenging, such as the Roaring Billy Falls Walk or the magnificent Routeburn Track (left and below). A short hike to the Blue Pools near Makarora or a jet boat trip from Haast in the south up the Waiatoto River gives visitors an initial impression of the park's stunning beauty. The longer hiking trails begin in Glenorchy at the northern end of Lake Wakatipu, or in the Matukituki Valley, which can be reached from Wanaka. Clean, basic cabins are also available for overnight accommodation.

FIORDLAND

Covering around 12,520 sq km (4,833 sq mi), New Zealand's largest national park is also considered the country's loveliest. Snow-covered mountains provide the backdrop for vast beech forests with giant, moss-covered trees that are often centuries old. The wide valleys formed by retreating glaciers feature a plethora of crystal clear rivers and serene lakes.

The park is home to around 700 endemic plants and rare animals, and owes its name to the fiords on the west coast that form underwater valleys reaching up to 400 m (1,312 ft) in depth. Only one of them, the Milford Sound (right and above; far right is Lake Te Anau), is accessible by road. The glacial landscape here gets up to 1,000 cm (394 in) of rain annually, providing ideal conditions for subtropical rainforests to flourish.

This area is still home to many plant and animal species that already existed millions of years ago on Gondwana, the supercontinent once located in the southern hemisphere. Trees here are often overgrown with carpets of lichen and climbing plants, while countless fern species flourish in the undergrowth. These seemingly impenetrable thickets are also home to unique birds while the glassy waters teem with dolphins, seals and Fiordland penguins, which are native to this region only.

The Milford Track is one of the most famous hiking trails in the world. It takes four days for the roughly 54-km (34-mi) route from the northern end of Lake Te Anau via the southern mountains as far as the Tasman Sea, through Fiordland National Park (main picture: Mackay Falls) to Milford Sound.

Papua New Guinea (above: stilt villages on the Sepik River) is only about 150 km (93 mi) off the Cape York Peninsula of northern Australia. The country comprises roughly 85 percent of the eastern part of the island of New Guinea while the rest is spread over a further 600 islands, the largest of which are New England and New Ireland.

The substantial differences in elevation – one quarter of the country lies above 1,000 m (3,281 ft) – account for the vast range of vegetation that exists here. Oak trees, bay trees and conifers dominate the mountains, while the low-lying areas boast palms, climbing plants, ferns and orchids.

Papua New Guinea's cultural diversity is also unique on the planet: Around 95 percent of the population is made up of Melanesians, who are divided into ever smaller clans that speak several hundred, mutually unintelligible languages. There are also small groups of Papuans (the island's indigenous inhabitants), splinter groups from Micronesia and Polynesia, and about 20,000 foreigners.

The Western Highland Province is inhabited by hundreds of traditional clans who gather in the provincial capital Mount Hagen every August for a festival of song and dance (below: festival participants sporting their white and orange stripes).

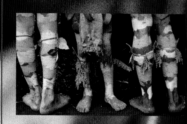

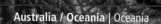

Main picture: Papua New Guinea's largest ethnic population is the Huli, who are often referred to as "wig men" on account of their elaborate headdress. Their abundance of adornments and vibrant body painting are an expression of their consummate creative skills, which have always impressed explorers and visitors.

FIJI ISLANDS

The majority of Fiji's islands are relatively close to each other compared to other similiar groups in the South Pacific: within a radius of only 250 km (155 mi). The two main islands, Viti Levu and Vanua Levu, are volcanic and feature high, jagged ranges that dot the interior. The climate is predominantly tropical, with the windward side on the south-east recording a hefty 3,000 to 5,000 mm (118 to 197 in) of annual rainfall. This feeds the dense mountain forests as well as the coastal mangroves and coconut palms. Meanwhile, less than half as much rain falls in areas protected from the wind. There, grasses dominate the landscape and cane sugar is a major crop. The largest island, Viti Levu, boasts bubbling hot springs and a number of rivers. Fiji is also famous for its coral reefs, which lie at a great range of depths. The islands are a mecca for soft coral diving.

The first humans are said to have settled on Fiji at least 3,500 years ago. What is unclear, however, is where these people came from.

Bora Bora Lagoon (main picture) is the stuff that South Sea dreams are made of. The "Pearl of the Pacific" is famous for its mighty volcanic stacks that jut out of the blue and turquoise sea.

FRENCH POLYNESIA

The six archipelagoes of French Polynesia (Society, Tuamotu, Marquesas, Austral, Gambier and Bass) are located in eastern Polynesia and their 118 islands cover a total area of about 4.5 million sq km (1,737,000 sq mi). One of the largest of the thirteen Marquesa islands is Nuku Hiva, which has dramatic coastal formations that drop nearly vertically into the sea. Its highest volcano is Poitanui on Uapu (1,232 m/4,042 ft). The Tuamotu archipelago, which consists exclusively of atoll reefs, is more than 1,000 km (621 mi) to the south-west.

A dance performance in Papeete, French Polynesia. Open your eyes and your heart, and you will soon understand why Polynesian culture reached its zenith on these islands.

The best-known island group is the Society Islands, some 1,500 km (932 mi) west of Tuamotu. It comprises by far the largest island, Tahiti, as well as Raiatea, Bora Bora and Moorea.

Tahiti, in the geographic heart of Polynesia, is also the economic and cultural center of the French overseas territory. Tahiti was made a French protectorate in 1842, and in 1880 a French colony. The other islands were taken into French possession by 1881. The islands are divided into the "Windward Islands" and "Leeward Islands", depending on their exposure to the south-east trade winds. Volcanic in origin, they boast lush tropical vegetation surrounded by rich coral reefs.

In 1643, Abel Tasman was the first European to discover the Fiji Islands. Their bright white beaches and turquoise-colored sea attract not only beach bums and divers, but favorable swells also offer excellent conditions for surfing (left).

The Golden Gate and the sparkling San Francisco skyline, the red sandstone towers of Monument Valley, the grandiose gorges of the Grand Canyon, the endless expanse of the prairie, the legacy of the Aztecs and Mayans, baroque pomp at the Popocatépetl, Highway 1 and Route 66, New York...from the green jungles of the Amazon and the ice caps of the world's highest volcano to the immense glaciers of Patagonia, the mysterious ruins of the Incas and the colonial heritage of the Europeans...the list seems never-ending. Welcome to the Americas!

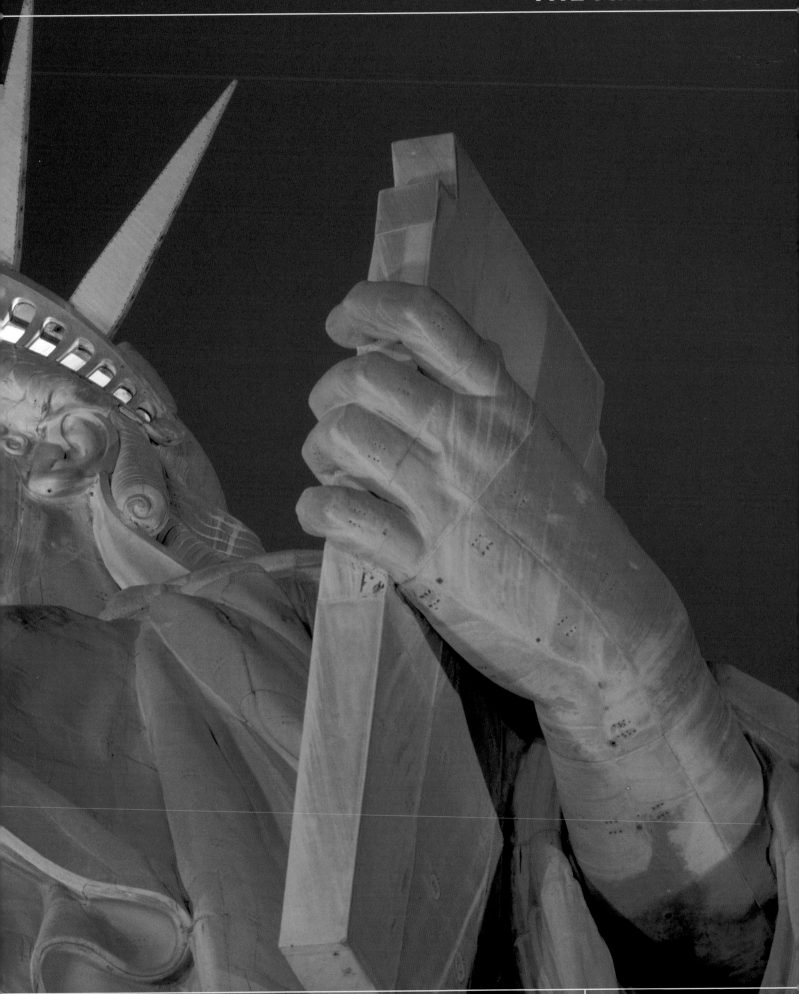

WOOD BUFFALO NATIONAL PARK

Two-thirds of Canada's largest national park, which covers about 44,802 sq km (17,294 sq mi), are located in Alberta; the other third is in the Northwest Territories. The park was founded in 1922 to protect the breeding grounds of the endangered whooping crane and the last remaining wood buffalos. The bison population (wood as well as prairie bison, which have also been released here, with both types frequently crossbreeding) is estimated at about 6,000 animals – the largest group of bison living in the wild anywhere in the world. The government also considered it important to protect the biologically important Peace-Athabasca Delta. Hunting in the wilderness is permitted only to the Cree and the Chippewa Native Americans who live here. There is practically no infrastructure here, with one access route runing north from Edmonton to the national park, along a total of 1,296 km (805 mi) of dirt track.

KOOTENAY

You take the Vermillion Pass to get to Kootenay National Park which, together with three other national parks including Banff, Jasper and Yoho, forms the Canadian Rocky Mountains UNESCO World Heritage Site. The picturesque Kootenay and Vermillion valleys traverse through the park, and the informative Fireweed Trail leads through a landscape that was destroyed by fires in 1968, but has since been replanted with young trees and luminous fireweed (rosebay willow herb). Marble Canyon is an impressive, 70-m-deep (230-ft) gorge cut through jagged limestone. The Paint Pots feature multicolored ochre that was used as sacred paint by the Ktunaxa Native Americans. At the entrance to Sinclair Canyon are the Radium Hot Springs – their healing powers were well known long ago to the Native Americans.

JASPER

Picture-perfect Canada: Jasper National Park in the Rocky Mountains is one of the most popular travel destinations in all of North America. Within its boundaries there are more than 800 lakes, most of which are fed by the surrounding glaciers. Lac Beauvert, for example, is a jade-green glacial lake situated near the town of Jasper, home of the famous Jasper Park Lodge, built by the former Grand Trunk Railroad to compete with the Banff Springs Hotel in the adjacent park. Jasper is not as overrun by visitors as Banff, making the many trails in the park a perfect way to experience the stunning landscape in relative solitude. A mountain train takes you up the ever popular Whistler Mountain, where breathtaking views of the region unfold below. Numerous trails also lead into the beautiful wilderness at Maligne Lake (left).

Main picture: Wood buffalo have massive skulls and enormous shoulders. Males can weigh up to a hefty 900 kg (2,000 lbs), making them larger than their prairie bison counterparts. Except during the mating season, when bulls engage in often bitter fights with their rivals, bulls and cows live in separate herds.

VANCOUVER

Vancouver is simply one of the loveliest cities in the world. Superbly situated on the idyllic northern Pacific Coast and surrounded by picturesque bays and the majestic mountains of the nearby Coast Range, this modern metropolis also has its share of glass skyscrapers, a quaint Old Town, spacious Stanley Park, sandy beaches, the Lion's Gate Bridge, as well as the futuristic Canada Place. Few cities harmonize so comfortably with the invit- ing wilderness nearby. Granville Island is an artificial leisure island under the highway bridges out on False Creek. The converted warehouses here were reassigned as restaurants, bars and shops, with artists and craftspeople working in their galleries. The past still shines brightly in Gastown while vibrant, exotic restaurants and shops are the focus in Chinatown. Vancouver is also a city of immigrants who do well to celebrate their cultures.

VANCOUVER ISLAND

Vancouver Island is a true paradise for the people of greater Vancouver – an island with a stunning natural environment totally separated from the urban bustle nearby, and yet in such close proximity to all of the comforts of the city. Victoria (right), the capital of Vancouver Island, is a former Hudson Bay Company trading fort.

Main picture: Cruise ships and Asian cargo ships are the main features of Vancouver Harbor, an important commercial hub that maintains a brisk trade across the Pacific.

BANFF

BANFF

In summer, dense vegetation thrives in places where it is sheltered from the wind in Banff National Park (main picture below). Fascinating adventures include a walk around Vermillion Lake, a journey on the Icefields Parkway and a visit to Herbert Lake (opposite page, from the top).

Banff National Park on the border of Alberta and British Columbia features snow-covered peaks, colossal glaciers, silent valleys, crystal-clear rivers – all of it still largely untouched. The elegant town of Banff sits below Cascade Mountain on the Trans-Canada Highway, enchanting visitors with its classy hotels, exclusive restaurants and shops, hot springs and of course stunning surroundings. The impressive Banff Springs Hotel was built solely because of the famous thermal hot springs that are the most popular attraction at the resort. If you wish to get away from the hustle and bustle, just make your way into the glorious hinterland. One of the best trails in the park takes you via wooden bridges and rock tunnels through Johnston Canyon. At the end of this difficult trail you will reach jade-green springs known as the Inkpots. Banff was the first Canadian national park (1885) and third in the world – after Yellowstone (1872) in the United States and the Royal National Park (1879) in Australia.

Only on rare occasions will you encounter an American lynx (left) or a coyote (far left) in the remote corners of Banff National Park. Founded in the year 1885, it is the oldest park in Canada.

Main picture: Water crashes down with a deafening roar over Horseshoe Falls, the Canadian side of Niagara Falls (*Niagara* is a Native American term meaning "thundering water").

TORONTO

Toronto is a surprisingly lively city. Ambitious construction projects indicate dynamic development, while traditional buildings such as Holy Trinity Church, a Catholic church from the 19th century, are protected heritage sites. Particularly worth seeing are Ontario Place, a futuristic leisure and shopping area on Lake Ontario that hosts rotating exhibitions, and the Harbourfront Centre, a contemporary arts and cultural center in converted warehouses located on the piers with shops, restaurants, waterfront cafés, art galleries and theaters as well as the Queen's Quay and York Quay Promenades. Toronto Islands, linked with the city by ferry, is a tranquil sanctuary featuring quiet canals, gentle strolls and a historic amusement park for children. The CN Tower is the city's emblem and is visible from vast distances. The viewing platform offers superb views over the city and its surroundings. Other highlights include the BCE Place, a bold skyscraper with a light-flooded atrium and Yorkville, Toronto's "Greenwich Village".

NIAGARA FALLS

Niagara Falls – a very popular travel destination for honeymooners – are located on the short but powerful Niagara River, which flows north from Lake Erie into Lake Ontario in Canada. The border between the USA and Canada runs through the middle of the falls.

Known for centuries by Native Americans as Thundering Water, the first white man to see Niagara was a Jesuit priest by the name of Louis Hennepin, who came in December 1678. The huge volume of water drops more than 50 m (164 ft) over the escarpment in a massive cloud

Niagara Falls are on the border between the USA and Canada, and are split by tiny Goat Island. The falls produce an average of 4,200 cu m (150,000 cu ft) of water per second.

of mist and spray. The river is actually split into two channels by tiny Goat Island: the large Horseshoe Falls are on the Canadian side and the smaller American Falls are on the U.S. side. Rainbow Bridge links the two countries. Table Rock to the west, next to the horseshoe-shaped falls, or the Minolta Tower, are recommended as observation points. The best view is afforded by the "Maid of the Mist" which sails right past the falls. The more adventurous visitor will take a "Journey Behind the Falls", a particularly impressive and unforgettable experience.

Rising boldly above the Toronto skyline, the CN Tower (left) at 555.3 m (1815 ft) was the tallest free-standing structure in the world for thirty-one years (Burj Dubai now holds that title). CN stands for Canadian National, the railway company responsible for its construction, which only took 40 months.

Built in Québec City by Canadian Pacific Railway in 1893, the luxury Château Frontenac hotel (main picture), towers high above the Saint Lawrence River. The river is an important means of transport and is about 1 km (0.6 mi) wide where it flows through the city.

GASPÉSIE PENINSULA

The Gaspésie Peninsula stretches northward from New Brunswick and eastward from Quebec. It makes up part of the southern shore of the Saint Lawrence River and extends as far as the Gulf of Saint Lawrence. To the south it is separated from New Brunswick by Chaleur Bay and the Restigouche River. Dense spruce forests and craggy cliffs stretch down to the sea while hiking trails crisscross the Chic-Choc Mountains. Grand Metis is known for its gardens and Sainte-Anne-des-Monts for its good salmon. Miguasha National Park on the south coast is considered to be the world's most important vertebrate fossil site.

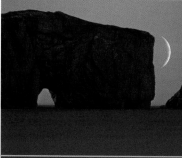

QUÉBEC CITY

The capital of the province of the same name is the heart of francophone Canada. More than ninety percent of the roughly 170,000 residents here speak French and the cityscape exhibits strong European influences. In fact, Québec City is the only North American metropolis with an intact city wall, while the Old Town's narrow alleyways are somewhat reminiscent

The parliament buildings (top) were built in Second Empire style and completed in 1886. The gem of the Lower Town is the painstakingly restored Place Royale (center). The narrow streets of the Old Town are reminiscent of old Paris (bottom).

of old Paris. Originally founded on the banks of the St Lawrence River in 1608, the buildings in the settlement beneath Cap Diamant have unfortunately burned down on several occasions, forcing the residents to retreat to the promontory and build Haute-Ville, the "Upper Town", which is linked via cog railway with the Lower Town.

The name of the Gaspésie Peninsula (left) derives from the Native American word "gespeg" meaning "where the land ends" or "end of the world". The Micmac were already here in 1534, when mariner Jacques Cartier landed and began a brisk trade with the locals. Far left and middle: Images from Miguasha National Park.

Sightseeing attractions include the Escalier Casse-Cou, a harrowingly steep staircase linking the Haute-Ville with the Quartier Petit-Champlain in the Basse-Ville, and the Place Royale, a former marketplace in the Lower Town. The Musée de la Civilisation provides insight into the city's history. La Citadelle, which dates from the early 19th century, is located at the east end of the city wall in Haute-Ville and has been a base for the only French unit of the Canadian Army since 1920. The Cathédrale Notre-Dame was built in 1647 and recalls

The Basilique-Cathédrale Notre-Dame (above) is the oldest stone church in Canada. Construction began in 1647 on the site of a chapel that had been built in 1633 by the city's founder Samuel de Champlain that burnt down in 1640.

French rule. The Maison Chevalier gives an indication of how the city's wealthy families lived in the 18th and 19th centuries. The luxury hotel Château Frontenac, built in 1893, resembles an oversized European castle. The Parc des Champs-de-Bataille, once the scene of a battle between the English and the French on September 13, 1759, is today one of the largest municipal parks in North America. The narrow alleyway Rue du Trésor adds a touch of Parisian charm to Canada.

MONTREAL

Montreal (above, with the market hall dome towering over the Old Town) was founded by French Catholics in 1642. Today, seventy-five percent of the city's residents can still claim French ancestry.

Situated at the confluence of the St Lawrence and Ottawa Rivers, Montreal quickly grew into a prosperous center of trade. The French influence remains strong in Vieux-Montreal, the lovely Old Town featuring a good number of historical buildings and narrow streets on the southern slopes of Mont Royal, while an air of urban life prevails in the inner city. After Paris, Montreal is the second-largest city in the world where French is spoken. In the winter, residents take refuge in the underground city – "la ville souterraine" – with its network of tunnels, passageways and shopping malls. The Basilique Notre-Dame, a splendid Catholic church (below), was built by prominent Protestant architect James O'Donnell.

City lights: A view of the glittering
city from Montreal's 223-m-high (732-ft)
Mont-Royal.

ALASKA

KOBUK VALLEY

The valleys of the Kobuk River recall the days when ancestors of the Inuits and Native Americans arrived in Alaska via the land-bridge from Siberia. Scientists believe it was some 12,000 years ago that they migrated to North America, when the same vegetation grew in the Kobuk Valley as today in the tundra, but at the time it had not yet been flooded by the ocean separating the two continents. Founded in 1980, this national park features astonishing sand dunes that rise up to 30 m (98 ft) high and extend across an area of 40 sq km (15 sq mi). Especially worth seeing here is a place known as Onion Portage, where giant herds of caribou (above) have arrived via this ford for thousands of years – only to be awaited by hunters on the shores. Countless weapons and tools have been excavated from the early encampments here that span a period of nearly 10,000 years.

GATES OF THE ARCTIC

In northern Alaska, two particu-larly striking peaks rise up like silent guardians from the Brooks Range to form a natural barrier between the valleys of the south and the seeminlgy endless plains of the north. Robert Marshall, a scientist and explorer who lived on the Koyukuk River as well as in North Fork between 1929 and 1939, named them the peaks "Frigid Crags" and "Boreal", but they are better known as the "Gates of the Arctic", also the name of the national park that was founded here in 1980 and extends to the north beyond the giant mountains. It is a vast area of mountains, rivers, lakes and wholly untamed nature, home to only a few Inuit. At the Anaktuvuk Pass the Inuit even established a small settlement in order to wait for the annual migration of the giant caribou herds there. The national park is four times the size of Yellowstone.

DENALI

Mount McKinley and the surround-ing glaciers, forests and lakes were all placed under protection back in 1917. In those days only a few adventurers were able to enjoy the beauty of the park, but when the Denali Highway was completed in 1957, ordinary folks could also discover the glory of the highest peak in the USA. Denali National Park offers nature in its unadulterated state, having remained virtually unchanged despite tourism. It owes its almost paradisiacal state mainly to the fact that private vehicles are not allowed to enter the area.

WRANGELL-ST. ELIAS   GLACIER BAY

The American bald eagle has been the national bird of the United States since 1782. These majestic creatures live mainly in Alaska and their wingspans of up to 2.4 m (8 ft) make them one of the most impressive birds in the world.

Wrangell-St Elias is the largest national park in the United States and is also home to the country's second-highest peak after Mount McKinley (6,194 m/20,323 ft): Mount St Elias, at 5,489 m (18,009 ft). More than one hundred glaciers here form the largest ice field south of the Arctic Circle. The Wrangell-St Elias wilderness area is the largest of its kind in the States and features impressive gorges and raging torrents where few traces of human existence can be seen except in the two copper towns of McCarthy and Kenicott. It became a national park in 1980.

"And here, too, one learns that the world, though made, is yet being made; that this is still the morning of creation; that mountains long conceived are now being born; that moraine soil is being ground and outspread for coming plants; to make the mountains and valleys and plains of other predestined landscapes, to be followed by still others in endless rhythm and beauty" – John Muir, October 1879. Little needs to be added. Nowhere else can you observe the constant transformation of nature as easily and as intimately as in Glacier National Park.

MOUNT SHASTA

Mount Shasta (main picture) is a 4,317-m-high (14,164-ft) volcano in northern California that towers gloriously above the rolling landscape. Petrified lava flows can be clearly seen beneath the snow. A mountain road with breathtaking views takes you up to 2,400 m (7,974 ft), but beyond that only experienced mountaineers should attempt the difficult ascent to the peak. On the south-west side is the quaint village of Mount Shasta City.

MOUNT RAINIER

Mount Rainier (above) is 4,392 m (14,410 ft) high and boasts the largest mass of ice in a single mountain range in the continental United States (i.e., not including Alaska and Hawaii). For Native Americans it is a holy mountain. William Fraser Tolmie, a brave physician in search of healing herbs, was allegedly the first white man to have ventured into its foothills. The first settler here, James Longmire, set up his farm at the foot of the volcano at the end of the 19th century. Things are still very much the same as they were then, with rugged landscapes and vast forests dominating Mount Rainier National Park.

MOUNT ST. HELENS

On the morning of May 18, 1980, Mount St Helens gave the people of the Pacific Northwest quite a jolt as an earthquake caused a massive volcanic eruption. Not only was a large section of the mountain blasted away, but the ash that was expelled made night out of day for nearly a week. The mountain slumped to a height of 2,550 m (8,367 ft) and the glacial melt devastated entire forests. The area has been protected since 1982, and on a clear day the volcano can be viewed from the Johnson Ridge Observatory. Seismic activity continues to make St Helens dangerous, the last small eruption occurring in 2004.

OLYMPIC

From its majestic mountains all the way to the rugged coast, Olympic National Park offers visitors spectacular alpine scenery, with jagged peaks, pristine lakes and powerful waterfalls juxtaposed with the wildly romantic Pacific seaboard with its craggy cliffs and sandy beaches. The park is also home to the Hoh Rain Forest, which is not only unique within the United States, but also the largest temperate rain forest in the western hemisphere. Formed by the region's heavy precipitation, this stunning forest has been a protected nature preserve since 1909.

West of Port Angeles, the commercial center of the park, is Lake Crescent which teems with fish. A road leads to the Sol Duc Hot Springs. From Port Angeles, a panoramic route takes visitors up to the Hurricane Ridge Plateau.

Main picture: The tall art deco towers of the Golden Gate Bridge, which are visible from almost any high point in the city, are two of the most recognizable icons of West Coast. When the structure was completed in 1937 it was the longest suspension bridge in the world.

SAN FRANCISCO

attractions are the Golden Gate Bridge, Fisherman's Wharf, the marina at the end of Hyde Street, Chinatown with its restaurants and shops, the Victorian houses on Alamo Square, the bustle of Market Street, trendy districts such as South of Market and of course a ride on the cable car (below).

The "City on the seven hills" (there are officially 43 hills) is regarded as one of the most attractive metropolises in the world. Founded in 1776 by Spanish explorers and originally called Yerba Buena, it received its present name in 1847, after Mission San Francisco de Asis founded by Father Junipero Serra. The first gold discoveries in January 1848 brought on the rise of the city as an important trading center and seaport. Even the catastrophic earthquake of 1906 could not slow the boom. Among its main

THE REDWOODS

Three nature reserves in northern California – Jedediah Smith, Del Norte Coast and Prairie Creek – owe their existence to a nature conservation movement focused primarily on saving the redwoods. Together with Redwood National Park (above), which is home to the great horned owl, North America's largest long-eared owl, they form a unified reserve. Redwoods, close relatives of the sequoias, reach heights of more than 100 m (328 ft) and live an average of 500 to 700 years with some reaching more than 2,000 years of age. The tallest trees are in the Tall Trees Grove near Orick. Prairie Creek is home to a dense rainforest, and the Del Norte Coast has a rugged coastline. Giant redwoods can also be seen on Mill Creek in Redwoods State Park and on the superb Avenue of the Giants.

HIGHWAY 1

Author Robert Louis Stevenson called this place the "most beautiful convergence of land and sea on earth". Highway 1 (above and main picture at Big Sur) is a spectacular route, particularly the stretch between San Francisco and Los Angeles. Secluded sandy beaches, rugged coastlines, romantic mission churches and picturesque towns line this stunning road covering more than a thousand miles from Washington and Oregon in the north down to the California-Mexico border.

LOS ANGELES

Los Angeles (above: Sunset Boulevard) is the second-largest city in the United States by population. In terms of surface area, however, it has no rivals. Greater Los Angeles covers 1,200 sq km (463 sq mi). The "City of Angels", founded in 1781 as "Pueblo de los Angeles" and still a relatively insignificant town throughout the 19th century, has never become a melting pot like New York City. Instead, it was and still is made up of a multitude of autonomous towns.

Mann's Chinese Theater, a movie palace built in 1927 by Sid Grauman that resembles an ornate Chinese temple, recalls the golden years of Hollywood. A location for many festive film premieres, legendary stars including Elizabeth Taylor, Humphrey Bogart and John Wayne are immortalized here in the cement with their hand or footprints.

Elegant towns such as Beverly Hills and Bel Air are effectively independent, floating like islands within the city. Around Los Angeles, the beaches of Santa Monica and Malibu as well as theme parks such as Disneyland become the main attractions.

Cypress Point (main picture) is one of
the most popular viewpoints along the
California Pacific coast between Los
Angeles and San Francisco. The gnarled
cypress tree (Lone Cypress), isolated on
a rock jutting out into the sea, is quite
possibly one of the most photographed
trees in the world.

The Merced River has dug itself deeply into the primeval landscape of this glorious park and formed a deep, elongated valley, at the bottom of which are the visitor center and some lodges. Yosemite Valley is dominated by two giant rock faces: Half Dome (above) and El Capitan. The latter, at 2,307 m (7,590 ft), is an absolute mecca among rock climbers, its 910 m (3,100 ft) face presenting one of the most dramatic challenges in the world for that sport. The magnificent Half Dome rises to 2,695 m (7,569 ft) from the valley floor and looks as if its other half simply broke off. This rock was formed around 250,000 years ago by powerful masses of ice at a time when humans did not yet roam the continent and when Glacier Point, today one of the most attractive viewpoints in the American West some 100 m (328 ft) above the valley, was still hidden under a thick layer of ice. In fact, the first humans first arrived in Yosemite Valley back in the Ice Age. They would have even experienced Tenaya Lake when it was still a glacier. Powerful natural forces did indeed shape this valley, giving form to the granite, but that process is still not complete. Yosemite Falls and Bridal Veil Falls are still at work on the valley floor and walls.

Yosemite National Park (main picture with El Capitan lit by the evening sun and the Merced River in the foreground) is one of the oldest national parks in the United States. The first areas were declared nature reserves as early as the 1860s and in 1905 it reached its present size. Many of the main attractions are situated in the roughly 10-km-long (6-mi) Yosemite Valley, in the heart of the park. Must-sees include the impressive peaks such as El Capitan or Half Dome as well as the Yosemite Falls (left), which plunge 739 m (2,425 ft) down the rock face.

JOSHUA TREE, DEATH VALLEY

Around one-fifth of Death Valley is situated at sea level or lower. Badwater (main picture, bottom) is the lowest point in North America at 86 m (282 ft) below sea level.

JOSHUA TREE

The true beauty of this national park can best be appreciated on a hike through the rolling hinterland where Joshua trees are silhouetted against the often breathtakingly blue sky north-east of Palm Springs. They are the silent guardians of the high desert. Related to the Yucca tree, these cactus-like plants can reach heights of up to 12 m (39 ft). A group of Mormons named the tree after an image of the Prophet Joshua praying with raised hands – the irregular branches reminded them of their prophet, who promised to show them the way to Paradise.

A paved road leads through dense groves of these trees and teddy bear chollas, which best reveal their full beauty in the evening light. The trails in Hidden Valley and along the Barker Dam are particularly beautiful. Other plants in the park are the creosote bush, which emits a poisonous substance to destroy competing plants, and the palo verde tree, whose wood is green because it photosynthesizes with both its trunk and branches.

DEATH VALLEY

Both glorious and dreaded, Death Valley in south-eastern California covers an area of approximately 10,000 sq km (3,860 sq mi) and is situated majestically between the Panamint and Amargosa ranges. The desert floor here (right) can reach temperatures in summer of more than 50 °C (122 °F).

Among the natural beauties in Death Valley National Park are the Devil's Golf Course (top) with its mosaic of salt crystals, Golden Canyon (middle), and Zabriskie Point (bottom).

Death Valley was made into a national monument in 1933, then a national park in 1994. The first white men to enter the valley came in 1849 as part of a wagon train headed for the riches of the California Goldrush. After taking what was meant to be a shortcut, they got stranded in the blistering heat. They persevered for twenty days before being rescued. One of the settlers is said to have shouted, "Goodbye, Death Valley!", which explains the name of the valley.

In the evening, the play of colors and light between the "holy trees" of Joshua Tree National Park is breathtaking (left). *Joshua Tree* is also the name of a U2 album voted by Rolling Stone Magazine as one of the top 500 albums in pop music history.

LAS VEGAS

Las Vegas, the glittering gambling metropolis in the Nevada desert, has fascinated visitors since the 1940s with its casinos and flashing neon lights. In those days, Bugsy Siegel, an infamous underworld boss from the East Coast, opened the first gambling palace in this otherwise desolate expanse: the Flamingo Hotel. Gambling was legalized in Las Vegas as early as 1931. Casino after casino began popping, and Bugsy Siegel became ever richer from his (almost) honest work. The city comes alive in the evening when the bright neon signs flicker along the Strip, the famous entertainment boulevard in Las Vegas, and the gambling-happy tourists are brought in by the busload. It was not until the 1990s that Las Vegas transformed itself into a giant theme park. As gambling is prohibited to anyone under the age of 21, "entertainment for the entire family" has become a priority to draw adults.

Main picture: Vast hotels like the Luxor (modeled after pyramids of Egypt) and the New York, New York, are palaces of entertainment sometimes featuring rollercoasters and special effects in their lobbies – and of course giant casinos. Only one thing seems to be missing: clocks. Vegas is always open!

YELLOWSTONE

It is the microorganisms in the Grand Prismatic Spring in Yellowstone National Park that give the soil and water their vivid colors (main picture). Opposite page from top: A fascinating diversity of landscapes, set away from the paved roads.

Explorer and trapper John Colter was the first white man to ever see the area that is now Yellowstone. He told of hot springs shooting out of the ground, of bison and bears, and praised the area as one of the great paradises of the American West.

Indeed, the earth below the park is in an ongoing state of upheaval here. The Grand Canyon of Yellowstone and the bubbling geysers here remind us of ancient volcanic eruptions, and there are more than 300 hot springs within the park. Cold filters its way down into hot chambers nearly 2 km (1.2 mi) below the surface where it is then heated and expelled again through narrow channels as a mixture of steam and water. Official catwalks take visitors through the misty landscape where geysers constantly emit foul-smelling sulfurous smoke.

The idea to transform the area into a national park originally came from the members of the Washburn-Langford-Doane expedition, which began its exploration of the region as early as 1870. Finally, in 1872, Yellowstone was declared the first national park of the United States.

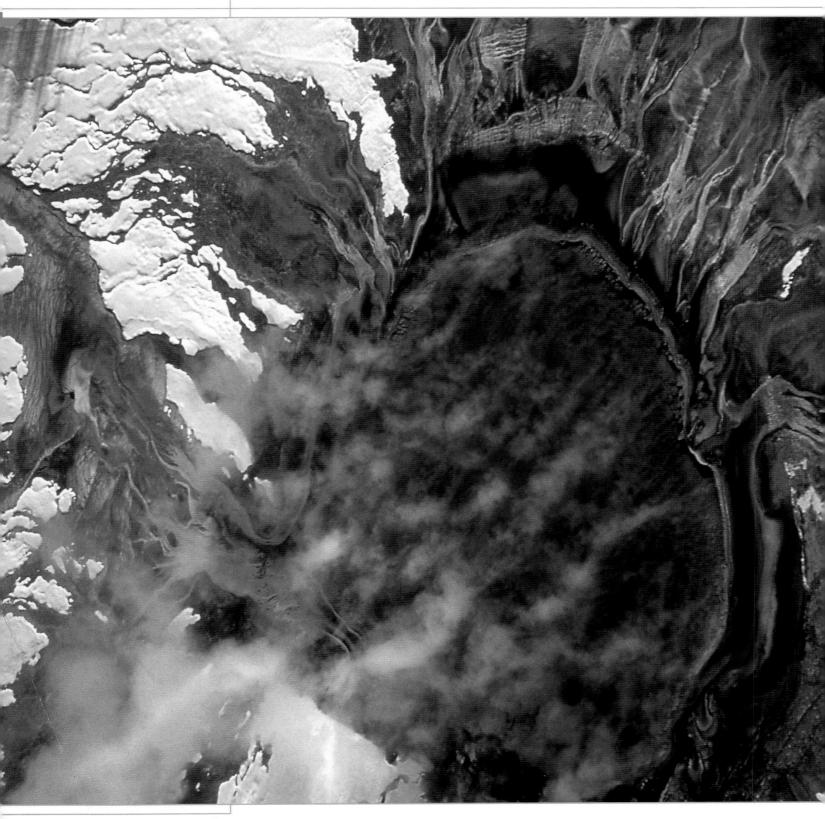

The oldest national park in the United States is a majestic wilderness of mountains, rivers, lakes and more than 300 geysers. Left: The hot waters of the White Dome Geyser are heated underground and then erupt in a giant plume.

THE GRAND TETONS

Grand Teton National Park was established in 1929 and is one of the most beautiful natural landscapes in the western United States. The peaks of the Teton Range are particularly magnificent (main pictures). Bottom: The Tetons with Jackson Lake in the foreground.

Below is an image of Grand Teton National Park in the early evening with its rugged peaks standing out against the wild sky like the sharp teeth of a giant shark. All the summits here are indeed over 3,000 m (9,843 ft) high, but their jagged form makes them appear much higher.

The most impressive mountains are Grand Teton (4,197 m/13,770 ft) and Mount Moran (3,842 m/12,606 ft). Between them lie the white masses of glacial fields while down in the valley the alpine meadows are covered in blossoming wildflowers in spring. Jenny Lake is the most attractive of six lakes strung together throughout the park like pearls on a necklace. A boat hire shack and a few cabins are the only signs of civilization. Four other lakes – Leigh, Bradley, Taggart and Phelps – nestle in the pristine valleys. Although a paved road runs through a great portion of the park, you rarely feel crowded by other people here. Jackson Lake, the largest of the six lakes, is along the road between Yellowstone and Grand Teton and is fed by mountain streams as well as the mighty Snake River.

Grand Teton National Park (left) is in north-west Wyoming, a few miles south of Yellowstone. The two parks are linked by the John D Rockefeller Jr. Memorial Parkway.

CANYONLANDS, ARCHES, DEAD HORSE POINT

CANYONLANDS

ARCHES

The Canyonlands in southern Utah are among the most exciting landscapes on our glorious planet. Accessible only to Native Americans and skilled riders during the first half of the 20th century, this terrain was ultimately declared a national park in 1964. The full beauty of the region can really only be appreciated on foot or on horseback, with many of the trails leading through deep gorges and hidden valleys. It is a fairytale world of colorful rock formations with the Green and Colorado rivers flowing through the park like green ribbons.

The stone archways and portals here have been worn out of the rock by wind and weather over a period of 150 million years. Protected by the government since 1929, they have only been part of Arches National Park near Moab, Utah, since 1971.
Arches Scenic Drive takes visitors to some of the most impressive vista points, while walks along Park Avenue, a path with steep rock faces on either side, leads out to Balanced Rock. Other attractions include breathtaking stone portals such as North Window and the Delicate Arch

(above), which is reached by taking a 3-km (2-mi) footpath and is as high as a seven-story building. Then there is Landscape Arch (below) which, at 90 m (295 ft) in length, is even listed in the Guinness Book of World Records.

Main picture: Sunset in Canyonlands National Park. A 450-m-long (1,476-ft) trail leads up to Mesa Arch, the most astonishing rock arch in the reserve.

DEAD HORSE POINT

Only a few miles from Moab is Dead Horse Point, probably the most spectacular state park in Utah. From atop the 600-m-high (1,969-ft) outcropping, which is part of an even larger escarpment, visitors here can enjoy superb views of the Colorado River, which meanders westward through a magnificent landscape of colorful rock formations and labyrinthine canyons. These stunning areas can really only be explored in an all-terrain vehicle, on horseback or on foot.

The forces of nature needed more than 150 million years to fashion this geological spectacle. Before the 20th century, giant herds of mustangs still grazed on the surrounding mesas, but were driven onto the peninsula by cowboys, caught by lasso and then broken in. Legend has it some of the horses died of thirst on the plateau, despite being able to see the river, because they couldn't find a way down. Only nocturnal mammals like coyotes and foxes now live on Dead Horse Point.

BRYCE CANYON

ZION

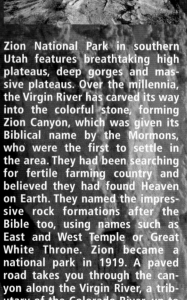

The red rock towers of Bryce Canyon rise like organ pipes from the stony ground. These colorful limestone formations, eroded by wind and weather over the course of millions of years, boast imaginative names such as Thor's Hammer, Queen's Castle, Gulliver's Castle, Hindu Temples and Wall Street. Nowhere else has nature been this capricious, not even in the Grand Canyon.

John Wesley Powell was the first white man to explore the Canyon in about 1870. The national park owes its name to Ebenezer Bryce, who built a farm in Bryce Canyon but soon moved on to Arizona. Apparently, the arduous task of spending weeks on end trying to find his cattle in the nooks and crannies here finally got to him. Bryce Canyon has been a national park since 1924. Native Americans have a more interesting name for the area: "red rocks standing like men in a bowl-shaped canyon".

Zion National Park in southern Utah features breathtaking high plateaus, deep gorges and massive plateaus. Over the millennia, the Virgin River has carved its way into the colorful stone, forming Zion Canyon, which was given its Biblical name by the Mormons, who were the first to settle in the area. They had been searching for fertile farming country and believed they had found Heaven on Earth. They named the impressive rock formations after the Bible too, using names such as East and West Temple or Great White Throne. Zion became a national park in 1919. A paved road takes you through the canyon along the Virgin River, a tributary of the Colorado River, up to the Temple of Sinawava, 13 km (8 mi) away. From there, a hiking trail takes visitors to Weeping Rock, a mossy overhanging rock, as well as to Angel's Landing, a striking chunk of mountain.

Main picture: Bryce canyon with its organ pipes made from stone. Other attractions include Bryce Amphitheater.

Arguably one of the most beautiful valleys in the world, Monument Valley on the Utah-Arizona border is on that list of "eighth wonders". It is indeed a magical world of red rock formations and perhaps the most recognizable symbol of the classic American Southwest. The countless films that have been shot here have transformed it into a near-mythical landscape. Harry Goulding, the owner of a trading post here, was the first to introduce John Ford – the director of such film classics as "Fort Apache", "The Searchers" and "Stagecoach" – to this impressive natural set, where colossal sandstone towers and stony spires rise out of the desert into the sky like monuments to the gods themselves. They boast fanciful names such as "Left Glove" and "Right Glove"; one slim rocky needle is known as "Totem Pole", while three rock needles standing in a line, once known as the "Three Sisters", have been renamed as "Big W" for John Wayne, who shot so many films here. They form a giant W when silhouetted against the sky. The valley is only accessible via a 22-km-long (14-mi) circuit route while the onward journey is only possible with a Navajo tour guide. The money is a donation to tribal coffers.

Main picture: Monument Valley south of Moab, Utah, has become famous through John Ford's many western films. The Navajo Indians' Tribal Park there was made a conservation area in 1960.

The cliff houses of the Anasazi (a disputed term) are visible proof that these Native Americans, who mysteriously migrated away from their lands in the 12th and 13th centuries, were able to build lasting settlements in this inhospitable region (main picture Mesa Verde).

MESA VERDE

The oldest and best-preserved adobe houses of the Anasazi, or Ancient Pueblo Peoples, can be found on the long, flat mountain called Mesa Verde (Spanish for "Green Table"), which is about 2,600 m (8,530 ft) high. The area was made into a national park back in 1906, and archeologists have found and restored entire villages in and among the gorges and cliffs here. Many houses were built into the seemingly inaccessible cliffs, leading researchers to believe they sought protection here from enemies.

Of the roughly 4,600 adobe houses in the park, many have been very well maintained. The best-known include the four-story Cliff Palace, whose 220 rooms and twenty-three *kivas* (ceremonial rooms) accommodated over 200 people; the Long House in Rock Canyon with 181 rooms and fifteen *kivas*; and the Spruce Tree House, built for about 110 people and featured 114 rooms and eight *kivas*. The pueblo was rediscovered by white men in the winter of 1888, when two cowboys found themselves facing the walls of Cliff Palace while looking for lost cattle.

CHACO CANYON

The term "Chaco Culture" denotes the period of greatest prosperity for the Anasazi, a somewhat sensitive name meaning either "ancient ones" or "ancient enemies" that refers to Ancestral Pueblo Peoples who lived as simple farmers in multistory dwellings or pueblos. From 850 to 1250, the canyon was their spiritual and cultural center, and they established large communities that were linked by a network of roads.

The characteristic feature of these settlements are the so-called "cliff dwellings" – houses built into nat-ural cliff faces. In Chaco Canyon there are twelve large pueblos and numerous smaller settlements that housed a total of between 6,000 and 10,000 people. Half-sunken round and oval buildings are known as "pit houses", while *kivas* are round ceremonial chambers with a diameter of up to 22 m (72 ft). The best-known is Pueblo Bonito, which was built on a semicircular area covering about 12,000 sq m (129,120 sq ft) and had space for thirty-six *kivas*. The Pueblo Bonito had 800 rooms on four levels.

GRAND CANYON

The Colorado River meanders its way for 446 km (277 mi) through this breathtakingly beautiful system of gorges that are between 5.5 and 30 km (3.5 and 19 miles) wide and up to 1,800 m (5,906 ft) deep (main picture).

In 1540, the Spaniard López de Cárdenas was the first European to see the magnificent panorama of the Grand Canyon, but it took until the middle of the 19th century before the vast area was accurately mapped.

The origins of the Grand Canyon are still not entirely clear. Presumably, the Colorado River began to carve a path through the rocky plateau around six million years ago and, over the course of time, the gorge grew. John Muir, an influential and passionate naturalist, called it the "grandest of God's terrestrial cities". Wind and weather obviously contributed to the shaping of rock cliffs and bizarre rock formations, and the sequence of sedimentary layers in the stone documents the various geological periods. Fossils that were found in the canyon provide important information on life in primeval times. Temperatures in the canyon can rise to 50 °C (122 °F), but only a few exceptionally resilient plants and animals are capable of withstanding this heat including some species of cacti and thorn bushes. Rattlesnakes, black widow spiders and scorpions also call it home.

TAOS PUEBLO, ACOMA PUEBLO, SANTA FE

TAOS AND ACOMA PUEBLOS

The Spanish named the Native Americans they found in the Four Corners region of the Southwest "Puebloans" because of their vast settlements, or pueblos, with terraced slopes and interconnected dwellings which, presumably for security reasons, could only be accessed via ladders and through hatches in the roof. The Puebloans include a number of culturally related tribes such as the Keresan, Tiwa, Hopi and Zuni who believe themselves to be descendants of the Ancient Pueblo Peoples.

The Taos Pueblo (main picture) is just 5 km (3 mi) outside of the city of Taos, the "Soul of the Southwest". It has been there for nearly 1,000 years without changing much. Indeed, while TV sets now flicker in the local living rooms, and the women shop in the nearby supermarkets, these multi-story houses still look more or less exactly the same as they did in 1540, when the Spaniard Coronado came to the area in search of the fabled golden cities. The Spanish were very disappointed when they found out that the golden light came only from the sun. Legend has it that Acoma Pueblo (above), also known as "Sky City" because of its location on a 112-m-high (367-ft) plateau, was already settled at the start of the Common Era. What is certain, however, is that the village has been inhabited for 1,150 years, making it one of the oldest continuously inhabited communities in the States. Coronado also visited Acoma Pueblo and called it the "best fortress in the world".

SANTA FE

Santa Fe, the capital of New Mexico and the second-oldest town in the U.S. after St Augustine, Florida, still has a strong Spanish character. The heart of this artists' paradise is the Plaza, a square enclosed by adobe houses with galleries and workshops where Ancestral Puebloans spread their blankets under the porch roofs to sell local turquoise jewelry.

The historic flavor of the city can best be appreciated in the Palace of the Governors, the oldest public building in the United States, which is opposite one of Santa Fe's finest churches, San Miguel Chapel. It is also the oldest church in the United States. The city fathers jealously guard the historical charm of their city: In Santa Fe, neither skyscrapers nor faceless office blocks are permitted, while Spanish ambience and Native American cultures have entered into an exceptionally flamboyant relationship.

CHICAGO

The metropolis on Lake Michigan (main picture) is the third-largest city in the United States. After the 2008 presidential elections, the city was renamed "Obama City". Barack Obama began his political career here before making it to the White House.

SKYLINE

Chicago was already an important transport and trading hub in the state of Illinois back in the 19th century. During the "Roaring 1920s", Al Capone's "Windy City" gained a deservedly dubious reputation as a metropolis of gangsters. For two days in October of 1871, a devastating fire destroyed almost the entire city. From among the many old buildings, only the historic Water Tower still stands today. The new Chicago was built on top of the charred ruins of the former city, and proved a perfect chance to show the enterprising spirit of the inhabitants. Aside from New York, no other city in the United States has a more impressive skyline than Chicago.

THE LOOP

The Loop, an area of downtown Chicago encircled by the "L" (elevated mass transit railway), is bordered by the Chicago River in the north and the west, Michigan Avenue in the east and Roosevelt Avenue in the south. It is basically the heart of this fascinating metropolis. State Street, the largest pedestrian zone in the world, lures visitors with its department stores, boutiques, restaurants, cinemas

Traffic rarely stops inside the Loop (top) even at night. Bottom: LaSalle Street Station.

and theaters. Even the sidewalk is full of surprises, among them the City of Chicago Public Art Program's 16-m-high (53-ft) untitled sculpture by Pablo Picasso at the Richard J. Daley Civic Center Plaza; the "Flamingo, Alexander Calder's giant spider in front of the Chicago Federal Center;, the "Universe", a giant mobile by the same artist that hangs in the lobby of the Sears Tower; and "The Four Seasons", a 20-m-long (66-ft) mosaic wall by Marc Chagall in what is now the Chase Tower Plaza.

Chicago became a virtual El Dorado for architects after the great fire of 1871, which almost completely destroyed the city, and they still seem to have more freedom here than in New York or San Francisco, for example. Left: A modern office block downtown. Opposite page: Chicago Tribune Tower.

CHICAGO BLUES

Gifted artists such as Muddy Waters, Howlin' Wolf, Elmore James and Little Walter all left a permanent mark on the Chicago Blues and their music is still popular today. As a genre, it forms part of the soundtrack for a journey through African American history, when the blues developed as an independent style from popular traditional songs. Like the rock 'n' roll of the 1950s, the Chicago Blues also emerged from the Mississippi Delta Blues of the South.

Murals on the south side (top) recall the early days of Chicago blues. Bottom: A still life with bass drum and trumpet case in Blue Chicago.

Before World War II, Chicago already boasted a lively music scene firmly rooted in Glenn Miller's big band swing sound, but it was less rootsy than the Chicago blues that would soon develop. Muddy Waters brought his version of the "dirty" blues from Clarksdale, spicing it up with a bit of electric guitar. Later blues greats including John Lee Hooker from nearby Detroit and Howlin' Wolf from Memphis, Tennessee, followed in his footsteps, helping to create a sound that greatly influenced a number of styles including rhythm and blues, country, rock 'n' roll and jazz, a genre that is unthinkable without the "blue notes", or worried notes. Jazz and blues still characterize the sound of the city in Chicago today.

"Then I'm walking in Memphis / Walking with my feet ten feet off of Beale …". American singer-songwriter Marc Cohn immortalized Beale Street (main picture) in the chorus of his hit, "Walking in Memphis", successfully covered by Cher just a few years later.

OAK ALLEY PLANTATION

Before the Civil War ended slavery, there were countless cotton and sugar-cane plantations scattered along the Mississippi whose owners commissioned grandiose estates for themselves known as "Plantation Houses". The most famous of them is Oak Alley Plantation. These mansions exude the kind of nostalgia that is evoked when people speak of the "Old South". Locally, however, they are not usually referred to as plantation houses but "antebellum homes", meaning pre-war houses. Since many of the owners had made their fortune on the backs of slaves, the number of plantations declined rapidly after the Civil War.

NASHVILLE

Nashville, in northern Tennessee, is a city that lives off of country music – both emotionally and economically speaking. The most important record companies, music publishers and studios are all based on Music Row and most visitors and tourists flock to Broadway which, after costly renovation work, has been restored to its former splendor.

MEMPHIS

Most people visit Memphis in the south-western corner of Tennessee because of the music. Famous Beale Street, for example, which was named after a forgotten war hero, is lined with restaurants and music clubs. The city is also a popular destination because of Graceland (above), the former country mansion of Elvis Aaron Presley, the "King of Rock 'n' Roll".

Forty miles west of New Orleans, on "Plantation Trail" near Vacherie, is the Oak Alley Plantation (left). The approach avenue is lined by live oaks that were planted as long as 300 years ago. The mansion (opposite page, interior) was built in 1839, in the Greek Revival Style.

NEW ORLEANS

The French established "Nouvelle Orléans", as it was then called, back in 1718. It quickly became home to settlers from what is now Canada, Germany, Scotland as well as large numbers of "free" Africans who came to create a truly multicultural city in the middle of the American South. The Spanish, French and African influences eventually melded here to create Louisiana Creole culture. After the French sold the territory to the

The whole city parties during Mardi Gras, but "Fat Tuesday", as Shrove Tuesday is known in New Orleans, is the big day (above) Top: Bourbon Street, the heart of the French Quarter.

United States in 1803 in the Louisiana Purchase, many plantations were set up in and around New Orleans and a very wealthy "Southern Aristocracy" emerged. In the 20th century, oil in the Gulf of Mexico inspired another economic boom.
The "Big Easy", as New Orleans is known, was devastated by Hurricane Katrina in August 2005, and at the end of August 2008, the city was only just spared another catastrophe.

Mount Desert Island, which takes up the largest portion of Acadia National Park, is covered in sweeping forests of pine, birch, blue lupines, deep green ferns and numerous types of wildflowers (main pictures).

Acadia National Park was founded in 1919 and is one of the most popular parks in the United States. Visitors arrive in large numbers on Mount Desert Island, especially in the fall when large swaths of forest transform into a sea of magical autumn colors. The changing leaves in fall are something of an event, with news of the current status broadcast via telephone and the Internet. Acadia is known for its particularly intense display.

The 19th-century Bass Harbor Lighthouse in Acadia National Park is one of the most attractive lighthouses on the New England coast. From there, the journey continues to the dreamy port of Bass Harbor. Then a drive along the asphalted Park Loop Road and up Cadillac Mountain takes visitors to Thunder Hole on Sand Beach, where the Atlantic Ocean roars deep into caverns in the rock cliffs. After that it's on to Jordan Pond, a large, serene lake. Paved roads take visitors into the wooded hinterland and far from the circuit road you can hear the mysterious call of the loon, a diving bird that is also known as the "Nightingale of the North".

The Bass Harbor Lighthouse (left) in Acadia National Park, Maine, is one of the most beautiful in New England.

CAPE COD

This Massachusetts peninsula thrives on the rugged charm of the Atlantic Ocean and the hustle and bustle of popular resort towns such as Hyannis. Provincetown, known locally as just "P-town", is a romantic village with narrow alleyways and flower-bedecked houses that once belonged to former ships' captains. Pilgrim Monument, an impressive granite

Cape Cod National Seashore is one of the peninsula's most impressive spots. Far from the main road, lonely dunes provide for a beautiful contrast to the bustle of the coastal towns.

tower, commemorates the first pilgrims to set foot on American soil here. "Old King's Highway" winds along the coast passed quaint villages, antiques shops and bed & breakfasts reminiscent of historic New England. In between there are wonderful expanses of marshland and charming ponds. On the southern Cape Cod coast there is noticeably more activity where locals and holidaymakers are attracted to Hyannis by the hotels, golf courses, go-carting tracks and restaurants.

New York, New York – so much more than a mere city, the Big Apple is both a symbol and a likeness of the American Dream itself. For some it is a place to be in the middle of it all, for others it may be a Babylon to avoid if at all possible. Whatever your preference, however, New York does have something for everyone It's loud and hectic and overwhelming at times, but it is a multicultural Eden that is capable of reinventing itself every single day.

"The town presented itself as gigantic, confusing, unfathomable and beautiful ... with blinding rows of windows and dark urban canyons," Jack Kerouac once wrote about New York Main picture: The concrete canyons of Manhattan.

If New York is the "City of Cities", then Times Square (main picture, when it was still accessible by car) at the intersection of Broadway and Seventh Avenue is not just the center of the city but also the center of the urban world. Bette Midler probably said it best: "When it's 3 p.m. in New York, in London it's still 1938."

Five different boroughs form the entity that is New York City: the Bronx, Manhattan, Queens, Brooklyn, and Staten Island. It is a world made of many smaller worlds in which one only need turn a corner to change between them. The classic New York experience begins when the taxi driver turns around and asks, "Where ya from?" And when it isn't New York, the coy and somewhat sympathetic smile that crosses his face will unfailingly be followed by a series of rants about the traffic and the crazy people in this metropolis of metropolises. But as soon as you ask him if he wouldn't rather live somewhere else where everything wasn't so hectic, the answer, given with a gleem in his eyes, is unfailingly, "No way, man, this is NEW YORK!"

FINANCIAL DISTRICT

A statue of George Washington stands before the New York Stock Exchange (above), the largest securities trading center in the world. The exchange is located inside a grandiose neo-classical building designed by George B. Post that was opened in 1903, but May 17, 1792, has been decided on as the date of the exchange's foundation – the day when Alexander Hamilton, the first Treasury Secretary of the United States, met with the most important brokers of the day under a buttonwood tree on Wall Street to sell them government bonds and pay off the vast debts that had been incurred by the Revolutionary War.

DOWNTOWN

Downtown Manhattan comprises the best-known neighborhoods in New York. Greenwich Village was a lively district for artists and trendy types, but a number of other neighborhoods like SoHo, TriBeCa and the East Village have become serious competition for the attentions of locals and tourists alike. SoHo stands for "South of Houston", a district full of alleys and side streets below Houston Street. TriBeCa is short for "Triangle Below Canal Street", and the East Village used to be known as the Lower East Side. Chinatown (above) is south of Canal Street while Little Italy is all around Mulberry Street.

Among New York's most recognizable icons are the Empire State Building, the United Nations Building on the East River, and the Chrysler Building. An entire herd of elephants was once herded across the Brooklyn Bridge (far left) to convince skeptics of the bridge's solidity.

MIDTOWN

The heart of New York City beats on Times Square. Huge shopping malls and themed restaurants characterize the area, which was once farmland. Broadway (above) runs diagonally across Midtown Manhattan.

FIFTH AVENUE AND CENTRAL PARK

Fifth Avenue has been New York's luxury boulevard since the 19th century. It runs from Washington Square down to the Harlem River, dividing the city and its streets into "East" and "West". Central Park (above) is the "lungs" of the city.

UPTOWN

The lifeline of Harlem is 125th Street (above). Taking Convent Avenue you get to Sugar Hill, north of which are Washington Heights with the Morris-Jumel Mansion, a grand villa in the style of Southern plantation estates.

MIAMI, MIAMI BEACH

The MacArthur Causeway was opened in 1997 and forms an almost 2.5-km-long (1.5-mi) link between the southern tip of Miami Beach and the mainland (right). It takes just a few minutes to get from the office towers to the beach – and this is what life in Miami is all about: the beach. The city (above: a hip-hop party; far right: a "sexy body contest") is avant-garde and progressive as well as being a gateway to the Spanish-speaking world of the Caribbean and South America. The Latin American influence gives it a vibrant and cosmopolitan feel and

more than 50 percent of the population speaks Spanish – even higher than cities like Denver or San Diego.
Out on Key Biscayne, Miami turns tropical. The island was christened the "Little South Seas" in the old

days because it served as the backdrop for Hollywood films meant to be set in Hawaii and Tahiti. From Biscayne Bay, visitors get a fascinating view of the skyline of Downtown Miami (above). Coconut Grove, with its elegant

boutiques and southern street cafés, is the place to see and be seen. In the evening, the most popular spot is South Beach, the southernmost section of Miami Beach. This narrow spit of land was derided as "God's waiting room" until the 1980s, because it was a favorite retirement area for impoverished pensioners. Then came the cult TV series "Miami Vice", and the sad nursing homes transformed into "Miami Nice". The pastel-shaded Art Deco hotels on Ocean Drive were given a facelift, and wealthy entrepreneurs turned on the style.

FLORIDA KEYS

The Florida Keys – small islands in the far southern reaches of the state (above) – wouldn't even be marked on the map had it not been for businessman Henry Flagler's ingenious idea to link them via bridges, thus incorporating them into Florida as the "American Caribbean". Initially, a railroad linked Miami and Key West, but a hurricane tore it away. It was then replaced by the "Overseas Highway", a 200-km-long (130-mi) bridge that carries US Route 1 through all of the keys. Key West, once known as a tropical paradise and hangout, has since become a busy resort with a distinctly Caribbean ambience. Author Ernest Hemingway lived there in a house on Whitehead Street that has since been turned into a museum and opened to the public (below).

THE EVERGLADES

The Everglades offer an ideal for a number of endangered species including aquatic birds like the snowy egret and sea-dwelling mammals such as the West Indian manatee, or sea cow. The Mississippi alligator, which grows up to 6 m (20 ft) in length, is also at home here (main pictures, from left to right).

Mangrove woods and marshes overgrown with sawgrass form a unique ecosystem in southern Florida and offer a perfect habitat for a fascinating range of animal and plant life. The Everglades cover an overall area of 5,661 sq km (2,185 sq mi) that extends from the Tamiami Trail in the north to Florida Bay in the south, and from the Florida Keys in the east to the Gulf of Mexico in the west. A national park since 1947, Native Americans originally referred to the area as "pay-hay-okee", meaning the "sea of grass".

The low altitude and lack of natural drainage have caused the region's high precipitation to collect here, which ultimately formed a vast network of swamps. Unfortunately, the complex ecosystem of the Everglades is seriously threatened by intensive agriculture, growing drinking water consumption in local towns and even overfishing. Thus, the fauna and flora are still endangered despite extensive preservation efforts. In the last fifty years alone, up to 90 percent of bird and 80 percent of fish species have died out.

Great blue herons, snakes, raccoons and frogs all feel at home in the marshy landscape of the Everglades (from left).

CAPE CANAVERAL, WALT DISNEY AMUSEMENT PARKS

CAPE CANAVERAL

NASA (the National Aeronautics and Space Administration), an organization set up for the peace-

ful exploration of space, was established on October 1, 1958. Eleven years earlier, on July 8, 1947, the former Ministry of War had moved its rocket test center to Florida's east coast. Soon after, the first manned Mercury and Gemini spacecraft had orbited earth. Apollo 11, the first expedition to the Moon, was launched from Complex 39 on Merritt Island, just adjacent to Cape Canaveral, which later became the permanent home of the Kennedy Space Center in 1964.
Far left: The control room as it was at the time of the Apollo mission.
Left: A spacesuit on display.

WALT DISNEY AMUSEMENT PARKS

On October 1, 1971, "the Mouse"
arrived in Florida and bestowed
upon the hitherto insignificant
town of Orlando an undreamed of
boom – Disney World. Almost forty
years later, it is still a viable operation, even though competitors
like Universal and Sea World have
opened up nearby.
Indeed, Mickey Mouse & Co. now
reign over an entire empire: the
"Magic Kingdom", which is the
actual theme park with Mickey
and his friends; the "Epcot Center", where technological experi-
ments are demonstrated in a playful and very entertaining way; and
the "Disney MGM Studios", a mixture of a theme park and real film
and TV studio. Additional attractions include leisure facilities such
as the "Walt Disney World Village",
three separate aquatic parks, and
"Pleasure Island", which features
nightclubs, cinemas and shops.

HAWAII

They say in Hawaii that when the lava flows, Pele, the goddess of fire, is angry. Nowhere else can you observe volcanic activity as intimately as on Hawaii's "Big Island", where two of the most active volcanoes in the world are part of the Hawaii Volcanoes National Park (main picture). Lava still pushes its way up from the depth of the oceans to the earth's surface.

The Polynesians, who came to Hawaii as early as 500 BC, called the islands "Heaven" or "Paradise". They would still be right. It is indeed a Garden of Eden for locals as well as visitors seeking a bit of tropical sunshine. The islands include Oahu, Kauai, Molokai, Lanai, Kahoolawe, Maui, and the Hawaii. At the time of the kings, who ruled the islands before they were usurped by the United States, traditional "chants" that told of life in the villages were still sung. Today, the hula, a dance in honor of the gods that was originally exclusively for men is still performed at various celebrations. Insets, from left: Excursion boats on the most famous beach in Hawaii, Waikiki in Honolulu on the island of Oahu; a tropical forest on Kauai; a surfer at Pipeline.

The Cathedral Metropolitana in Mexico City (main picture, top) is the largest religious building in the Americas. It dominates the Zócalo, the second-largest urban open space in the world. El Ángel (main picture, bottom), the golden angel at the Monumento a la Independencia, looks down over the Paseo de la Reforma from its 40-m (125-ft) column.

THE CAMPUS OF THE UNIVERSIDAD NACIONAL AUTÓNOMA DE MÉXICO

The first university in Latin America was founded in Mexico City in 1551 by King Philip II. Prior to being awarded autonomous status in 1929, the university originally comprised a collection of separate buildings in the historic heart of the city. It was only during the 1930s that plans were drawn up to building a university campus combining all of the institutes in one complex. The final plans were implemented from 1949 to 1952 at the Pedregal de San Ángel, then located outside the city. The master plan for the university's design was the work of architects Mario Pani and Enrique del Moral. Although they consistently applied the principles of contemporary architecture and modern urban development, they also managed to incorporate local traditions and building materials. Particularly remarkable is the successful integration within the architecture of works by artists such as Diego Rivera, José David Alfaro Siqueiros and others.

HISTORIC CENTER, XOCHIMILCO

According to unofficial figures, Mexico's capital is one of the fastest growing metropolitan areas in the world today. The metropolis lies at an altitude of 2,240 m (7,349 ft) above sea level, in a wide basin in the central highlands

From top to bottom: The National Palace, built in 1523 on the east side of the Zócalo; a giant mural by Diego Rivera inside the palace; the Palace of Fine Arts (above), built in the historic heart of Mexico City between 1904 and 1934, representative of the country's European heritage.

and on the site of the pre-Columbian city of Tenochtitlán. The former Aztec capital was founded in about 1370 on a number of islands in the Lago de Texcoco. Following the conquest of Tenochtitlán the city was almost completely destroyed by Spanish conquistadors in 1521. They then built their churches and colonial buildings on the ruins of where Aztec temples, palaces and sanc-

The university buildings embody tradition and modernity as well as the visual arts. The library by Juan O'Gorman (far left) and the rectorate tower by Enrique del Moral, Mario Pani and Salvador Ortega Flores (middle and left with a mural by Siqueiros) are typical examples.

tuaries once stood. Some of these heavy buildings, standing on typically soft, unstable ground, are now slowly threatened by subsidence. Aztec artefacts continue to be unearthed during construction work in the historical heart of Mexico.

A number of Mexico City's most significant historic buildings are grouped around the main square of Zócalo. The Templo Mayor, dedicated to the Aztec gods Tlaloc and Huitzilopochtli, is the most important relic from that era. The National Palace has been the scene of key political events and now serves as the president's residence. Paintings by Diego Rivera (1886–1957) depicting scenes from Mexico's history can be seen on the staircase and in an

Traces of the Aztec culture are still found today in the Templo Mayor (top) and in the "floating gardens" made of reed islands in Xochimilco (above).

upstairs gallery. The Metropolitana is the largest cathedral in the Americas and embodies a mix of styles from Renaissance to neoclassical. Magnificent patrician houses such as the Palacio de Marqués de Jaral de Berrio document Mexico's economic advancement. Architectural highlights of the 20th century include the Art Nouveau Palace of Fine Arts and the opera house, opened in 1937. The "floating gardens" (Chinampas) in Xochimilco, south of Mexico City, are today still reminiscent of the man-made water landscape created by the Aztecs in their capital Tenochtitlán.

EL VIZCAÍNO

There is a unique marine habitat comprising the lagoons Ojo de Liebre and San Ignacio as well as several coastal lakes that extends along the Pacific Coast about halfway along the Baja California peninsula. Gray whales cavort here between December and March after travelling about 8,000 km (4,971 mi) from their summer territory, the Arctic Bering Sea, in order to mate and give birth in these warmer, calmer waters. Almost half of all gray whales worldwide are born in the waters of Baja California. Blue whales, humpback whales (main picture), seals, sea lions and elephant seals also frolic here. Five of the seven sea turtle species still in existence are found here as well, while thousands of migratory birds spend the winter in the coastal regions each year.

In addition to whales, marine mammals such as the northern elephant seal (top), and endangered reptiles like the green sea turtle (middle, a newborn), and the loggerhead sea turtle (bottom) also thrives in this protected region.

BAJA CALIFORNIA

The Baja California (Lower California) peninsula extends over 1,150 km (715 mi) from north to south, from Ensenada to Cabo San Lucas. It runs parallel to the Mexican coast, thus separating the Gulf of California from the Pacific Ocean. With a maximum width of 240 km (149 mi), the peninsula is divided into two federal states: Baja California Norte and Baja California Sur, north and south, respectively. The landscape of this sparsely inhabited region is mostly impassable, inhospitable and barely accessible in many areas – but it is an Eldorado for naturalists. The vegetation is dominated by succulents and cacti including the giant cardon cactus (above) and the islands of the coast are a paradise for birds. The world's largest population of blue-footed booby (below) lives here, for instance.

Built in the 18th century, the Palacio de Gobierno in Morelia (main picture) has arcaded balconies on two floors.

EL TAJÍN

Recent research indicates that El Tajín's origins go back as far as the second century. The ruins can be divided into three different sections: El Tajín, Tajín Chico and the Hall of Columns. The focal point of each is formed by rectangular or trapezoidal squares lined with pyramids. The most famous of them is the Pyramid of the Niches with its six platforms dedicated to the god of rain and wind. It originally boasted 365 elaborately decorated niches, suggesting a link with astronomical calendar calculations. El Tajín is thought to have once been a center for pelota, a ball game played as a tribute to the storm god, to whom the losing players were sacrificed. The ball could only be moved with the hips, knees or elbows and thrown through a ring. Archaeologicial discoveries made at the complex indicate that El Tajín enjoyed a close relationship with Teotihuacán, reaching the zenith of its power following the fall of the latter in about 800. The city was destroyed and abandoned about 400 years later, in around 1200.

XOCHICALCO

The pre-Columbian ruins known as Xochicalco are located around 100 km (62 mi) south of Mexico City. The fortified complex, which experienced its heyday during the Epiclassic period (650–900) following the downfall of Teotihuacán, was an important political and cultural center that reflected a variety of ethnic influences. Interestingly, however, it has not yet been possible to assign Xochicalco to a specific civilization.

The snakes on the plinths of the Temple of the Feathered Serpent frame human figures (above).

MORELIA

Morelia, the capital of Michoacán located about 250 km (155 mi) west of Mexico City, enjoyed a rapid rise shortly after being founded by the viceroy of New Spain in 1541. Its first church, the Renaissance-style Iglesia de San Francisco, was consecrated in 1546. The building was attached to a monastery that today houses a museum of handicrafts. Twenty other churches were subsequently built and several historical colleges are also testimony to Morelia's role as an important intellectual center.

Santuario de Guadalupe is a baroque church in Morelia's Old Town (interior décor from 1915).

The friezes and columns of the southern ball court in the pre-Columbian city of El Tajín feature meticulously carved reliefs depicting a jaguar (left) and the sacrifice of a pelota player (far left).

TEOTIHUACÁN

Situated about 50 km (31 mi) northeast of Mexico City, Teotihuacán comprises one of the most important ruins in Mesoamerica. The huge city complex had already been abandoned for more than 700 years when the Aztecs discovered it in the 14th century. The core of the surviving main buildings and the central north-south axis date from around 200 BC. The Temple of Quetzalcoatl and the large pyramids were built about 200 to 300 years later. With around 150,000 residents, the city was easily the largest

The Pyramid of the Sun (top) was built on an area that marks the very heart of Teotihuacán. The complex is decorated with splendid murals such as that of the priest with his magnificent headdress (bottom).

in the Americas by about the year 350. Its wealth was largely based on obsidian mining, a volcanic rock used to make tools, implements and weapons. The decline of Teotihuacán began in the seventh century and the city was finally abandoned in about 750. In addition to the more than 2-km-long (1.2-mi) and 40-m-wide (125-ft) Street of the Dead, the most important constructions include the around 65-m-high (213-ft) Pyramid of the Sun, the somewhat smaller Pyramid of the Moon and the Temple of Quetzalcoatl. Other outstanding buildings are the carefully restored Palacio de Quetzalpapalotl with its lovely murals and stonework, as well as the Yayahuala, Zacuala and Tepantitla Palaces.

POPOCATÉPETL, OAXACA, MONTE ALBÁN

Santo Domingo (main picture) is considered Oaxaca's loveliest baroque church. Largely rebuilt at the beginning of the 18th century following earthquake damage, a Dominican monastery (today the Centro Cultural Santo Domingo) with several cloisters also used to belong to the church.

POPOCATÉPETL

At 5,465 m (17,931 ft), the snow-covered "smoking mountain" is the second highest peak in Mexico after Citlaltépetl at 5,700 m (18,702 ft). This stratovolcano has been unusually active again since 1994 and often emits a plume of smoke. The first major eruption following nearly 200 years of dormancy occurred in back in 2000. Although no lava was released during the eruption, the residents of the capital just 60 km (37 mi) away cast a worried look at "Popo" as gas and ash from eruptions have hindered air traffic and public life in Ciudad de México on several occasions in recent years – most recently on December 1 and 2, 2007.

OAXACA

The city of Oaxaca has a wealth of colonial-era grandeur as well as Zapotec and Mixtec culture on offer, and yet it retains a rather provincial flair despite the hustle and bustle. There is a large indigenous population here and the state has the highest percentage of indigenous-language speakers. The Plaza de Armas, which is the site of the cathedral, was rebuilt after an earthquake in 1730 and appears to be somewhat badly proportioned. The Iglesia de Santo

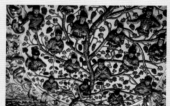

The interior of Santa Domingo is a symphony of polychrome and gilded stucco (top). The family tree of the founder of the Dominican order (bottom) is an unusual feature.

Domingo is smaller and seems inconspicuous from outside, but the interior is breathtaking. An unimaginable twelve million gold pesos have been built into the church over a period of 200 years. Similarly impressive is the Museo de las Culturas de Oaxaca in the Centro Cultural Santo Domingo, with pre-Columbian finds from near Monte Albán including the world-famous Mixteca treasure from Grave No. 7. The Museo de Arte Prehispánico exhibits Rufino Tamayo's private collection of pre-Spanish artefacts. The city's markets are also worth visiting.

The Franciscans, Dominicans and Augustinians signaled the Christianization of the country by building monasteries on the slopes of Popocatépetl south of Mexico City Far left: The Nuestra Señora de los Remidos Monastery with the volcano in the background. Left: Murals in the Cathedral of Cuernavaca.

MONTE ALBÁN

The region around the city of Oaxaca has been settled since the sixth century BC. It was originally the Olmec people who excavated the mountain above Oaxaca Valley, but the resulting city, Monte Albán, later became the religious center of the Zapotec, who were highly developed in mathematics and writing. As Monte Albán came under the increased influence of Teotihuacán, it lost importance as a cult site and was gradually abandoned

The giant areal of Monte Albán (top) contains advanced pyramids and palace buildings (middle). The extraordinary relief slabs with the peculiar "danzantes" are on display in the local museum (bottom).

by its up to 20,000 inhabitants after the year 800. Monte Albán served the Mixteca as a massive necropolis for a short period from 1250 but then declined as a result of Aztec incursions in the area (1490). The special features among these attractions include the strangely decorated human figures on the Building of the Dancers, Tunnels connect the temples with a structure that was thought to have been an observatory.

The ruins of one of the most impressive Mayan cities are in the middle of the tropical jungle of Chiapas in southern Mexico. Although they had been discovered in 1784, the ruins of Palenque (main picture) were only systematically excavated in the 20th century.

CAMPECHE

Following it was founded in 1540, Campeche served as the starting point for the Spanish crown's conquest of the Yucatán. The important port soon became a lucrative target for notorious pirates such as Henry Morgan and William Parker, who plundered Campeche repeatedly. The hexagonal, over 2.5-km (1.8-mi) city wall was built between 1668 and 1704 and the defensive fortification with its four bastions ("baluartes") is one of the best-preserved in the Americas. Today the bastions and two forts house museums, galleries and botanical gardens. Exports of the red fabric dye, palo de tinte, is what inspired Campeche's second golden age in the 19th century and many magnificent buildings from this era have also survived: beautiful city palaces, the Teatro Toro, a number of churches built between 1540 and 1705, and the baroque but rather somber Catedrál de la Concepción San Francisquito, built on the site where the first mass is said to have been held in the New World in 1517.

PALENQUE

Palenque, a Mayan city that reached the zenith of its influence between the sixth and eighth centuries, was built between the third and the fifth centuries, when most important structures were erected. The glyphs in the Temple of the Inscriptions have been deciphered and constitute the most significant written records of Mayan culture. The untouched burial chamber of the Mayan Prince Pacal was discovered in the pyramid in 1952.

Directly adjacent to the "palace", with its high tower, is the Temple of the Inscriptions, a stepped pyramid with a temple construction on the roof platform (top). Almost all of the buildings are decorated with elaborate reliefs (bottom).

Inside the most famous temple, the 20-m-high (66-ft) Templo de las Inscripciones (Temple of the Inscriptions), are sixty steps leading into the crypt at a depth of 25 m (80 ft). Similar to the Egyptians, the Palenque pyramids were also burial chambers, the valuable objects from which are now on display in the Museo Nacional de Antropologíca in Mexico City. Opposite the Temple of the Inscriptions stands the "palace" where the royal family lived. Its 15-m (49-ft) tower was used for astronomy while a tabletop on the upper floor functioned as an altar.

The cathedral of Campeche (far left) is the oldest on the Yucatán Peninsula. The cobbled alleyways of the Old Town with its brightly colored buildings hold particular appeal (middle, left).

On March 21 and September 21, the sun falls on the giant El Castillo pyramid in Chichén Itzá in such a way that a shadow in the form of a serpent winds down the steps to meet a stone carved as a serpent's head at the bottom (main pictures, top). Below: A stone sentinel.

UXMAL

Uxmal, like the town adjacent to it, was an important urban and ceremonial center from the eighth to the 10th centuries. The central building is the almost 40 m (131 ft) high Pyramid of the Magician. The imposing construction, which was dedicated to the rain god Chac, is in fact the fourth building to have been constructed on this site of former temples. The expansive Governor's Palace stands on a 15-m-high (49-ft) platform decorated with an impressive stone mosaic frieze. The front elevations of the Nunnery, the House of the Tortoises and the Dovecote also feature detailed stone mosaics. The peculiar features of the friezes on the façade of the great palace of Sayil are surpassed only by those of the pillar ornaments. The triumphal arches over the once cobbled streets in Labná and Kabah are rare Mayan architectural treasures. The Palace of the Masks in Kabah owes its name to the roughly 250 stone masks of the god Chac on the front elevation. There is also a ball court in the complex.

CHICHÉN ITZÁ

These ruins extend over an area of 300 ha (741 acres) in the northern Yucatán and are the legacy of two pre-Columbian civilizations: the Maya and the Toltec. The cult site is thought to have been founded by the Maya in roughly 450. Large constructions followed in characteristically grand Mayan style such as the Complex of the Nuns or the main church. Groups influenced by the Toltec eventually moved into the abandoned Maya cult center in the 10th century and initiated a second golden age that lasted around 200 years. The transition to a Toltec-influenced

Chichén Itzá is characterized by a stylistic mix of ancient regional cultures with those of the Maya. The reclining figure here, known as "Chac Mool", in the Temple of the Warriors is an example (top). The skulls of those sacrificed were displayed (bottom) on a tzompantli, a foundation wall decorated with skull reliefs.

sculptural and relief style that featured warrior figures and graphic atlases is clearly recognizable. The observatory (Caracol) and the Quetzalcoatl pyramid known as the Castillo are representative of this epoch and have other monumental structures (Temple of the Jaguar) as well as a variety of ball courts grouped around them.

Situated on a giant platform, the Governor's Palace (main picture, in the foreground) is a masterpiece of Mayan architecture. Behind it stands the Pyramid of the Magician. Uxmal declined in importance from the 11th century and was finally abandoned by around 1200.

The longest-living barrier reef in the northern hemisphere is located off the coast of Belize on the edge of the continental shelf. It is made up of a variety of reef types comprising around sixty-five different coral species, their bizarrely shaped thickets and columns creating an ideal habitat for countless creatures. In addition to almost 250 species of aquatic plant this fantastic diversity also includes around 350 mollusk species, sponges, shellfish and about 500 fish species (above), from eagle rays to goliath groupers. Heavily endangered marine creatures such as manatees, hawksbill turtles and loggerhead sea turtles also inhabit this protected area. The islands (cayes) off the coast are mostly covered with either mangroves or palms. Accessible cayes in the area include Ambergris Caye, 58 km (36 mi) north of Belize City, and the Turneffe Islands. In addition to the underwater world, which often affords visibility of up to 30 m (65 ft), the reef's other attractions include the bird sanctuary on Half Moon Caye and the Blue Hole, a collapsed underwater cave.

Spectacular diving territory: the Blue Hole (main picture), in the Belize Barrier Reef 80 km (50 mi) east of Belize City. These coral reefs were described by Charles Darwin as early as 1842. An underwater cave collapsed here around 10,000 years ago when the land sank into the ocean. The circular "blue hole" with a diameter of 300 m (328 yds) is 125 m (410 ft) deep.

The Agua Volcano rises steeply behind the Arco de Santa Catalina in Antigua Guatemala. Despite earthquake damage, the former capital of Guatemala is one of the loveliest Spanish colonial-style cities in the world (main picture).

ANTIGUA GUATEMALA

The Spanish conquerors founded the "noble" and "royal" city of Antigua in the highlands of Guatemala at the foot of three volcanoes in 1543 – the former settlement here had been destroyed in a mudslide. During the decades that followed, the capital of the Spanish colonial empire in Mesoamerica, situated at an altitude of 1,500 m (4,922 ft), developed into a virtual metropolis with up to 70,000 inhabitants. San Carlos de Borromeo, the first papal university in Central America, was founded here in 1675.

Built in Italian Renaissance style, Antigua, with its checkerboard layout, flourished for two centuries before being destroyed by an earthquake in 1773. The impressive ruins and rebuilt churches, cathedrals, monasteries, palaces and townhouses are testimony to the city's former economic, cultural and clerical significance. Today, the grandiose baroque colonial buildings still make it possible to see why Antigua (above: an Easter procession) was considered the loveliest capital in the New World.

TIKAL

Situated in north-eastern Guatemala, Tikal is home to one of the most important Mayan ruins in Central America (above, a vase fragment testifying to the high quality of their ceramic work). The site was first settled in around 800 BC. A giant complex of temples and palaces was built starting in the third century.

Tikal is located in a national park that covers around 600 sq km (232 sq mi) in the middle of a primeval forest that is home to a great many animals. During Tikal's golden age (550–900), up to 90,000 people lived in this temple city. To date, more than 3,000 buildings and complexes have been excavated in the 15-sq-km (6-sq-mi) area that was the city center – magnificent palaces as well as simple huts and ball courts. The most spectacular are the five gigantic temple pyramids, one of which is 65 m (213 ft) high and is the highest of all Maya constructions. In about the year 800 this cult site comprised twelve temples all built on one giant platform. Archeologists have also unearthed implements, cult items and burial objects.

QUIRIGUÁ

Monumental columns and elabo-rate calendars are among the highlights of the archeological site of Quiriguá in the remote eastern corner of Guatemala, close to the border with Honduras. The first inhabitants settled here in about AD 200, but this Mayan city did not reach the height of its prosperity until the eighth and ninth centuries, a fact that is reflected in a wealth of art treas-ures from the time. Like many Mayan cities, however, Quiriguá was then abandoned for centuries for reasons unknown.
One important turning point in the history of this city came during the regency of Cauac Sky (right, depicted on a column) with the beheading of the mighty ruler of Copán in 738, upon whom Quiriguá had been politically dependent for many years.
The city, its prosperity being mostly based on the trade in goods such as jade and obsidian, consequently rose to become a center of political power. The majority of the famous monumen-tal stelae date from this golden age in the eighth century. The elaborate and finely worked sculptures on the monolithic sandstone blocks are sculptural masterpieces and depict political and military events – including the very execution on the main square mentioned above that led to the city's rise.

The ruined Mayan city of Copán boasts incredibly detailed stelae dating from the eighth century (main pictures left and right: stelae B and N) that depict Mayan rulers and their various deeds.

RÍO PLÁTANO

The Río Plátano Biosphere Reserve, which covers an area of 830,000 ha (2,050,930 acres), extends from the north coast to the interior of Honduras to an elevation of more than 1,300 m (4,265 ft) above sea level. The largely mountainous region covers about seven percent of the country's terri-tory and features a variety of habitats. Lagoons and mangrove forests alternate with pristine beaches while coastal savannah with beak rush sedge and other marsh plants meets palms and lowland pines. Tropical and subtropical rainforests with all of their biodiversity can be found deeper in the interior. The reserve's inhabitants include jaguars, pumas and ocelots, king vultures and harpy eagles, mana-tees, tapirs and pacas, as well as a number of monkeys. In addition to the indigenous Miskito, Pech and Tawahka peoples, the Garifuna (an ethnic group of Caribbean and African descent) and Mestize also live here. There are also archeological sites with Mayan remains as well as traces of another pre-Columbian civilization.

COPÁN

The 30 ha (74 acres) of ruins at Copán are in north-western Honduras, close to the border with Guatemala. Copán was one of the most important city-states that thrived during the Mayan golden age in around 700. One of the earliest descriptions of Copán is that by Diego García de Palacio from 1570, but the city was not actually excavated until the 19th century. Hundreds of ruins are thought to still exist under the earth mounds in the Copán Valley.

The Acropolis – a complex of interconnected constructions in the shape of pyramids, temples and

This monumental stone head of the mythical giant Pauahtun was part of a colossal statue and now lies at the foot of Temple 11.

terraces – forms the center of what has been excavated to date. Altar Q, in which the names of sixteen rulers of Copán are carved, is especially remarkable. The Hieroglyphic Stairway is Copán's most important monument. Close to 2,500 glyphs cover the sixty-three steps and form the longest Mayan text to date. It pays tribute to the achievements of the dynasty from its founding through to the opening of the staircase in the year 755. The ball court with three marker stones, which occurs in this form only in Copán, is also worthy of note. Fourteen altars and twenty stelae, dating back to between 618 and 738 have also been restored. The base of the elaborately decorated Stela H conceals two fragments of a golden figure.

The animals of the Río Plátano Biosphere Reserve include (from far left) mantled howler monkeys, white-nosed coatis, white-faced capuchins and three-toed sloths.

Poas Volcano is 2,704 m (8,872 ft) high and has two crater lakes. The water in the one is cold and clear while the lower crater (main picture) is an acidic lake with a diameter of 1,300 m (4,000 ft) and a depth of 300 m (963 ft). Sulfuric gas is emitted continually while the water shoots up like a geyser.

Geographically, Central America begins at the Mexican Isthmus of Tehuantepec, but there is a major geological border further to the east: the North American and Caribbean plates meet almost directly on the border between Guatemala and Honduras/El Salvador. This means that the land bridge from Honduras to South America is "Caribbean", which is indeed true of its climate (with few exceptions) and makes its plant and animal biodiversity unequalled anywhere in the world. Species from North and South America that once developed independently of one another intermingle here, for example. Cultural exchanges between the Mexican civilizations and South America also took place via the continental bridge which, at the Panama Canal, is only 46 km (29 mi) wide.

The volcanoes of the Cordillera Central and the Cordillera de Talamanca rise to an elevation of more than 3,400 m (11,155 ft) to the south of a gigantic rift, filled in part by the expansive Lago de Nicaragua. Some of them are still active like the 1,633-m (5, 358-ft) Arenal Volcano (main picture) in Costa Rica. This is due to the pressure exerted by the Pacific Cocos Continental Plate, which is sliding below the Caribbean Plate on the southern Costa Rican coast.

Tiny Costa Rica has a number of national parks within a relatively small area that are all still climatically very different: from the humid, tropical Caribbean side to the arid regions in the Pacific side, and from the marsh areas in the east to the rain forests of the central highlands and the dry forests of the north-west with its prickly bushes. Both coasts of the country also serve as breeding grounds for sea turtles, the inspiration for the Tortuguero National Park, which is only accessible by boat.

The Arenal Volcano (left), situated at the southern end of the lake of the same name and surrounded by a belt of tropical rainforest, is one of seven active volcanoes that rise out of the Cordillera Central, which traverses the country from the north-west to the south-east. Costa Rica's spectacular mountains of fire are situated east of the island's capital San José, on the edge of the Valle Central. Some of them have crater lakes such as Irazú and Poás, which feature geyser-like eruptions of muddy water and steam. Arenal erupted again in 1968 after being dormant for centuries and the crater now emits a constant plume of smoke.

GUANACASTE

This region in north-western Costa Rica covers 100,000 ha (247,100 acres) and comprises three national parks and smaller protected areas. It extends from the Pacific coast over the 2,000-m (6,562-ft) mountains of the interior down to the lowlands on the Caribbean side. Guanacaste encompasses coastal waters, islands, sandy beaches and coastal cliffs as well as streams and rivers in mountainous and volcanic landscapes, including the active composite volcano Rincón de la Vieja. No less than thirty-seven areas of wetland, mangroves and tropical rainforest are found here as well as tropical dry forest (in the background above) where the trees shed leaves during the hot season. This last remaining area of intact tropical dry forest in Central America measures around 60,000 ha (148,260 acres) and is one of the largest protected forest areas of its kind in the world.-

COCOS ISLAND

Cocos Island (in Spanish, *Isla del Coco*) is 550 km (342 mi) off the south-west coast of Costa Rica and boasts magnificent natural resources and tropical rain forests. Its isolated location has meant that numerous endemic plant species have been able to thrive here. There are also three bird, two reptile and more than sixty endemic insect species. The island's coastal waters are also part of a national park and are home to large fringing reefs with thirty-two coral species as well as a wealth of marine fauna. In addition to sharks (above, a scalloped hammerhead shark) there are another 300 fish species living in these waters.

The Talamanca and La Amistad reserves provide the ideal habitat for around 250 reptiles and amphibians as well as more than 200 mammals including the jaguar (main picture), puma, ocelot and tapir.

TALAMANCA AND LA AMISTAD

The cross-border reserve shared by Costa Rica and Panama boasts the greatest biodiversity of fauna and flora in the world. It covers the Central Cordillera de Talamanca from southern Costa Rica to western Panama and ranges from sea level all the way up to an elevation of roughly 3,800 m (12,468 ft). The wide spectrum of very diverse habitats and landscapes is predominantly covered with tropical rain forest, which has been growing here for 25,000 years (below). Above the lowlands are cloud forests and areas of sub-alpine paramo with bushes and grasses as well as areas with evergreen oaks, moors and lakes. Its topographic and climatic variety as well as its geographic location at the juncture between North and South America mean that the park has no shortage of unique flora and fauna. In addition to diverse finches, hawks and eagles, the vibrant acorn woodpeckers that benefit from the park's oak trees (above middle) contribute to the diversity of the indigenous bird species. The lovely long-tailed silky flycatchers (above right) live in montane forests above 1,800 m (5,906 ft). The magnificent quetzals (above left) are also among the region's feathered inhabitants. Archeological finds even indicate that human beings had been living in this region thousands of years ago but the research is still in its early stages. Today around 10,000 members of the indigenous Teribe, Guaymí, Bribri and Cabécar ethnic groups live in reserves located within the protected area.

Sunken shipwrecks, nothing uncommon in the waters off the Bahamas, attract giant fish shoals, welcome prey for sharks and barracudas (main picture).

Tropical sun, white sandy beaches, rustling palms and the blue sea – in short, the Bahamas (left, a market in Freeport on Grand Bahama). Among the most popular travel destinations in the world, the attractions in Nassau and Freeport are mostly geared toward activities and luxury vacationing while the Family Islands offer a bit more of the solitude and tranquility associated with paradise. "It's better in the Bahamas" was the islands' tourist slogan for many years. Lying on a white sandy beach, forgetting everything under palms waving in

the gentle wind, and washing away your cares in the pleasantly warm waters you might be tempted to agree. Pastel-colored houses in the blazing sunshine, vibrant corals and turquoise water. The Bahamas indeed provide the perfect holiday atmosphere. Left, a starfish off San Salvador, where it is said Columbus landed during his first voyage west. Right, a Caribbean flamingo. This island nation comprises about 700 islands and has been independent since 1973. Among the best-known islands are New Providence Island with the capital Nassau, Cable Beach and Paradise Island as well as Grand Bahama with Freeport, the islands' economic hub and the home of a great many gambling casinos. The Family, or Out, Islands are only accessible via light aircraft or by boat. The British influence can still be felt everywhere and, combined with the jet-set atmosphere in Nassau and Freeport and the Caribbean charm of the Family Islands, it contributes to some of the islands' appeal. The water is warm and clear and the reefs off the Bahamas are among the loveliest in the world.

HAVANA

"Queen of the Caribbean" is just one of Havana's epithets (above, the Malecón). Pastel hues envelop the city and the romanticism of "son" rhythms fill the air while flaking plaster walls play the bolero of decay. At Havana's legendary Tropicana nightclub (right), Cuba's most beautiful women dance in the most exotic of costumes. Indeed, Havana is not only one of the oldest but also one of the most fascinating cities in the New World. To protect the merchant harbor, where all the gold and silver transports were shipped from the Americas back to Spain, the Spanish built mighty fortifications between the 16th and the 18th centuries. The Old Town was laid out in a checkerboard plan in which the grid of streets is frequently broken up by spacious squares. The main square, Plaza de Armas, features impressively restored colonial buildings such as the Palacio del Segundo Cabo. One of the most attractive baroque structures is the Palacio

de los Capitanes Generales. Also worth seeing are the old palaces of the former nobility with their wrought-iron balconies. Among the religious buildings in town, the Cathedral (above right) stands out. Completed in 1704, Alejo Carpentier once called it "music that has become stone". Right: A staircase in the Old Town.

VIÑALES

Bizarrely shaped *mogotes*, steep cone-shaped rocks created 150 million years ago, rise out of the valley in Viñales. They were once part of an extensive cave system that has since collapsed – what remains are the rock formations that lie in the valley like gigantic boulders. It is the main tobacco-growing region of Cuba.

Main picture: Havana is teeming with classic cars, many of them lovingly done up and used as taxis in Cuba.

One of the first mayors of Santiago de Cuba (main picture, El Morro Fortress) was conquistador Hernán Cortez, who used it as a base from which he ultimately conquered territories that are now Mexico.

CIENFUEGOS

The first inhabitants of this port town were the Spanish. The French came later, mainly from Bordeaux, New Orleans or Florida. When the city gained in importance thanks to the export of sugar it was laid out along a grid in neoclassical style. In the process of redesigning the town, planners tried to realize their vision of a healthy city environment, hence the straight roads, which were meant to aid in circulating air – in the 19th century it was believed that bad air was the main cause of disease.

The houses in Cienfuegos are generally only two floors high so that each apartment and all rooms are flooded with light. The layout of the squares reflects the importance placed on public life. Building styles were then fused in later construction phases and yet it still creates the impression of a harmonious entity. Aside from the residential buildings, the Governor's Palace, the San Lorenzo School, the cathedral, the Teatro Tomás Terry and the Palacio de Ferrer (Casa de la Cultura) are also worth visiting.

SANTIAGO DE CUBA

Cuba's second-largest city is situated in a sheltered bay fringed by the foothills of the Sierra Maestra. The magical Parque Céspedes is the focal point of the Old Town, with the Casa Diego Velázquez, built in 1516, Cuba's oldest building. The attractive Hotel Casa Grande, now a colonial museum, is worth visiting. The blue and white Ayuntamiento (town hall) and the Catedral de Nuestra Señora de la Asunción were all built at the turn 20th century. The Museo del Car-

The El Morro Fortress towers high above the entrance to the port of Santiago de Cuba. it was built as a defense against pirates and hostile colonial powers (main picture).

naval in the Calle Heredia is also worth a visit. The Moncada Barracks, north-east of the center, has become a sort of pilgrimage destination for fans of the Cuban Revolution. It is here that Fidel Castro and a handful of friends undertook their daring and now legendary first attempt to topple the Batista Regime in 1953. But the attack on the barracks failed and the revolutionaries either landed in jail or were shot. The Santa Ifigenia Cemetery is arranged in a grid style like the cemetery in Havana and is definitely worth seeing. The El Morro Fortress is now home to the Museo de la Piratería.

Once the residence of a rich merchant, the Palacio de Ferrer is now a cultural center (left). Other unusual buildings in Cienfuegos are the Governor's Palace (far left) and the cathedral.

TRINIDAD

Trinidad, founded in 1514 on the central southern coast, is one of the most beautiful cities in Cuba. Many of its buildings date back to the 18th or 19th centuries, when the city prospered thanks to the robust sugar trade. The Plaza Mayor has remained almost unchanged since those times, preserving its historic appearance with some beautifully restored houses. The historic sugar mills in the neighboring Valle de los Ingenios, the Valley of the Sugar Mills, are worth a trip and can best be see from the tower of Manaca-Iznaga.

CAMAGÜEY

Camagüey was named after Cama güebax, the Native American tribal territory where the town was originally founded. Camagüey's economic significance as the capital of a prosperous region of sugar production and cattle breeding afforded it a certain autonomy, inspiring a unique architecture that still gives the city a special character today. One of the most attractive squares in the Old Town is the Plaza San Juan de Dios, built in the 18th century.

JAMAICA

"Xaymaca" – "the land of forest and water" – is how the indigenous Arawak named their little slice of paradise in the Caribbean Sea. It is a fitting name for this place, which is separated from Cuba by the up to 7,240-m-deep (23,754-ft) Cayman Trough. Discovered by Christopher Columbus for the Spanish Crown in 1492, it has been a parliamentary monarchy within the British Commonwealth since 1962. The partly swampy coastal regions, characterized by mangroves and coconut palms, feature a number of good swimming beaches. About two-thirds of the island is comprised of a heavily karstified limestone plateau. Jamaica rises in elevation as one travels from west to east, and forms of the tropical cockpit or cone karst can also be found in abundance in Cockpit Country. The eastern Blue Mountains are home to the 2,292-m-high (7,520-ft) peak of the same name, the island's highest point. Jamaica offers a wide variety of natural ecosystems with densely overgrown mountains, rolling hills, fern-covered river valleys and breathtakingly beautiful beaches. Especially stunning is the sight of the waterfalls gushing from the tropical greenery into the turquoise sea.
Bottom: Dunn's River Falls. Top: Cockpit Country. Left: The island's north coast.

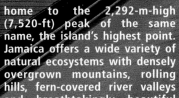

PUERTO RICO

The easternmost island of the Greater Antilles was the last Spanish bastion in the Caribbean before it fell to the United States in 1898. In 1950 the islanders were asked whether they wished to remain a U.S. colony or to become an autonomous protectorate of the United States. Three-fourths voted for the latter. The Old Town of San Juan is worth seeing with its narrow alleyways, old houses with beautiful wooden balconies, and the massive fort. It shows the importance of the town and the port. Since 1822 La Fortaleza has been the seat of the Governor of Puerto Rico and as such the oldest continuously used government building in the western hemisphere. At the eastern tip of the island is the mile-long, golden sand beach of Luquillo, a draw for locals and visitors.

DOMINICA

The climax of any visit to the third-largest of the Lesser Antilles is the Morne Trois Pitons National Park, founded in 1975 and featuring misty rain forests, lakes and waterfalls. This nature reserve, which covers nearly 7,000 hectares (17,297 acres), offers a unique habitat for a number of plant and animal species. Nearly 150 bird species populate these forests and the various volcanic formations surrounding the still-active Morne Trois Pitons Volcano are of breathtaking beauty. Roughly fifty fumaroles, hot springs and five active volcanic craters can be found between the rugged and densely overgrown canyons. Hot mud bubbles up from one boiling lake. The Emerald Pool (above) also owes its unusual hue to the elementary powers at the center of the earth.

The Caribbean is perfect for cruising. Modern ships are like floating Las Vegas hotels, offering everything from department stores to saltwater swimming pools. Pictured here: The *MV Galaxy* (main picture) anchored in Montego Bay, Jamaica.

TRINIDAD AND TOBAGO

This island republic consisting of the two main islands of Trinidad and Tobago as well as several smaller islands is situated north-east of Venezuela and forms the southern part of the Caribbean island arc. Trinidad, the largest of the Lesser Antilles islands, received its name from the three prominent mountain chains that traverse the island and reach elevations of 941 m (3,087 ft). The considerably smaller island of Tobago is located 32 km (20 mi) to the north-east of Trinidad and is also traversed by a densely forested mountain range, this one only reaching elevations of up to 576 m (1,890 ft).

Both islands were "discovered" for Spain by Christopher Columbus in 1498. The Spanish had fully colonized Trinidad by 1552, but in 1797 it was taken from them by the British. In 1814, Tobago also became a British colony and in 1888 it was united with Trinidad. In 1962 the state of Trinidad and Tobago gained its independence, and since 1976 it has been a republic within the British Commonwealth.

Trinidad and Tobago is primarily famous for its carnival. Nowhere else in the Caribbean can you see such stunning costumes (left) and nowhere else do stilt runners (below), fire-eaters, and calypso and limbo rhythms enchant locals and visitors to the degree they do here.

ST. LUCIA

St Lucia, birthplace of Derek Walcott, winner of the Nobel Prize for Literature, has lovingly been called by the British and the French "The beautiful Helena of the West Indies". Indeed, both European nations have had great influence on the history of the island – it changed hands between the two powers fourteen times until it finally became British in the Treaty of Paris in 1815. Since 1979, St Lucia has been independent but it has remained a member state of the British Commonwealth. Even more exciting than a visit to the capital, Castries, is a trip around the island to the Pitons Nature Reserve (above), an area near Soufrière in the south-west that covers roughly 30 sq km (12 sq mi) and is well worth the time. The cone-shaped twin peaks of the Gros Piton (770 m/2,526 ft) and Petit Piton (743 m/2,438 ft) form a landmark of the Lesser Antilles that is visible from vast distances. Created during a volcanic eruption, they were described by Walcott as the "Horns of the Caribbean". The nature reserve includes the mountain ridge, a field of solfataras with fumaroles and hot springs as well as some adjacent marine areas. Nearly sixty percent of the underwater area was once covered in coral, but Hurricane "Lenny" (1999) destroyed much of this. The establishment of zones where fishing is forbidden has now led to a recovery that has made the area around the Pitons one of the most biodiverse in the entire Caribbean.

People in Trinidad and Tobago begin work on their elaborate sequin and feather costumes weeks before the actual climax of carnival in February (main picture). The festival here is the second-largest in the world after the one in Rio – some of the Rio costumes are actually made in Trinidad and Tobago.

Giant anthropomorphic monoliths are the main attraction at the excavation sites in the park of San Agustín. Many of the larger-than-life stone figures and heads are characterized by their wide mouths and huge, predator-like canine teeth (main picture).

SANTA CRUZ DE MOMPOX

On the banks of the Río Magdalena, roughly 250 km (155 mi) south of Cartagena, is one of the oldest and most beautiful colonial cities in Colombia. For a long time, Santa Cruz de Mompox was an important inland port on the trade route to Cartagena. Today the Río Magdalena flows through another riverbed and the town has lost its importance. The historic heart of the city, with its harmonious architecture in Spanish colonial style is more like an open-air museum unique to Colombia. Instead of the customary central square, Mompox boasts three squares that form its center – La Concepción, San Francisco and Santa Bárbara – all linked by the Calle de la Albarrada. Each square has its own 16th-century church. Santa Bárbara's is the most unusual, with a baroque steeple, decorations in the shape of palm trees on the balcony and stucco-work, as well as flowers and lions. The Calle del Medio also has some beautiful buildings such as the church and hospital of San Juan de Dios.

CARTAGENA

Founded in 1533, this port city quickly developed into a flourishing center for the trade in gold and slaves thanks to its favorable location on the Caribbean coast. In the middle of the 16th century, however, attacks by pirates became more frequent and so the city was fortified. When the English buccaneer Sir Francis Drake captured Cartagena in 1586, a 12-m-high (39-ft) and up to 18-m-thick (60-ft) defensive wall was built. The largest fortification wall in the New World,

Top: Cartagena's gigantic fortifications had to withstand several attacks over the centuries. Bottom: The Church of San Pedro Claver.

it managed to once again withstand attacks by the British in the 18th century. These events are still commemorated today by a cannonball that got stuck in the church of San Toribio. The Old Town has three distinct districts: San Pedro, comprising mainly upper-class manor houses with their magnificent portals and flower-bedecked inner courtyards; San Diego, mainly a residential and commercial district; and Getsemaní, which was mainly for the working class and is now dominated by people of African descent. The cathedral (16th century) and the Palacio de la Inquisición are worth seeing here.

The most unusual structure in Santa Cruz de Mompox is the octagonal baroque steeple of Santa Bárbara, which has its own balcony (far left). Another gem is the San Francisco Church with its red and white façade (left). In the middle is a view across town from the bell tower of the San Agustín Monastery.

TIERRADENTRO

The archaeological park of Tierradentro in the Cordillera Central in southern Colombia is littered with subterranean tombs that are unique in South America for their size as well as their access staircases. Above-ground, several figures have been found that were cut into the stone. The discoveries probably date back to an ancient farming culture with a highly developed cult of the dead.

SAN AGUSTIN

Just south of Tierradentro in southern Colombia is the most important archeological site in the country, and one that features the largest collection of religious monuments and megalithic sculptures in South America. The region around the excavation site, in the area where the Río Magdalena rises, was already settled in the 5th century BC. The most impressive discoveries are the idolos: stone figures of humans and animals that recall the statues of the Mayan gods in Central America.

CANAIMA

In the language of the Camaro-coto Indians who live here, the name "Canaima" represents a somewhat sinister god who manifests all evil within himself. By contrast, the national park – which covers about 3 million ha (7.4 million acres), the second-largest in Venezuela – captivates with its overwhelming positive natural beauty. Located in the south-east of the country, on the borders with Guyana and Brazil, the park extends across the magnificent landscape of the Gran Sabana. It is fille with dense vegetation and spectacular waterfalls such as the Salto Ángel, the Salto Kukenam and the cascades of the Canaima Lagoon, which plunge over breathtaking cliffs. Between 3,000 and 5,000 species of flowering plants and ferns are said to exist here – many of them indigenous. Aside from savannah it also features impenetrable montane forests and scrubland. On the many *tepuy*, or flat-topped mountains, a special, even enterprising

vegetation has developed that includes carnivorous plants. Of the roughly 900 plant species that have been recorded on one of these *tepuys*, at least one-tenth are indigenous. Colorful butterflies, hummingbirds and parrots flutter through these forests while on the ground, mammals like great anteaters, giant arma-

dillos, giant otters, forest dogs and ocelots prowl around. The Catalan Captain Félix Cardona Puig was the first white man to see the powerful Salto Ángel waterfall in 1927. It was ultimately named after the American pilot, Jimmy Angel, however, who flew there in 1933, with his single-engine propeller plane.

The highest waterfall in the world, Salto Ángel (main picture and inset), plunges some 1,000 m (3,281 ft) from the north-eastern side of the roughly 2,500-m-high (8,202-ft) Auyántepui.

Franciscans began to construct San Francisco only a few years after the city was founded in 1534. The church and convent were completed in 1580 and make up the largest existing historical architectural complex in all of South America (main picture).

QUITO

Quito, located at an elevation of 2,850 m (9,351 ft), is the oldest town in South America. The volcano-fringed upper basin was settled by the Caras Indians in pre-Inca days. Under Huayna Cápac it developed into the second-largest administrative center of the Inca Empire. Spanish conquistadores ultimately destroyed this northern-most outpost of the Incas and in 1534, Spanish Sebastián de Belal-

In the middle of the high altar of the San Francisco Church stands an Immaculata, an "Immaculate Virgin" (top), carved by Bernardo de Legarda in 1734. The artful pulpit with its polychrome figures (bottom) is yet another jewel of colonial baroque art.

cázar founded "San Francisco de Quito" on its ruins. The historic center of Quito today is the place with the highest density of colonial art treasures in South America. The Church and Convent of San Francisco, the largest and oldest place of worship in the city, was built by the so-called Quito School of Art, which combines the influences of Spanish, Italian, Moorish, Flemish and South American indigenous art.

CUENCA

When the Spanish arrived here, it was already an important settlement known as Tomebamba, originally founded by the Cañaris Indians and later taken over by the Inca. But by the time Gil Ramírez Dávalos arrived and established Santa Ana de los Ríos de Cuenca here in 1557, only the ruins of the Inca ruler Huayna Cápac's former metropolis remained. It had been destroyed in the war between the last two Inca kings.

The Spanish built Cuenca using a grid style around a central square, the Plaza Abdón Calderón, and it is here that the heart of the city still beats. The Old Cathedral with its squat bell tower from 1557 stands here. The New Cathedral, just opposite, dominates the cityscape. When the city experienced a period of prosperity in the second half of the 19th century thanks to the sale of quinine and handmade straw hats, many of the old houses were "modernized". Now, the unusual combination of local and European architectural features is what gives the city its special flair.

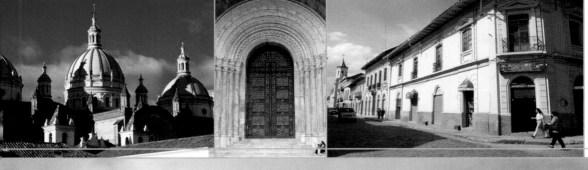

For many local people, Cuenca, the "Athens of Ecuador", is the most beautiful city in the country. Cobbled streets and brightly painted colonial houses make for the special charm of Cuenca's Old Town. Far left: The mighty towers of the New Cathedral and its portal (center).

About 1,000 km (625 mi) off the west coast of Ecuador, out in the middle of the Pacific Ocean, is a spot where hot magma from the core of the earth developed into a spectacular archipelago consisting of twelve larger and more than 100 smaller volcanic islands. The oldest in the eastern-most part developed some 2.4 to 3 million years ago. Fernandina, in the west of the archipelago, is the youngest island, notching up just 700,000 years. Three major ocean currents flow around the archipelago including the Humboldt Current, which brings cold water from the icy polar regions right up to the Equator. Other currents bring life from the tropical and subtropical regions of Central and South America as well as the Indo-Pacific region, all of which have made the Galapagos Islands a swirling melting pot of the most diverse species. The geographic isolation of the archipelago also offered the optimum conditions for flora and fauna to develop in complete isolation. Charles Darwin's visit in 1835 ensured the enduring worldwide fame of the islands. Observing species of finches here that were nearly identical but which had developed different beak shapes according to the specific island they were on allowed him to gain valuable insights for the development of his theory of evolution. The Galapagos archipelago is a paradise for birds and reptiles alike, but very few mammals have managed to make their way there. In fact, most of the animals living on this group of islands are indigenous. Particularly spectacular species include the flightless cormorant, the Galapagos land iguana, the marine iguana, and of course the graceful and beautiful Galapagos tortoise.

Primeval species such as the Galápagos land iguana (main picture) were able to thrive on the remote Galapagos Islands off the coast of Ecuador. Galapagos tortoises (left), the largest living tortoises, can reach a weight of more than 200 kg (441 lbs). Marine iguanas (far left) feed on anything they find in the sea.

The first white person to discover Machu Picchu was the American Hiram Bingham in 1835. Bingham called the settlement Machu Picchu, meaning "Old peak", in reference to its location below the Huayna Picchu, or "Young peak". Simply put, everything seems mysterious about this Inca settlement, which sits like an eagle's eyrie on top of a flat mountain at an altitude of 2,430 m (7,973 ft) and is hidden in the tropical montane forest of the eastern Andes. What makes this place above the Río Urubamba Valley so fascinating is not just the amazingly well-pre-

served buildings but also the unique harmony between architecture and nature. The structures are perfectly adapted to the uneven terrain around them. Speculation continues to this day as to the significance of this town, which was never discovered or even noticed by the Spanish colonists. Perhaps it was no more than an attempt by the Inca to also colonize the easterly slopes of the Andes. All that is certain is that the city was built around 1450 and abandoned again just one hundred years later. The complex is divided into two areas: the agricultural zone out on the steep mountain slopes, with terraces for arable farming that were integrated into a sophisticated irrigation system, and the unfortified urban district with palaces, temples and residential buildings. Among the most remarkable structures are the Round Tower, the Sun Temple and the Temple of the Three Windows.

Main picture: One of the best examples of perfectly integrating architecture with its surroundings is the "Forgotten City" of Machu Picchu, situated in a high-altitude landscape of stunning beauty. The Inca settlement, also known as the "City of the clouds", was built on several terraces on a high plateau.

The giant stone blocks of the Inca fortress of Sacsayhuamán (main picture), above Cuzco, look as if they were stacked by the hands of giants. It is still not certain how the blocks, some weighing more than 200 metric tons, were brought here – the Incas had no wheels or rollers.

Cuzco is one of the oldest cities in the New World that still exists today. This region was already settled by farming peoples in about 1000 BC, and about 2,000 years later it became the focal point of the powerful Inca Empire. According to one creation myth, the city, located at 3,400 m (11,155 ft) above sea level, is said to have been founded in about 1200 by Manco Cápac, the first mythical Inca ruler of the Kingdom of Cuzco. Over the 300 years or so that followed, Cuzco developed into the most sumptuous Inca city in the empire and became the political, religious and cultural heart of their realm. Most of the temples and palaces were built during this imperial period, which began with the accession to power of King Pachacútec (1438). It is said that numerous buildings were clad in gold and copper plates. In 1533, the conquistador Francisco Pizarro brutally conquered the city. Cuzco was destroyed and missionaries built their churches and monasteries on top of the ruins of the Inca temples in order to extirpate the memories of indigenous traditions.

A view cross the rooftops towards the Cathedral of Cuzco (left), built in the 17th century in the Renaissance style.

Main picture: Jaú National Park, Mamirauá and Amanã nature reserves, and Anavilhanas Ecological Station encompass the largest protected area of rainforest in the Amazon Basin. The region's dense tropical rain forest and floodplain forests are one of the most biodiverse areas on earth.

MANAUS

The capital of the Brazilian state of Amazonas is situated on the banks of the Rio Negro, in the heart of the rain forest. Founded in 1669 as a Portuguese fort, Manaus developed into a flourishing metropolis during the rubber boom at the turn of the 20th century but increased use of synthetic rubber products then caused a dramatic downturn in the city's prosperity. It was only after Manaus was declared a free trade zone in 1967 that it once again recovered from the decades of decline. The city is the seat of the Universidade Federal do Amazonas, established in 1965, and plays an important role in regional tourism as the jumping off point for excursions into the Amazon basin. Reminders of the rubber boom include the market halls (Mercado Municipal Adolfo Lisboa), which were built in a cluster around the port in 1902, their cast-iron construction a Gustave Eiffel design; and the Palácio Rio Negro (1910), a well-preserved city villa that once housed the regional government and today serves as a cultural center for visitors. The famous opera house, the Teatro Amazonas, towers gracefully over the port (above), its dome decorated with 36,000 ceramic tiles that were imported from Alsace, France. Although the theater was officially opened on December 31, 1896, it wasn't actually completed until 1898.

The Amazon is by far the largest river system on earth: its catchment area alone is larger than Western Europe. The river is only called the Amazon after its confluence with the Rio Negro 18 km (11 mi) downstream from Manaus. In its middle reaches it is called the Solimõe, into which three tributaries flow: the Maranón, the Huallaga and the Ucayali, all of which rise in the Andes. The other tributaries – the Rio Negro, Rio Madeira, Rio Tapajós and Rio Xingu – are of great size as well. The difference between the ebb and flow in the Amazon can be up to 15 m (49 ft). After Manaus the river is very sluggish and seldom less than 5 km (3 mi) wide, except near Óbidos where it narrows to 2 km (1.2 mi) and can reach depths of 100 m (328 ft). Scientists have theorized that the source of the primeval Amazon was originally in what is today the Sahara. What has been proven is the fact that the river originally flowed in the opposite direction, namely into the Pacific. South America and Africa, then one continent, began to split apart 70 million years ago. The upthrust of the Andes then began at the same time as the American Plate slid westward under the East Pacific Plate. For a long time the river flowed westward through Guayaquil. The current direction only dates from about six million years ago. In general, the soils of the Amazon rain forest region – the largest continuous forest area on earth – are oddly low in nutrients, making human encroachment an issue. Intentional fires to clear land as well as unregulated logging have forced the government to put huge areas under protection – often unsuccessfully. When Europeans arrived in about 1500, there were about two million Indians here; today they number no more than 50,000. Whole tribes were decimated, enslaved, or succumbed to epidemics introduced by colonists.

Insets, clockwise from top left: Dense Amazon rainforest; an ocelot, under threat from fur hunters; Kayapó Indians; the Rio Negro at a width of 2 km (1.2 mi) near Manaus; Yanomami Indians. The Brazilian Federal Indian Bureau FUNAI is committed to protecting indigenous Amazon peoples.

The ornate gold carvings are an impressive feature of the 18th-century baroque São Francisco Church in Salvador da Bahia. A magnificent wooden ceiling spans the opulently decorated nave (main picture).

OLINDA

Olinda's Old Town is known as the "Pearl of the Brazilian Baroque" and spans several palm-covered hilltops. "O linda situação para uma vila" was how the Portuguese described this "beautiful location for a city" before founding the settlement on the Atlantic coast in 1535. The Dutch went on to conquer the north-eastern territories of Brazil, including Olinda, at the beginning of the 17th century and initially razed the city to the ground before rebuilding it in Dutch style. The Portuguese then took it back after defeating Dutch troops at Guararapes in 1654. Many of the buildings that were destroyed in the 17th century have since been rebuilt or expanded.

Around twenty baroque churches and countless "passos" – small chapels – as well as monasteries such as São Francisco and São Bento remain as testimony to the city's tremendous religious significance. The Igreja da Sé, founded in 1537 and the cathedral of the archbishopric of Olinda and Recife since 1676, housed the first parish in the north-east.

SALVADOR DA BAHIA

In 1501, Italian seafarer Amerigo Vespucci landed at this site on the Atlantic coast where fifty years later Salvador da Bahia de Todos los Santos was founded. The city was Brazil's first capital, a title it held between 1549 and 1763. Running the extensive sugar and tobacco plantations here used to require a great deal of manpower that could not be supplied by Indian tribes alone. As a result, African slaves were brought in as

The sober exterior (top) of the baroque São Francisco Church belies an ostentatious interior filled with gilded sculptures, flower motifs and angels (bottom).

well, and it was here at Cafuá das Mercês that the first slave market in the New World took place back in 1558.

"Black Rome", Salvador's less flattering name from that era, consists of a lower city with an upper city that rises some 80 m (262 ft) above it. The port and the business district are down on the seafront while the palaces and churches typically claim the higher ground.

The São Francisco Monastery, founded in 1585, is the oldest Franciscan structure in Brazil. The tiles in the sacristy depict scenes from the life of St Francis (far left); in the middle is the belfry; left are medallions set in a wooden ceiling portraying the saints.

The two parts of the city are still linked via narrow alleyways, steep steps and footpaths, and an electric lift, the elevador lacerda, has been a convenient means of travelling between the two since the end of the 19th century. Salvador's upper city is the largest intact district of Renaissance buildings in Brazil. No fewer than 166 churches are testimony to the city's extravagant past, with the cathedral, the São Francisco Church, and the church of the Carmelite monastery among the most important buildings. This idyllically situated coastal city is probably the

The best-preserved colonial buildings are in the Pelourinho district where the Igreja de Nossa Senhora do Rosário dos Pretos (top) stands on the main square, Largo de Pelourinho. Bottom: The twin towers of the Igreja do Santíssimo Sacramento behind the rows of restored colonial-era buildings.

most exotic and eccentric city in the country. More than two-thirds of its residents are descendants of black African slaves, which has made Salvador da Bahia a melting pot of European and African religions, traditions and festivities. Some people even call it "The city of happiness" because of the many festivals and the easy-going ambience. The Pelourinho, a district with many colonial-era buildings, was made a UNESCO World Heritage Site in 1985.

Main picture: "God created the world in six days; the seventh day he dedicated to creating Rio" – the pride of Rio's inhabitants is perhaps most gloriously and colorfully expressed during Carnival.

When Portuguese seafarer André Gonçalvez arrived with his ships in expansive Guanabara Bay on January 1, 1502, he thought he had discovered an estuary. As a result, he called what he thought to be a river the Rio de Janeiro – January River. Very few cities in the world enjoy a location and a backdrop as breathtaking as Rio de Janeiro. Together with the 394-m (1,293-ft) Sugar Loaf mountain (above right), the famous statue of Christ with outstretched arms on top of the 704-m (2,310-ft) Corcovado mountain (above) is one of the most recognizable icons in the metropolis – if not in the world.

Founded on March 1, 1564, as the Cidade de São Sebastião do Rio de Janeiro, Rio is not only Brazil's former capital, but also the former capital of the Portuguese Empire. Right on the Atlantic, Rio boasts two of the world's most famous beaches: Copacabana and Ipanema (below).

662 The Americas | Brazil

PANTANAL

The Pantanal wetlands are located in the very south-eastern corner of Brazil, close to the border with Bolivia and Paraguay. During the torrential summer rains between November and April the substantial rivers systems of the Rio Cuiabá and Rio Paraguai flood a lowland area that is three times the size of Costa Rica to form a vast expanse of wetlands with shallow lakes, marshes and swamps. These annual floods function as a natural control mechanism that regulates the exchange of groundwater and freshwater as well as purifying the existing supply. The sediment and nutrients brought by the floodwaters then enable lush grasslands to develop here during the drier winter from the end of April to October, when the rivers once again subside. Pantanal's unique landscape – the largest wetland in the world – is particularly spectacular during these hot, humid months when the sky tends to possess a semi-permanent haze. It is then that the cerrado savannah begins slowly encroaching again on wide areas of the wetlands where beautiful hardwood trees such as the jatobá also grow.

Pantanal is the largest freshwater wetlands in the world and hardly any other tropical location boasts the same density of wildlife. Animals here include (from far left) black howler monkeys, giant otters, six-banded armadillos, jaguars and hyacinthine macaws.

IGUAÇU

Iguaçu Falls, where Brazil, Argentina and Paraguay meet, can be heard long before they actually come into view. Initially it is a faint gurgling that quickly swells into a deafening, thunderous roar. The Iguaçu River, lined with dense tropical vegetation and called the Iguazú in Argentina, is about 1 km (0.6 mi) wide where it approaches the horseshoe-shaped precipice. The falls then crash with impressive power over a cliff that is 2,700 m (850 ft) in length – an amazing natural spectacle. More than 270 individual waterfalls have been counted here.

The adjacent Iguaçu National Park on the Brazilian side covers an area of 1,700 sq km (656 sq mi) and provides refuge for a vast range of endangered species. Parrots and white-bellied nothuras flit around under the protection of dense forests while swifts build their nests in the craggy rocks between the waterfalls. This rain forest region is also home to jaguars, tapirs, ant bears and collared peccaries. Both the Argentinian and Brazilian sides were made UNESCO World Heritage Sites in the 1980s.

Iguaçu means "big water" in the language of the indigenous Guaraní Indians. Sunlight shines through the spray creating an enchanting rainbow (left) as almost two tons of water per second plunge into the gorge with a deafening roar.

LAKE TITICACA

Lake Titcaca can make some unique claims: with a surface area of 8,300 sq km (204 sq mi), it is the largest lake in South America; it straddles the border between Peru and Bolivia; and it lies at an elevation of 3,812 m (12,507 ft), the highest commercially navigable lake in the world. In addition to that, the natural landscape and the Inca ruins in the region around the lake are a

source of ceaseless fascination. The Isla del Sol, for example, contains Inca cultural and ritual sites. According to Inca legend, the island is the birthplace of the sun god. The Temple of the Sun (Templo del Sol), situated on the highest point of the island, is particularly shrouded in mystery. The Island of the Moon (Isla de la Luna) is also worth a visit. Beyond the geological islands on Lake Tit-

icaca, there are also a number of man-made floating islands on the lake (left). They were created in pre-Inca times by the Uros (Uru), fisher folk who live on these artificial islands. Initially they used reeds mixed with earth just to build the foundations of their houses on land. The continual rise in the water level, however, meant that they had to keep raising these foundations until some

of the houses began floating on the lake during the floods. Since this had advantages for fishing, the Uros decided to make a virtue out of necessity – the concept also afforded them protection from Inca attacks. The Uros simply retreated to their floating islands on the lake whenever there was threat of an invasion. The Uros also use reeds to make their stylized boats (below).

Lake Titicaca (main picture) in the Peruvian-Bolivian highlands is located at an elevation of 3,812 m (12,507 ft), and is 190 km (118 miles) long and 50 km (31 mi) wide.

ALTIPLANO

Western Bolivia is a high-elevation region dominated by impressive mountain ranges with expansive basins stretching between them. This contrast is especially visible along the border with Chile. The basin landscape of the Altiplano (literally meaning "high level") extends between the Cordillera Occidental (Western Cordillera) and the Cordillera Oriental (Eastern Cordillera) of the Andes and where elevations range between 3,600 and 4,200 m (11,812 and 13,780 ft). The 6,520-m (20,506-ft) Mount Sajama (left, with a church built of air-dried bricks in the foreground) in the national park of the same name is an eye catcher that is visible from great distances. With a permanent snowcap above 5,300 m (17,389 ft), Mount Sajama is a dormant volcano, but there is a very high degree of tectonic activity in the region, and volcanic eruptions and earthquakes are a frequent occurrence.

CORDILLERA REAL

This region is indeed worthy of the lofty name. Cordillera Real (or Royal Cordillera) is a fascinating range that extends east from Lake Titicaca, in Bolivian territory (above), its glistening high-altitude glaciers visible from afar when the sun is shining. In addition to the highest peak in the range, the 6,880-m (22,573-ft) Nevado del Illimani (above), there are a number of other peaks here that break the 6,000 m (19,686 ft) mark. They are so spectacular that passionate mountaineers from all over the world travel to South America to trek in the Cordillera Real.

TORRES DEL PAINE, LAUCA, ALERCE ANDINO

The granite peaks of the Chilean Torres del Paine (main picture) tower 3,050 m (10,007 ft) over the Southern Patagonian plains.

TORRES DEL PAINE

The mountains of the Torres del Paine range rise directly from the expansive, windswept plain. They consist of steep, seemingly impregnable peaks and massive granite formations with the 3,050-m (10,007-ft) Cerro Torre Grande as their highest point. Cerro Torre is then surrounded by the only slightly lower peaks of Paine Chico, Torres del Paine and Cuernos del Paine. This national park is Chile's adventure paradise and offers a wide range of hiking trails for both short day tours or longer treks that take visitors through the entire park and last several days. All of these fascinating excursions bring you through the glorious glacial landscape, over the Grey Glacier and along the swift-moving Río Paine river, which cascades into Lago Pehoe lake. Gnarled trees bracing themselves against the wind are a unique feature of the park, as are the colorful plains covered in wildflowers, endangered Andean condors, various waterfowl and endemic guanacos. Any trip to this region requires good preparation.

LAUCA

Chile is "an island on the mainland". To the north it is bordered by the world's driest desert, in the west by the waves of the Pacific and in the east by the peaks of the Andes. To the south, Chile dissolves into an array of islands that are then lost in the Antarctic Ocean. Lauca National Park is home to a number of permanently snow-capped, 6,000-m (19,686-ft) peaks that include superb volcanoes such as Parinacota (above) at 6,342 m (20,808 ft) as well as Lago Chungará, one of the highest lakes on earth.

ALERCE ANDINO

Alerce Andino National Park extends along the Seno and the Estuario de Reloncaví and is home to ancient conifers (related to the redwoods) that reach diameters of up to 4 m (13 ft) and heights of up to 50 m (164 ft). Many of the trees are around 1,000 years old. The famous Carretera Austral, Chile's loveliest route into the solitude of the south, also begins near Puerto Montt in Alerce Andino. This mixed paved and gravel road stretches along more than 1,000 km (621 mi) of rural Patagonia through forest and past lakes, fjords and snow-covered peaks. Some 100,000 people live in this wild region.

The granite peaks of Torres del Paine National Park in Chile rise up from the plains of Southern Patagonia like an impregnable fortress (left).

The heart of the Atacama Desert is the driest place in the world. The Humboldt Current, an ocean current off the Pacific coast, carries cold water from the Antarctic northward. Due to the lack of wind, the steep coastal mountains then trap fog rising from the ocean – and therefore the moisture – which keeps it from reaching the interior. This results in an extremely dry climate, with some places having never recorded any form of precipitation since records have been taken. To put it mildly, it is an inhospitable environment that can be very warm during the day and uncomfortably cold at night. Yet it is anything but monotonous. The ocher desert mountains and snow-covered volcanoes are as enchanting as the deep blue and green lagoons and the scattered oases. Above right is a salt lake in the Atacama with stratovolcanoes in the background. In the center is one of the loveliest of these, Licancábur at 5,916 m (19,410 ft). To the right is the Géiser el Tatio geyser field, which is typically at its most active in the early morning.

A booming economy does not always require a fertile landscape. The desert, too, has its riches. In this case, these riches made Chile a wealthy country back in the 19th century, initially with saltpeter, an essential raw material for the manufacture of gunpowder and artificial fertilizers. At that time, however, the Atacama did not yet belong to Chile. This vast region was shared by Peru and Bolivia, Chile having become involved in the saltpeter business only through a company in Antofagasta. In 1879, when the Bolivian government made an attempt to expropriate the

company, Chile made its move. The army occupied the town, instigating the Saltpeter War. Peru and Bolivia lost the war in 1883 and Chile then enjoyed a saltpeter monopoly. Most of the towns are derelict nowadays, but

new towns continue to appear elsewhere in the desert: Chuquicamata, for instance, not far from Calama. This small town was built up around the world's largest opencast copper mine. The vast, man-made crater is

At 6,893 m (22,616 ft), the Ojos del Salado (main picture), located in the Atacama Desert on the border between Argentina and Chile, is one of the highest volcanoes on earth as well as one of the tallest peaks in the Andes.

4 km (2.5 mi) long, 2 km (1.2 mi) wide and about 700 m (2,297 ft) deep. Several hundred thousand tons of rock are blasted here every day before being loaded onto giant trucks, crushed and washed. The mine generates one million tons of pure copper (99.6 percent) annually along with smaller quantities of valuable minerals, including gold and silver. Chuquicamata is expected to yield copper until beyond 2010 before the deposits become exhausted. The Chileans are optimistic, however: Other copper mines will replace them and the desert also holds other mineral reserves including sulfur, phosphate, gold, silver, manganese, molybdenum, rhenium and lithium. San Pedro de Atacama is the best jumping off point for exploring this impressive desert region (below right, the Adobe church in San Pedro). About 12 km (7.5 mi) to the west is the Valle de la Luna (above left) a bizarre, waterless erosion landscape created primarily by wind (since there is no precipitation). "Moon valley" is most impressive at sunset and at full moon when the sandstone glows in all manner of colors, from ocher-yellow and orange to deep red and violet, with everything bathed in pale white moonlight. Almost 100 km (62 mi) north of San Pedro de Atacama is the Géiser el Tatio geyser field. These geysers are really a sight for early risers. To reach the geysers, which should be visited before sunrise because it is only at dusk and in the early morning hours that they are at their most active, visitors must take a poor dirt road that leads past Licancábur volcano (5,916 m/19,410 ft). Bubbling up from dozens of holes in this volcanic landscape, they make for a fascinating spectacle against the clear blue sky of the rising sun. The geysers are situated at an altitude of 4,300 m (14,108 ft), making it one of the highest geyser fields in the world. The salt lake south of San Pedro covers an area of 3,000 sq km (1,158 sq mi). It is no shiny, white salt lake, but rather a crusty, brown-white clay mixture interspersed with salt crystals. There are a number of individual water basins in the lake, however, that form small, clear lagoons that are often frequented by flamingos. These lagoons are also at their best at sunset when the Salar shimmers in a variety of pastel tones and the flamingos stand as dark silhouettes in the water. The best view can be enjoyed at Lago Chaxa, which is about 50 km (31 mi) south of San Pedro. Above are the salt pans of the Atacama Desert.

RAPA NUI (EASTER ISLAND)

The tuff statues, some of which are several meters high, are impressive testimony to a lost Polynesian civilization on Rapa Nui, an island in the middle of the Pacific that measures just 164 sq km (63 sq mi) and belongs to Chile (main picture).

Two million years ago the Rano Kau volcano rose up out of the vast Pacific Ocean. The island that this uplifting created originally comprised seventy-seven smaller craters. At a distance of some 3,700 km (2,299 mi) from the South American mainland and around 4,200 km (2,610 mi) from Tahiti, Easter Island) is one of the most isolated places on earth.

The island was first settled as early as AD 400. A second wave of settlement is thought to have taken place in the 14th century, when the legendary King Hotu Matua arrived here with his Polynesian followers. The Polynesians called the island Rapa Nui, meaning "Big island". The main testaments to their culture are the several hundred "moais", tuff sculptures, measuring up to 10 m (33 ft) in height and standing on large platforms known as "ahu", and the Rongorongo script, a kind of pictorial writing. The significance of the moais has not yet been established. Dutchman Jacob Roggeveen reached the island, which is today inhabited by about 4,000 people, on Easter Monday 1722, which gave the island its present name.

The function or meaning of the *moais* – gigantic figures and heads made of tuff that were erected on Easter Island (left and far left) – remains a mystery.

Main picture: The Plaza de la Republica is one of the most popular nightspots in Buenos Aires. The 67-m (220-ft) obelisk at its center commemorate the founding of the city in 1536.

Porteños – or port residents – is what the residents of Buenos Aires call themselves, referring to the city's location on the western side of the Río de la Plata. Around three million people live in the city of "good air" (above a mural in the port district of La Boca), and almost fourteen million in the greater urban area – about one-third of the entire Argentinean population, which is of largely European descent. Founded by the Spanish in 1536 as Nuestra Señora Santa María del Buen Aire, the city had to be abandoned just five years later following bloody conflicts with indigenous populations. It was founded anew in 1580, was the capital of a Spanish viceroyalty from 1776 to 1810, and has been the capital of Argentina since 1880. The heart of the metropolis, with its grid layout, is the Plaza de Mayo with the Casa Rosada, seat of the state president. The Mothers of the Plaza de Mayo gather there on Thursday afternoons in silent protest against the crimes committed by the military dictatorship. Buenos Aires became famous as the birthplace of the tango (above) – "a sad thought that is danced", according to the Argentinean composer Enrique Santos Discépolo in his description of the "dance of the emotions", characterized by sensual passion and eroticism.

Main picture: The front of the Perito Moreno Glacier rises up to 60 m (197 ft) above Lago Argentino. Ice blocks are continually breaking off and crashing into the sea.

The park's thirteen glaciers form part of the Patagonian Ice Field which, covering 15,000 sq km (5,790 sq mi), is the largest continuous ice mass outside of Antarctica. There are also another 200 small glaciers not directly connected to the ice field. The most famous of these is the 30-km-long (19-mi), 5-km-wide (3-mi) Perito Moreno Glacier, which slowly pushes its "tongue" across a peninsula, cutting off a branch of Lago Argentino every three or four years. When the wall of ice is no longer able to withstand the pressure, the backed-up mass of water breaks through part of the glacier front and makes its way to the sea.

Bizarrely formed icebergs owing their ornate shapes to the harsh elements are a common sight south of the Antarctic Circle. Penguins often rest on them (right, main picture).

"It lies there, wilder than any other part of our earth, unseen and untouched," wrote Norwegian Roald Amundsen, the first person to reach the South Pole, in his travel journal in 1911. The Antarctic is a gigantic land mass almost completely covered with snow and ice. Only one-sixtieth of its surface area (with the ice shelf almost 14 million sq km/5.5 million sq mi) is free of ice while the rest is covered by ice with an average thickness of 2,500 m (8,203 ft) – it reaches thicknesses of over 4,500 m (14,765 ft) in spots. This ice expanse is not a flat surface either, but one that is traversed by high mountain ridges. One of the longest ranges on earth is found here, the Transantarctic Mountains, which extends diagonally across the continent over more than 4,800 km (2,983 miles). Only the highest peaks such as the 4,897-m (16,067-ft) Mount Vinson poke up through the gigantic ice mass. The Antarctic has never been truly settled by humans. The more than eighty research stations are home to about 4,000 people in the summer and about 1,000 in the winter.

King penguins are the second-largest penguin species and primarily inhabit the Sub-Antarctic Islands (left). They breed for the first time when they are six years old, the egg initially being incubated by the male in the folds of its belly. The incubation period lasts for a total of fifty-five days.

Index of images

Abbreviations:

A   Alamy
akg   akg-images
B   Bilderberg
C   Corbis
G   Getty Images
H   Huber
IB   The Image Bank
Ifa   ifa-Bilderteam
JA   Jon Arnold Images Ltd
L   Laif
P   Premium
PC   Photographer's Choice
RH   Robert Harding
S   Schapowalow

Sorted from upper left to lower right

World Imagery/Gavin Hellier, 489.3 Wildlife, 489.4 G/RH World Imagery/Gavin Hellier, 490/491 C/George Steinmetz, 491 L/Redux/ The New York Times, 492.1 ifa/Aberham, 492.2 P/Minden/ , Yoshino, 492/493 C/Martin Harvey, 493.1 G/Petersen, 493.2 P/Minden/ Lanting, 493.3 P/Stock Image, 494.1 Okapia, 494.2 Blickwinkel/Pflanzen, 494/495 M/Zak/ Paysan/Rosing, 495.1 A/WorldFoto, 495.2 A/Nick Greaves, 495.3 Lonely Planet Images/ Grant Dixon, 496.1 G/IB/Manoj Shah, 496.2 C/Howard, 496.3 C/Harvey, 496.4 Pix/Minden/Lanting, 496.5 G/fStop/Sean Russell, 496.6 Okapia, 496/497 Mauritius, 498/499 ifa/Aberham, 499 C/Yann Arthus-Bertrand, 500 G/Photonica/Jake Wyman, 500/501 G/ Axiom Photographic Agency/Ian Cumming, 501 L/Le Figaro Magazine, 502.1 C/Peter Johnson, 502.2 Okapia, 502/503 Eye Ubiquitous/Hutchinson, 503.1 A/Images of Africa Photobank, 503.2 pictureNEWS/Mario Vedder, 503.3 B/Klaus D. Francke, 504.1 P, 504.2 G/Stone/Paul Souders, 504/505 G/Gallo Images/Dave Hamman, 506 G/Gallo Images, 506/507 C. & W. Kunth, 507 P, 508.1 Clemens Emmler, 508.2 Clemens Emmler, 508/509 A/ImageState, 509.1 P, 509.2 Clemens Emmler, 510 Clemens Emmler, 510/511 ifa/JA, 511.1 Clemens Emmler, 511.2 C/Dave G. Houser, 512.1 Clemens Emmler, 512.2 C/Bob Krist, 512.3 Clemens Emmler, 512.4 Das Fotoarchiv, 512/513 Franz Marc Frei, 513.1 Clemens Emmler, 513.2 Clemens Emmler, 514.1 Das Fotoarchiv/Markus Matzel, 514.2 L/Riehle, 514.3 L/Heeb, 514/515 C/Gallo Images/Dennis, 515.1 L/Emmler, 515.2 P/Joubert/NGS, 516.1 C/Gallo Images/Martin Harvey, 516.2 C/Yann Arthus-Bertrand, 516.3 G/Riser/Michael Melford, 516.4 P/Minden, 516.5 L/G. Huber, 516/517 G/Riser/JH Pete Carmichael, 518/519 L/Le Figaro Magazine, 519 P/Transdia/HNnel, 520/521 H/G. Simeone, 521.1 ifa, 521.2 G/IB/Phillippe Burseiller, 521.3 L/Henseler, 522/523 C/TSM/Faulkner, 524/525 Clemens Emmler, 525.1 C/Yann Arthus-Bertrand, 525.2 C/Theo Allofs, 525.3 L/Emmler, 525.4 Transglobe/Schmitz, 526.1 Geospace/Acres, 526.2 ifa, 526.3 Don Fuchs, 526/527.1 P, 526/527.2 P/ImageState, 527.1 C/Gavriel Jecan, 527.2 C/Joe McDonald, 527.3 C/Fogden, 527.4 C/Jon Sparks, 527.5 Okapia, 528.1 Geospace/EDC, 528.2 G/Chesley, 528.3 P/Minden, 528.4 P/Minden, 528/529 Don Fuchs, 530.1 C/Paul A. Souders, 530.2 P, 530/531.1 P, 530/531.2 P/Panoramic Images/Lik, 531.1 A/David Noton Photography, 531.2 A/Mark Nemeth, 531.3 Okapia, 531.4 C/Yann Arthus-Bertrand, 531.5 Don Fuchs, 532.1 Blickwinkel/McPHOTO, 532.2 Don Fuchs, 532.3 Clemens Emmler, 532/533 ifa/JA, 534/535 P/StockImages, 535.1 Don Fuchs, 535.2 ifa/JA, 535.3 Don Fuchs, 536.1 Don Fuchs,

536.2 Don Fuchs, 536.3 C/Hans Strand, 536.4 P, 536/537 C/Yann Arthus-Bertrand, 538 Christian Heeb, 538/539 Tobias Hauser, 539.1 P/Stucke, 539.2 ifa/Held, 539.3 Panorama Stock, 540.1 P/Minden/de Roy, 540.2 C/Eurasia Press/Steven Vidler, 540/541 Clemens Emmler, 541.1 P/ImageState/Allen, 541.2 Tobias Hauser, 542.1 P/Schott, 542.2 P/Bunka, 542/543 Bilderberg/Burkard, 544.1 P, 544.2 L/Christian Heeb, 544/545 Christian Heeb, 545 Clemens Emmler, 546.1 Franz Marc Frei, 546.2 Franz Marc Frei, 546/547 Clemens Emmler, 547.1 G, 547.2 Holger Leue, 547.3 Clemens Emmler, 548.1 A/RH Picture Library Ltd., 548.2 C/Keren Su, 548/549 C/Charles & Josette Lenars, 550 C/Darrell Gulin, 550/551 C/Yann Arthus-Bertrand, 551 C/NewSport/Jeff Flindt, 552/553 P/Stock Images/Harris, 554.1 G/Taxi/Ambrose, 554.2 Vario Images, 554.3 P/Firstlight, 554/555 P/Minden/Brandenburg, 556 G/Panramic Images, 556/557 P/Yanagi, 558/559 P, 559.1 G/Visual Unlimited/Tom Walker, 559.2 C/Zuckermann, 559.3 P, 559.4 P, 559.5 ifa, 560.1 P/Bunka, 560.2 G/J. Squillante, 560/561 P/Orion Press, 561 P/Schwabel, 562.1 G/Stone/Chris Cheadle, 562.2 L/hemis, 562.3 B/Wolfgang Fuchs, 562.4 B/Wolfgang Fuchs, 562/563 L/Raach, 563.1 C/Blair, 563.2 G/Altrendo Nature, 563.3 L/hemis, 564.1 L/Heeb, 564.2 C/Rogers, 564/565 L/hemis, 566.1 C/T. Thompson, 566.2 P/Minden/J. Brandenburg, 566.3 C/Tom Silver/RF, 566/567 C/T. Allofs, 567.1 ifa/Warter, 567.2 P, 568.1 P, 568.2 P/Raymer, 568/569 C/Charles O_Rear, 569.1 L/Heeb, 569.2 Christian Heeb, 570.1 P/Kosuge, 570.2 P, 570/571 G/PC/Michele Falzone, 571.1 P/Gilchrist, 571.2 P/FirstLight/ Watts, 571.3 M, 572.1 C/Muench, 572.2 Christian Heeb, 572.3 Christian Heeb, 572.4 Christian Heeb, 572/573 Christian Heeb, 574.1 G/Stone/Marc Muench, 574.2 G/IB/Don Smith, 574/575 G/National Geographic/Philip Schermeister, 575 P/Sisk, 576.1 P/Flaherty, 576.2 P/Marr, 576.3 P/StockImage/Grunewald, 576/577.1 P/Sheumaker, 576/577.2 P/ImageState, 577 P, 578 P, 578/579 G/Stone/George Diebold, 580/581 P/Minden/Brandenburg, 581.1 P/Roda, 581.2 P/Minden/T. Fitzharris, 581.3 P/Minden/Brandenburg, 581.4 P/Minden/Mangelsen, 582/583.1 P/Gilchrist, 582/583.2 C/Ono, 583 P, 584.1 C/George H. H. Huey, 584.2 ifa/Panstock, 584.3 Rainer Hackenberg, 584/585 P, 585 C/Roberts, 586.1 Christian Heeb, 586.2 Christian Heeb, 586/587 L/Heeb, 588 P/Schott, 588/589 ifa/Nova-Stock, 590.1 C/Huey, 590.2 C/Muench, 590/591 C/Huey, 591.1 Christian Heeb, 591.2 Arco Images/NPL, 592/593 ifa, 593.1 P/Sisk, 593.2 C/Randklev, 594.1 A. M. Gross, 594.2 C/Craig Aurness, 594.3 C/Purcell, 594/595 ifa/TPC, 595.1 ifa/Siebig, 595.2 ifa/Siebig, 595.3 P/Stock Image/Frilet, 596.1

L/Heeb, 596.2 P/Schramm, 596.3 L/Heeb, 596/597 P, 597.1 P, 597.2 L/Multhaupt, 597.3 L/Falke, 598.1 C/R. Holmes, 598.2 L/Heeb, 598.3 C/A. Wright, 598.4 L/Jonkmanns, 598/599 Christian Heeb, 599.1 Das Fotoarchive/Moore, 599.2 C/Kulla, 599.3 ifa/JA, 600/601 P/Minden/C. Clifton, 601.1 C/Sohm, 601.2 G/Panoramic Images, 601.3 S/Atlantide, 601.4 Arco digital images/T. Sweet, 601.5 Avenue Images/G. Ercole, 601.6 Arco digital images/T. Sweet, 601.7 Avenue Images/J. Greenberg, 601.8 Arco digital images/T. Sweet, 602/603 Martin Sasse, 604.1 L/hemis, 604.2 L/Tatlow, 604.3 L/Artz, 604/605 Martin Sasse, 605.1 G/Panoramic Images, 605.2 L/Sasse, 605.3 L/Aurora, 605.4 L/Heeb, 606.1 L/Modrow, 606.2 P/Barbudo, 606.3 ifa/Panstock, 606.4 L/Modrow, 606/607 ifa/JA, 607.1 L/REA, 607.2 Avenue Images/W. Metzen, 608 L/Kristensen, 609.1 P/Mahlke, 609.2 C/Joe McDonald, 609.3 P/Mahlke, 609.4 ifa/Schulz, 609.5 P/Pacific Stock/J. Watt, 609.6 P/Minden/N. Wu, 610.1 L/Modrow, 610.2 P/Prisma, 610/611 P/Gorsich, 611.1 L/Heeb, 611.2 L/Heeb, 611.3 L/Heeb, 612/613 G/Art Wolfe, 613.1 P, 613.2 L/Heeb, 613.3 P/Cavataio/Pacific Stock, 614.1 L/Mayer, 614.2 L/Gonzales, 614.3 L/Mayer, 614/615.1 G/Stone/Robert Frerck, 614/615.2 P, 615.1 A/Robert Fried, 615.2 L/Heeb, 615.3 L/Heeb, 615.4 A/Geogphotos, 615.5 P/Roda, 616.1 Das Fotoarchiv/Knut Mueller, 616.2 A/Travis Rowan, 616.3 A/Guillen Photography/UW/ Mexico/Sea of Cortez, 616/617 G/Riser/Kevin Schafer, 617.1 C/George H. H. Huey, 617.2 C/Patricio Robles Gil, 618.1 C/Richard A. Cooke, 618.2 G/IB/Macduff Everton, 618/619 A/Aflo Co. Ltd., 619.1 C/Archivo Iconografico, 619.2 C/Angelo Hornak, 619.3 L/Heeb, 619.4 Bridgemanart.com, 620.1 P/Brimberg/NGS, 620.2 Pix/Raga, 620.3 A/Marion Kaplan, 620/621 L/Heeb, 621.1 A/Melvyn Longhurst, 621.2 A/Marek Zuk, 621.3 A/Marek Zuk, 621.4 Visum/Andreas Sterzing, 621.5 Bildagentur-online, 621.6 M/imagebroker, 622.1 C/George Steinmetz, 622.2 L/hemis, 622/623 H, 623.1 L/Heeb, 623.2 C/Jose Fuste Raga, 623.3 Andia/Mattes, 624.1 G/Picture Finders, 624.2 G/Picture Finders, 624/625.1 Marr, 624/625.2 Marr, 625 ifa/Panstock, 626 A/Images&Stories, 626/627 G/Giovanni, 628.1 L/heeb, 628.2 C/Macduff Everton, 628/629 L/Tophoven, 629.1 M/age, 629.2 C/Charles & Josette Lenars, 630 C/Yann Arthus-Bertrand, 630/631 NGS/Garrett, 631.1 Wildlife, 631.2 A/Arco Images, 631.3 Picture Press/Jürgen Sohns, 631.4 A/Danita Delimont, 631.5 C/R. A. Cooke, 632/633 L/Heeb, 633 G/Riser/Richard Ustinich, 634.1 L/Heeb, 634.2 A/Michael Patrick O_Neill, 634/635 H/Kiedrowski, 635.1 Okapia, 635.2 C/Kevin Schafer, 635.3 A/Kevin Schafer, 635.4 L/Hauser, 635.5 A/Oyvind Martinsen, 635.6 L/Hauser, 636

L/Kirchgessner, 636/637 C/Stephen Frink, 637.1 C/Stephen Frink, 637.2 P/Minden/G. Ellis, 638.1 L/Hauser, 638.2 M/age, 638.3 L/Hauser, 638.4 L/Hauser, 638.5 L/Hauser, 638.6 L/Hauser, 638/639 L/Hauser, 640.1 L/hemis, 640.2 Bildagentur-online, 640/641 L/Celentano, 641.1 L/Hauser, 641.2 L/Hauser, 641.3 L/Hauser, 641.4 Hackenberg, 642.1 C/Eye Ubiquitous/David Cumming, 642.2 P, 642.3 Das Fotoarchiv/Babovic, 642.4 C/Denis Anthony Valentine, 642.5 C/Eye Ubiquitous/David Cumming, 642/643 L/Sasse, 644.1 A/PCL, 644.2 A/Banana Pancake, 644.3 L/Falke, 644/645 L/hemis/Patrick Frilet, 646.1 LOOK/ Ingrid Firmhofer, 646.2 M/age, 646/647 G/Jane Sweeney, 647.1 A/Jeremy Horner, 647.2 C/Jeremy Horner, 647.3 C/Jeremy Horner, 647.4 C/Archivo Iconografico, 647.5 Das Fotoarchiv/Zippel, 648 G/Stone/Ke Fisher, 648/649 A/Kevin Schafer, 650.1 C/Pablo Corral Vega, 650.2 A/Mireille Vautier, 650/651 A/JA, 651.1 C/Tibor Bogntr, 651.2 A/North Wind Picture Archives, 651.3 Superbild/JTB, 652.1 A/Wolfgang Kaehler, 652.2 C/Yann Arthus-Bertrand, 652/653 P, 653.1 L/New York Times/Redux, 653.2 LOOK/ Per Andre Hoffmann, 654 L/Tophoven, 654/655 P, 656/657 L/Gonzales, 657 C/Vega, 658 C/Lehmann, 658/659 G/Reportage/Daniel Beltra, 659.1 P, 659.2 P, 659.3 M, 659.4 P/Pecha, 659.5 M/Wendler, 660.1 A/Rolf Richardson, 660.2 A/eMotionQuest, 660/661 L/Heeb, 661.1 Bildagentur-online, 661.2 A/Graham Corney, 661.3 L/Heeb, 661.4 S/Reinhard Kliem, 661.5 L/Piepenburg, 662/663 G/PC/John Lamb, 663.1 G/LatinCoIntent/SambaPhoto/Cassio Vasconcellos, 663.2 G/National Geographic/Richard T. Nowitz, 663.3 L/Heeb, 644.1 Okapia/Peter Arnold, 664.2 Okapia, 665.1 Blickwinkel/E. Hummel, 665.2 Biosphoto/ Theo Allofs, 665.3 G/Joel Sartore, 665.4 Still Pictures/Mike Oowels, 665.5 M/Wendler, 665.6 S/Atlantide, 665.7 Okapia, 666/667 A/Tibor Bognar, 667 P/Tansey, 668.1 C/Houk, 668.2 Woodhouse, 668.3 P/Japack, 668/669 G/IB/Andrew Geiger, 669.1 C/Pablo Corral Vega, 669.2 C/Hubert Stadler, 669.3 C/Pablo Corral Vega, 670.1 C/Stadler, 670.2 C/Anthony John West, 670/671 C/Galen Rowell, 671 P/Panoramic Images, 672.1 digitalvision/Woodhouse, 672.2 P/Hummel, 672/673 N.N., 673.1 C/Stadler, 673.2 C/Stadler, 673.3 C/Stadler, 674/675 L/Malherbe, 675.1 L/Le Figaro Magazine, 675.2 H, 676/677 S/H, 677.1 H/Bernhart, 677.2 L/Gonzales, 678/679 LOOK/ Michael Boyny, 680/681 P/Hummel, 681 P/Minden/Wiesniewski.

MONACO BOOKS is an imprint of Verlag Wolfgang Kunth

© Verlag Wolfgang Kunth GmbH & Co.KG, Munich, 2009

English edition:
Translation: Sylvia Goulding, Katherine Taylor
Editor: Kevin White for bookwise Medienproduktion GmbH, Munich

For distribution please contact:

Monaco Books
c/o Verlag Wolfgang Kunth, Königinstr.11
80539 München, Germany
Tel: +49 / 89/45 80 20 23
Fax: +49 / 89/ 45 80 20 21
info@kunth-verlag.de

www.monacobooks.com
www.kunth-verlag.de

Printed in Slovakia

All facts have been researched with the greatest possible care to the best of our knowledge and belief. However, the editors and publishers can accept no responsibility for any inaccuracies or incompleteness of the details provided.
The publishers are pleased to receive any information or suggestions for improvement.